T0338014

Financial Independence
(Getting to *Point X*)

Financial Independence (Getting to *Point X*)

A COMPREHENSIVE TAX-SMART WEALTH MANAGEMENT GUIDE

Second Edition

John J. Vento

WILEY

Published by John Wiley & Sons, Inc., Hoboken, New Jersey.
Published simultaneously in Canada.

For general information on our other products and services or for technical support, please contact our Customer Care Department within the United States at (800) 762-2974, outside the United States at (317) 572-3993, or fax (317) 572-4002.

Wiley publishes in a variety of print and electronic formats and by print-on-demand. Some material included with standard print versions of this book may not be included in e-books or in print-on-demand. If this book refers to media such as a CD or DVD that is not included in the version you purchased, you may download this material at http://booksupport.wiley .com. For more information about Wiley products, visit www.wiley.com.

Library of Congress Cataloging-in-Publication Data

Names: Vento, John, author.
Title: Financial independence (getting to point X) : a comprehensive
   tax-smart wealth management guide / John J. Vento.
Description: Second Edition. | Hoboken : Wiley, 2018. | Revised edition of
   the author's Financial independence (getting to point X), c2013. |
   Includes index. |
Identifiers: LCCN 2018021243 (print) | LCCN 2018021981 (ebook) | ISBN
   9781119510383 (Adobe PDF) | ISBN 9781119510352 (ePub) | ISBN 9781119510345
   (hardback)
Subjects: LCSH: Finance, Personal—United States. | BISAC: BUSINESS &
   ECONOMICS / Finance.
Classification: LCC HG179 (ebook) | LCC HG179 .V457 2018 (print) | DDC
   332.02400973—dc23
LC record available at https://lccn.loc.gov/2018021243

Cover Design: Wiley
Cover Images: © Axel Bueckert/EyeEm/Getty Images;
             © SchulteProductions/Getty Images

Printed in the United States of America

V10002590_071918

*This book is dedicated to the memory of my
parents, Rosario Vento and Concetta Giuffre
Vento, for the sacrifices and commitments they
made throughout their lives to provide their
children with the opportunity to live the
"TRUE" American Dream.
Momma and Poppa, I love you, miss you,
and think about you every single day!*

Contents

Foreword

Driving to work the other day, I saw a billboard with a simple statement: "We spend more time clicking 'like' than planning for retirement." Take a moment or two to let that thought sink in.

If you're like me, you probably find that proposition pretty disturbing, primarily because it rings so true.

By now thousands, maybe even millions, of Americans have seen that billboard noting that we spend more time choosing emojis, or even looking at billboards, than planning for retirement. I wonder how many of those people have actually started thinking about retirement. This is a pressing issue for those in their forties or older, but it's important for young adults, too. Cat videos and pictures of our friends' grandchildren are certainly more fun than dealing with financial matters. It's a lot easier to assume things will work out than it is to come up with a financial plan. But whether you have four years or 40 left in your working life, retirement gets closer every day.

If you ask most Americans what material thing they desire most, high on everybody's list is having enough money to do whatever they want without worry. Achieving financial independence, what John Vento calls "getting to *point X*," is such a common aspiration, but short of hitting a lottery mega-jackpot, most people have no idea how to get there. As contradictory as it may sound, the United States is the richest and most successful country in history, yet we are a nation of financial illiterates.

The vast majority of people graduate from high school or college with no understanding of fundamental financial concepts like how to make a budget, why it's important to start saving and investing at an early age to take advantage of the way the power of compounding makes your money grow faster, or how the wrong kind of debt can cripple their chances of achieving their financial goals.

Consider that currently only 17 states have some mandated financial literacy curriculum for students in high school. I saw an article recently that pointed out that 94% of American adults were unable to pass an 11-question test that asked basic financial questions like,

"If you purchase a bond and interest rates rise, what will happen to the price of the bond?" In today's environment, knowing the answer to that question could be pretty helpful.

Economically, we live in a different world than our parents did. For most people who don't work in government, pensions are a thing of the past; public pensions are threatened as well. We often hear about how New Deal and Great Society programs like Social Security and Medicare may soon be unable to fund their long-term obligations. We've made individuals responsible for funding their own retirements and financial futures, but haven't given them the resources and tools to do so.

Unfortunately, money doesn't come with a set of instructions, an issue of which John Vento, as both a Certified Financial Planner™ and Certified Public Accountant, is well aware. Like most Americans, John didn't learn about investing from his Italian immigrant parents. But they did share some priceless practical advice about money – "don't buy it if you don't need it" and "live within your means."

John has taken those moneywise principles and built upon them to create a holistic approach that provides not only a guidebook to financial literacy, but also a roadmap to financial independence. Over the years he has shared his experience and financial acumen to help hundreds of clients.

What makes John's approach, and this book, so helpful is the emphasis placed on strategically managing one's tax obligations. In fact, it's one of the first issues he addresses. Understanding tax strategies and managing your tax bill should be part of any sound financial approach, and with decades of experience, John is in an excellent position to help readers accumulate (and keep) personal wealth by combining holistic financial planning with a strategic approach to taxes.

One of the concepts that John introduces in this book is *Tax Alpha to the 2nd Power*^{SM}. The term *tax alpha* has been used in the investment world to measure the additional return earned from an investment by implementing sound tax strategies as part of the decision-making process. Taking it to the 2nd power is how John describes the additional return a financial planning client will realize by implementing sound tax strategies throughout all of their wealth management issues, and not just with their investment strategies. This edition also addresses the monumental changes to the US tax code that went into effect in 2018, which alone makes this volume worth reading.

John addresses important topics such as planning for retirement, managing your investments, and preserving your estate in accessible, down-to-earth language without burdensome industry jargon.

There's no denying that financial planning, choosing and managing investments, and minimizing your tax obligation are intimidating subjects, but they're not rocket science. Professional advice can make a big difference in achieving long-term goals.

The Chinese philosopher Lao Tzu famously noted that "A journey of a thousand miles begins with a single step." Financial literacy is the first step on your journey to achieving your financial goals and dreams. This book will provide you with the necessary tools, as well as a roadmap to getting to your very own *point X*, financial independence.

Bob Oros, *CEO of HD Vest Financial Services*

Preface

Living the American Dream

My first clients were quintessential examples of successful American Dreamers. They came to the United States from Italy after World War II with nothing, and they created a wonderful life for themselves and their children by working hard, living modestly, and saving. I confess I learned more from their example than from any college course or studies that I finished in order to earn my licenses. As you might guess, these clients were my parents.

Rosario Vento, my father, was born in the small town of Messina, Sicily, in 1923. My mother, Concetta Giuffre Vento, born in 1921, came from an even smaller village nearby called Sant'Agata. They lived through the Great Depression (which was as bad in Europe as it was in the United States), survived World War II by seeking shelter in the hills of Sicily, and were married shortly after the war's end. It was clear that opportunities in Sicily and throughout Italy were limited as a result of the devastation of war, so they made the difficult decision to place their hopes and dreams on a new life in America.

Because he could not afford to pay for two tickets, my dad initially came to America alone. After a year, he was able to afford to rent a small but comfortable apartment in Bensonhurst, Brooklyn, and had saved enough money to pay for a one-way ticket to the United States for my mother. She joined him, and they began the great journey of their life together, eager to work hard and reap the rewards of living the American Dream.

Neither one had more than an eighth-grade education, nor did either one speak English very well. After arriving in the United States, my father worked as a barber, and my mother got a job as a seamstress in a sweatshop. They had three children in quick succession and then, after a gap of eight years, one more (me). Together, they earned a modest income, but they always managed to live within their means and save what they could. They never owned a car; instead, they got around the city by walking or using public transportation.

They rarely went out to dinner; instead, they always prepared fresh, homemade meals. Before they spent a dime, they always asked, "Is this necessary?" If the item was in fact a necessity, they would then ask: "Is there a less expensive alternative?"

This was my parents' attitude toward money throughout their lifetime, in good times and bad. During the early years of their life in Brooklyn, they saved enough for a down payment on a house and obtained a mortgage, which they paid off over 30 years. They put all four of their children through college; one became a teacher, one a medical doctor, one a social worker, and one a certified public accountant and Certified Financial Planner™ (again, me).

After I graduated from college, I began helping my parents manage their finances, although, as mentioned, they taught me much more about money than I was ever able to teach them. Each year, I prepared a Statement of Financial Position and a Statement of Cash Flow for them, an exercise that, for me, was not only a pleasure but a reconfirmation of the values they had taught me. They always lived well within their means, were careful savers, and were usually able to add funds to their investable assets. Over the years, I was able to assist them in developing a well-diversified investment portfolio.

Ultimately, the year my mother turned 75, they achieved a financial milestone that they had never thought possible. I was sitting at their kitchen table, sipping the espresso that my mother always prepared for me whenever I came to visit. On this particular day, I was there to talk to them about their finances. To my great joy, I was able to look my mother straight in the eyes, and say: "Congratulations, you and Papa are millionaires!" The combined value of their home, their invested assets, and their cash totaled just over a million dollars – and of course they had no debt.

Words cannot do justice to the expressions on their faces and the tears of joy in their eyes. At that moment, my parents knew that they had accomplished one of their most cherished goals – financial independence. For them, the American Dream was not just a dream anymore; it was now their reality.

My mother passed away in 2006 and my father in 2011. They left this Earth knowing that they had lived comfortably and responsibly. They had been able to raise, care for, and educate their children, and they never became a burden to us. In fact, upon their passing, they were able to leave their children with a solid financial legacy that could be measured both in dollars and by example. This book is dedicated to them and to the hope that the guidance in these pages can help you achieve your financial dreams, too.

John J. Vento

Acknowledgments

I want to thank everyone who helped make this second edition possible.

First, I would like to thank Bob Oros for recognizing the value this book could have in increasing financial literacy throughout the country. His support by providing assistance from many of HD Vest's top specialists has truly taken the second edition to a whole new level. I am truly grateful to Clint Brookshire, Jonathan Dodd, James Hickey, Julie Marta, Chad Smith, and Carol Ventura for the value they added to this book by sharing their wealth of knowledge. I give my sincere thanks to Andrea Dorsett for coordinating this effort and Eric Ungs for his creative ideas.

I want to thank Annamarie Gentile for her contribution and expertise in the area of estates, trusts, and elder care planning. I also want to thank Jerry Filipski for his contribution to the business retirement planning section. The advice and guidance these experts provided raised the bar in both of these areas.

Many thanks to my entire staff for their support and assistance throughout this project. I would like to give a special thanks to Kim Riccio, our firm's tax manager, for her unmatched expertise in researching the latest tax laws. She has been my go-to person for almost two decades. I also want to give a special thanks to Norman J. Axelrod, our firm's senior tax manager, for all his fact checking, research, and proofreading.

I can't thank Carly Racioppi enough for managing this project, proofreading the transcript, adding her insight, and never hesitating to give me her honest opinion. She proved herself as a tremendous asset to this second edition.

When I wrote the first edition, my three children, John, Christine, and Nicole, were teenagers and assisted me every step of the way in putting my words and thoughts on paper. That experience opened their minds to the world of business and finance, and they have all since graduated college with degrees in accounting and finance. My daughters have recently started their professional careers, Christine at KPMG Deal Advisory and Nicole at Goldman Sachs as a financial analyst. My son, who is also a CPA now, recently left Pricewaterhouse-Coopers to join my firm as a senior accountant. They have put in countless late nights and weekends in assisting me with this book. The word "proud" does not do justice to how I feel about them and the fact that they have decided to follow in my footsteps with a career in finance.

Last but not least, to my wife Doreen: I can't thank you enough for sharing your life with me and for the amazing mother you have been to our children. You have shown not only me, but our children as well, the true meaning of life. Happiness is being married to your best friend. Thank you for being the most important person in my life and my biggest supporter.

J. V.

Introduction

Getting to *Point X*

Every kid over the age of five knows this expression. It can refer to many things, but the strongest image for most of us is an ancient, moldy pirate's map showing precisely where a long-lost treasure is buried. This book was written to help you discover your own "buried treasure." Of course, this is not a child's game. It is a guide to the necessary knowledge (with a special focus on **Tax Alpha to the 2nd Power**^SM facts and strategies) to help you accumulate the wealth you need to lead the life you desire.

I have been a certified public accountant (CPA) and a Certified Financial Planner™ (CFP®) for many years. I started my career working for KPMG (one of the Big Four accounting firms) and then established my own practice in 1987. I have worked one-on-one with literally thousands of individuals, assisting them in their pursuit of a secure financial future. I have helped these people pursue their financial goals, and this has given them and me tremendous pleasure. However, I have also seen people who, for many reasons, have been unable to achieve financial security. Needless to say, this is unfortunate.

With this book, my hope is to help everyone find financial security and financial independence: from the eager teenager who just received his first paycheck; to the dual-income couple in mid-life who are paying their mortgage, putting their kids through college, and perhaps helping aging parents; to the retired grandmother who wants to make sure her estate is in good order for the benefit of her loved ones. By combining financial planning with tax strategies, this book may help readers increase their personal wealth and pursue their financial independence, a position I refer to as *point X*.

Financial Literacy and the Move Away from Capitalism

Before I explain in detail how to reach *point X* – financial independence – I want to talk a bit about how and why I came to write this book. The term *financial literacy* is not new, but it appears in our general lexicon more and more frequently these days, especially since the worldwide financial crisis of 2008. For the first part of the decade that preceded this crisis, the unsettled economy had been described by the *Wall Street Journal* and other sources as "the New Norm." Experts believed that this recession unleashed a "new normal," where the spendthrift ways indulged in by many before the 2008 crisis had been substituted with an increasing interest in saving, general frugality, and the need to develop a stronger sense of financial literacy.

As a result of the 2008 economic meltdown, it became stunningly obvious that many people have not managed their finances in such a way as to provide financial freedom for themselves and their families at any stage of their lives – much less after they retire. In fact, many financial organizations report that most (yes, most!) Americans currently reaching retirement age – the infamous baby boomers – have not planned or saved adequately for retirement.

Somehow over the past several decades – I believe since the end of World War II – many people in our society have come to believe incorrect notions about money. These financial myths include such ideas as:

- "Owning your own home is everyone's right."
- "The real estate market will always rise."
- "You can live 'large' on credit and never pay any consequences."
- "If you need to work, you can always find a job."

These myths – a warped conception of the American Dream – exploded in a puff of smoke in 2008. (In fact, they were eroding for many years, but most people failed to heed the warnings.) As a result, many people have suffered financially, some tragically. Many of us were disenchanted by this new norm in our society, as can be seen by the move towards socialism in the United States and abroad. The lessons in frugality learned by earlier generations – people who lived through the Great Depression of the 1930s and World War II – had been lost. Many Americans were living way beyond their means, and they now had to pay up.

As a result of the 2008 Great Recession and its aftermath, we all must now relearn some essential financial truths, become financially responsible, and prepare for the financial realities of life. In other words, we must become *financially literate*. We must learn all we can about our money so that we can make the most informed financial decisions in all facets of our lives.

In my opinion, the millennials were the generation that was most significantly affected by the financial crisis of 2008 and experienced first-hand the consequences of the financial blunders of the baby boomers, their parents. This younger generation has come to realize the importance of being financially responsible. Many of them were caught up in the financial hardships experienced by their parents and neighbors. They saw foreclosures on homes in their neighborhoods, families being torn apart because of lost jobs, and the inability to meet the most essential living expenses. Many millennials have been unable to afford to rent their own apartments, let alone to own their own homes, which has caused many young adults to move back in with their parents. The promises made to them that working hard and going to college would result in a terrific paying job simply were not true. Some have lost all hope of ever being able to pay off their burden of student loan debt. This feeling of hopelessness has left many of them disenchanted by capitalism, which has resulted in an increasing number of millennials openly admitting that they would prefer a socialist society.

According to a new YouGov study commissioned by the Victims of Communism Memorial Foundation, 44% of millennials would prefer to live in a socialist country, with another 7% saying the same about communism. Only 42% said they would choose to live in a capitalistic country like the United States, according to the survey of 2,000 millennials. There is definitely a generational divide between the baby boomers and the millennials on this matter.

I am hopeful that the major improvements in the US economy over the past several years will turn around this attitude against capitalism. With the declining unemployment rate, increase in economic growth, and hope for prosperity, I am confident that this generation will begin to believe in the true American Dream once again; this country is in fact the land of opportunity and not the land of entitlements. The baby boomer generation must take responsibility that they, and not the younger generation, created this socialist mentality. It may take decades to reverse this perception of what being an American should represent, but I am hopeful that it will happen sooner rather than later.

In many ways, the millennials are similar to the generation that lived through the Great Depression. I believe that this generation will not only survive, but will prosper from the lessons learned through their life experiences. The millennials will not repeat the same mistakes made by their parents' generation. I am very optimistic about their future, as well as the future of all Americans. For this reason, this book and the guidance it provides will be essential in teaching all generations of Americans that there is hope in achieving their own financial independence, *point X*. The first step we must take as a society is to educate ourselves in becoming financially literate.

Financial literacy means having a firm understanding of fundamental financial concepts and strategies, and the ability to manage money responsibly in order to work towards financial security. Financial literacy is essential to the financial stability of individuals and families, as well as the overall economic health of society as a whole.

Point X: Our Fundamental Financial Goal

Point X is literally and fundamentally the point at which we can stop working for our money and our money starts working for us. It is the spot at which our savings and investments alone generate enough income to support our chosen lifestyle, and allow us to continue to live that lifestyle without having to work for a paycheck. It is the place where we have achieved true financial independence.

For most of us, getting to *point X* is our most fundamental financial goal. It is the position we hope to achieve so that we can retire. Even if we do not wish to retire from productive and enjoyable work, we all still yearn to arrive at *point X* – often sooner rather than later – to feel financially secure and financially free.

What that number may be in terms of dollars is different for each of us. Some people can manage rich full lives on a modest income, and seem to be able to find their *point X* with ease and clarity. Others have multimillion-dollar annual incomes, yet still find themselves living way beyond their means and view getting to *point X* as an arduous and perhaps an impossible journey. How you determine your personal *point X* depends on several variables, including:

- Understanding your present standard of living
- Projecting how you want to live after you retire (or after you stop receiving a paycheck)
- Figuring out how many years of saving it will take for you to reach *point X*
- Figuring out how many years of financial independence you hope to enjoy after you reach *point X*

Determining your personal *point X* also involves some mathematical calculations, including:

- The rate of return you hope to achieve on your investments
- The effects of inflation and taxes on your investments before and after you retire

Although this process of defining *point X* may look like grad-school calculus right now, I promise you it is really not all that difficult, and my purpose in writing this book is to explain this process in the simplest way possible.

Ten Key Issues to Comprehensive Wealth Management

No matter how you define your particular *point X*, whether it is an annual income of $25,000 or an estate of $250 million, you need to understand and effectively deal with 10 fundamental wealth management issues. They are:

1. Committing to living within your means and conscientiously saving for the future
2. Understanding taxes and how to effectively minimize your tax obligation
3. Realistically defining your standard of living, including your net worth and your current cash flow
4. Managing debt
5. Insuring yourself and your family in case of extreme illness or death
6. Protecting your property
7. Planning for the education of yourself and your children
8. Investing intelligently and productively
9. Planning for retirement
10. Preserving your estate

Throughout our lives, we are in a perpetual state of change, financially and otherwise. Our needs and wants are constantly altering along with our income and our standard of living. What may seem like a financial priority at the age of 18 (buying a car; paying for college or graduate school) is probably quite different by the age of 30 (purchasing a first home or planning for the birth of a child). At 60, we may be considering retirement while simultaneously paying for a child's college education or an elderly parent's care.

What makes these financial issues even more challenging is that our economy is also in a constant state of change.

Throughout our lives, we will encounter many questions and problems relating to money, but every one of them will fall, in some way, under one or more of these 10 key wealth management issues. It is important that you understand them and work within them productively – that you become financially literate. Depending on how you prepare and handle each of these wealth management issues will determine how successful you will be on your path to financial independence, *point X.* Moreover, these issues are interrelated, and how you deal with one very often will have an effect on how you treat the others. For example, if you fail to manage debt properly, you will find it difficult to save for a home of your own, your child's education, or your retirement. Or, if you neglect to properly insure yourself against sickness or premature death, your spouse and family could be wiped out.

Woven into the issues of wealth management is a common variable. Throughout this book, I provide facts and strategies that will focus on minimizing this most significant expenditure, that is, *taxes.*

Our Biggest Expense

Have you ever gotten to the end of the week, the month, or the year, and asked yourself *where did all my money go?* Many – maybe most – people are baffled by this question and do not understand how, even if they are earning a respectable salary, their entire salary could be used up, particularly when they were not especially extravagant. They find themselves with little or no savings, or even worse, in additional debt.

What do you consider to be your biggest expense? Most people think it is their mortgage or their rent. Others who have children in college feel sure that it is those endless educational expenses. Still others who may have serious health issues may believe it is their perpetual doctor, hospital, and prescription bills.

Well, I promise you, it is none of the above. It is taxes!

Yes, that is where most of your money has gone – and continues to go: taxes, taxes, and even more taxes. For 2018, the maximum federal income tax rate is 37%. On top of that, the combined Social Security tax rate is 15.3% (half paid by the employer and half paid by the employee). Employers also have to pay additional payroll taxes under the Federal Unemployment Tax Act (FUTA) and State Unemployment Tax Act (SUTA). Depending on where you live, you may also be paying well over 10% of your paycheck on state and local taxes; for example, New York City residents pay a combined state and city income tax, which is as high as 12.7%.

If payroll taxes were not enough, we also pay income and capital gains taxes on our other earnings, such as income from investments. We pay sales tax on many items we purchase, and we pay numerous excise taxes and other special taxes on many items we frequently do not even think about, such as alcohol, tobacco, and fuel. We pay for certain licensing fees, registration fees, parking meters, tolls, tickets, and summonses, all of which are forms of taxation. We also pay real estate taxes, school taxes, water and sewer taxes, mortgage recording taxes, and transfer taxes on property. If you choose to give large gifts to a friend or family member, you may be subject to a gift tax. Clearly the government will tax you to death; in fact, ironically it already taxes you for dying – a little something called estate tax.

If you take a close look at how much you pay for various taxes, chances are this number would be more than 50% of your overall expenditures. Keep in mind that some of these taxes are hidden but nevertheless included in your cost of living.

So what would be the single most important expenditure for you to focus on in order to keep more of what you make and dramatically increase your savings? The answer, of course, is taxes – taxes, taxes, and more taxes.

But the fact is that most people completely overlook the importance of minimizing their taxes in order to help maximize their wealth accumulation. You must implement a "tax alpha" strategy for each of the wealth management issues discussed throughout this book. Tax alpha's focus in the past has revolved around the investment decision-making process and has fallen short in addressing all of the wealth management issues throughout an individual's lifetime.

Throughout this book, I have now exponentially created *Tax Alpha to the 2nd Power*^{SM} by optimizing sound tax strategies and applying them throughout the entire financial planning process. I provide hundreds of *Tax Alpha to the 2nd Power* facts and strategies that will help you accelerate your wealth accumulation and dramatically increase your chances of reaching *point X*, financial independence.

Take a Financial Planning Checkup

Before we begin to discuss hard figures, you should evaluate your financial situation by completing the Comprehensive Wealth Management Questionnaire. This questionnaire will help you start thinking about the financial issues you have under control and others that may need attention.

COMPREHENSIVE WEALTH MANAGEMENT QUESTIONNAIRE

The following 20 questions will assist you with identifying your financial strengths and weaknesses and in setting your financial goals toward the pursuit of achieving financial independence, your very own *point X*.

1. Do you save 10% or more of your gross income (pay yourself first) before determining your standard of living? If you answered *no,* read Chapter 1, "Committing to Living Within Your Means."
2. Do you have easily accessible funds to cover at least three to six months of your living expenses in case of an emergency? If you answered *no,* read Chapter 1, "Committing to Living Within Your Means."
3. If you have a desire for a special purpose (e.g., a home, a special vacation, a wedding, or a business startup), do you have plans for accumulating those funds? If you answered *no,* read Chapter 1, "Committing to Living Within Your Means."
4. Do you know if you are taking advantage of every tax deduction and tax credit available to you? If you answered *no,* read Chapter 2, "Understanding Taxes," and pay particular attention to the **Tax Alpha to the 2nd Power** facts and strategies at the end of each chapter.
5. Do you know the value of your financial net worth? If you answered *no,* read Chapter 3, "Determining Your Financial Position."
6. Do you have a clear understanding of your *cash inflows* and *outflows?* If you answered *no,* read Chapter 3, "Determining Your Financial Position."
7. Do you maintain a zero balance on your credit cards and maintain no other high-interest rate loans? If you answered *no,* read Chapter 4, "Managing Debt."
8. Do you know whether you have the most favorable terms on your home or investment property mortgage(s)? If you answered *no,* read Chapter 4, "Managing Debt."
9. Do you have medical insurance that covers basic medical expenses as well as catastrophic medical expenses? If you answered *no,* read Chapter 5, "Insuring Your Health and Life."

10. Do you (or your parents) have a plan for paying for nursing home or long-term home health care costs? If you answered *no,* read Chapter 5, "Insuring Your Health and Life."

11. Do you have long-term disability insurance to help pay your expenses if you or your spouse were unable to earn an income? If you answered *no,* read Chapter 5, "Insuring Your Health and Life."

12. Will your family receive sufficient funds from your life insurance policies upon your death or the death of your spouse to ensure your family's continued support and lifestyle? If you answered *no,* read Chapter 5, "Insuring Your Health and Life."

13. Do you carry a minimum of $1,000,000 in personal liability insurance? If you answered *no,* read Chapter 6, "Protecting Your Property with Insurance."

14. Are your assets that you cannot afford to replace properly covered by insurance (e.g., car, home, fine jewelry, art)? If you answered *no,* read Chapter 6, "Protecting Your Property with Insurance."

15. Do you have sufficient funds set aside to pay for your children (or grandchildren) to attend college? If you answered *no,* read Chapter 7, "Paying for College."

16. Do you know if you will be financially ready to retire or become financially independent at your desired age? If you answered *no,* read Chapter 8, "Planning for Retirement."

17. If you are changing jobs or retiring, are you confident that you understand your financial options and are making the right choices? If you answered *no,* read Chapter 8, "Planning for Retirement."

18. Do you fully understand the different investment choices (stocks, bonds, mutual funds, exchange-traded funds [EFT], etc.) available to you? If you answered *no,* read Chapter 9, "Managing Your Investments."

19. Do you (and your spouse) have a will? Has it been reviewed by an attorney within the past five years, and was it drafted in your current state of residence? If you answered *no,* read Chapter 10, "Preserving Your Estate."

20. Do you (and your spouse) have a health care proxy and power of attorney? If you answered *no,* read Chapter 10, "Preserving Your Estate."

How to Use the Questionnaire

To answer many of these questions, you will need to gather certain documents including copies of your will, health care proxy, insurance policies, and banking and brokerage statements. After you have answered these questions completely and honestly, you will quickly be able to identify the major wealth management issues you need to focus on.

Many of these issues should be addressed no matter what your age or situation. For example, even if you are single and still in your twenties, you should have sufficient health insurance, be saving for the proverbial rainy day, and be planning financially for retirement, if only by participating fully in your company's retirement plan. Also, you may need a will, a health care proxy, and a power of attorney. If you are married, have children, and own a home and other valuable property, additional issues will become increasingly important, like sufficient life insurance, health insurance, and property insurance. As you get into your fifties and beyond, you will be more and more concerned with paying for your children's education, possibly caring for aging parents, and (again) saving for retirement.

All of these subjects are addressed in detail in subsequent chapters of this book.

The Power of This Book

Becoming financially independent is not something that happens by chance; it requires focus, discipline, determination, sacrifice, and a lot of hard work. If you are serious about achieving financial independence and are willing to make the commitment to do what it takes, then this book will provide you with the necessary tools to pursue your financial goals. In short, I will guide you toward reaching your own personal *point X*, financial independence.

Using financial planning strategies – the 10 key issues to comprehensive wealth management – and many real-life (though anonymous) client stories – I show how to navigate through the most critical factors that affect you and your family's financial life. Most importantly, I explain how to employ current **Tax Alpha to the 2nd Power** facts and strategies in order to save hundreds – and perhaps thousands – of dollars every year. By doing so, you will not only minimize your biggest expense, you will maximize the money you can put into your pocket (or your investment portfolio), helping you reach financial independence.

Thus, this book is a complete resource for anyone concerned with building wealth and financial security in today's no-guarantee financial environment. It is my hope that this comprehensive and up-to-the-minute book will become the essential financial guide for every individual and every family.

What's New in the Second Edition

2018 has marked a year of fundamental change to America's tax system, so the timing could not have been better for me to refresh the content of this book. The Trump administration's Tax Cuts and Jobs Act, which is designed to stimulate America's economic growth primarily by lowering income taxes, is the most significant tax reform since the Reagan era. I have detailed many of these tax law changes throughout the book, especially in the "*Tax Alpha to the 2nd Power* Facts and Strategies" section at the end of most chapters. This will provide you with some of the newest tax-planning strategies that you may want to consider putting into place right away. With such sweeping changes, it is critically important that you obtain an understanding of how these modifications will specifically impact your financial future.

This edition also includes a new Chapter 11, titled "Starting Your Own Business." Although this chapter is not part of the personal 10 Wealth Management Issues, it will cover the path by which so many entrepreneurs have reached their own *point X*. I will share with you my experience over the past 30 years of helping hundreds of small business owners achieve financial independence. The chapter concludes with an explanation of what the Tax Cuts and Jobs Act will mean for your small business, as well as *Tax Alpha to the 2nd Power* facts and strategies for wealth accumulation.

Considering that there are more people today aged 65 and older than ever before in history, according to the US Census Bureau, it would be remiss of me not to include a section on elder care planning. Chapter 10, "Preserving Your Estate," will now provide some guidance on how to plan and ultimately prepare for long-term care costs for you, your parents, or your grandparents.

These major changes and updates to the second edition will ensure that you continue to be on the right path to achieving and maintaining your financial independence, *point X*. Whether this is your first time reading my book, or you have studied the first edition in detail, you will find this information to be invaluable in achieving your financial goals and dreams.

CHAPTER 1

Committing to Living Within Your Means

There is no dignity quite so impressive, and no independence quite so important, as living within your means.

—Calvin Coolidge,
30th president of the United States

We all want to live the American Dream. Beginning with the earliest European settlers, Americans have sought the heights of success and prosperity for themselves and their children, and have believed firmly that we can achieve it, no matter our race, religion, nationality, or gender. All it takes is hard work and discipline.

The American Dream Becomes the American Nightmare

Our country was founded on the conviction that it was the land of opportunity and prosperity – that was the definition of the American Dream. In the early years of our country's existence, infinite real estate was available for the taking, a great boon for a basically agrarian society. If you wanted more land, all you had to do was pack up your wagon, travel farther west, and claim it. If you were willing to work hard, you could earn an honest living, rear and educate your children, and save for your family's future. These principles stood firm for almost two centuries.

Nevertheless, perhaps because of the decades of affluence that followed World War II, this land of "equal opportunity" turned into the land of "expected entitlements." People came to believe that living beyond their means – usually on credit – was acceptable, and "living large" became the norm. Younger people no longer thought they needed to save for a down payment on a house, a new car, or a luxurious vacation. They could just put the costs on a credit card or take out a loan. Even professional financial institutions fed into this false sense of affluence, giving credit cards, large home mortgages, and home-equity loans to people they knew full well could never pay them off. This distorted definition of the American Dream significantly contributed to the financial crisis of 2008 and turned this dream into a nightmare for many people. Although the road to recovery was a long and painful one since 2008, many people have since dug themselves out of this hole by following the very principles I have outlined in this book.

If my parents were able to come to a foreign land with only an eighth-grade education, barely able to speak the language, and end up as millionaires, certainly anyone blessed with the education and opportunities available to most Americans today can become financially independent. Anyone can get to *point X* – the point at which you can support yourself and your family financially with your *investments*, not a salary. All it takes is knowledge of good financial practices and the discipline to carry them out.

Living Within Your Means: The Essential Step

The single most important step you must take to become financially independent is to commit to living within your means. This sounds obvious; this sounds easy. But believe me, it is not!

Amazingly, many people do not understand what "living within your means" actually implies! I believe that the definition of "living within your means" is living on *less than* your take-home salary and any other resources you receive, such as income from an annuity or a trust. Living within your means does *not* mean existing from paycheck to paycheck. Living within your means does *not* mean living on credit or on loans. Living within your means does *not* mean turning to parents or friends to pay the tab when you cannot quite meet the rent or need to buy a new computer. It means not only figuring out how to pay for your needs and wants, but budgeting your income so that you still have a little money left over.

Paying Yourself First

In addition to living within your means, if you are ever going to get to *point X*, you must also *save* money. (You will ultimately need to invest this money productively, but I'll cover that in Chapter 9, "Managing Your Investments.") I call this exercise *paying yourself first*. Therefore, "living within your means" includes not only such necessities as shelter, food, utilities, and clothing, but also payment into your personal savings. Ideally, that payment should be 10% or more of your gross pay. You may think that this is impossible, but once you get started, you will realize how easy it can be. And, of course, if you can afford more, by all means, put those funds in savings or invested assets.

The following is an example of how this could work and how this will help you achieve financial independence. If you are earning $52,000 a year, that is $1,000 a week gross income, and you are probably bringing home about $700 of that after taxes. If you *pay yourself first* by funding your 401(k) plan with 10% of your gross income, that is $100 per week (or $5,200 a year), which may earn a rate of return with compounding over the time invested. If you start saving that at age 21 and retire at age 65, you will have saved $228,800 over those 44 years. Also, that $100 you save affects your take-home pay by only $70 (assuming a 30% tax rate), so you will be taxed on $900 instead of $1,000 per week, which means you will bring home $630 instead of $700 per week. Yes, that is $70 less money you have to spend on your needs and wants, but you get the full benefit of $100 saved. Assuming you can earn 7% per year on your 401(k) investments over the 44-year period,[1] you may be able to accumulate $1,383,829 by the age of 65. I believe that saving now is a small price to pay for financial independence in the future. I do not know any easier way to achieve financial independence. By the way, this does not even factor in employer matching dollars, which can significantly increase your savings.

"Paying yourself first" must be as much a necessity to you as the roof over your head, the food on your table, and the clothes on your back. It is not a luxury; it is not something you will start doing next week or next month or next year, but it is an essential expense that you must pay *now*.

---

[1]The rates of return shown above are purely hypothetical and do not represent the performance of any individual investment or portfolio of investments. They are for illustrative purposes only and should not be used to predict future product performance. Specific rates of return, especially for extended time periods, will vary over time. There is also a higher degree of risk associated with investments that offer the potential for higher rates of return. You should consult with your representative before making any investment decision.

Know the Difference Between What You Need and What You Want

If you asked most people to define the necessities (or essentials) of life, they would probably say: shelter, food, and clothing. I have just added another essential to that list: saving money on a regular basis, or paying yourself first. However, defining what is essential (and not essential) in terms of shelter, food, clothing, and savings requires some additional attention:

- Shelter should not be the biggest house in the best neighborhood decorated with the most expensive furniture (*not essential*); instead, shelter means a house or apartment that gives comfort and safety to your family, which you can pay for and maintain with the money you have available (*essential*).
- Providing food for yourself and your family does not mean eating out every night at the fanciest restaurants or even ordering in from the local pizzeria or Chinese restaurant (*not essential*), but it means preparing healthy meals from foods paid for within a food budget you have established (*essential*).
- Clothing does not mean buying the latest $200 jeans or other overpriced designer apparel (*not essential*), but it means planning for your family's clothing needs based on a well-thought-out budget (*essential*).
- In terms of saving money, you need not try to sock away 25% of your salary, especially if money is tight (*not essential*); you simply need to get in the habit of saving 10% or more of your gross pay (*essential*).

In other words, you need to begin to discriminate between the nonessentials and the essentials, your wants and your needs.

In working with the finances of thousands of people over the past 30 years, I have noticed one common trait in everyone who ultimately achieves financial independence: They experience anxiety every time they are faced with the decision to make a purchase that is not essential. Whether it is an expensive cup of coffee or an expensive car (or even a not-so-expensive car!), if they buy it, they experience anxiety and guilt. In other words, for these people, the pain of purchasing a nonessential item exceeds the pleasure.

Usually, when faced with such a decision, instead of acting impulsively, they ask themselves if the purchase is necessary.

(Do I need a new suit for my first day at a new job?) If the answer is *no*, they are comfortable with the decision. *(I can wear my old suit; I'll have it dry-cleaned and pressed, and no one will know that I've had it for three years.)* If the answer is *yes (My old suit is looking a little worn – and having a new suit will help me to feel confident on my first day on the job!)*, they always look for a less-expensive alternative. *(Can I find an equally good suit at another store or on sale? Will a less-expensive suit look just as good – and make me feel just as self-confident?)*

The fact is, most Americans view this *essential* versus *nonessential* concept in completely the opposite way. Many people believe it is imperative to "keep up with the Joneses," to quote that old-fashioned expression, which implies a perceived necessity to appear as affluent as our friends, neighbors, and professional colleagues. Other expressions such as *shop till you drop* and *retail therapy* are now commonplace in our world, and are considered acceptable, amusing, and even cool! *Shopping till you drop* is thought by many people to be as beneficial to one's health as an afternoon of bicycling in a park; *retail therapy* is firmly believed to be a form of entertainment and even an antidote to anxiety and stress.

We are supposed to feel good about racking up thousands of dollars on our credit cards, and many people actually do get immense pleasure from excessive shopping (at least until the bills arrive). As for putting money into the bank instead of splurging on a new big-screen TV – forget it. This behavior has nothing to do with providing the *essentials* of life; it has to do with satisfying our *wants*, not our *needs*. And, of course, more often than not, it has everything to do with whether or not we are living beyond our means.

Discerning the difference between *essentials* versus *nonessentials*, *wants* versus *needs*, is imperative if you are going to live within your means, save sufficient money, and ultimately get to *point X*. You may need to train yourself to associate anxiety and guilt instead of pleasure with making those exciting, but nonessential, purchases. You may need to frequently remind yourself and members of your family that short-term gratification from buying nonessentials is not nearly as important or satisfying as achieving the long-term goal of financial security. When the pain you associate with sacrificing your financial future is greater than the immediate gratification of providing yourself and your family with nonessential items, you have mastered the skills necessary to becoming financially independent.

DAILY FINANCIAL AFFIRMATION

Securing my own and my family's financial future is my number-one priority.
I live within my means.
I always pay myself first.
I say *no* to nonessential purchases.

****

After you have written down this daily financial affirmation, say it out loud. Then post copies of it around your house in places where you (and other members of your family) will see it repeatedly throughout the day – in the center of your refrigerator door, on your bathroom mirror, and on your bedside table. Post another in your workplace, such as next to your telephone or on your computer screen saver. Place a copy in your wallet or purse. Consciously read your Daily Financial Affirmation first thing in the morning and last thing at night. During the day, if you experience a moment of weakness and are about to spend money on a nonessential expenditure, read your daily financial affirmation out loud once again.

Simple Saving

A traditional savings account is the first place you should consider putting the money you are paying yourself. Having enough cash on hand to see you through an illness, injury, job loss, or other financial emergency can help you avoid taking on debt or tapping into your retirement assets. It is just a smart move.

How much you save will depend on your needs, responsibilities, and comfort level. My rule of thumb suggests that you should have enough cash in savings to cover at least three months of expenses for couples with both partners earning an income, and you should have enough cash in savings to cover six months' expenses if you are single or married with only one spouse earning an income. If you fear that your job is in jeopardy or you think it will take you longer than six months to get back on your feet financially should you lose your job, you should try to have even more in savings. Also, if you are saving for anything other than the proverbial rainy day, such as for a house, wedding, new car, or special trip, count these funds as extra.

Given the relatively low interest rates offered at this time on cash instruments (which include savings accounts, money market funds, and certificates of deposit, or CDs) and the fact that the current rate of inflation is higher than the interest rate, you may actually be losing money on the ultimate purchasing power of your savings. However, do not let this alarm you too much. Saving in this way is still an essential part of getting to *point X*. Also, these savings come with Federal Deposit Insurance Corporation (FDIC) insurance of up to $250,000 per depositor, so your money is safe.

What Is the FDIC?

It is important to understand the added safety and reduced risk of saving your money with the protection of the FDIC. For some people, having the peace of mind of knowing their money is guaranteed to be returned to them is priceless. Traditional types of bank accounts, such as checking accounts, savings accounts, and CDs, are insured by the FDIC. Banks also may offer what is called a *money market deposit account*, which earns interest at a rate set by the bank and usually limits the customer to a certain number of transactions within a stated period of time. All of these types of accounts generally are insured by the FDIC up to the legal limit of $250,000 per depositor, per institution, and sometimes even more for special kinds of accounts or ownership categories. For more information on deposit insurance, go to the FDIC website at www.fdic.gov.

Many banking and brokerage institutions also offer consumers a broad array of investment products such as mutual funds, annuities, life insurance policies, stocks, and bonds. Unlike traditional checking or savings accounts, however, these nondeposit investment products are *not* insured by the FDIC. Many people are under the false impression that if they purchase something through their bank, they will be protected by the FDIC. This clearly is not the case and you must always understand the risks associated with putting your money into non-FDIC-insured accounts.

Saving for Special Situations

There's an old saying: "All work and no play makes Jack a dull boy." We could adjust that adage slightly and say, "All saving and no *splurging* makes Jack a dull boy." But perhaps it is the word *splurge* that needs the adjustment.

Getting to *point X* primarily refers to achieving ultimate financial independence, the point where you can stop working for your money, and your money can start working for you. But for most of us throughout our lives, other expensive essentials (and nonessentials) will undoubtedly present themselves, and these will require special savings. These might include major purchases, such as buying a first home, paying for your own or a child's lavish wedding, celebrating a daughter's "sweet 16" birthday party or your parents' 50th wedding anniversary, or finally taking a lifelong dream vacation, such as going on a safari in Africa or a trip to the Far East.

When planning for these special events and purchases, you need to view them as requiring additional savings, beyond your cash security savings, and add them as line items to your budget. You might even consider opening separate savings accounts to help you budget for these special situations, and earmark these funds for that special purpose. Nevertheless, you should never sacrifice your primary long-term goal of achieving financial independence in order to meet these other shorter-term desires.

Easier Said Than Done

Granted, a world of difference exists between knowing what to do and *actually* doing it. We know that in order to reach *point X* and become financially independent, we must spend less than we make and save more from our salaries, or *pay ourselves first*. But now comes the hard part: We must actually do it! The prospect can be overwhelming, both emotionally and financially.

We live in a society of instant gratification; we want more and we want it now, whether it is a daily $5 cappuccino from the local coffee house, a $500 pair of shoes, a $50,000 car, or a $500,000 house. These examples may be exaggerations, but many of us feel bad about ourselves if we seem to be faring less well financially than our friends and colleagues. We feel a need to maintain a high standard of living, even if that standard of living is based on borrowed money and is measured in such superficialities as expensive coffees and prestigious labels. Also, as discussed, many of us have learned to experience excessive spending as pleasurable, not painful. These emotional factors attached to living within our means can be troublesome, powerful, and difficult to overcome. But, like dieting, it is essential to your health that you become aware of these feelings and correct them.

For many people, the reality is that they have already dug themselves into a huge financial pit, and getting out of it is going to be time consuming and painful. They may need to pay off thousands of dollars of credit card debt (see Chapter 4, "Managing Debt") or enormous school loans (see Chapter 7, "Paying for College"), before they feel that they can begin to seriously save. This is daunting, to be sure, but not hopeless.

Stop the Insanity

Albert Einstein defined insanity as "doing the same thing over and over again and expecting a different result." If you have been living beyond your means and not saving – and wondering why you never have any money – now is the time to stop the insanity! Stop splurging on small nonessentials and start saving for the big essentials, the greatest being your own and your family's financial security. You must commit to living within your means, discriminate between nonessential wants and essential needs, and save for your future. It is your treasure, and ultimately, it is your *point X.*

 AN ACTION PLAN FOR COMMITTING TO LIVING WITHIN YOUR MEANS

- **Make the serious commitment to live within your means.** Discuss this commitment with your spouse and children, and urge them to commit as well.
- **Pay yourself first.** Include saving money in your budget, just as you do any other essential living expense.
- **Open a savings account. Save 10% or more of your gross pay.** Ask your bank to automatically move the designated amount from your checking account to your savings account.
- **Keep sufficient cash available** to cover three to six months of your basic living expenses, depending on your needs.
- **Place the "Daily Financial Affirmation" in key places** around your house where you and members of your family will see it frequently.
- **If you are saving money for a special purpose, add that amount to your budget** as an additional line item, and consider opening a separate account for that purpose.
- **Complete the Comprehensive Wealth Management Questionnaire** (see the Introduction) to assist you in establishing your financial priorities and goals.

CHAPTER 2

Understanding Taxes

The hardest thing in the world to understand is the income tax.

—Albert Einstein,
father of modern physics

Taxes are the price we pay to live in our society. Our federal and state income taxes pay for everything from roads, public schools, public libraries, and hospitals to national parks, dams, the US military services, and the salaries of all the people who work for the US government, including the President of the United States. Our taxes also pay for Social Security, Medicare, and other social services. Although we want, need, and appreciate these services, many of us fear that a tremendous amount of money is wasted in the management of government – and we are paying for it.

The fact is, the average American family pays more than one-third of its income in federal, state, and local income taxes – and even more in property taxes, excise taxes, sales taxes, and other hidden taxes, such as taxes on cigarettes, liquor, and certain luxuries. So this means that the average person works all day Monday and most of Tuesday for the government, and then they work the rest of the week for their own benefit. Just another reason to hate going to work on Mondays! In other words, for just about everyone, taxes are our biggest personal expense, by far.

In order to reach *point X*, it is imperative that you understand the basics of our tax system. You must practice careful and creative tax preparation and planning, so that your personal tax burden does not deplete your income unnecessarily, and your wealth can accumulate quickly and safely. Tax laws are incredibly complicated, and there is no reason for you to read or understand the virtually infinite ins and outs of the often arcane US Tax Code. Most people do need help from professional tax advisors to benefit from tax strategies; however, you should have enough basic knowledge about taxes and the tax system to ask the right questions and find the appropriate help to suit your own unique financial and tax needs. And that is what this chapter provides: an understanding of the basics you need to know to be financially literate.

A Brief History of the US Tax System

I begin this chapter with a very brief history of taxes in the United States, so that you can be prepared for what is to come. I remember sitting in my first history class as a child and my teacher saying, "The reason we study history is because our history tends to repeat itself."

The subject of taxes has been a significant part of American history since long before the American Colonies became the United States of America. Every schoolchild remembers the Boston Tea Party of 1773, when the citizens of Boston dressed as Native Americans and dumped tea into Boston Harbor to protest Britain's unfair taxation on tea throughout the Colonies. This rebellious act played a strong role in the start of America's Revolutionary War.

Actually, taxes had already been a part of the American Colonial government since almost the moment the first Colonists arrived. In addition to taxes imposed by Britain, each individual Colony imposed local taxes on themselves. The first property taxes were imposed on Colonists as early as 1634, less than 15 years after the Pilgrims landed at Plymouth Rock.

However, in the early years of the new nation, taxes were imposed by the individual states, not the federal government. The Articles of Confederation, the predecessor to the United States Constitution, was proposed by the Continental Congress in 1776 (the same year that body declared the independence of 13 former colonies from Great Britain) for the governing of their affairs and mutual interest. This was ratified by all 13 new states from 1778 to 1781 during the American Revolution for their mutual benefit. Article VIII of this document provided that all taxes for the common treasury be allocated to each of the states based on the estimated value of land, buildings, and improvements under the laws and authority of each state.

The Articles of Confederation was replaced by the United States Constitution, which created a national government, commencing in 1789. Article I, Section 2 *apportioned to the states direct taxation* and the number of representatives in the House of Representatives based on the populations of the states as defined by that section. Except for tariffs on imports, virtually all power for taxation rested with state and local governments, and until the mid-nineteenth century, many of the states relied on property taxes as a major source of revenue.

Income Taxes and the Sixteenth Amendment of 1913

After the American Revolution, tax on personal income was imposed by some state governments, but only in a small way. The first federal income tax was adopted as part of the Revenue Act of 1861 to pay for the Civil War, but it was allowed to lapse after the war was over. However, by the late nineteenth century, the increasing importance of intangible property, such as corporate stock, caused the states to shift to other forms of taxation. In 1913, the Sixteenth Amendment to the Constitution, which permitted the federal government to directly levy an income tax on individuals and corporations, was ratified.

The Sixteenth Amendment defined income as "all income from whatever source derived." In 1926, the law was organized as the US Code, or the Internal Revenue Code, and included tax on income, estates, gifts, excise, and certain other things. Over the years, particularly in 1954 and 1986, the Code was revised and expanded, but essentially it remained as it was devised almost 100 years ago.

Federal income tax rates have fluctuated wildly since they were established in 1913. In 1913, the proponents of the federal tax assured citizens that the federal tax on income would be small. The opponents of the income tax urged that, at least, there should be a provision to the Sixteenth Amendment capping the tax rate at no more than 10%. However, in 1918 when the government required money to fight World War I, the federal income tax rate was increased to an astonishing 77% for those in the highest income bracket.

Significant income tax cuts have been made over the years, usually based on the belief that tax cuts would spur economic growth. One such series of cuts was made during the 1920s; unfortunately, the last such cut in that series, made in 1928, was followed by the stock market crash in 1929 and the Great Depression. Taxes were raised again in the latter part of the Depression and reached new heights (94%!) during World War II, again in an effort to pay for a very

Exhibit 2.1   **Highest Marginal US Income Tax Rate: 1913 to 2018**

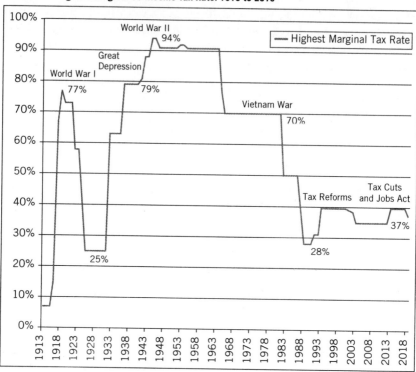

necessary war. Income tax rates were reduced significantly during the Johnson (1960s), Nixon (early 1970s), and Reagan (1980s) presidencies, and again between 2001 and 2008 during George W. Bush's presidency. Although Obama raised rates again during his presidency, President Donald Trump reduced rates across the board through his sweeping 2018 tax reform, the Tax Cuts and Jobs Act. Exhibit 2.1 illustrates the dramatic changes in income tax rates since 1913.

The Emergence of State and Local Income Taxes

Although individual states have taxed individuals since even before the formation of the US Constitution, most of these were taxes on property. Today, many states and some localities continue to rely heavily on property taxes as well as on retail sales taxes. By the 1920s, many states had adopted taxes on income for both individuals and corporations, similar in definition and structure to the taxes imposed by the federal government. The states generally taxed residents on all of their income, including income earned in other states, as well as income earned by nonresidents in a particular state. (For example, many people who earn income in New York City live in the nearby states of New Jersey, Connecticut, and even Pennsylvania. As a result, they are taxed by New York State.)

Where Are We Now with Regard to Taxes?

For the past several years, the federal income tax rates have hovered between 10% for those in the lower income bracket and 39.6% for those in the top income bracket. (Refer back to Exhibit 2.1, which shows income tax rates from 1913 through 2018.) As a result of President Trump's comprehensive tax reform act in 2018, we are seeing a decrease in income taxes across the board for nearly all levels of income. Although I am hopeful that the nation will enjoy a continued downward trend in tax rates, legislation can clearly change dramatically with a new administration or national crisis. Therefore, it is very important that you take into consideration the possibility of any future tax increases when implementing tax-saving strategies. As I have said repeatedly, minimizing your largest expenditure (taxes) is critically important to your wealth accumulation plan and to your ability to reach *point X*. You should refer to Appendix C for some basic concepts and definitions of various types of taxes.

Organizing and Retaining Your Records

Tax records should be carefully kept on a year-round basis – not thrown in a drawer or shoebox and then hastily assembled just for your annual tax appointment. Without tax records, you can lose valuable deductions by forgetting to include them on your tax return, or you may have unsubstantiated items disallowed if you are audited.

Generally, returns can be audited for up to three years after filing; however, the IRS may audit for up to six years, if it discovers substantial unreported income. The three- and six-year limits start with the filing of a tax return; if no return is filed, the time limit never starts to run. In other words, if you have failed to file a return, you can be audited and taxed at any time.

Which Records Are Important?

The following are some of the records that you will need to retain for tax purposes.

- Records of income received
- Tax-deductible expense items

- Home improvements, sales, and refinances (for homes with profit potential of $250,000 or more)
- Investment purchases and sales information
- Documentation for inherited property
- Medical expenses
- Charitable contributions (records vary with value of gift)
- Interest and taxes paid
- Records on nondeductible IRA contributions

How Long Should Records Be Kept?

Just how long you should keep records is partly a matter of judgment and a combination of state and federal statutes of limitations. Because federal tax returns can be audited for up to three years after filing (six years, if underreported income is involved), it is a good idea to keep most records for six years after the return filing date.

Some records are worth keeping permanently, partly because of long-term needs and partly because they take up very little room. Consider permanently retaining a copy of each year's tax return. Contracts, real estate buy-and-sell records, and records of property improvements should be retained for seven years after the property is sold.

If you are in business, your record requirements are more extensive.

As many businesses and individuals turn to paperless filing systems, it has become much easier to retain records for longer periods of time. The IRS accepts digital records, so thanks to technology, it now makes sense to keep your tax documents permanently in an electronic form. Going paperless can reduce the clutter, benefit the environment, and make files more accessible. Just keep an external backup drive or temporary paper copies to protect you from losing your important data.

Tax-Preparation Services

It is now undoubtedly clear to you that calculating and paying your income taxes is a complicated process, and the annually changing laws and codes affecting taxes make the job even more difficult. Bear in mind that you are legally responsible for your tax returns whether you prepare them yourself or hire someone else to prepare them for you. You have several choices.

Internal Revenue Service

One obvious resource for help with tax preparation is the IRS. Under certain circumstances, the IRS will prepare your federal income tax return if it is simple and you do not itemize your tax deductions. I would not recommend taking this approach, however, because it is not a function of the IRS to advise on strategies that can reduce your tax obligation; also, the IRS will not prepare any required state and local income tax returns.

Even if you would prefer to do your taxes yourself or hire a private professional preparer, the IRS offers many publications to help with tax planning and preparation. Check out the IRS website (www.irs.gov) for further information.

Tax Planning and Preparation Software

In general, two kinds of tax-related software are available: tax planning and tax preparation:

1. Planning programs help you to look into different strategies for managing taxes.
2. Preparation programs, such as TaxAct[1] or TurboTax® software packages, guide you through the preparation process.

If your taxes are relatively simple, these programs can save you time and money. However, if you have experienced major life changes (marriage, divorce, a significant inheritance), invest in the stock market, or are self-employed, you should probably secure the help of a tax professional.

Hiring a Tax Preparer

Most taxpayers conclude that preparing their own taxes is simply too difficult and time-consuming, and they turn to private professionals for help. A professional tax preparer helps you prepare the most accurate tax return and protects you from liability. A good tax preparer should also provide *advice* on tax strategy and help manage

---

[1] HD Vest Financial Services® and TaxAct, Inc. are wholly owned subsidiaries of Blucora, Inc. (NASDAQ: BCOR). HD Vest Financial Services® is the holding company for the group of companies providing financial services under the HD Vest name.

more complex tax problems. In fact, if your tax preparer is not saving you many times the cost of his or her tax preparation fee in tax saving strategies, then it may be time to look for another *tax advisor.*

Tax advisors come in a number of forms, with varying credentials and degrees of competence. The four most common are tax preparers (or nonlicensed services), enrolled agents (EAs), certified public accountants (CPAs), and tax attorneys, described in the following paragraphs. Appendix A offers a more in-depth overview of various professionals who can help you with your wealth management goals. You can also visit IRS.gov for more information on each of these designations.

Nonlicensed National and Local Tax Services   These preparers can be found in such companies as H&R Block and independent local firms. They must now register with the IRS and pass tests to prove that they have the minimum acceptable competence to prepare tax returns. These services are best if you have straightforward, simple returns.

Enrolled Agents   EAs are required to pass an extensive examination on various topics of taxation and must meet minimum continuing education requirements annually. They are also licensed and authorized to represent you before the IRS, should you be audited.

Certified Public Accountants   CPAs are highly trained and have passed complex and extensive examinations in the areas of accounting, taxation, auditing, and business law in order to be licensed. They must obtain advanced degrees that include rigorous courses in both accounting and taxation. They must also meet a minimum work experience requirement before they can be granted a license. CPAs are required to meet minimum continuing education requirements on an annual basis and are authorized to represent you before the IRS, should the need arise. They also must adhere to a fiduciary standard to their clients.

Tax Attorneys   These are lawyers who specialize in tax planning, and are most appropriate for those who have a complex tax situation that could result in legal problems, such as the sale of a business or a messy divorce.

Frankly, if you are committed to reaching *point X,* I strongly recommend that you secure the services of a professional tax advisor – one who is appropriate for your income and tax needs. In addition, you should schedule at least one additional meeting during the year, preferably before or after tax season, to discuss all of your tax planning and financial needs and goals.

Accumulating Wealth Through Tax Planning

As mentioned, our single largest expenditure is our tax obligation. When you factor in federal, state, and local income taxes and then Social Security and Medicare taxes, at current tax rates, more than 35% of our paychecks go toward taxes. Then, when you consider sales tax, cigarette tax, fuel tax, excise tax, property tax, estate and gift tax, this number can easily exceed 50% or more of your income.

So, if our single largest expense is taxes, then tax planning can be the most significant step you can take toward saving money and accumulating greater wealth. The government requires you to pay no more than the amount of taxes you are legally obligated to pay, but, believe it or not, the majority of people pay much more simply because they do not spend the time to understand more about tax planning. You should consider the tax consequences when making any major financial decision, whether it is buying a house or taking out a loan for your child's college education.

Tax Avoidance *Is Not Tax* Evasion*!*

The term *tax evasion* has a scary connotation. Most of us know that tax evasion (not paying our taxes by illegal means, such as under-reporting income or overstating deductions) is illegal. People have been known to spend time in jail for tax evasion. Tax evasion is illegal, pure and simple.

Tax avoidance, however, is perfectly legal. Tax avoidance is the legal utilization of the tax code to one's own advantage; in other words, you can reduce the amount of tax you pay by means that are within the law.

What Is Tax Planning?

Tax planning is just another way of saying *tax avoidance.* It is a way to maximize the amount of money you keep by minimizing the amount of taxes you pay. Tax planning means educating yourself on the many ways to avoid overpaying your taxes. By focusing on tax avoidance techniques, you will be able to minimize your taxes and maximize your wealth accumulation. More than any other method by far, this is the most efficient way to save money and accumulate wealth without dramatically altering your lifestyle.

Specifically, tax planning involves taking every tax deduction, tax credit, and tax deferral method allowed in the tax code, and using it to your advantage. You must make tax planning part of your everyday life, and always ask yourself: *Is this the most tax effective way to handle this financial situation?*

How Do I Learn About Tax Planning?

I suspect that after reading the preceding paragraph, you may be feeling completely overwhelmed. What is more, you are probably ready to really chew me out. (*Sure this guy knows about taxes – he is a CPA with an MBA in taxation.*) And that is true. Tax deductions, tax credits, and tax deferrals are second nature to me: studying these tax laws and strategies is what I do all day long. If you are like most people, your knowledge of taxes is probably limited. You bring your receipts to your tax accountant every year (if that), and hope for the best. Do not feel intimidated – that is normal.

However, becoming educated about taxes is not really that difficult, and once you begin to see how much money you will save by taking advantage of various tax credits and other tax-related advantages, you will become very motivated. Actually, you have already taken the first step in your educational process by reading this chapter. You should also read other books, journals, and articles, particularly those that address your professional and personal concerns. I would recommend visiting some well-known personal finance websites, which are packed with tax and financial planning strategies, such as Fox Business at foxbusiness.com/category/personal-finance.html and Yahoo! Finance at finance.yahoo.com/personal-finance. Beyond that, speak to your employer's human resources department about any and all employee tax-related benefits available to you, and make sure you act on them. Finally, communicate with your tax accountant and financial advisor. You need to do this more than once a year at tax time, when he or she is busiest. Instead, set up a meeting during the summer months, when most tax people have the time to really focus on your needs and think creatively on your behalf.

In the meantime, I have concluded each chapter with my top *Tax Alpha to the 2nd Power*[SM] facts and strategies as they relate to the key wealth management issue covered in that chapter. I believe that these sections will be the most valuable to you in your wealth-accumulation process. Read them carefully, and discuss them with your tax advisor to ensure that you are not paying a penny more in taxes than the law requires.

Tax Benefits

You can help reduce the amount of tax you owe by taking advantage of any number of tax benefits available to you. The goal of tax planning is to choose which tax benefits make the most sense for you and then implement them.

These tax benefits are how Congress rewards you for making certain types of financial decisions. For example, you may be able to reduce your total income (and therefore your progressive tax rate) if you contribute money to a retirement account, such as a 401(k) or IRA plan. This is Congress's way to motivate you to save for your retirement.

The income tax system is voluntary. You are free to arrange your financial affairs in such a way to take advantage of any tax benefits. *Voluntary* does not mean that the tax laws do not apply; you must pay your taxes. However, *voluntary* does mean you can choose to pay less tax by managing your finances in a way to minimize your taxes.

Before you focus on your particular concerns, you need to get an accurate picture of your true net worth, figure out where your money is coming from (and going to) at this very moment, establish your financial goals, and begin to budget for the future. Chapter 3, "Determining Your Financial Position," shows you how to do this. After all, you cannot get to *point X* if you do not know precisely where your starting point is before you begin your financial journey.

Tax Cuts and Jobs Act of 2017

On December 22, 2017, President Donald Trump signed the Tax Cuts and Jobs Act into law. As the largest change to America's tax system in over three decades, this law is a sweeping overhaul of both the individual and corporate tax codes. Trump's reform is designed to stimulate America's economic growth by lowering income taxes for the vast majority of Americans, as well as by creating jobs in the United States. We have already seen some of the effects of this tax reform through the 2017 stock market rally, as well through our paychecks, since we are now able to keep more of our hard-earned money. The combination of these two factors alone is sure to accelerate your arrival to financial independence, getting you closer to your *point X.*

This book reflects the latest tax law changes under the Tax Cuts and Jobs Act, and I have included many of the latest provisions in the **Tax Alpha to the 2nd Power** facts and strategies section at the end of each chapter. Many provisions in President Trump's tax reform law outlined throughout this book are generally effective from January 1, 2018 through December 31, 2025, unless specifically noted. After

2025, with some exceptions, the rules revert back to the laws that existed in 2017; this is called a sunset provision. However, it is highly expected that these provisions will be made permanent before they are due to expire. It is also important to note that the corporate tax changes covered in Chapter 11 are not part of the sunset provision, as they have already been made permanent.

The following are some highlights of the most significant changes that will affect *individuals and their families*. For more specific details on each of these items, please refer to the **Tax Alpha to the 2nd Power** facts and strategies in the relevant wealth management chapters to follow. The Tax Cuts and Jobs Act of 2017 has:

- Lowered individual income tax rates and set them at 10%, 12%, 22%, 24%, 32%, 35%, and 37%
- Almost doubled the standard deduction
- Repealed the personal exemption
- Limited the opportunity for individuals to write off up to $10,000 ($5,000 for married filing separately) in state and local income taxes or sales tax and property taxes
- Increased the Child Tax Credit to $2,000 per qualified child and make up to $1,400 of this amount refundable
- Maintained the Child and Dependent Care Tax credits
- Maintained the Adoption Tax Credit
- Eliminated the alimony payment deduction for the payer and the inclusion as income to the payee for those divorced or separated after December 31, 2018
- Repealed the moving expense deduction
- Eliminated all miscellaneous itemized deductions, which were previously deductible subject to the 2% floor
- Limited casualty losses
- Expanded the deduction for charitable contributions from 50% to 60% of the income base
- Continued the Earned Income Tax Credit
- Almost eliminated the Alternative Minimum Tax (AMT)
- Limited the tax break to current and future homeowners by limiting the mortgage interest deduction
- Eliminated the Home Equity Loan interest deduction
- Expanded the medical expense deduction by allowing a deduction in excess of 7.5% of adjusted gross income instead of 10%
- Eliminated Obamacare's health insurance individual mandate penalty tax starting 2019

- Expanded the use of 529 educational savings plans beyond undergraduate and graduate school
- Continued the current retirement savings plans incentives provided through employers, as well as through the Individual Retirement Accounts (IRAs)
- Doubled the amount of the exemption for Estate and Gift tax
- Allowed for a deduction of 20% of qualified business income

With such sweeping changes, I would highly encourage you to work with a tax professional to understand how this tax law will specifically impact your financial future. Utilize this book as a learning tool and to present topics of discussion with your financial advisor and tax professional.

 TAX ALPHA TO THE 2ND POWER^{SM} **FACTS AND STRATEGIES FOR WEALTH ACCUMULATION**

Here are several tax facts and strategies that will address your wealth accumulation goals at an exponential rate, which will help put you on the path to financial independence, *point X*.

- Maximize your tax deductions.
- Take full advantage of every tax deduction and credit.
- If possible, shift income and deductions to the tax year that will result in lower taxes.
- If possible, shift income among family members to take full advantage of lower tax brackets.
- Defer the payment of taxes to future years through the use of tax-deferred accounts.
- Maximize your tax-free sources of income.
- Meet with your employer's human resources department to ensure that you are taking advantage of all tax-free fringe benefits available to you.
- Speak with your tax and financial advisor quarterly, or at least twice a year, not just at tax time.
- Update Form W-4 to adjust your tax withholdings through your employer, to ensure you are not dramatically overpaying or underpaying your taxes based on the most recent tax law changes. Although most people like a big tax refund at the end of the year, this simply means you are giving the government an interest-free loan. There is no easier way to improve your cash flow than by adjusting your exemptions so that you are not overpaying your tax with each paycheck.

(continued)

- Refer to this book and other tax references periodically to keep you on track with your finances and to ensure you are using relevant and current **Tax Alpha to the 2nd Power** facts and strategies.
- Make tax planning part of your life. Always ask yourself, *Is this the most tax-effective way to handle this financial situation?* By far, this is the most efficient way to save money and accumulate wealth, without dramatically altering your lifestyle.

AN ACTION PLAN FOR UNDERSTANDING TAXES

1. **Carefully read through and study this chapter and Appendix C.** By doing so, you will have begun to acquaint yourself with the basics of the US tax system and the process of taxation. Remember, this is your biggest expense, and you need to become aware of ways to keep it in check, if not reduce it.
2. **Begin to take control of your own taxes.** Create a file or files and save appropriate paperwork in an organized and comprehensive way. Check and update these files monthly throughout the year, and then go through them again when you are preparing to file your taxes.
3. **If you prepare your tax returns yourself,** use one of the recognized tax preparation programs, such as TaxAct[2] or TurboTax®, to help guide you through the preparation process.
4. **If you decide to hire a professional tax preparer,** find a highly qualified tax advisor who best suits your needs. (Appendix A describes the differences between various professionals.)
5. **Consult with your tax advisor throughout the year,** and not just when it is time to prepare your tax return, to identify additional tax and financial saving strategies.
6. **Familiarize yourself with current *Tax Alpha to the 2nd Power* facts and strategies** at the end of each chapter so that you can discuss them with your tax advisor and incorporate them into your financial life.
7. **Make conscientious tax planning a part of your life.** It is one of the best ways to amass wealth and reach *point X*.

---

[2]See footnote 1.

Determining Your Financial Position

A budget is telling your money where to go instead of wondering where it went.

—Dave Ramsey,
American businessman, author, and radio host

Now that you have taken the extremely important step of committing to living within your means, and you understand that taxes are a significant expenditure in your life, you need to determine what your financial situation currently looks like. This does not mean simply knowing your annual salary or identifying how much you take home in every paycheck – although that is definitely part of it. In order to live within your means, you must have a precise understanding of your financial assets, liabilities, and net worth, by preparing a *statement of financial position.* You also need to know – and to track on a regular basis – where all your personal funds are coming from and going to: This is your *statement of cash flow.* Finally, after taking a careful look at your current financial position, you must determine your financial goals, whether for the next 5 years, 10 years, or throughout your retirement years. Only then can you realistically budget for the future – and of course, reach *point X.*

Figuring Your Financial Net Worth

You cannot get to *point X* unless you know your starting point, and to determine that, you need to figure out precisely how much you are worth – financially, that is. Figuring your financial net worth involves preparing an essential document: a personal statement of financial position.

To help guide you in its preparation, I have put together a sample statement of financial position, shown in Exhibit 3.1, based on the financial lives of a hypothetical couple, James and Patricia Loomis. Much of the discussion in this chapter uses the information in Exhibit 3.1, so you can use it to follow along. (I have many clients who are similar to James and Patricia, but the Loomises are purely fictional.) In addition, to help you prepare your own personal statement of financial position, I have provided a blank worksheet, shown in Exhibit 3.2.

Case Study: How One Couple Learned They Were Spending More Than They Earned

James and Patricia Loomis are a successful – albeit fairly typical – American couple in their late thirties. They have been married for 12 years and have two children, a boy and a girl, ages 10 and 8. They live in an upscale suburb of Cleveland, Ohio. James is a lawyer who worked for seven years for a local Cleveland firm, but he decided to go out on his own five years ago. He now has a successful practice, and he also owns the small office building that houses his practice. He purchased this building for $900,000 and still owes $740,000 on the mortgage. The current estimated fair market value is only $750,000 because real estate values have decreased over the past several years in their area. At the time, purchasing the building seemed to be a better idea than paying rent to a landlord. His law practice is the tenant in the building and pays rent to James, who in turn uses this rent money to pay the building's mortgage.

Patricia has managed to juggle caring for her family and work-ing as a part-time writer since the birth of her children. Before having children, she worked as a journalist for several years at a newspaper in Cleveland. When she left the newspaper, she rolled over her 401(k) into an IRA. She is self-employed as a writer for a financial book author and gets paid $25,000 per year for providing this service. James and Patricia bought a rather large

Exhibit 3.1   James and Patricia Loomis, Statement of Financial Position

James and Patricia Loomis

Statement of Financial Position as of December 31, 2017

Assets		Liabilities and Net Worth	
Cash/Cash Equivalents		**Liabilities**	
Cash	$5,250	Current:	
Money Market	10,600	Credit Card 1 – H {at 12%}	$6,000
Savings Account	–	Credit Card 2 – W {at 8%}	–
CDs	10,000	Current Liabilities	$6,000
Total Cash/Cash Equivalents	$25,850		
		Long-Term:	
Invested Assets at FMV		Credit Card 1 – H {at 12%}	$100,000
Business Owned	$28,000	Credit Card 2 – W {at 8%}	750,000
Office Building {Paid $900,000}	22,000	Auto 1 Note Balance – H {at 10%}	42,000
Investment Portfolio {100% Stocks}	28,500	Auto 2 Note Balance – W {at 0%}	25,000
Variable Annuity {100% Stocks}	18,500		5,500
IRA – H {100% Stock}		Mortgage – Office Building – 30 Years at 9% Fixed, 25 Years Remaining	12,000
IRA – W {100% Money Market}	740,000		
SIMPLE Plan-IRA – H {100% stock}	460,000	Mortgage – Primary Residence – 30 Years at 6.5% Fixed, 20 Years Remaining	13,000
529 Education Savings Plan			4,000

(Continued)

Exhibit 3.1 (*Continued*)

James and Patricia Loomis

Statement of Financial Position as of December 31, 2017

Assets

Liabilities and Net Worth

Life Insurance – H (Cash Surrender value)	350	Student Loans 1 – H (at 3%)	50,000
(Face Value $300,000)		Long Term Liabilities	$1,347,000
Total Investments	$951,850		
Personal Use Asset at FMV			
Primary Residence (Paid $600,000)	$700,000	**Total Liabilities**	$1,353,000
Personal Property and Furniture	20,000		
Auto 1	28,000	**Net Worth**	$392,700
Auto 2	20,000		
Total Personal Use	$768,000		
Total Assets	$1,745,700	**Total Liabilities and Net Worth**	$1,745,700

Note to financial statements:

H = Husband
W = Wife
FMV = Stated at the current fair market value

40

Exhibit 3.2 Statement of Financial Position

Statement of Financial Position As of December 31, 20 __ __

Assets	Liabilities and Net Worth

Cash/Cash Equivalents

Cash

Money Market

Savings Account

CDs

Total Cash/Cash Equivalents

Invested Assets at FMV

Business Owned

Office Building

Investment Portfolio {   }

Variable Annuity {   }

IRA – H {   }

IRA – W {   }

SIMPLE Plan-IRA – H {   }

529 Education Savings Plan

Liabilities

Current:

    Credit Card 1 – H {at   %}

    Credit Card 2 – W {at   %}

    Current Liabilities

Long Term:

    Credit Card 1 – H {at   %}

    Credit Card 2 – W {at   %}

    Auto 1 Note Balance – H {at   %}

    Auto 2 Note Balance – W {at   %}

    Mortgage – Office Building -   Years at   % Fixed,   Years Remaining

    Mortgage – Primary Residence -   Years at   % Fixed,   Years Remaining

(Continued)

Exhibit 3.2 *(Continued)*

Statement of Financial Position As of December 31, 20 _ _

Assets		Liabilities and Net Worth	
Life Insurance – H (Cash Surrender value)			
Face Value		Student Loans 1 – H (at %)	_____
Total Investments	_____	Long Term Liabilities	_____
Personal Use Asset at FMV			
Primary Residence (Paid $)		**Total Liabilities**	_____
Personal Property and Furniture			
Auto 1	_____	**Net Worth**	_____
Auto 2	_____		
Total Personal Use	_____		
Total Assets	_____	**Total Liabilities and Net Worth**	_____

Note to financial statements:

H = Husband
W = Wife
FMV = Stated at the current fair market value

house about 10 years ago for $600,000, which was a stretch for them financially. The house currently has a fair market value of $700,000, and the Loomises owe $460,000 on their mortgage.

In terms of other anticipated expenses, they know that they need to start saving for their children's education. The public schools in their town are excellent, so private school costs for elementary and high school for the Loomis kids are not an issue. However, James and Patricia know that they will be sending their children to college within the next eight years, and they will be paying college costs for at least six years. For two of those years, they expect they will need to pay for two children's college costs at the same time. It is also likely that their children, who are good students, will want and need financial help from James and Patricia in order to go to graduate school.

James and Patricia do not foresee having to care for aging parents. Patricia's parents have both already died and James's parents are financially comfortable with adequate long-term care insurance.

At this moment in their lives, James and Patricia are feeling financially sound. But is this accurate? A statement of financial position will provide a clear picture of their true *financial net worth*. This will begin to point out areas that may not feel problematic now but should be addressed before they become overwhelming in the future.

Measuring Net Worth

A personal statement of financial position measures your financial net worth by assigning values to all of your financial assets and liabilities. Once you have identified the specific amounts of your assets and liabilities, you simply subtract the total of your liabilities from the total of your assets, and that amount is your financial net worth. This calculation represents one of the most basic accounting equations: $(A - L = NW)$, or *assets* minus *liabilities* equal *net worth*. Let us walk through the process.

Identifying Assets

Your first step in this process is to identify every financial asset you have. An asset is simply anything you own that has a value, including cash, investments, your primary residence (if you own it), any other real estate you own, your automobiles, retirement accounts, furniture, and jewelry. Once you have identified all the assets you own, you should classify them in the following three categories: cash and cash equivalents, invested assets, and personal-use assets. These are described in the following paragraphs and referred to in the statement of financial position shown in Exhibit 3.1.

1. *Cash and cash equivalents* include cash on-hand, bank accounts (savings and checking), money market accounts, and Treasury bills (T-bills). These accounts reflect what is called *liquid cash*, or money that is readily available for emergencies. James and Patricia have $25,850 in cash and cash equivalents, as can be seen on their statement of financial position.

2. *Invested assets* are all assets that are reasonably expected to generate income. (These, of course, are the most important assets in achieving financial independence or getting to *point X*, since these are the assets that will be working to make money for you.) Examples of invested assets include a privately owned business, an investment portfolio, retirement accounts, and fixed and variable annuities. James and Patricia have $951,850 in invested assets, which are stated at current fair market value on their statement of financial position.

3. *Personal-use assets* are the assets that, in effect, measure your standard of living. Personal-use assets typically do not generate income; instead, they require you to use additional resources to maintain or replace them. This would include a primary home, a vacation home, automobiles, furniture, jewelry, and artwork. James and Patricia have $768,000 in personal-use assets, which are stated at fair market value on their statement of financial position.

It is worth noting that for the past several decades, until the economic crash of 2008, many people considered their homes to be an *invested asset,* not a *personal-use asset.* This was because, during this period, real estate in the United States boomed, and many people made substantial financial killings by buying and selling houses; in other words, we experienced a real estate bubble. Sadly, that bubble burst, and many people who could not afford their homes lost them through bank foreclosures and short sales. Fortunately, over the past several years, the real estate market has recovered, and many homeowners who managed to keep their homes are now much better off financially. The lesson to be learned here is clear. Real estate does go up in value, but it also can go down in value. The fact is, your home and vacation home should always be considered personal-use assets, not invested assets.

Listing Liabilities

Liabilities include any financial obligations you may have that require you to make payments, either currently or in the future. When you list your liabilities on your personal statement of financial position, they fall into two categories:

1. *Current liabilities:* full payments that are due within one year (i.e., short-term loans).
2. *Long-term liabilities:* payments that can be stretched out for one year or longer (such as student loans, business loans, mortgages, and home-equity loans).

When listing liabilities, be sure to include their terms as well as their current outstanding balance. Terms refer to the interest rates being paid, the number of payments to be made, and any prepayment penalties. (It will be essential to know and list these terms when evaluating your debt, which is discussed in detail in Chapter 4, "Managing Debt.")

James and Patricia have current liabilities of $6,000 and long-term liabilities of $1,347,000. Therefore, their total liabilities are $1,353,000. (Technically, the current portion of their long-term liabilities, which are the payments that they are required to make over the next 12 months, should also be listed as current liabilities. However, for ease and clarity, I have not made this distinction, and I have included only $6,000 of their credit-card debt as current.)

Calculating Your Financial Net Worth

Now that you have listed all of your assets and liabilities, the moment of reckoning has come. When you subtract your total liabilities from your total assets, you will know your personal financial net worth.

The number that represents your financial net worth (and indeed, your entire personal statement of financial position), may well be an eye-opener for you. It will reveal your financial strengths and weaknesses. For some people, this is a positive experience, making them feel financially secure and sound. However, for many people (maybe even the vast majority), these calculations often reveal areas that need improvement and may even uncover serious financial problems. Nevertheless, identifying and facing financial realities serves as a starting point for putting your financial house in order.

Analyzing a Statement of Financial Position

In James and Patricia's case, their financial net worth as of December 31, 2017, is $392,700. At first glance, this appears quite positive for a couple who is not yet 40 years old. However, despite the fact that they have significant assets (a privately owned business, an office building, and an expensive home), they have a false sense of financial security and are a long way from achieving *point X*.

To put it another way, if the Loomises liquidated all of their assets and paid off all of their liabilities, they would be left with $392,700 (cash) in their bank account. If they took this money and invested it prudently, they might be able to generate a 5% return on their invest-ments.[1] This would provide them with an income of $19,635 per year before taxes. At this time, their annual income is $216,876 (as shown later in the statement of cash flow, Exhibit 3.3), which allows them to maintain their current standard of living. Note that this number is *more than 10 times* what they can reasonably expect their current financial net worth to generate.

Clearly, they have not accumulated a sufficient amount of invested assets to allow them to be financially independent. (Chapter 8, "Planning for Retirement," discusses in detail how the Loomises can close this gap so that they can achieve financial independence by the time that they are ready to retire.)

At the moment, they have a number of weaknesses in their state-ment of financial position. First, as we have discussed, for a married couple in their late thirties, a financial net worth of $392,700 is not sufficient to meet their long-term financial needs. In addition, they have only $25,850 in cash or cash equivalents available in case of an emergency, which is also not sufficient. Their goal should be to have at least three months' income, which, in their case, would be approx-imately $54,000.

In addition, their invested assets are not as strong or positioned as well as they should be. Among their invested assets is James's office building, which (as mentioned) he purchased for $900,000 in 2006, but after the real estate crash of 2008, is now valued at only $750,000. Although real estate values throughout the country

---

[1]The rates of return shown above are purely hypothetical and do not represent the performance of any individual investment or portfolio of investments. They are for illustrative purposes only and should not be used to predict future product perfor-mance. Specific rates of return, especially for extended time periods, will vary over time. There is also a higher degree of risk associated with investments that offer the potential for higher rates of return. You should consult with your representative before making any investment decision.

have recovered from their lows, office buildings in his town are still struggling. Furthermore, James's investment portfolio, variable annuity, and IRA accounts are 100% invested in stock. This is not a well-balanced portfolio, and he may be taking on too much risk. Conversely, Patricia has 100% of her IRA account in money market funds, which are currently paying 0%! It seems clear that they need professional guidance and management from a financial advisor to help them diversify their investments so that they can both minimize their risks and maximize their returns.[2]

With regard to their retirement accounts, they have a total of only $55,500, which includes a variable annuity and their IRA accounts. As a couple, they always had an excuse for not funding their retirement account and instead chose to buy an expensive home, go into private practice, and purchase an office building. Although their tax advisor encouraged them to do so each year, they chose to delay funding their retirement accounts. This is not enough for a couple in their late thirties, and they will need to make significant contributions to their retirement accounts going forward to be able to retire comfortably in their late sixties. (Again, for more information, see Chapter 8, "Planning for Retirement.")

They have set aside only $4,000 for their children's education, and their firstborn will be attending college within the next eight years. Given the current cost of a college education, they need to start fully funding their children's 529 plans and other educational saving plans. (For more information about preparing financially for your own children's educational needs, see Chapter 7, "Paying for College.")

Currently, James is covered for only $300,000 of permanent life insurance; Patricia is not covered at all. Given their family needs, they are significantly underinsured, and in the event of James's death, Patricia would not be able to maintain their current standard of living. They should increase the amount of life insurance coverage on both of their lives. (Life insurance options are explored in Chapter 5, "Insuring Your Health and Life.")

With regard to liabilities, the Loomises also have some financial issues that must be addressed. Currently, they are carrying $34,000 in credit-card debt ($6,000 of which is included as a current liability) at the rate of 12% per year, and $22,000 at the rate of 8% per year. They have a $28,500 car loan at 10% and an $18,500 car loan at 0% interest. James also has an outstanding student loan for $50,000

---

[2]Diversification does not assure or guarantee better performance and cannot eliminate the risk of investment losses.

at 3% interest. They have clearly been living well beyond their means, and since their cash outflows consistently exceed their cash inflows, they have been forced to accumulate large amounts of credit-card debt. This unfortunately is very common for couples who are always trying to keep up with the Joneses. They need to consolidate their high-interest debts and lower their overall interest rates and monthly payments. (The one exception is the 0% car loan. Based on this low interest rate, they should continue to make these payments.)

James's office building has a mortgage of $740,000, which is almost equal to the building's current fair market value. Unfortunately, they will not be able to refinance this loan because of the extremely high debt-to-asset ratio (close to 100%). Nevertheless, they should make an attempt to secure a loan modification with their existing lender, but this may be difficult to accomplish given the building's reduced value.

Conversely, James and Patricia are in a perfect position to refinance the mortgage on their home and should be able to lower their rate from 6.5% to the current 30-year rate of 4.5%. They should also take out an additional $100,000 from their equity in the home. It is extremely important to note that under the tax reform act of 2018, interest on home-equity loans is no longer tax-deductible and is limited to acquisition indebtedness. See Chapter 4, "Managing Debt," for more details on this new tax law. This $100,000 should be used to wipe out all of their credit-card debt ($56,000), as well as James's ($28,500) auto loan, which totals $84,500. They will continue to make payments on their low-interest rate personal loans (auto loan at 0% and student loan at 3%). The balance of $15,500 (from the $100,000) should be added to their cash reserves.

The new mortgage of $560,000 at 4.5% interest over 30 years will cost them approximately $34,049 per year ($2,837.42 per month), compared to the $37,920 ($3,160 per month) they are currently paying on their old home mortgage. You can speak with a home mortgage loan officer or use a financial calculator to go through the various what-if scenarios based on your mortgage choices.

This reduction of $3,871, together with the reduction of the payments on their credit-card debt of $5,712 and James's auto loan of $7,656 (see loan payments under Exhibit 3.3), improves their current cash flow by a total of $17,239 per year.

Some financial advisors believe that you should never pay off unsecured debt (such as credit-card debt) with secured debt (such as a home mortgage). However, I personally believe that under the right circumstances, this can absolutely be the right thing to do, as the example of the Loomises so strikingly shows.

An Important First Step

Analyzing your statement of financial position is an important first step to developing financial goals and implementing prudent financial strategies that will help you get to *point X.* Moreover, the figure that represents your current financial net worth is perhaps the most significant number in your quest to financial independence. You need to calculate this number once a year in order to measure your success. Personally, I always analyze and update my statement of financial position at the end of the year to assist me in establishing my financial goals for the upcoming year, which are always a part of my New Year's resolutions. I strongly recommend that you do the same.

Making Sense of Cash Flow

Building your personal financial net worth requires minimizing your liabilities and increasing your assets, particularly your invested assets. Therefore, in addition to calculating your net worth, you need to get a firm grip on where your money is coming from – and, perhaps even more important – where it is flowing to. In other words, you need to create a detailed personal statement of cash flow.

Quite simply, a statement of cash flow will show all of your *cash inflows* and all of your *cash outflows* (as we refer to them in the accounting profession) for a designated period of time, usually one year. As discussed in Chapter 1, the secret to achieving financial independence (getting to *point X*) is to live within (and ideally below) your means, and to *pay yourself first* (i.e., save money). If your cash inflows exceed your cash outflows, then you will have discretionary income, which can (and should) be used to add to your savings, or your accumulated wealth.

However, if your cash outflows are greater than your cash inflows, then you are living beyond your means, are surely accumulating debt, and are severely limiting your chances of getting to *point X.* As with the statement of financial position, I have created a sample statement of cash flow (shown in Exhibit 3.3), representing the current financial life of James and Patricia Loomis, and will refer to it to help you identify relevant issues of your own. In addition, I have provided a blank statement of cash flow worksheet for your personal use (shown in Exhibit 3.4). Before you can begin filling in your worksheet, you will need to gather copies of your pay stubs, most recent income tax return, and bank and credit-card statements for the preceding 12 months.

Exhibit 3.3 James and Patricia Loomis, Statement of Cash Flow Before and After Recommendation

	James and Patricia Loomis Statement of Cash Flow (Before Recommendations) For the period January 1, 2017 to December 31, 2017		James and Patricia Loomis Statement of Cash Flow (After Recommendations) For the period January 1, 2017 to December 31, 2017		Net Cash Flow Increase
Inflows					
Self-Employment Income – H	–		–		
Wage Income W2 – H	$190,000		$190,000		
Self-Employment Income – W	25,000		25,000		
Wage Income W2 – W	–		–		
		$215,000		$215,000	
Dividend Income		840		840	
Interest income		280		280	
Net Rental Income ($78,000		756		756	
Rental Income Less Mortgage on Office Building $77,244)					
Total Inflows		**$216,876**		**$216,876**	
Outflows					
Invested Assets (Pay Yourself First)					
SIMPLE Plan Contributions – H	$5,000		$5,000		
IRA Contribution – W	1,500		1,500		
Dividend Reinvested	840		840		
Interest Reinvested	280		280		
Total Outflows to Invested Assets		**$7,620**		**$7,620**	

Housing

Mortgage Home	$37,920	$34,049
Rent	–	–
Cable	1,650	1,320
Cell Phone	1,980	1,584
Cleaning	4,800	2,400
Electricity	1,950	1,950
Gardener/Snow Removal	1,800	1,800
Insurance (Home)	2,350	2,350
Gas	1,220	1,220
Internet	540	540
Maintenance and Repairs	1,200	1,200
Phone (Landline)	480	–
Supplies	640	640
Property Tax (Home)	5,200	5,200
Water and Sewer	1,250	1,250
Total Outflows to Housing	$62,980	$55,503 $7,477

(Continued)

Exhibit 3.3 *(Continued)*

	James and Patricia Loomis Statement of Cash Flow (Before Recommendations) For the period January 1, 2017 to December 31, 2017	James and Patricia Loomis Statement of Cash Flow (After Recommendations) For the period January 1, 2017 to December 31, 2017	Net Cash Flow Increase
Transportation			
Bus/Taxi Fare	$840	$840	
Fuel	6,230	6,230	
Insurance	2,800	2,380	
Licensing	90	90	
Maintenance	400	400	
Tolls	310	310	
Other	125	125	
Total Outflows to Transportation	$10,795	$10,375	$420
Family Risk Management			
Health	–	–	
Life	1,400	1,400	
Long-Term Disability	1,200	1,200	
Long-Term Care	–	–	
Other	–	–	
Total Outflows to FRM	$2,600	$2,600	

Food					
Groceries	$4,545		$4,545		
Dining Out	10,400		5,200		
Other	600		600		
Total Outflows to Food		15,545		10,345	$5,200
Personal Care					
Clothing	$2,000		$2,000		
Dry Cleaning	850		850		
Hair/Nails	680		680		
Health Club	1,200		600		
Medical – Out of Pocket	5,000		3,000		
Organization Dues or Fees	350		350		
Other	–		–		
Total Outflows to Personal Care		$10,080		$7,480	$2,600
Entertainment					
CDs	$520		$520		
Concerts	1,200		1,200		
Live Theater	600		600		

(*Continued*)

Exhibit 3.3 *(Continued)*

	James and Patricia Loomis Statement of Cash Flow (Before Recommendations) For the period January 1, 2017 to December 31, 2017	James and Patricia Loomis Statement of Cash Flow (After Recommendations) For the period January 1, 2017 to December 31, 2017	Net Cash Flow Increase
Movies	380	380	
Sporting Events	500	500	
DVDs/Blu-rays	350	350	
Other	—	—	
Total Outflows to Entertainment	$3,550	$3,550	
Loans Payments			
Personal	—	—	
Student 1 – H	3,328	3,328	
Student 2 – W	—	—	
Credit Card 1 – H	3,792	—	
Credit Card 2 – W	1,920	—	
Auto Loan 1 – H	7,656	—	
Auto Loan 2 – W	4,625	4,625	
Total Outflows to Loan Payments	$21,321	$7,953	$13,368
Taxes			
Federal Income Tax	$38,000	$38,000	
Self-Employment Tax – H&W	19,125	19,125	

FICA/Medicare	–	–
State Income Tax	9,400	9,400
Other	235	235
Total Outflows to Taxes	$66,760	$66,760
Gifts and Donations		
Charity 1	$2,400	$2,400
Charity 2	1,200	1,200
Charity 3	500	500
Total Outflows to Gifts and Donations	$4,100	$4,100
Professional Fees and Legal Obligations		
Accounting & Legal Fees	$600	$600
Alimony	–	–
Payments on Lien or Judgment	–	–
Other	–	–
Total Outflows to Professional Fees and Legal Obligations	$600	$600

(Continued)

Exhibit 3.3 (*Continued*)

	James and Patricia Loomis Statement of Cash Flow (Before Recommendations) For the period January 1, 2017 to December 31, 2017	James and Patricia Loomis Statement of Cash Flow (After Recommendations) For the period January 1, 2017 to December 31, 2017	Net Cash Flow Increase
Child Care and Other Expenses			
Child Care	$3,000	$2,400	
Clothing	800	800	
Domestic Help, Babysitting	240	240	
Lunch Money	1,050	1,050	
Medical	250	250	
Organization Dues or Fees	300	300	
School Supplies	250	250	
School Tuition	–	–	
Toys/Games	600	600	
Other	200	200	
Total Outflows to Child Care and Other Expenses	$6,690	$6,090	$600
Pet Care and Other Expenses			
Food	–		
Grooming	–		
Medical	–		

56

Toys		–		–
Other		–		–
Total Outflows to Pet Care and Other Expenses				
Personal Expenses				
Cash Withdrawals	$1,200		$1,200	
Dues/Subscriptions	600		600	
Education	–		–	
Gifts (Birthday, Holiday, etc.)	1,200		1,200	
Vacation/Travel	3,500		3,500	
Other	500		500	
Total Outflows to Personal Expenses		7,000		7,000
Total Outflows		219,641		189,976
Discretionary Cash Flow*		**$(2,765)**		**$26,900**
				$29,665
				$29,665

*Cash inflows less cash outflows.

Exhibit 3.4   Statement of Cash Flow

Statement of Cash Flow
For the period January 1, 20 _ _ to December 31, 20 _ _

Statement of Cash Flow (After Recommendations)
For the period January 1, 20 _ _ to December 31, 20 _ _

INFLOWS

Self-Employment Income – H

Wage Income W2 – H

Self-Employment Income – W

Wage Income W2 – W

Dividend Income

Interest Income

Net Rental Income

Total Inflows

OUTFLOWS

Invested Assests (Pay Yourself First)

SIMPLE Plan Contributions – H

IRA Contribution – W

Dividend Reinvested

Interest Reinvested

Total Outflows to Invested Assets

Housing

Mortgage Home

Rent

Cable

Cell Phone

Cleaning

Electricity

Gardener/Snow Removal

Insurance (Home)

Gas

Internet

Maintenance and Repairs

Phone (Landline)

Supplies

Property Tax (Home)

Water and Sewer

Total Outflows to Housing

(Continued)

59

Exhibit 3.4 *(Continued)*

Statement of Cash Flow For the period January 1, 20 _ _ to December 31, 20 _ _	Statement of Cash Flow (After Recommendations) For the period January 1, 20 _ _ to December 31, 20 _ _

Transportation

Bus/Taxi Fare

Fuel

Insurance

Licensing

Maintenance

Tolls

Other

Total Outflows to Transportation

Family Risk Management

Health

Life

Long-Term Disability

Long-Term Care

Other

Total Outflows to FRM

Food

Groceries

Dining Out

Other

Total Outflows to Food

Personal Care

Clothing

Dry Cleaning

Hair/Nails

Health Club

Medical – Out of Pocket

Organization Dues or Fees

Other _____ | _____ | _____

Total Outflows to Personal Care

Entertainment

CDs

Concerts

Live Theater

Movies

Sporting Events

DVDs/Blu-rays

Other _____ | _____ | _____

Total Outflows to Entertainment _____

(Continued)

Exhibit 3.4 *(Continued)*

		Statement of Cash Flow			Statement of Cash Flow (After Recommendations)	
		For the period January 1, 20 _ _ to December 31, 20 _ _			For the period January 1, 20 _ _ to December 31, 20 _ _	

Loan Payments

Personal

Student 1 – H

Student 2 – W

Credit Card 1 – H

Credit Card 2 – W

Auto Loan 1 – H

Auto Loan 2 – W

Total Outflows to Loan Payments

Taxes

Federal Income Tax

Self-Employment Tax – H&W

FICA/Medicare

State Income Tax

Other

Total Outflows to Taxes

Gifts and Donations

Charity 1

Charity 2

Charity 3

Total Outflows to Gifts and Donations

Professional Fees and Legal Obligations

Accounting and Legal Fees

Alimony

Payments on Lien or Judgment

Other _____

Total Outflows to Professional Fees and Legal Obligations _____

Child Care and Other Expenses

Child Care

Clothing

Domestic Help, Babysitting

Lunch Money

Medical

Organization Dues or Fees

School Supplies

School Tuition

Toys/Games

Other _____

Total Outflows to Child Care and Other Expenses _____

(Continued)

63

Exhibit 3.4 (*Continued*)

Statement of Cash Flow
For the period January 1, 20 _ _ to December 31, 20 _ _

Statement of Cash Flow (After Recommendations)
For the period January 1, 20 _ _ to December 31, 20 _ _

Pet Care and Other Expenses

Food

Grooming

Medical

Toys

Other

Total Outflows to Pet Care and Other Expenses

Personal Expenses

Cash Withdrawals

Dues/Subscriptions

Education

Gifts (Birthday, Holiday, etc.)

Vacation/Travel

Other

Total Outflows to Personal Expenses

Total Outflows

Discretionary Cash Flow*

*Cash inflows less cash outflows.

64

Identify Your Cash Inflows (Your Sources of Income)

Begin your statement of cash flow by summarizing all of your sources of income. This includes your annual salary (or salaries, if you have multiple incomes, or if you are figuring cash flow for a couple and both husband and wife work). Include any freelance or self-employment income, interest or dividend income, pension, Social Security income, and any and all other sources of income you may have. Do *not* include any earnings from tax-deferred accounts such as 401(k)s, IRAs, and annuities, because these are not available to pay for cash outflows. However, if you received *distributions* from these tax-deferred accounts, then you should include them as part of your cash inflows. Finally, these figures should reflect your gross pay, or before-tax income. Your taxes are most definitely listed under cash outflows.

James and Patricia Loomis's cash inflows include James's salary of $190,000 (which he budgeted for himself from his law practice), Patricia's part-time self-employment income of $25,000, dividend income of $840 from their investment portfolio, and interest income of $280 on their money market accounts and CDs. Finally, they also have cash inflow from the office building, where James's law practice is the tenant. The rental income of $78,000 offsets the mortgage payment of $77,244, providing them with an additional $756 per year. As can be seen on the statement of cash flow, their cash inflows total $216,876.

Identify Your Cash Outflows (Your Expenses)

Cash outflows include *essential* items (e.g., housing, food, clothing, and transportation), as well as *nonessential* items, or basically everything else you spend money on throughout the year. List each one of these basic items as a subheading (*Housing, Food, Personal Care, Entertainment,* etc.), then go through your checkbook and credit card statements and summarize these payments in as much detail as possible. (Do not worry if you are not absolutely perfect; general trends will show up fairly quickly.) Some items will remain constant, such as your mortgage, your car loan payments, and your student loan payments. Others, however, may fluctuate, or jump out as excessive.

Your cash outflows should also include items that many of us do not commonly consider as part of our personal or family budget. For example, in the spirit of paying yourself first, the first line items under the heading of *outflows* on your statement of cash flow should be your savings (10% or more of your gross pay), including 401(k) contributions and any reinvested dividend income. In other words, these funds should be considered an essential outflow of money, as important as your rent or mortgage, electricity bill, or grocery bill.

Also, all your tax payments (even those paid through your employer), should be highlighted and included as part of your cash outflows, including all tax payments from your income such as federal income tax, FICA and Medicare, and state and city income tax.

Separating Essentials from Nonessentials

Once you have listed your cash outflows in as much detail as possible, take some time to analyze your statement very closely. Begin to identify which items are *essential,* and which are *nonessential;* which ones are *needs,* and which are *wants.* If you are married, go through your statement with your spouse. You should even show it to your older children, particularly teenagers who may be racking up big bills with an automobile, cell phone, or other expenditures.

At first glance, certain items may appear to be necessities, such as shelter, food, clothing, and transportation. However, with a closer look, these apparent necessities can begin to look more like luxuries. For example, your house may be costing you more than you can really afford. You may have no trouble meeting the basic mortgage payment, but your electricity and gas bills, your lawn and garden maintenance, and your property taxes may be through the roof. A close analysis of your cash outflows might suggest that it could be worthwhile moving to a smaller house or a less expensive neighborhood.

Transportation costs – or more specifically, the cost of maintaining automobiles – are another area where the line between necessity and luxury can blur. Is owning a $50,000 car really that important? In a household with teenagers who drive, the need for two or even three cars may seem imperative, but are the costs becoming prohibitive? Like a house, the cost of a basic automobile may not be unaffordable, but the price of gasoline, insurance, and maintenance can put a big dent in a family budget.

With a close look at your statement of cash flow, items that are completely nonessential are sure to jump out. Costs for such indulgences as manicures, theater tickets, or expensive birthday gifts may suddenly seem not only excessive, but frivolous. Also, small cuts, when added together, can turn into big savings for you and your family.

And let's not forget the power of bargaining. Not everything sells for the asking price. Most financially successful people view bargaining as a game and do not experience any feeling of embarrassment for doing so. Even a billionaire like President Donald Trump is always looking for a bargain. As he said in his book, *Think Like a Billionaire*, "Don't be obsessive about it, but check through your bills from time to time. You should also always feel comfortable bargaining for goods and services. I do it all the time, and I'm one of the richest men on Earth."

Consider the following analysis of the Loomises' statement of cash flow. It should inspire additional ideas for ways your family can cut costs.

Analyzing a Statement of Cash Flow

James and Patricia Loomis's cash outflows (before the changes) have been broken out in the following categories:

- Invested assets: $7,620
- Housing: $62,980
- Transportation: $10,795
- Family risk management and insurance: $2,600
- Food: $15,545
- Personal care: $10,080
- Entertainment: $3,550
- Loan payments: $21,321
- Taxes: $66,760
- Gifts and donations: $4,100
- Professional fees and legal obligations: $600
- Child care and other expenses: $6,690
- Other personal expenses: $7,000

In all, the Loomises' cash outflows total $219,641, leaving them with a discretionary cash flow of negative $2,765. (Cash inflows of $216,876 minus cash outflows of $219,641.)

In other words, James and Patricia are spending $2,765 more per year than they are bringing in. Also, like many people, they are subsidizing their overspending by increasing their credit-card debt. If they continue on this path, they may never achieve financial independence. They clearly need to make changes in their cash flow so that they can increase their invested assets (pay themselves first), turn their discretionary cash flow from negative to positive, and ultimately use the excess discretionary positive cash flow to pay down their debt.

As part of the analysis of their statement of financial position, they (working closely with their Certified Financial Planner™) were able to uncover a strategy that consolidated most of their debt and reduced their cash outflow by $17,239 (credit card and car loan payments by $13,368 and the mortgage payment by $3,871). By closely analyzing their statement of cash flow, they were able to further improve their cash flow by eliminating some of the nonessential expenses. Finally, they (again, through working with their tax advisor, financial planner, and insurance agent) were able to find some additional creative ways to save on taxes and other important expenses.

How One Family Cut Basic Costs

After the Loomises held a family meeting (which included their two children, even though their kids are relatively young), they were able to begin to identify which of their basic expenses were absolutely essential and which were nonessential. With a little cooperation and compromise, they identified those expenses they could either minimize or eliminate. (As mentioned, these figures are listed in detail on James and Patricia Loomis's statement of cash flow, shown in Exhibit 3.3. It will help if you refer to it throughout this discussion.)

They started with their housing expenses. In addition to reducing their mortgage payment, they were able to make some substantial cuts in their home maintenance costs. They eliminated two (of the five) television cable boxes they had in their home, reducing their cable cost by $330 per year. All family members agreed that they would not use their cell phones beyond the minutes allowed under their family plan, which saved them $396 per year. Because each family member had his or her own cell phone, they decided to eliminate the household landline, which saved them an additional $480 per year.

With regard to their house itself, James and Patricia discussed the possibility of moving to a smaller, less expensive home, acknowledging that they lived in one of the largest homes in their neighborhood, which was truly a nonessential expense. Even though they agreed that a home this size was not a necessity, they were not willing to downsize at this time. They were emotionally tied to the home, and they felt this was the best place to raise their children. They did make a commitment that once their children were away in college, they would revisit this financial issue and make the decision of downsizing at that time. Still, with regard to the house, everyone agreed to keep their rooms clean and tidy so that their cleaning service could be cut from once a week to every other week, for a savings of $2,400 per year. With these relatively small sacrifices – all nonessentials – along with debt restructuring, their total housing cash outflows were reduced by $7,477 per year.

After taking a close look at their transportation costs, the Loomises found that the only item they could reduce was their auto insurance. They contacted their insurance agent, who made them aware of a number of discounts they could be entitled to, such as increasing their deductible and taking a defensive driving course. By taking advantage of these offers, they were able to reduce their auto insurance by 15%, or $420 per year.

After closely examining their other insurance costs (listed under "family risk management" in Exhibit 3.3), they realized they were underinsured and therefore were not able to reduce their expenditures in this area; in fact, they needed to increase them. James and Patricia made a commitment to meet with their life and disability insurance agent to discuss their insurance needs and to make sure they had sufficient coverage.

Under the category of food, both James and Patricia were surprised that, on average, they were spending $200 per week dining out, which came to a whopping $10,400 per year. They agreed that they would reevaluate the type of restaurants they dined at, and would try to limit their dining out to no more than twice a month. This would reduce their dining out cost by $5,200 per year.

Under the personal care category, James agreed to eliminate his monthly fitness club membership, since he had not been to the gym in over two years. Although Patricia kept her membership, they were able to save $600 per year.

With the help of their CPA, they were able to make a creative alteration to their out-of-pocket medical expenses. Because their health insurance plan is an HSA-qualified high-deductible health plan (HDHP), they were able to set up a tax-deductible *health savings account* and contribute $5,000 (for 2018 this could be as much as $6,900), which they typically paid for out-of-pocket medical expenses. (See Chapter 5, "Insuring Your Health and Life," for more details on health savings accounts.) Because they are in a 40% marginal tax bracket, this saved them $2,000 per year in income taxes. As a result, they were able to reduce their out-of-pocket medical costs to $3,000 per year, net of their tax savings.

Concerts, theater, and sporting events are among the most important things the Loomises do as a couple and as a family, so their entertainment costs remained unchanged.

As a result of their loan consolidation, their loan payments (credit card and car loan) were reduced by $13,368 and their mortgage payment by $3,871, which added $17,239 to their discretionary cash flow. (Refer back to Exhibit 3.3, the Loomises' statement of cash flow.) After a brief conversation with their CPA, who reviewed their statement of cash flow, they realized that they could take advantage of the child and dependent care credit on their tax return. Their accountant told them that, based on their adjusted gross income, they were entitled to a tax credit of 20% (of up to $3,000) of their child-care expenses for one dependent, and up to $6,000 of expenses for two or more dependents. Because their total child care cost was $3,000, they were entitled to a tax credit of 20% of this cost ($600). They were eligible for this credit because both of them work and need to pay for childcare for their children, both of whom are under the age of 13. In addition, because they had not taken this deduction before, their tax accountant was able to amend their tax returns for the past three years, and he secured a total refund of $1,800. This deduction will continue to add $600 per year to their discretionary cash flow until their children reach age 13.

James and Patricia were amazed that they had gone from a negative cash flow of $2,765 to a positive cash flow of $26,900, and they were able to add $29,665 (about 15% of their annual income) to their discretionary cash flow. They decided they would use the extra money to fund James's SIMPLE (savings incentive match plan for employees) IRA (an additional $7,500) and Patricia's IRA account (an additional $4,000). By funding these accounts, they further reduced their tax liability by an additional $4,600 (40% of the $11,500 IRA deduction), giving them even more discretionary cash flow. They also made a commitment to establish a 529 plan for both their children's educations and fund it with $10,000 per year.

They were also finally able to commit to purchasing the proper amount of life insurance (for both James and Patricia) and long-term disability coverage (for James), which came to $5,000.

After making all these essential financial commitments, they still had an additional $5,000 and decided they would use this money to pay down James's $50,000 student loan. They realized that, if they were to make this additional payment annually, they might be able to eliminate this loan within five years.

Finally, the Loomises made a commitment to meet with their tax advisor at least once during the year (in addition to their annual tax visit) to discuss further tax-saving strategies. They believed that, in addition to the items they had already identified, they could reduce their taxes even further with proper tax planning. With all these cost-cutting efforts, the Loomis family has come a long way toward the right path to achieving financial independence, *point X.*

By asking yourself these sorts of detailed financial questions and answering them honestly, you may be able to cut your own monthly expenditures by as much as 15%, as the Loomises did – or perhaps even more.

Little Things Mean a Lot

If you and your family work closely to identify areas in your life where you could minimize expenses, you could easily save $10, $20, or even $30 a day. Consider: By saving $20 per day, you would be saving $140 per week, about $608 per month, and $7,300 per year. If you are 30 years old, and if you invest that savings of $7,300 annually for 35 years (until you are 65 or about retirement age) at an assumed 8% rate of return, you will amass $1,257,914. To assist you in coming up with a number of easy ways to save money, see Appendix B, "101 Ways to Save $20 or More per Week."

Establishing Your Financial Goals

By classifying your cash outflows as *essential* or *nonessential,* you begin to acknowledge and separate your *needs* from your *wants.* As a result, you start to determine your true standard of living (or lifestyle) that you want to be living, the one you are actually living, and the one you need to be living if you want to get to *point X.*

Defining Your Lifestyle – What Do You Consider "Wealth"?

In our society, *wealth* is often defined as earning enormous paychecks; amassing huge investment portfolios; owning cavernous houses filled with expensive furniture and state-of-the-art electronics; driving multiple, high-end automobiles that cost in the six figures; owning vacation homes and enjoying luxurious vacations at ski resorts, Caribbean islands, and European capitals; having closets bursting with designer clothing (even for infants) – and the list goes on. Even so-called "middle-class" folks seem to want these things, perhaps on a slightly less-exalted scale, but the quest for material goods is the same.

Of course, none of these things are necessities, even for the truly wealthy; they are things we *desire*. But if we cannot afford them, some of us have been known to go into enormous debt to buy them, causing immense stress for ourselves and our families. This is a book about personal finance, so I am not going to discuss the social and emotional challenges often associated with great wealth – the workaholism, the strained marriages, the lack of time for children, the loss of friendships – even the diminishing of personal integrity and what we call the *soul*. What my parents considered the "American Dream" – the freedom to work hard in order to have a secure and happy life for themselves and their children – has become warped.

The fact is, *wealth* need not mean aspiring to possess a breathtaking amount of money. For some people, wealth may mean living in a small house in a less affluent neighborhood so that they can afford to send their children to the best colleges. For others, wealth may mean giving up luxurious material goods in order to work in a lower-paying, but personally rewarding career, such as teaching, social work, or the arts.

It is imperative that you define what *wealth* means to you. In other words, you need to be clear about what standard of living (or lifestyle) you aspire to and how you propose to achieve it financially. And the curious fact is, no matter what you choose, you can still get to *point X*. As I have noted before, I have had clients who earn hundreds of thousands – even millions – of dollars annually, yet struggle to pay their monthly bills; at the same time, I have had clients who live on modest wages, yet are well on their way to a secure retirement.

Getting to Point X – and the Places in Between

Remember, this is a book about how to get to *point X* – the place where we can stop working for our money and our money starts working for us. For most people, *point X* means retirement, pure and simple. This is because it takes most middle-class people several decades to amass sufficient resources so that they no longer need to pull down a paycheck.

At the same time, for most people, a comfortable retirement is not their only financial goal – nor should it be. In addition to saving for retirement, most of us want to buy a house, educate our children,

take a vacation every year, and give our families a few special indulgences such as an expensive wedding. We may want to start a business
or buy into a professional practice of some kind. What is more, some
people have responsibilities that are sure to incur great expense, such
as the need to support an aging parent or provide lifelong care for a
disabled child.

Therefore, by definition, your financial goals include additional
items beyond getting to *point X*. As with your overall lifestyle, only *you*
can decide what those goals are.

Your Financial Goals: What Is Most Important to You?

Although I cannot tell you what is most important for you personally, as a Certified Financial Planner I will express professional opinions about the value of certain financial decisions. By completing the
Comprehensive Wealth Management Questionnaire in the introduction to this book, you will be able to identify your most significant
financial goals and then be able to prioritize them in order of their
importance to you. Here are my thoughts and recommendations:

- **Paying yourself first (saving):** As I have said repeatedly, unless
  you have an extraordinarily high-paying job, expect to receive
  a large inheritance, or know for certain that you will win
  the lottery, you must save your money and pay yourself first.
  You need to have cash in savings for that rainy day – in my
  opinion, enough cash to cover at least three to six months'
  worth of living expenses. To reach your other financial
  goals, including *point X*, you need to pay yourself first. (See
  Chapter 1, "Committing to Living Within Your Means.")
- **Paying off your debts:** You should pay off most of your
  debt – especially high-interest credit card debt – as quickly as
  possible, before you can begin to save seriously. If paying off
  your existing bad debt is one of your goals, turn to Chapter 4,
  "Managing Debt."
- **Saving for retirement:** If you are in your twenties, the prospect
  of retirement probably seems incredibly remote, especially if
  you are planning a wedding, buying a house, or expecting a
  new baby. However, I cannot say it more strongly: If you want
  to get to *point X*, you need to begin planning for retirement and
  saving for it *now*. (I discuss this in detail in Chapter 8, "Planning
  for Retirement" and provide proof in Chapter 12, "The Time
  Value of Money.")

- **Buying a home:** Most people are eager to own their own home, which is typically a good financial decision, but, remember, you should consider your house as a *personal-use asset*, not as an investment asset. Aside from being certain that you can afford the mortgage and maintenance costs, you should plan to hold on to a property for at least a decade, since owning a home is a long-term proposition. Today, owning real estate can be a good way to diversify your investment risk, and a well-chosen house or other property will most likely increase in value over a period of years, but bear in mind that it will take time.

- **Owning your own business:** Many people dream of owning their own business or buying into an existing practice, such as a medical, dental, or law practice. The financial ramifications of starting your own business are complicated. Still, owning your own business can be an excellent road to *point X*. Although the financial benefits of owning and operating your own business can be significant, so is the risk and time commitment required to achieve success. Before going into business for yourself, you must fully understand what you are getting yourself into. (See Chapter 11, "Starting Your Own Business," for a full analysis of this topic.)

- **Educating your children:** For me, educating my children was a top priority. I believe strongly that educating children is the best way to insure their financial future. With that said, not every child needs to obtain a four-year college degree. For those children who are not as studious, they may possess special skills and talents that they can further by attending a trade school. Do not buy into the falsehood that going to college will guarantee you a good job. We need plumbers, carpenters, electricians, and other blue-collar skilled citizens, and many of these jobs pay much better than white-collar jobs.

  These days, paying for college (and private elementary and high school, if that is your wish or need) is not only incredibly expensive, but is full of financial pitfalls. (See Chapter 7, "Paying for College," for a full analysis of this issue.)

- **Funding unexpected situations:** Some people have unexpected or problematic situations in their life, such as the care of a disabled child or aging parent, which are among their most important financial priorities and require careful financial planning. There are a number of ways to arrange financially for these types of issues. (See Chapter 5, "Insuring

Your Health and Life," and Chapter 10, "Preserving Your Estate" for more information.)

- **Funding special purchases:** We all have dreams – most of which cost money – whether it is a trip around the world, the ownership of a ski chalet in Utah, or a state-of-the-art gourmet kitchen. Unfortunately, in recent decades, many of us have gotten into the habit of buying expensive items on credit. It used to be that if you wanted a new car, an expensive wedding, a trip to Paris, or a remodeled kitchen, you saved up for it. These days, people frequently put such purchases on credit cards or take out loans, creating big debts with high interest rates. Big mistake! You need to save.

Finding Trusted Advisors

To effectively take care of all your financial needs, you will very likely need the help of several professionals, including a financial advisor, a tax advisor, a lawyer, and an insurance advisor. Please refer to Appendix A, "Selecting a Trusted Advisor," to assist you in evaluating the qualifications and the type of advisor that would be most suited to assist you. Selecting a trusted advisor to guide you to financial independence is perhaps one of the most important decisions you can make on your journey to *point X*.

If you do not pay attention to the tax consequences of your financial position, you may be paying significantly more in taxes than the law requires. Therefore, you must include tax planning as part of your overall wealth accumulation strategy. Using an approach that takes advantage of these *Tax Alpha to the 2nd Power*^SM facts and strategies will maximize your financial position.

TAX ALPHA TO THE 2ND POWER^SM FACTS AND STRATEGIES FOR DETERMINING YOUR FINANCIAL POSITION

When preparing your statement of financial position and your statement of cash flow and then considering your ongoing financial goals, it is imperative that you take your tax issues into account. Here are several tax facts and strategies that will address your wealth accumulation goals at an exponential rate, which will help put you on the path to financial independence, *point X*.

(continued)

This *Tax Alpha to the 2nd Power* facts and strategies section has been sub-divided into the same categories listed on IRS Form 1040, for ease of reference.

FILING STATUS AND EXEMPTIONS

- Make sure you choose the proper filing status when filing your income tax return, because this will determine the standard deduction you may claim, as well as the tax rates that will apply to your level of taxable income. If you qualify as *head of household*, be sure to take advantage of this filing status, because it can decrease the amount of taxes you will pay.
- If you use a tax preparer to file your income tax return, they are now required to do due diligence in verifying your head of household status, the American opportunity tax credit, earned income tax credit, and child tax credit, or they may be subject to a preparer penalty of $500 per occurrence.
- If one or both of your parents qualifies as your dependent, you may claim *head of household* status even if they do not live in your home. To qualify, you must pay more than half of your parent's household expenses.
- **The $4,150 personal exemption per taxpayer, spouse, and each qualifying dependent has been eliminated, starting January 1, 2018, which could disproportionally affect larger families.**

INCOME

- Find a job for your dependent children to help fund some of their living expenses. **Each child can earn up to $12,000 in 2018 without having to pay any federal income taxes.**
- For 2018, if your company paid adoption expenses up to $13,840 you can exclude that from your income for tax purposes. A nonrefundable tax credit for the same amount is available for qualified adoption expenses; however, you cannot take both for the same adoption expenses.
- If you live and work in a foreign country and you meet the requirements of either the foreign bona fide residence test or the physical presence test, you may be able to exclude up to $104,100 of foreign earned income (employee or self-employed) in 2018. If you qualify for the foreign earned-income exclusion based on either of these tests, you may also be able to exclude actual housing expenses in excess of $16,656 from your federal taxable income. Depending on your qualifying foreign income and foreign location, special rules and limitations apply.
- You can shelter up to $5,000 of income in a dependent care flexible spending account with pretax dollars to assist in making child care more affordable. Parents can take advantage of the FSA and child care credit, both of which remain in place, but you are not permitted to use both of these breaks to cover the same child care costs.
- You may be able to avoid the tax on gain from the sale of your principal residence if you owned and used the home for at least two years during the

five-year period ending with the date of the sale. For a single individual, you may be able to exclude $250,000 of the gain. For a married couple filing jointly, you may be able to exclude up to $500,000 of the gain. This tax-free income is by far one of the most favorable reasons for home ownership.

ADJUSTMENTS TO GROSS INCOME

- **Starting in 2018, you will no longer be able to take an adjustment to income for moving expenses, with a few exceptions related to active U.S. Armed Forces service.**
- **The Tax Cuts and Jobs Act eliminated the alimony payment deduction for the payer and the inclusion as income for the payee.** For any divorce or separation agreement executed after December 31, 2018, the Act provides that alimony and separation maintenance payments are not deductible by the paying spouse. It also repeals the provision that considered these payments as income by the receiving spouse. I predict there will be a dramatic increase in the number of divorces in 2018 since there will be a rush to get them finalized before the end of the year.
- Any divorces finalized before January 1, 2019, will be grandfathered in; therefore allowing the continued deduction for qualifying alimony and reporting of payment received as income. It is important to note that any modifications made to an existing divorce agreement will then be subject to the new rules. Exercise extreme caution before modifying any preexisting divorce agreement.
- The educator deduction of $250 has been retained under the new tax law and will be adjusted for inflation annually. K-12 teachers, instructors, counselors, principals, and aids qualify for this deduction. You must work at least 900 hours per year and this includes qualified expenses such as books, supplies, equipment, software, professional development, and other teaching-related materials.

ITEMIZED DEDUCTIONS

- **The Tax Cuts and Jobs Act almost doubled the standard deduction to $12,000 for individuals (single and married filing separately), $18,000 for heads of household, and $24,000 for married couples filing jointly.** Taxpayers age 65 or older, as well as blind people, get $1,300 more per person ($1,600 if unmarried). With these significantly higher amounts, very few people will be itemizing their deductions starting in 2018.
- **Charitable contribution deductions have been expanded from a 50% to a 60% limit on adjusted gross income.** Therefore, you will be able to deduct a larger amount in charitable donations, assuming you qualify to itemize your deductions.
- If you are planning to make a large charitable contribution to a qualified charitable organization, you should consider making a gift of property such as

(*continued*)

stocks, bonds, mutual funds, or real estate that has increased significantly in value, instead of a cash donation. The full fair-market value of the property is tax-deductible as a charitable contribution if you held it for one year or more, and the gain will not be subject to tax. Therefore, you will not only increase your charitable contribution deduction, but you will also avoid paying the capital gains tax on the profit.

- If you will be itemizing your tax deductions and expect to be in a higher tax bracket this year than next, consider prepaying your January mortgage payment in December. Not only will you get the tax break on this year's tax return, but the tax break will be higher if you expect to be in a lower tax bracket next year. This may be a wise strategy to implement in a year that you receive a large bonus, commission, or perhaps make a gain on a sale of property or other investments.

- Increase your tax-free income by making sure your employer reimburses you for all business expenses you paid that are within the guidelines set by your employer and the IRS. Some examples are business travel, meals and entertainment, work car expenses, and continuing education. It is more important now than ever before, since, **beginning in 2018, job-related expenses that were not reimbursed by your employer will no longer be allowed as an itemized deduction.**

- You can still write off personal gambling losses to the extent of winnings, as long as your itemized deductions exceed your standard deduction. **Starting January 1, 2018, in addition to gambling losses, you can now write off gambling expenses, such as traveling, supplies, forms, etc., to the extent of gambling winnings.**

- **Starting in 2018, you will no longer be able to take an itemized deduction for casualty and theft losses, unless they are attributable to a federally declared disaster.**

- **Starting in 2018, you will no longer be able to take an itemized deduction for such items as tax preparation fees, safety deposit boxes, and other personal investment related expenses, as well as other miscellaneous items that were previously deductible and subject to the 2% AGI limitation.**

- The loss of the unreimbursed employee business expenses can be remedied by speaking to your employer about setting up an accountable plan to reimburse you for these out-of-pocket work expenses, even if it means reducing your salary to allow for this. Since you are no longer allowed to take these deductions as an itemized deduction, this is a must. This will give you an opportunity to pay for these work-related expenses in pretax dollars.

- It is important to now *allocate costs* such as a tax preparation fee to the individual schedules prepared, such as Schedule C for self-employed or Schedule E for rental properties. These costs are deductible under these schedules, but no longer deductible on Schedule A as a personal itemized deduction.

- You should pay all of your IRA fees directly from your IRA account since you are no longer allowed an itemized deduction for these fees on your Schedule A.
- **Starting January 1, 2018, high-income taxpayers will benefit from the elimination of the overall limit on itemized deductions, since it has now been repealed.** In 2017, the total amount of itemized deductions was reduced by 3% of the amount by which your adjusted gross income exceeds $261,500 for single taxpayers and $313,800 for married taxpayers.
- The most controversial aspect of the tax reform act regarding individual taxpayers had to do with the state and local tax (SALT) itemized deduction. **Starting in 2018, a cap has been placed limiting the total itemized deduction for state and local income tax or sales tax, as well as real estate tax, to $10,000 or $5,000 if married filing separately.** Many high-income-tax states, such as California, Oregon, Minnesota, Iowa, New Jersey, Vermont, the District of Columbia, and New York, will be negatively affected by this change.
- If you own unimproved investment or non-income-producing land, you should make a section 266 election under the new tax law. This election would allow you to capitalize any real estate taxes and interest to the cost of the land rather than deducting it in the current year. You can elect to capitalize one or both of these costs. If you otherwise would not be entitled to a deduction because of the new limitations, you would then be able to deduct these costs as part of your cost basis upon the sale of your property. This election must be made on an annual basis and requires a statement to be attached to your tax return.
- Individuals who reside in high-tax states now have a much bigger incentive to move to a low income tax state such as Texas or Florida. By moving to a low-tax state and establishing residency there, not only will you avoid paying the higher state and local income tax, but you also will not suffer from the loss of these tax deductions.
- With the significant changes mentioned above, I believe that millions of taxpayers will no longer be able to benefit from itemizing their personal tax deductions. With the reduction and elimination of many previously deductible items, the standard deduction may become the better choice for most. **This move toward simplification of personal tax preparation should make preparing your tax return much easier and should also dramatically reduce the odds of an IRS tax audit going forward.**

TAX AND CREDITS

- **The Tax Cuts and Jobs Act lowers individual income tax rates and sets them at 10%, 12%, 22%, 24%, 32%, 35%, and 37%, giving Americans the opportunity to keep more of what they make.** The majority of Americans will be seeing this rate cut in their paycheck starting February 2018.

(continued)

- The vast majority of taxpayers that were subject to the AMT tax in the past were in that position because of the required add-back in the AMT calculation for state and local income tax, sales tax, real estate taxes, and miscellaneous itemized deductions. **As a result of the reduction and elimination of some of these itemized deductions, the add-back items will be virtually eliminated, making very few taxpayers subject to this added tax in the future.** These changes have dramatically simplified our tax system.
- The tax reform act will permanently adjust the Alternative Minimum Tax (AMT) exemption amounts for inflation and make them significantly higher starting in 2018. The AMT exemption amount in 2018 for single and head of household is $70,300, married filing jointly is $109,400, and married filing separately is $54,700.
- The income thresholds at which the AMT exemption amounts begin to phase out have been dramatically increased to $500,000 for individuals and $1,000,000 for joint filers.
- If you finalize an adoption and pay qualified adoption expenses before the end of the year, you may qualify for the adoption credit. For example, the maximum adoption credit for 2018 is a nonrefundable credit of $13,840 (this will be adjusted annually for inflation). For 2018, the amount of the credit phases out starting with adjusted gross income of $207,580 and is totally phased out at $247,580 (this will be adjusted annually for inflation).
- **Starting 2018, you may be able to claim a child tax credit of $2,000 for each qualifying child who is younger than age 17 at the end of the year.** The maximum refundable amount of this credit is $1,400. **The threshold at which these credits begin to phase out was increased substantially to $400,000 for married taxpayers filing a joint return and $200,000 for other taxpayers.**
- **Starting 2018, a new nonrefundable credit of $500 for qualifying dependents, who are not your qualifying children, may now be available to you.**
- If your children are 17 years old or older or you care for elderly relatives, you can claim a nonrefundable $500 credit under the new and expanded rules.
- The Child and Dependent Care Credit, which allows parents to deduct qualified child care expenses, is still alive and well under the new tax law. This has been expanded to $1,050 ($3,000 cost × 35%) for one child or $2,100 for two children under 13 years of age. To qualify for the maximum credit, your adjusted gross income would have to be under $15,000. The credit is decreased by 1% for every $2,000 of income earned over $15,000, until you reach $43,000. Any adjusted gross income level of $43,000 or higher will receive a maximum credit of $600 ($3,000 cost × 20%) per child or $1,200 ($6,000 cost × 20%) for a maximum for two children.
- If you have a qualifying dependent of any age who is disabled and lives with the taxpayer for more than half of the year, you may still qualify for the dependent care credit described above.

- **The marriage penalty, which would penalize taxpayers where both the husband and wife earn income, has been eliminated, except for those in higher tax brackets.** For example, if two single individuals each earned a taxable income of $80,000 for the year, both of these individuals would fall under the old 25% tax bracket. However, if they got married on December 31, 2017, their combined income would be $160,000. This would put them in the old 28% tax bracket, and they would therefore pay more money as a married couple than they would have if they remained single. Under the new tax brackets, they would fall into the 22% marginal tax rate, regardless of whether they got married or not. Under this new tax law, you no longer get penalized for being married unless your combined income is greater than $600,000.
- **Effective January 1, 2018, the "kiddie tax" has been changed by now applying ordinary and capital gains rates applicable to trusts and estates to the net unearned income of a child.** Kids receive the first $1,050 free of tax, the next $1,050 at the single tax rate, and anything over $2,100 at the trust and estate tax rate. Taxable income attributable to earned income is taxed according to an unmarried taxpayers' brackets and rates. The child's tax is now unaffected by the tax situation of the child's parent or the unearned income of any siblings. The kiddie tax applies to unearned income for children under the age of 18. It also applies to those who, at the end of the year, were 18 years old or full-time students age 19 to 23 and did not have earned income that was more than half of their own support.

PAYMENTS

- Do not use the government as your banker. When cash flow is tight, you may be tempted to pay your other bills before you pay any necessary taxes to the government, but *do not do it*. The government charges stiff penalties and interests and should always be the lender of last resort.
- If you discover that you have not taken advantage of any tax deductions or tax credits that you were entitled to, you can file an amended return to claim an additional refund. Generally, the statute of limitations is three years from the date you filed your tax return. Therefore, if you uncover a recurring error, you can file a claim for a refund for the last three years of tax returns. This is a great way to improve your cash flow, and it is another reason why you should meet with your tax advisor throughout the year.
- You may be able to qualify for the earned income credit if you have qualifying children and meet certain requirements, and in limited cases, you may also qualify for this credit if you do not have children. For example, in 2018, the maximum earned income credit with three or more qualifying children is $6,444 and $520 if you do not have qualifying children. The amount of this credit is based on your income level and how many children you have. If you are a low-income earner, this credit is definitely worth consideration.

AN ACTION PLAN FOR DETERMINING YOUR FINANCIAL POSITION

You now understand the importance of preparing your statement of financial position and calculating your true financial net worth and your current cash flow. You should also be getting a firmer grip on your personal financial goals and how to reach them – including, of course, getting to *point X*. Here is a quick action plan to both get you started and keep you going:

1. **Prepare your personal statement of financial position.** In order to know your true financial net worth, you need to prepare this statement, and update it once a year. Use the worksheet shown in Exhibit 3.2 to assist you.
2. **Prepare your personal statement of cash flow** in as much detail as possible. Working together with your spouse and children, identify and eliminate as many nonessential expenditures as possible. Use the worksheet shown in Exhibit 3.4 to assist you.
3. **Pay yourself first.** Use the money you save to decrease your debt and increase your invested assets.
4. **Define your lifestyle.** Carefully figure out what *wealth* means to you, and then figure out how you can plan to financially achieve and support that lifestyle. Of course, discipline yourself and members of your family to live within your means, no matter what sort of lifestyle you choose.
5. **Find a highly qualified tax advisor** who best suits your needs and work with him or her closely throughout the year to identify additional tax- and money-saving strategies.
6. **Familiarize yourself with current *Tax Alpha to the 2nd Power* facts and strategies.** Discuss them with your tax advisor frequently throughout the year, and incorporate them into your financial life.
7. **Set long-term goals.** Annually, set goals for where you would like to be financially one year from now, five years from now, and in your retirement years. Revisit these goals throughout the year to make sure you are on track.

4

Managing Debt

Debt is the slavery of the free.

—Publilius Syrus,
ancient Latin writer and former slave

Case Study: How Two Doctors Went Bankrupt in Only a Few Years – What Not to Do

In March of 2006, through one of my seminars, I met a young, recently married couple from Baltimore. Both Peter and Suzanne Ellis were physicians who had recently completed their residencies and were about to embark on their careers. Peter was an internist, and Suzanne was a gynecologist and pediatrician. At the time we met, both Peter and Suzanne had found positions in existing practices. Of course, they were no longer interns, but they were the low doctors on the totem pole in their respective practices, and, like most young professionals, had much to learn. Nevertheless, one of their dreams was to set up a full-service family practice where they would work together, and they wished to make that happen as soon as possible.

Peter and Suzanne were eager to talk to me. They had some fears about the fact that they were starting their professional and married lives with a combined student loan debt of more than $500,000. Yes, this is a lot of money, but I was not terribly concerned. They were both only 30 years old, and I believed that their medical careers would provide them with the opportunities to make a well-above-average income for many years to come. However, I advised them to take their time, save up for larger purchases (such as launching their mutual practice or buying a house), and avoid credit card or other sorts of bad debt.

Despite my advice, they started off on the wrong foot. Wait – let me rephrase that: Peter and Suzanne made just about every financial mistake imaginable, and then some. In fairness to Peter and Suzanne, they were often led astray by bankers and mortgage lenders who, in my opinion, exercised behavior that bordered on the criminal.

Instead of deciding to work for four or five years with other doctors in established practices (to learn the realities of the day-to-day life of a doctor and the business of running a medical practice) and saving their money, they immediately borrowed more than $400,000 to establish a family practice of their own. The bank (which was a specialty cash-flow lender) was willing to provide the funds based on Peter and Suzanne's *potential* income (future cash flow), not their financial reality, which was, quite literally, no cash, no patients, absolutely no experience managing a medical practice, and a half million dollars' worth of student loan debt. But Peter and Suzanne were feeling flush with their success (or the idea of it), and none of the advice provided by the so-called experts from their banks hinted that they might be living in a dream world – or more to the point, in a financial nightmare.

And things got worse. While they took out their business loan, they leased two cars, a Mercedes-Benz and a BMW, which they viewed as rewards for their hard work during medical school as well as symbols of their (potential) success. The monthly payments on the car leases seemed affordable, and, again, the financing company was more than willing to put up the money for the loans.

Peter and Suzanne found a location for their new practice, and they moved ahead with leasing the space, but it needed lots of renovation to become useable as a medical office. They thought the renovation would take three or four months, so they both kept their respective positions. Still, with both working full time and building out a medical office at the same time, they ran into several challenges. The construction ran into additional delays and ultimately took 11 months to complete, not the 4 months they had originally planned, which, for one thing, adversely affected their business loan. Still, their bank said, "No problem," and instead generously offered to defer the payment on their business loan. These deferred payments were simply added to the principal of their loan. Therefore, on top of the $400,000 they borrowed to build out the office, they now owed an additional $40,000 in interest, which had accumulated over the additional 11 months.

During the months they were waiting for their office to be ready, they also decided to look for a house to buy so they could get out of the relatively small one-bedroom apartment they were renting in downtown Baltimore. They met with a realtor who, in turn, introduced them to a mortgage broker. They soon found their dream home (five bedrooms, five baths, a beautiful yard, an in-ground pool, etc.), which was selling for "only" $1,400,000. They still had no savings for a down payment or cash for the closing costs, and the earnings from their jobs just barely covered their monthly expenses. But, shockingly, the mortgage broker was able to work with a bank to provide them with some creative financing.

The bank was willing to give Peter and Suzanne 80% financing if the seller was willing to provide an inflated purchase price on their contract and then give back a seller concession for that amount. In essence, the seller agreed to artificially increase the contract price of the home so that Peter and Suzanne would qualify for a larger loan. (With this type of loan, at the closing, the seller agrees to lower the price, which ultimately allows the borrower to borrow more than 80% of the purchase price. This was a very common practice before the housing collapse of 2008. The banks, the lawyers, and the government regulators were fully aware of this practice and encouraged it to promote home ownership.) The bank was also "nice enough" to make it an *interest-only loan* with negative amortization. This meant that Peter and Suzanne were paying only part of the monthly interest on their mortgage loan; meanwhile, the principal balance increased every month, making the monthly payment more affordable in the short term. The mortgage broker also provided them with a *combo loan*, which allowed them to take on a home-equity loan for the remaining 20% of the purchase price.

Peter and Suzanne were overjoyed. Their particular American Dream (two successful doctors, practicing together in their own office, and living in a beautiful home) seemed to be coming true very quickly, and they had not had to come up with a cent to pay for any of it. Or so it seemed, at least for a short period of time. They moved into their big new house and furnished it completely, putting most of their purchases on multiple credit cards, which banks and other financial institutions were only too eager to give them.

By the time the renovation of their office was finally done, they were already having a difficult time making their monthly payments for their home mortgage, car leases, credit cards – and of course all their business loans and expenses. Also, at this time, Peter quit his salaried position to focus full-time on building up their new practice.

Suzanne continued with her position because they felt it could be useful to have at least some guaranteed income coming in.

But life is full of surprises, and something unexpected happened. Not long after their office was finished and Peter began the practice, they learned they were going to have a baby. Although they were becoming more and more worried about their finances – and a child would certainly add to their financial burdens – they were thrilled. To complicate matters, six months into her pregnancy, Suzanne had to stop working for medical reasons and remain resting at home. Then, after the birth of their beautiful and healthy baby boy, she insisted on staying home for an additional six months to care for their new son.

Throughout this time, Peter was not earning enough through his practice to be able to draw a salary; in fact, he began tapping into his personal credit cards for an additional $150,000 just to keep the practice and his family afloat. Not only were Peter and Suzanne sinking under their financial obligations, in late 2008, soon after the birth of their son, the national (and international) economy spiraled into a severe recession.

People were not spending money unless it was absolutely necessary, making it very difficult for Peter to bring new patients into his practice. Banks were no longer making loans unless they knew for certain that the loans could be paid back. As a result, Peter and Suzanne couldn't borrow from Bank *A* to make their payments to Banks *B*, *C*, or *D* and so on, a practice they had become quite good at. The credit card companies lowered their credit limits and started to demand repayment of loans that were greater than a certain limit. Real estate prices tumbled, and the house they had paid $1.4 million for only two years earlier was appraised for only $800,000, making it impossible for them to sell the house without still owing a $600,000 debt, with no hope of ever being able to repay it.

Although Peter began to be able to draw a small salary from the practice and Suzanne went back to work full time at her original position, their liabilities exceeded their assets by more than $1.5 million, and their cash outflow far exceeded their cash inflow. They had no choice but to seek bankruptcy protection against their creditors.

Today, they are finally starting to see the light at the end of the tunnel. They were forced to sell their home in a short sale; they gave up their fancy cars; and they are now finally living within their means. The bankruptcy eliminated all of their credit card debt, and they were able to renegotiate the terms of their business loans, which put them in a position that will allow them to pay their monthly obligations. The damage they did to their credit took seven years to repair, and there is no telling how many years the stress has taken off their life spans.

Basic Principles for Managing Debt

Peter and Suzanne's story sounds incredible, but not only is it true, it is surprisingly similar to the financial life stories of thousands of Americans who are living far beyond their means. Over the past decade, many people have experienced severe financial difficulties because of the national and world economic crisis. Although the economy has started to improve over the last few years, many people had lost their jobs and could not find work and, as a result, had to go into severe debt.

However, for many others, their financial crises are the result of irresponsible behavior toward money. The fault lies with individuals, as well as financial institutions and our own government, who failed to regulate, and in fact encouraged, this type of behavior. Although history tends to repeat itself, I am hopeful that reading this chapter will prevent you from doing the same.

Peter and Suzanne's story could have had a much different ending if they had simply taken seriously my basic financial advice, described in the following sections.

Learn the Meaning of Financial Responsibility

Being financially responsible implies learning the basics of personal financial literacy: figuring your net worth, figuring and carefully watching your cash flow, and learning about the other financial tools required to make you secure. In Peter and Suzanne's case, they were clueless about their personal financial situation while working toward opening a medical practice, which is a business proposition that requires a tremendous amount of financial savvy (see Chapter 11, "Starting Your Own Business"). They made no efforts to teach themselves about personal and business financial practices until it was too late.

Ironically, had Peter and Suzanne followed the guidance of Chapter 11 of this book, they may have been able to avoid Chapter 11 of the United States bankruptcy code.

Live Within Your Means and Always Pay Yourself First

Peter and Suzanne started their life together at "less than zero" financially by a huge amount; they had student loans of more than

$500,000. Had they begun working in established practices, figured out how much they could earn as medical doctors, figured out their net worth, created a thoughtful and realistic cash flow, and, most of all begun saving, they could have moved toward the lifestyle that represented their American Dream on a much surer footing and probably fairly quickly.

Know (and Respect) the Difference Between Wants and Needs

Peter and Suzanne *wanted* to share a successful medical practice, but they *needed* to learn more about the real life of a doctor and to begin saving for their goals. They *wanted* a lavish and beautiful home, but they *needed* a roof over their heads. They *wanted* to drive expensive automobiles and have all the other trappings that indicated success, but they *needed* a car (maybe two), some furniture, and some savings for unexpected surprises (like a baby). Even with their student loans, they could have bought a small house, decorated it modestly, and started saving for their joint family practice. They might even have bought a larger house where they could have both lived and worked. In any case, they did not need it all *now*.

Learn to Say No

Of course, they should have been saying *no* to many things from the beginning. I am not saying they should have deprived themselves of every luxury, but they should have known that *if it looked too good to be true, it probably was* – to quote a useful cliché. For example, the ease at which they were able to get both a large business loan and a home mortgage loan should have been red flags to them, especially because they originally felt uneasy about carrying their student loans. They should have said *no* to starting their own medical practice before they were ready. They should have said *no* to owning an enormous, expensive house when a modest one would have served them well for many years. They should have said *no* to driving two expensive cars, when two more modest cars would have been sufficient. And they should have said *no* to buying all the items that resulted in their maxed-out credit cards.

Although many of my clients have had difficulties with debt, Peter and Suzanne's story is one of the most extreme tales of poor debt management I have ever witnessed. Managing debt is critical if you want to achieve *point* X. However, as Peter and Suzanne's story illustrates, managing debt can be complicated and difficult, even for intelligent, well-meaning people, and it can get out of hand quickly and disastrously.

To achieve financial independence, you must first fully understand the concept of debt, and then you must make sure your own personal debt is under control.

Good Debt Versus Bad Debt

Debt. In a funny way, the word alone conjures up dank Dickensian prisons in the backstreets of London, with families chucked inside, starving, because they owe the local butcher, baker, and candlestick-maker. *Debtors' prisons,* as these sorts of places were known, imprisoned people (together with their families) who were unable to pay their bills. Although the act of being imprisoned for nonpayment of debt was outlawed in the late nineteenth century, in today's world of relatively trouble-free bankruptcy, some financial experts believe it might not be a bad idea to bring it back. I do not agree; however, I sometimes believe it is far too easy for people to walk away almost scot-free from gross financial irresponsibility. As a society, we need to move away from rewarding people for bad behavior and penalizing them for good behavior.

Conversely, for many people, debt is a scary concept, although it need not be. The fact is, not all debt is *bad debt*; indeed, some debt is not only good, it is essential for establishing good credit, and it can be an important factor in growing your wealth and helping you reach *point X*. In any case, understanding the difference between *bad debt* and *good debt* is imperative to becoming financially literate and financially independent.

Basically, *good debt* is money that people borrow for purchases and situations that, in the long term, will help them amass wealth and ultimately reach *point X*. Some examples of *good debt* include student loans, business loans, certain investment asset loans, and some personal-use asset loans (such as an affordable home mortgage).

In contrast, *bad debt* is money that people borrow (usually on a credit card) for the purchase of nonessential expenditures, as well as many personal-use assets. (Recall from Chapter 3 that personal-use assets are assets that define your lifestyle, such as homes, automobiles, boats, jewelry, works of fine art, etc.) These items have value, but they require additional expense to maintain them, and, in some cases (such as with a car or boat), they depreciate over time. Thus, another way to define *bad debt* versus *good debt* is to consider whether the item is an *essential* or *nonessential* expense; is it a *need* or is it a *want?*

For example, if you wish to become a doctor, you may *need* to take out a student loan to pay for your education, putting you in substantial debt for many years. However, ultimately, you will be able to use your education to earn an above-average living. As a result, this is *good debt*. However, if after you have earned your degree, you *want* to buy all the accoutrements that supposedly define success or an affluent lifestyle, like luxury cars and large houses, you can put yourself in serious financial straits, as Peter and Suzanne did. This, of course, is *bad debt*.

When you do not use debt properly, that can lead to significant financial hardship and can prevent you from ever becoming financially independent. However, when you use debt to leverage yourself in the pursuit of accumulating wealth, it can be a very powerful tool.

Credit Card Debt

The most common form of consumer debt is credit card debt. In our world, we can use a credit card to charge anything from a tube of toothpaste to a three-week cruise in the Adriatic. However, if we do not pay off the credit card charges when the bill arrives, the money used to buy the items purchased with the card become *debt*. And credit card debt is like cancer: If you do not properly control it, it can kill you – financially, that is.

Ideally, you should use credit cards only as a convenient form of payment, which is often safer than using cash. Nevertheless, you should pay any credit card charges at the end of each billing month. If you cannot afford to pay your complete credit card balance at the end of each month, whether you have used it to buy a sweater or a sofa, you are *going into debt* to pay for the item or items you have purchased. Not only that, but you are going to *pay interest* on those purchases – sometimes quite a large interest – so the item is costing you much more than you originally thought.

Basically, when you start using your credit cards without paying them off, you are subtly (or perhaps not so subtly) indicating that *you cannot really afford the purchases you have made*. To put it another way, these purchases are very likely *nonessential*; they are *wants* rather than *needs*. And when you begin charging true *essentials* on your credit cards, such as food, medications, or diapers, and are unable to pay for them when the bill comes due, you may well be on the brink of financial disaster.

The Insatiable Credit Card

Credit card companies sometimes offer teaser rates of 0% so that you will use their credit card and maintain a running balance for a few months. Do not fall for this: It is a trap that lures you in until you have charged more than you can pay for, and then they sock you with a double-digit interest rate after the teaser rate period ends. Likewise, some retail stores offer 10%, 15%, and even 25% discounts on purchases, if you are willing to apply for an in-store credit card. Do not be lured in unless you can pay off the purchases when the bill shows up in your mailbox. Again, it is just a way to make you feel that you can afford a host of *nonessentials*. Credit cards can eat you alive.

To understand the voracious nature of credit cards and what it can mean to your financial future, consider the following scenario. Your end-of-summer vacation week is coming up and you have no plans. You look in your newspaper's travel section or go online and find a great vacation package to Quebec for you and your spouse. This vacation will cost you $1,750 – plus you have always wanted to go to Quebec. (Note the term *want*.) You book the trip, have a nice week away, and then with all of the incidentals and souvenirs included, you realize that your trip actually cost you closer to $2,500. At the end of the month, you have a few other unexpected bills, so you do not have the cash available to pay for the trip when the bill arrives, and you leave the charges on your card.

Over the next four months, several old friends come to visit from out of town, and you decide to entertain them at a few expensive restaurants and throw in a couple of Broadway shows and some sporting events; before you know it, you have added another $1,500 on your credit card.

Now winter is approaching and you *need* a new winter coat. While you are out shopping, you see a few great buys on sweaters, and simply cannot resist a pair of expensive boots. Suddenly, you have added another $1,500 to your credit card.

Now, it is a week before Christmas, and you realize that you have not purchased any gifts for your relatives and friends. You do not have a lot of extra cash, but, yes, you do have that credit card. There goes another $2,500.

Without really thinking about it, you have just spent $8,000 over just a few months for the purchases of any number of nonessential items – all *wants*, not *needs*. You even have justified this in your own mind, since your monthly minimum payment is only $150, an amount you can comfortably cover each month.

However, let us take a closer look at this scenario. You now have an $8,000 credit card balance, the interest rate on your card is 22% (not unusual), and the monthly payment is $150. The fact is, if you pay only the minimum each month, *it will take you almost 18 years to pay off this credit card balance;* even worse, *you will end up paying $23,430 in interest.* In other words, over the 18-year period, *you would be paying a total of $31,430* for those nonessential items that you originally thought cost you $8,000, four times more than you expected. These purchases – and the undisciplined financial planning – have robbed you of the potential to save that $31,430 toward reaching your financial independence, or *point X.*

Every time you use a credit card to pay for a nonessential item that you cannot afford to pay for at the end of the month, you are severely jeopardizing your financial future. Money can compound quickly, or grow exponentially, almost magically, if it is saved. The power of compounding can be your *best friend* or your *worst enemy,* depending on whether you choose to be a *saver* or a *spender.* (For a detailed discussion on the power of compounding, see Chapter 12, "The Time Value of Money.") This same powerful tool has the *opposite* effect if you borrow money or maintain a large balance on your credit cards. Your debt can compound as quickly and magically as your savings. You cannot accumulate wealth if you are maintaining balances on your credit cards.

Paying Down Credit Card Debt

When I evaluate a client's statement of financial position, I very often discover that he or she is maintaining credit card balances and paying double-digit interest rates (sometimes as high as 20% or more) on this debt. At the same time, the client has money sitting in bank savings accounts or invested in other assets that are earning a lower rate of return than the interest the client is paying on his or her credit cards. In situations like these, it is sometimes wise to use the available cash to pay off the credit card debt.

Let us assume you are paying your credit card company 20% interest on a $5,000 credit card balance, and, at the same time, you have $12,000 in a savings account earning 1% interest as well as $20,000 in an aggressive mutual fund account, where you hope to earn 9% per year over the long run while taking on a great degree of risk. If you had the following choices, which one would you choose?

1. Would you want to earn 1% on your money in your savings account (taxable as ordinary income) with FDIC insurance?

2. Or would you want to possibly earn 9% (while taking on a great deal of risk) through an aggressive mutual fund (possibly taxable at capital gain rates)?
3. Or would you want to save 20% interest tax-free on $5,000, guaranteed, by paying off your credit card balance?

The answer is obvious: You would pick option 3, which is 20% guaranteed tax-free savings. Therefore, if you have high credit card balances, your best investment choice would be to *eliminate that debt.* (One caveat: If you use your savings or investments to pay off your credit card debt, you must not turn around and run up more credit card debt as soon as your cards are clear. Sooner or later, you will run out of money, and you will find yourself in even worse financial shape.)

Other Surprising Resources for Reducing Debt

If you do not want to raid your savings or money market accounts, you can consider other potential resources for putting your out-of-control credit card debt back in line. Here are a few suggestions.

Take Out a Home-Equity Loan   If you own your own home and have sufficient equity, you might want to consider taking out a home-equity line of credit and using it to pay off your credit card debt. A home-equity loan can help you in several ways. First, by using the loan to pay down the credit card debt, you are trading 18% to 20% interest (on your credit cards) for 4% to 5% interest (on the home-equity loan). The other advantage to a home-equity loan is that although it spreads your payments over many years, it can help you improve your monthly cash flow. Although the tax deductibility of the interest on a home-equity loan is no longer available starting January 1, 2018, it can still be a useful tool in lowering your cost of financing and bringing down your monthly obligation. Please be aware that credit card debt is unsecured and home-equity loans are secured against your home. In other words, debtors can put a lien against your house with a home-equity loan.

Borrow Against Your Life Insurance   If you have a whole-life insurance policy, you can borrow against it and use the money to pay your debt. However, *be sure to pay it back.* If you die before the loan from the policy is paid off, the outstanding balance (plus interest) will be deducted from the death benefit of the policy, and your beneficiaries will pay the price.

Borrow Against Your 401(k)   If you have a healthy 401(k) account, you may be able to borrow up to 50% of its value or $50,000, whichever is less. The interest is lower than credit cards, plus you are borrowing from yourself, not a bank or mortgage lender.

Bear in mind that borrowing from your 401(k) can have severe drawbacks, including these:

- You will be paying back the loan and its interest with after-tax dollars.
- You must repay the loan within five years.
- If you leave your job before you fully repay this loan, you will have to pay the balance of what you owe *immediately*. If you do not repay it, that amount will be treated as a distribution to you, and you will be taxed accordingly. You may also be subject to an additional 10% penalty by the IRS, unless you qualify for one of the exceptions.

I am not a big fan of borrowing from your 401(k) plan, but I do believe it is better than using a credit card.

Borrow from Family and Friends   If you find yourself deep in credit card debt, consider borrowing from your parents, your sister, your rich single aunt, or your best friend to get rid of the money-sucking interest on a high credit card balance. However, be sure to arrange to pay them back quickly – preferably with interest – to not only preserve good relationships, but to be sure that you treat this transaction as business (not a gift).

Reducing Credit-Card Debt the Old-Fashioned Way

What if you do not have lots of extra cash in savings, a thriving 401(k) account, equity on real estate or a life insurance policy, or a rich aunt, and yet you have run up $10,000, $15,000, $20,000 or more in credit card debt? You are probably anxious and frightened about this situation (and if you are not, you should be). But all is not lost; you can actually reduce your debt the old-fashioned way: Pay it back yourself.

Here are some constructive actions you can take to get yourself back on track financially if faced with off-the-charts credit card debt:

- **Stop using your credit cards.** While it is financially wise to have one or two (but not 10) active credit cards, stop using them until you pay them off. After you have paid them off, do not run up nonessential charges again. (Note: *Do not* cancel all of your credit cards. Canceling your cards can have a negative effect on your credit score. When deciding which credit card to keep, always keep the one that you have had the longest: This will help you maintain an overall higher credit score. More information about credit scores is provided at the end of this chapter.)
- **Consider using a prepaid credit card or a debit card.** Visa and MasterCard offer both types of cards. *Prepaid credit cards* are prefunded reloadable cards requiring payment in advance, after which you can use the card until the payment is depleted. You can use them anywhere you can use credit cards, as well as at ATMs. *Debit cards* provide electronic access to your bank accounts, and most relay a message to the bank to withdraw funds from a designated account. You can use debit cards as you would use cash or a check.
- **Know the enemy.** Paying off credit card debt is war! You need to know yourself (and your apparent weakness for buying *nonessentials*), and you need to know and understand the details of the credit cards you have been abusing. How many cards do you have? What is the sum of all your credit card debt? What interest rates are you being charged? How quickly can you pay this down?
- **Reduce your interest rates.** Many financial institutions will lower your interest rates if your credit is good – and sometimes even if it is not so good. Contact the institution and plead your case, or put higher-interest-rate balances on lower-interest-rate cards.
- **Set a due date to repay your debt.** As with any long-term project, it helps to have a firm goal in terms of time. Depending on how much debt you have, give yourself a date when you want to finish paying off your debt. Recheck your date each month, and make sure you are making significant progress.
- **Give yourself a break.** Paying off credit card debt is admirable and rewarding, but it is like dieting – it takes strength and discipline, and you occasionally need to have a treat. This does not

mean you should charge a trip to Paris on your newly cleared credit card – in fact, avoid anything having to do with credit cards. But perhaps, using cash, buy yourself a new outfit or go out for an evening at the theater. In other words, spend a little money – just do not put it on a credit card.

Auto Loans

Buying a car is usually the first major purchase any of us ever make. However, unless you are a 17-year-old boy who has saved up his caddying tips to buy a third-hand jalopy, or unless you have significant disposable cash, you are most likely going to have to take out an auto loan to purchase a new car. Many people buy cars frequently (the average American buys a new car about once every four years), and many families have multiple cars, sometimes one for each member of the family. In this day of expensive cars, the purchase of an automobile is almost as complicated as the purchase of a house (and I am not even referring to buying a luxury automobile like a Lexus or a Mercedes-Benz). Moreover, buying a car is a very significant addition to your personal debt and potentially a real roadblock to getting to *point X*.

Like any major purchase, you need to research the automobile market thoroughly before you choose the car and the financial requirements that best suit your need. You must decide if you want to buy a used ("preowned") car or a new car, which you will own when you pay off your loan, or if you want to lease a car, which you will return at the end of the lease's term, like renting a house instead of buying it.

For many people, the price of a car they can afford really depends on the amount of a monthly loan payment they can add to their budget. I would recommend not allocating more than 15% of your monthly take-home pay towards a car loan payment. You can use the calculator found at www.calcxml.com/do/aut06 to provide you with some guidance on how much of a car you can actually afford to finance.

Another option you will want to consider is whether leasing or purchasing an automobile will make the most sense for you. Although leasing has become a very popular way to obtain a new or used car, it may not be as attractive as some people think. If you are willing to own a car for 5 or more years, in general, purchasing would be much less costly in the long run than leasing would be. At the end of your loan payment, you will have a car that you will own outright and have equity in. You can use the calculator at www.calcxml.com/calculators/should-i-lease-or-purchase-an-auto to determine if financing or leasing would be the best option for you.

Also, in addition to the auto loan or the cost of the lease, you must consider the fact that you need to maintain your car, which can be expensive. Moreover, your car comes with a host of other necessary costs: insurance, annual license plate fees, and, of course, the cost of gasoline.

Given their high cost both to purchase and maintain, automobiles can be among the most treacherous purchases we make, not only financially but also psychologically. For many people, automobiles symbolize relative status. Are you a Mercedes-Benz or a Ford Taurus type? There is nothing wrong with wanting to own a Mercedes – unless you take out a loan for one when all you can really afford is the Taurus.

Most of us consider a car to be a necessity, an essential expense, a *need* rather than a *want*. However, among the many decisions involved in buying a car, some entail giving in to very expensive *wants* (a new Mercedes), rather than more economical *needs* (a used Ford). If you live within a city, public transportation would be a much more economical alternative, even if you occasionally have to use a taxi or Uber.

Student Loans

Whenever you make an investment in yourself and your future that may provide you with a better life and higher income, then the money you borrow to achieve that goal should be considered *good debt*. Therefore, if you need to take out a loan (or loans) to attend college or pursue an advanced degree or professional license, you should feel comfortable that you are incurring *good debt*. With that said, be careful not to buy into the notion that everyone needs to go to college. Also keep in mind that, if you don't maintain good grades, you may never get that high-paying job you were counting on, which can quickly turn this good debt into bad debt. This will be discussed further in Chapter 7.

If you have low-interest-rate student loans, you need not be in any rush to pay them off. Nevertheless, make sure you make every payment on time, so that you can improve your credit score. (More information on credit scores is provided at the end of this chapter.) Also, student loans may allow a useful tax deduction. You may be able to deduct up to $2,500 of student loan interest paid from your taxable income if you qualify under the income threshold. For 2018, the maximum $2,500 of student loan interest may be deductible if the taxpayer's modified adjusted gross income is below $65,000 for single and head of household taxpayers and below $135,000 for married taxpayers filing jointly. The amount of the student loan interest that is deductible is phased out with higher modified adjusted gross income (MAGI), until there is no deduction for singles and heads of households with $80,000 MAGI and married filing jointly taxpayers with $165,000 MAGI. Although student loan interest is considered consumer debt, if you use it wisely, your return on investment could far exceed your cost of interest. In other words, it is *good debt.*

Home Mortgage Loans

On a national – and perhaps an international – level, we are still in the process of digging ourselves out of one of the most serious financial debacles since the Great Depression of the 1930s. A large part of the problem had to do with a serious (in my opinion, almost criminal) mishandling of home mortgage loans.

For several years leading up to the 2008 meltdown, banks were sometimes lending money for the purchase of a home without even verifying a person's income (with loans called *no-income-verification loans*) or his ability to repay the mortgage loan. If the bank determined that someone could not afford the mortgage payment, the bank would simply adjust the terms and provide an interest-only loan, an adjustable rate loan, a balloon payment loan, or some other form of creative financing so that the borrower could purchase a little piece (and sometimes quite a large piece) of the "American Dream."

Some banks even allowed seller concessions, which simply was an inflated sales price so that a person could buy a home and receive 100% financing. (This practice is still legal today. How is this possible?) You did not even need to come up with closing costs because the banks worked those fees into the financing. In some situations, people were buying homes with no money down and walking away with money at the closing. To make matters worse, the easy-credit policies during this period artificially increased the value of homes (demand for homes was greater than the supply) and provided consumers with an entitlement mentality that justified their unsustainable standard of living.

But, of course, as we know, it ultimately all came crashing down. It may now take us decades to correct this irresponsible behavior.

Everyone was to blame: the federal government (the deregulators), the banks (lenders), and even the consumers (borrowers). We all should have known better. Bankers were drinking and driving, consumers went along for the ride, and the government continued to pour the wine, until they crashed the economy into the Great Recession of 2008.

It is hard to believe that it has already been a decade since the financial crisis. Although many of these aggressive lending programs and practices have been eliminated, there are still programs sponsored by the federal government, such as the Federal Housing Administration (FHA), and state-sponsored programs, such as the State of New York Mortgage Agency (SONYMA). These programs allow as low a down payment as 3.5% of the purchase price with credit scores of 580 or higher. Let's hope that history does not repeat itself here.

Owning a Home: Not Necessarily Good Debt

The notion of owning a home has long been a significant facet of the American Dream. Since the economic boom in the years following World War II, Americans came to believe that possessing a home of their own was almost a right. They certainly thought owning a house made sound financial sense, mostly because, for several decades, the value of a home escalated, sometimes very quickly.

One of the valuable lessons learned during the Great Recession of 2008 is that the value of homes can in fact go down, sometimes substantially. Buying a home and expecting its price to go up in the short term is not a sure thing. The purchase of a home may be a good decision (and taking out a home mortgage can be considered *good debt*), but only if you can meet certain criteria.

Before you begin picking out your dream home in your favorite neighborhood, you need to figure out precisely how much house you can actually afford. To help you with this choice financially, use the calculator at www.calcxml.com/calculators/home-affordability to determine how much of a home you can actually afford.

For example, if your current income is $80,000 from all sources, your monthly auto payment is $300, your minimum monthly credit card payment is $250, and your monthly student loan payment is $300, how much of a home can you afford? Before we can answer this, we also must make further assumptions that you will be taking a 30-year mortgage, can obtain a 4% interest rate, and have $70,000 available for a down payment. Based on these facts and the guidelines I have set for home affordability, you can afford to purchase a home for $329,732 with a $259,732 mortgage. Your monthly payment on this mortgage would be $1,240. This is without the real estate tax and insurance, which sometimes is added to your monthly mortgage payment when paid directly by the bank.

According to Doreen Vento, home lending officer with CitiBank, "The best way to determine how much you can comfortably afford to spend on a mortgage payment is by looking at this through the eyes of a mortgage lender, the bank. Banks typically use the following ratios as a guideline in determining how much a prospective homeowner can comfortably spend on a monthly mortgage payment. The first one is referred to as a front end ratio, which includes the mortgage principal payment, interest, real estate taxes, and homeowners' insurance. These amounts should not exceed 28% of your gross income. The second one is referred to as a back end ratio, which includes the mortgage principal payment, interest, real estate taxes, homeowners' insurance, and all other debt payments (credit card, car loans/leases, and student loans). These amounts should not exceed 43% of your gross income. These percentages will vary depending on your credit score."

Moreover, in my opinion, before you can buy a house, you need to have saved 20% of the total cost of the home as the down payment, as well as all closing costs. Finally, before you buy, you should compare the costs of renting versus the costs of purchasing. If you cannot afford the monthly payments and costs of maintaining a home, you may need to rent rather than buy, or scale down your *wants*.

Also, given the high costs of acquiring (and ultimately selling) a house, you must be committed to living in this home for at least 10 years for it to begin to potentially increase in value. In addition, you should tally the everyday costs of home maintenance: property taxes, homeowner's insurance, heating, electricity, gas, and so forth. Finally, you also need to consider the cost of ongoing home maintenance: painting, major repairs, etc. And note: I have not mentioned those wonderful cosmetic accoutrements (also known as *nonessential wants*) – the new furniture, the beautiful decorations, the renovated family room in the basement, the gorgeous deck, and the in-ground pool.

A house should meet your basic living standards (*needs*), and should not be based on your ego (*wants*). Still, a house can increase in value if you hang on to it for many years and maintain it well. It can also help you financially in other ways.

Why a Mortgage Is Still Good Debt

The reason a home mortgage is usually considered *good debt* is that, from the moment you buy the house, it offers certain financial reliefs and leverage. For starters, your home mortgage interest may be tax-deductible. The mortgage interest deduction on your personal residence can only be taken on mortgage debt of up to $750,000, down from $1 million prior to 2018. This applies only to mortgages taken after December 15, 2017. It is important to note that preexisting mortgages prior to this date are grandfathered in at the $1 million level. The interest on home-equity debt can no longer be deducted at all, whereas up to $100,000 in home-equity debt could have been considered previously. This deduction has been eliminated for all home-equity loans, even if they predated the new law. Therefore, if you are in the 40% tax bracket and are paying 6% interest on your mortgage, your after-tax cost for financing may actually be only 3.6%, which is 6% less the 40% tax savings. Please note, real estate taxes are also tax-deductible. Starting January 1, 2018, this is capped at $10,000 for most taxpayers (capped at $5,000 if married filing separately), along with your state and local income tax or sales tax.

After you have been paying your mortgage for a few years and have built equity in your home, you can use the equity to leverage other purchases or financial needs.

When comparing the costs of owning a home versus renting, take the tax savings into consideration. If you pay rent, that expense is not tax-deductible and therefore does not provide the same advantages as paying a mortgage does. Also, in some situations, especially if you plan to live in your house for several years, the money you would be spending in rent could be building up as equity. This is when a mortgage becomes *good debt*.

Refinancing a Home Mortgage

During the past two decades, a record number of Americans have refinanced their home mortgages because of historically low interest rates. The ultimate purpose of refinancing your home mortgage is to lower your costs of financing so that you free up more cash that can be used toward reaching financial independence, or *point X.*

To determine whether it makes sense to refinance your mortgage, you need to perform a breakeven analysis. Quite simply, you must determine the number of months it will take you to recover the costs of refinancing from the interest cost you will be saving.

Generally speaking, if you plan on living in your home past your breakeven period, then refinancing may be the right decision for you. The breakeven period is not determined by the cost of the new loan divided by the reduction in the monthly mortgage payments; although many bankers and mortgage brokers use this as a comparison point, it does not tell the whole story.

Mortgage refinancing is a complex and potentially expensive process in which you pay off one or more existing debts with a new home loan. Therefore, before you refinance, you need to know what your upfront closing costs will be, what your current and new interest rates will be, and a number of other details. Closing costs to refinance your mortgage can include loan origination fees, appraisal fees, attorney fees, mortgage recording tax, and so forth. In some cases, these costs could be as high as 2% of your loan amount.

However, if the figures work, every month after your breakeven point would result in a savings to you. In some cases, you may actually be able to reduce the number of years on your loan without increasing your monthly payment. There are numerous possibilities and what-if scenarios you need to consider when refinancing. To determine if you should refinance your mortgage, you can use the calculator at www.calcxml.com/calculators/refinance-calculator.

To clarify how to determine your true breakeven point, consider the following example. Let us assume that you owe $200,000 on your current mortgage, you are paying 6% per year, and you have 20 years remaining on this loan. Let us also assume you can refinance this loan and obtain a new mortgage at 4% with the same 20-year term. If the bank and other fees associated with refinancing this loan come to $3,000, how many months will it take for you to recover your upfront closing costs and then ultimately have a true savings as a result of refinancing?

Using the above financial calculator and inputting all of the facts in this example, we have determined a breakeven number of months to be 14. Therefore, if you plan on staying in your home more than 14 months, refinancing would be a wise financial choice for you. Your monthly payment would be reduced from $1,433 to $1,212, putting an extra $221 each month into your free cash flow. You can ultimately save $53,016 in interest throughout the 20-year life of this loan.

You should go through this example with your own set of facts to determine your breakeven point in terms of months.

Get Professional Advice

For most people, buying a home is the single most significant purchase they will make throughout their lifetime. Do not rely on your gut instincts or your emotional *wants*. Do the hard research into the financial aspects of making this huge purchase.

Also, do not rely solely on the advice of your real estate broker or mortgage broker, because they may not always have your best interests in mind. Before making a final decision about the purchase of a house, consult with your tax and financial advisor.

Business and Investment Loans

The best investment you can make is in yourself. For some people, this means furthering their education (see Chapter 7, "Paying for College"); for others, it means going into business for themselves (see Chapter 11, "Starting Your Own Business"); and for some, it may mean both.

Going into business for yourself could be one of the most rewarding decisions you could make, but it could also be one of the costliest mistakes of your life. You should never jump into a business venture without first determining the likelihood of its success and your reasonably expected rate of return on your time and investment. From my more than 30 years of experience, I can tell you firsthand that starting your own business could be one of the quickest roads to financial independence. Sadly, for many, it could be the quickest road to financial ruin. If you do not study this carefully and fully comprehend the risks, then this potential *good debt* could easily become a *bad debt.*

If you believe you have a great business plan that has a high probability of success and profit, can reasonably be expected to exceed your cost of financing, and has an acceptable return on investment, then this may be considered *good debt.* Every time you evaluate a business opportunity or investment, you must do your best to determine not only your hard and soft costs, but also your opportunity costs for entering into this business venture. *Opportunity costs* represent what you would have been able to earn with that money if you had invested it elsewhere.

Although the best investment you can make is an investment in yourself, do not take out any sort of business loan without researching it carefully. Consult with others who have gone into similar practices or businesses, study appropriate literature, and discuss the financial details with your tax and financial advisor. The same applies to investment loans.

Understanding Credit

What is *credit?* Credit is the act of borrowing money with the agreement to pay it back at some future date. In fact, credit sounds suspiciously like *debt*, which includes all the subjects we have just covered (auto loans, student loans, home mortgages, business loans, and, curiously enough, *credit* cards). Indeed, the process of establishing good credit involves precisely these sorts of common loans.

As with debt, there is good credit and bad credit. If you have *good credit*, it means you pay what you owe on time; *bad credit* means you have a history of not paying your bills on time and letting debts (again, very often credit card debt) build up, usually with high, speedily compounding interest rates. *Good credit* paves the way to getting to *point X*; *bad credit* is almost always a serious roadblock to reaching financial independence.

A Word About "No Credit"

You may also have *no credit.* This means that you have never borrowed money from a commercial lender (such as taking out a credit card), and there is no record of your payment history.

Note that many boarding school and college students away from home for the first time have no credit in their own names, but credit card companies and retail shops are quick to try to lure students into "establishing credit." This can be a good thing so long as the student pays his or her bills. However, it can be a tragic situation if the student takes out a host of credit cards, runs up huge balances, and then either leaves his or her parents to pay them off, or is not responsible. Before they even venture out into the workplace, they could end up with huge debts and very likely a shaky credit history.

Actually, some people prefer to maintain a no-credit history, or what is known as a *nontraditional credit history*. If this is your choice, be sure to pay your bills (rent, telephone, utilities, medical) in a timely way, and save all your receipts for up to three years. Then, if you want to apply for a loan of any kind (such as an auto loan or a home mortgage), you can use your receipts to prove your good credit.

Establishing and Maintaining Good Credit

The trick to establishing and maintaining good credit is pretty basic. At the most fundamental level, you need to:

- Open a checking account.
- Apply for a low-interest credit card.
- Keep your credit card balance low – or, better yet, pay it off every month.
- Finally, pay all your bills on time, never missing a payment.

Beyond these fundamentals, you may also go after the bigger-ticket items like an auto loan or a home mortgage. How you handle these loans will affect your *good credit* – but conversely, the state of your credit will affect whether you will be permitted to take out these loans in the first place.

Establishing and maintaining good credit also involves living within your means financially and even paying yourself first. Toward that end, you need to establish a budget for all your expenses, and then, of course, stick to it. (If necessary, reread Chapters 1 and 3.)

Only when you understand your financial realities (and not your "dream lifestyle") can you create a budget that is appropriate for your financial situation and that you can maintain effectively. This involves being realistic about your spending habits, and knowing where you are spending most of your money. (Save your receipts, and study your bills each month.) It also means saving up for expensive items – new furniture, vacations, a down payment on a house – and not putting these items on your credit card, unless, of course, you can pay them off at the end of the month. Staying on budget will assure that you will not only have *good credit*, but that you will be on your road to *point X*.

Your Credit Report and Your Credit Score

Your credit report is like your school report card, and your credit score is the grades you have that represent how financially responsible or irresponsible you have been. Understanding how to get your credit report as well as what it takes to improve your credit score is an important part of achieving and maintaining financial independence throughout your lifetime.

What Is a Credit Report?

Anybody who has ever used a credit card or made a loan payment has a credit report: It is a formal statement (like a school report card) that sums up, among other things, all your "credit" behavior, such as timely payments, missed payments, and the number of credit cards you have. Your credit report determines whether you are in sound financial shape.

These reports are made to (and through) three major credit reporting agencies that maintain information on your credit history. These three agencies are:

1. Equifax Credit Information Services
   P.O. Box 740241
   Atlanta, GA 30374
   1-866-349-5191
   www.equifax.com
2. Experian (formerly TRW)
   P.O. Box 4500
   Allen, TX 75013
   1-888-397-3742
   www.experian.com
3. TransUnion
   P.O. Box 1000
   Chester, PA 19016
   1-800-888-4213
   www.transunion.com

Lenders, employers, landlords, and other service providers buy your credit information in the form of a credit report to help them decide whether to approve your application for a loan, credit card, job, or housing, or to offer you a product or service at a particular rate.

What Is Included in Credit Reports?

Your credit reports from Equifax, Experian, and TransUnion include the following information:

- **Personal information:** Compiled from credit applications you have filled out in the past, this information normally includes your name, current and recent addresses, Social Security number, date of birth, and current and previous employers and your employment history.

- **Credit history:** The bulk of your credit report consists of details about credit accounts that were opened in your name or that list you as an authorized user (such as a spouse's credit card). Account details, which are supplied by creditors with which you have an account, include the date the account was opened, the credit limit or amount of the loan, the payment terms, the balance, and a history that shows whether you have paid the account on time. Closed or inactive accounts stay on your report for 7 to 11 years from the date of their last activity, depending on the manner in which you paid them.
- **Credit report inquiries:** Credit reporting agencies record an inquiry whenever your credit report is shown to another party, such as a lender, service provider, landlord, or insurer. Inquiries remain on your credit report for up to two years.
- **Public records:** Matters of public record obtained from government sources such as courts of law – including liens, bankruptcies, and overdue child support – may appear on your credit report. Most public record information stays on your credit report for years.

What Is Not Included in Your Three Credit Reports?

None of the credit reports from Equifax, Experian, and TransUnion include information about your checking or savings accounts, bankruptcies that are more than 10 years old, charged-off or debts placed for collection that are more than 7 years old, gender, ethnicity, religion, political affiliation, medical history, or criminal records. Also, your credit score (discussed in the next section) is generated by information on your credit report, but it is not part of the report itself.

Checking Your Credit Report

You should check your credit report on a regular basis, at least once a year – and ideally two or three times a year, because the reports and your credit scores are constantly in flux. The three major credit reporting bureaus, Experian, TransUnion, and Equifax, are required by law to give you a free copy of your credit report each year on request. Call 1-877-322-8228 or go to www.annualcreditreport.com to order your free credit reports.

You should take a close look at these reports to ensure that they are accurate and complete. If you identify errors or accounts that you do not recognize, you should report this to the credit bureaus immediately. These problems could jeopardize your credit score and may also be a warning of possible identity theft (discussed in the next section of this chapter).

What Is a Credit Score?

Your credit score, called a FICO score (named for the Fair Isaac Corporation), is a mathematical model designed to predict credit risk, based on data contained within your credit report; in effect, your credit score summarizes your credit information. Lenders typically review your credit report and credit score to determine whether to extend credit (i.e., whether to lend you money) and on what terms. A higher score usually means you pose a lower risk to the lender, who will, in turn, be more likely to offer you favorable interest rates.

Several factors can affect your credit score, including these:

- **The number of loans you are carrying:** These include a home mortgage, auto loans, student loans, retail store credit cards, and bank credit cards.
- **Types of credit used:** Creditors prefer a variety of loans – mortgages, auto loans, store credit, and so forth.
- **Payment history:** The credit score takes into account whether you have repaid your loans in a timely manner and consistently.
- **The length of your credit history:** The longer your credit history, the higher your score.
- **Public records:** Have you filed for bankruptcy? Have reports been made for lack of alimony payments or child-care payments? If so, these factors will affect your credit score adversely.
- **New accounts:** Have you added new accounts to your debt, and if so, how many? Try to maintain no more than three or four credit cards, because more than this can lower your FICO score, which would make you appear to be a higher credit risk to a lender.
- **Inquiries into your credit file:** Have lenders requested copies of your credit information? Fair Isaac's research shows that opening several credit accounts in a short period of time can be an indication of greater credit risk to the lender.

As the information contained in your credit report files changes over time, so might any new scores based on your data. Your credit score from a month ago may have changed if there has been any recent activity on your credit file.

Your credit score is by far the most important factor that creditors look at to determine whether you are a credit risk. Credit scores range from 280 to 850, with the higher value representing lower credit risk. (In other words, the higher your score, the easier it should be for you to obtain credit.) The median score ranges from 690 to 720. A poor credit score (below 600) can cost you the ability to access additional credit, insurance, utility services such as telephone and electricity, a rental unit, and even a job. Conversely, an excellent credit score (720 or above) will increase your chances of a loan approval, as well as attractive interest rates and terms. This, of course, will indicate that you are headed in the right direction to becoming financially independent.

How to Improve Your Credit Score

If you would like or need to improve your credit score, here are a few good suggestions:

- **Watch your percentage of debt.** Make sure your debt (including all bills and loans) remains under 36% of your gross annual income.
- **Use credit accounts regularly but conservatively.** Pay them off completely each month, as soon as the bill arrives.
- **Pay all of your bills on time.** The sooner the better.
- **Reduce the amount you owe.** Pay off your credit cards and other loans as quickly as possible. (See the section on paying down credit card debt earlier in this chapter.)
- **Maintain credit cards that you have held for long periods of time.** If you have accounts at retail stores or credit cards that you have had for years, keep them open. Use them conservatively – and pay off balances at the end of each month. Creditors like to see that you have sustained long-term credit.
- **Get rid of your newest credit cards.** Cancel any cards you have applied for within the past six months, unless you have moved high-interest balances to cards with lower-interest balances. Do not apply for new credit cards until the balances on old cards are clear.

- **Avoid applying for new loans.** Creditors like to see that you can handle different types of loans, including auto loans, home mortgages, and student loans. However, do not take on more debt simply to improve your credit score. This is seen as a negative.
- **Check your credit reports regularly.** You are permitted one free credit report each year; however, ideally, it is better to check them more frequently.
- **Fix disputes quickly.** Do not let disputes go beyond 30 days or into collection.

Preventing Identity Theft

So you followed all the rules, paid all your bills on time, and have maintained a terrific FICO score. Now you must also be prepared to take the necessary steps to protect it. Identity theft has become a widespread problem throughout the country. Identity theft occurs when someone steals your (financial) identity: In other words, they borrow money in your name, take out credit cards, open bank accounts, file tax returns using your name, or simply sign your name to a letter.

For identity theft scam artists to steal your identity, they need only some of your personal information, like your name, current address, Social Security number, date of birth, and perhaps your mother's maiden name. If the scam artist gets his hands on your current credit card, driver's license, or birth certificate you will then become very easy prey. These criminals steal millions of identities each year by going through trash cans at people's homes and workplaces. They will call or email you and represent themselves as government officials or financial institutions. They will fill out change of address forms on your behalf to get utility bill information. They will copy down your credit card number and use it to make purchases. Today, one of the top causes of identity theft comes from cyber theft, in which these criminals access your personal information online and by hacking government institutions, businesses, and any other source that contains personal information. Perhaps the most notable theft was the Equifax breach of 2017, which we will talk about in the next section of this chapter. They will steal anything they can get their hands on to get your personal records.

Do not become a victim of identity theft, and always be on the alert. Never provide anyone with your personal information unless you know who that person is. To protect yourself against identity theft, you must be proactive and always on the defensive. You should take the following 12 steps immediately:

1. Check your credit report today and on an annual basis.
2. If you believe you are being electronically hacked, you should immediately shut down your computer and unplug all of your devices.
3. Buy a good shredder, and keep it handy so you can use it before discarding any sensitive personal documents.
4. File a police report if any of your personal financial information has been lost or stolen.
5. Immediately close any bank or brokerage accounts that have been accessed without your knowledge.
6. If you think you have been a victim of identity theft, put your credit report on fraud alert with all three credit bureaus.
7. Never print or write your telephone number, driver's license number, or Social Security number on your personal or business checks.
8. Do not sign the back of your credit card, and definitely do not leave it blank. Instead write in "Photo ID Required."
9. Always keep your PINs and passwords in a safe and secure location.
10. Do not put your credit card number or vendor account numbers on your checks when making payments.
11. Make a photocopy of everything in your wallet today and lock it up in a safe or some other secure place. If your wallet is lost or stolen, you will have all of the relevant information such as account numbers and phone numbers to make the necessary calls to cancel them.
12. Report any identity theft to the Federal Trade Commission. You can also complete and submit IRS Form 14039, Identity Theft Affidavit, especially if you believe your tax return was involved and someone tried to claim a refund on your behalf.

The Equifax Breach

On September 7, 2017, Equifax, one of the three national credit reporting agencies, announced a cybersecurity incident potentially implicating 143 million Americans. Then on October 2, 2017, they increased that amount by 2.5 million more Americans, making this one of the largest data breaches in US history. More specific details of this announcement is posted on their website.

Nearly half of the United States population may have had their personal information stolen, such as their names, birthdates, Social Security numbers, and driver's license numbers. Equifax is still sorting through this disaster and trying to determine whose data has been exposed.

Rather than waiting around to find out if you were one of them, you should visit Equifax's website at www.equifaxsecurity2017.com and enter your last name and last six digits of your Social Security number. The site will tell you whether it is likely or not that your data has been exposed, and it will put you on a list to get more information. You can also sign up for a year's worth of free credit monitoring.

If you have been identified as one of the Americans who may have been exposed to this data breach, you should take the following four steps immediately to protect yourself:

Check your credit report and look for suspicious items through the three credit report agencies, such as new accounts being opened and lenders that you are not familiar with.

Place a credit freeze on your profile with the three credit agencies. This stops new accounts from being opened in your name. This may create an inconvenience for you, since you will have to unfreeze your accounts if you want to apply for new loans or make your credit history known to potential employers. I think this is worth the inconvenience.

Check your credit card statements and pay special attention to cards you do not use often. The initial reports from the breach were that hackers may have been making charges on underused cards.

File your income tax return early and notify the IRS if you believe you have been a victim of identity theft. The filing of false tax returns to claim refunds from the government using someone else's identity was the most common cyber scam in 2016, according to the Better Business Bureau.

Analyzing Your Debt

The essential starting point to debt management is analyzing your debt. To do this, take another look at your statement of financial position (see Exhibit 3.2 in Chapter 3). Your personal statement of financial position is a snapshot of where you stand financially today.

As discussed in Chapter 3, *debt* refers to all of your financial liabilities, or all the financial obligations you have to pay currently (within one year) and in the future (one year or longer). Gather together all the supporting documentation for your liabilities, and check the terms of these liabilities. (The terms include balances outstanding, monthly payments, interest rates, number of payments remaining, and any prepayment penalties.)

Identify the debt that you have incurred to finance your lifestyle, and focus on reducing and eliminating this type of debt going forward. If your consumer debt balances are high, you will need to implement a debt management program. A properly structured debt management program helps you identify which debt you need to eliminate first, along with the necessary steps you need to take to make your monthly payments easier to handle. Your number-one priority should be to retire the debt with the highest interest rate while still making all of your required monthly payments. If there are less expensive alternatives, such as swapping high-interest credit cards for low-interest credit cards, you should take advantage of these lower rates. I have seen many cases where clients have shopped around for lower-rate credit cards and then used this as a means of negotiating with their current credit card companies for a more attractive rate. Never assume that the interest rate you are paying is the lowest rate available to you. Negotiate, negotiate, and then negotiate. It will make a difference in the long run. You should also consider consolidating your consumer debt, as long as you can lower your overall interest rate.

As part of the debt analysis, you will also need to evaluate your existing mortgage and apply the principles discussed above under mortgage refinancing. If you go through the breakeven analysis and come up with a favorable breakeven point, take advantage of the lower rate. You should carefully consider the pros and cons of using your home as collateral to refinance and consolidate unsecured consumer debt, such as credit cards and car loans.

If you have financial difficulties, your unsecured consumer creditors are very unlikely to take your property for nonpayment. Very often, you can renegotiate these loans and perhaps obtain forgiveness of debt. If you have a very weak balance sheet where your liabilities exceed your assets, then debt forgiveness may be an option before bankruptcy.

Conversely, if you have a very strong balance sheet and your assets significantly exceed your liabilities, you may want to consider consolidating your high-interest consumer debt into your mortgage refinancing. You will not only be able to lower your cost of interest, but you will still be able to write off the interest to the extent that it is part of your home acquisition indebtedness. Please remember that any excess amount borrowed over this amount may not be tax-deductible. I would recommend this only to individuals who have already accumulated a comfortable financial net worth and believe their probability of defaulting on their loans does not exist.

Once again, you cannot move forward effectively and efficiently on the road to financial independence until you clean up the liabilities section of your statement of financial position – your debts. Minimizing your liabilities and reducing your costs of financing will allow you to accumulate more invested assets much more rapidly.

If you do not pay attention to tax consequences while managing debt, you may be paying significantly more in taxes than the law requires. Therefore, you must include tax planning as part of your overall debt management strategy. Using a financial planning approach that takes advantage of these *Tax Alpha to the 2nd Power*[SM] facts and strategies will maximize your ability to build wealth while reducing debt.

 TAX ALPHA TO THE 2ND POWER[SM] FACTS AND STRATEGIES FOR MANAGING DEBT

Here are several tax facts and strategies that will address your wealth accumulation goals at an exponential rate, which will help put you on the path to financial independence, *point X*.

- **The mortgage interest deduction on your personal residence and second home can be taken only on mortgage debt of up to $750,000,** down from $1 million ($375,000 for married filing separately, down from $500,000). This only applies to mortgages taken after December 15, 2017. It is important to note that preexisting mortgages prior to this date are grandfathered in at the $1 million level.
- **The interest on home-equity debt can no longer be deducted at all, whereas up to $100,000 in home-equity debt could have been considered previously.** This deduction has been eliminated for all home-equity loans, even if they predated the new law. I believe many people will start paying down these home-equity loans now that they are no longer tax-deductible.
- **Under the Tax Cuts and Jobs Act of 2017, the tax deductibility of mortgage interest is limited to only acquisition indebtedness.** The term acquisition indebtedness means any indebtedness which is incurred in acquiring,

constructing, or substantially improving any qualified residence of the taxpayer and is secured by such residence. Acquisition indebtedness also includes any indebtedness secured by such residence resulting from the refinancing of the indebtedness meeting the requirements of the previous sentence, but only to the extent the amount of the indebtedness resulting from such refinancing does not exceed the amount of the refinanced debt.

- **If any interest paid on loans is in excess of the acquisition indebtedness described in the previous point, it is generally not tax-deductible and treated as personal interest.** If you can show (have an audit trail) that this excess was used as a business or investment loan, it may then be deductible under a separate set of rules. The tracing principle allows you to deduct interest paid from borrowed money on your personal residence for business or investment purposes by making a 10-T election. This will allow you to trace the borrowing to the activity it relates to and deduct the interest against that activity. *This election must be attached to your tax return in the year of borrowing and then applies thereafter.*
- If you pay points to a bank as prepaid interest, they are deductible over the term of the loan, unless they are paid on the purchase or improvement of your principal residence. In this case, they would be deductible in the year you pay them.
- Investment interest paid to buy or carry investments is deductible up to the amount of net investment income. If you do not have investment income, you may not deduct investment interest paid. The investment interest paid in excess of net investment income may be carried forward and deducted in future years when you have net investment income. You may not deduct interest paid on loans used to buy or carry tax-exempt securities.
- If you incur a nonbusiness bad debt, you can deduct it as a short-term capital loss. For example, if you make a personal loan to a family member or friend, you expect to get repaid, and you are not normally in the business of making loans, you may be able to take this as a loss on your income tax return. You will have to prove that this was a bona fide loan, and it should be put in writing along with its terms.
- Normally if a debt is cancelled or forgiven, it must be included in your gross income for tax purposes. If, however, you were insolvent immediately before the cancellation, or it occurred as part of a Title 11 bankruptcy case, it would generally not be taxable to the extent of your insolvency.
- Student loan interest may be deductible (above the line deduction) up to $2,500 from your taxable income, if you qualify under the income threshold. The maximum $2,500 of student loan interest may be deductible if the taxpayer's modified adjusted gross income is below $65,000 for single and head of household taxpayers and below $135,000 for married taxpayers filing jointly. The amount of the student loan interest that is deductible is phased out with

(continued)

higher modified adjusted gross income (MAGI), until there is no deduction for singles and heads of households with $80,000 MAGI and married filing jointly taxpayers with $165,000 MAGI.

- **Student loan debt forgiveness because of the death or total and permanent disability of the borrower is now exempt from income tax after December 31, 2017.**

AN ACTION PLAN FOR MANAGING DEBT

1. **Become crystal clear about the difference** between *bad debt* (very often high credit card debt) and *good debt* (such as home mortgage loans, student loans, and business loans).
2. **If you have a large balance on your credit card(s),** make every effort to pay it off as quickly as possible and to maintain a zero balance on your cards.
3. **If you have significant high-interest credit card debt,** consider using cash from savings or investments to pay off the balance. Or consider other ways to get rid of high-interest credit card debt, such as borrowing from your life insurance or 401(k). It is important to get rid of the debt, but be very careful if you borrow from other sources.
4. After you have paid off your cards, **do NOT run up the balance on your card again!**
5. **If you have no credit-card debt, check your credit reports and your credit scores carefully.** You may need to use your credit cards a bit more frequently—yet prudently—to ensure that your credit score is healthy.
6. **If you have an outstanding auto loan or lease,** check it carefully. Are the fees and costs you are currently paying in line with your budget? Could you scale back on automobile costs? If you are making payments on more than one automobile, could you eliminate one or more family cars?
7. **If you have a student loan,** make every payment on time to maintain good credit. Check to see if you qualify to deduct student loan interest as an adjustment to income.
8. **Avoid taking out a business loan for a fledgling business** until you have researched your business idea thoroughly. (See Chapter 11, "Starting Your Own Business.") Discuss new business plans in detail with your tax advisor or a financial planner.
9. **If you are considering buying a home,** calculate carefully how much you can realistically afford to pay for a house. Do not forget that you will need to pay

20% (my recommendation) of the price as a down payment, plus closing costs, in cash. Consult a financial expert to help you make this decision.

10. **Credit reports:** Request a copy of your credit report from each of the three credit-reporting agencies at least once a year. (By law, you are entitled to one free copy from each agency each year.) Better yet, pay the minimal fees to check these reports two or three times a year.

11. **Credit score:** If your credit score is under 720, take steps to raise it.

12. **Identity theft:** Take steps to avoid identity theft. If you fear you are the victim of identity theft, report it immediately to the three credit-reporting agencies and the Social Security Fraud Administration.

13. **Equifax Data Breach:** Find out if you were one of the victims. You should visit Equifax's website at www.equifaxsecurity2017.com. If you are identified as potentially affected, follow the four steps identified above.

CHAPTER 5

Insuring Your Health and Life

If we are wise, let us prepare for the worst.

—George Washington,
first president of the United States

Even a sound, carefully planned investment strategy can fall apart if you have not prepared properly for unforeseen problems concerning your health and life. If you or a member of your family is hit with a prolonged illness, a severe injury, a disability, or death (especially of the primary wage earner), the planning and investing you have so carefully developed can quickly disintegrate.

The premiums you pay for health and life insurance will provide you with the peace of mind that comes with knowing that your assets and family will be protected, if and when the unexpected happens.

Having the right kind of health and life insurance at the appropriate stages of life is as important as the insurance itself. The type and extent of insurance you need will change throughout your lifetime. The family health and life risk management issues that are important to a young couple are normally dramatically different from those that are important to an older couple in their retirement years. For example, a young couple may need health insurance to cover prenatal care or life insurance to replace the income lost if one of the spouses should die before the children are grown. In contrast, an older retired couple may have little need for life insurance but may want to protect themselves against the high cost of long-term care, and they therefore need to consider investing in long-term care insurance.

The major health and life risk management issues are:

- Health (or medical) insurance
- Disability insurance
- Long-term care insurance
- Life insurance

Each of these issues is discussed in this chapter. Your particular situation will determine what type of insurance you need, what kind of policy or policies will work best for you, and the amount of coverage you should carry.

Choosing a Health Insurance Plan

Health insurance is imperative, no matter what your circumstance–young or old, single or married, childless or raising a family. Without proper health insurance, a serious illness or accident experienced by you or any member of your family can bankrupt you and rob you of all your savings. And given the high cost of health care these days, it can happen very fast.

Nevertheless, even with today's government-mandated healthcare, as of early 2017, the CDC reports that nearly 29 million Americans are not covered by health insurance, and that includes 3.6 million children. This is an appalling and frightening statistic. Obamacare did expand the number of Americans covered by health insurance. Clearly, this has had a positive effect on many families that did not have coverage in the past. Unfortunately, this came at an extremely high cost to everyone else who did have health insurance, because at the end of the day, it is a zero-sum game. When you provide free healthcare coverage to millions of people, it may be free to them, but ultimately, this cost has to be picked up by someone. The burden fell on hardworking middle-class Americans, who had to pay significantly more for their health insurance coverage. Even when this cost was passed along to employers, ultimately it resulted in many middle-class Americans receiving little to no salary increases since Obamacare's inception.

I often meet people who tell me that they do not have health insurance coverage. Very often these are younger people who do not think they need coverage, individuals who have not been able to maintain a long-term job, and very often self-employed individuals who are struggling to pay their bills. Usually, their reason is that they simply cannot afford to pay the high premiums. My response to this way of thinking is that you cannot afford to be *without* health insurance coverage. All it takes is one major illness or accident, and you can be completely wiped out financially. A prolonged visit to the hospital for a week or two could easily cost you several hundred thousand dollars. Adding this type of unexpected debt to your finances can hold you back and may even prevent you from ever becoming financially independent. If you truly are not able to pay for health insurance, you will want to find out if you are eligible for Medicaid or some other government-sponsored health insurance program. If you cannot be covered under Medicaid, then you have no choice but to purchase some other form of health insurance, even if the policy covers only catastrophic illness or accident. In my opinion, health insurance is not a choice; it is a necessity that you simply cannot do without. Life is about choices, so eliminate some of your wants and replace them with this vital need.

If you have never purchased insurance, it may be helpful to define some of the following terms before we get into the types of policies that may be available to you. These terms may also be useful for understanding the remaining sections in this chapter, as well as Chapter 6, "Protecting Your Property with Insurance."

- A *premium* is the amount you would be periodically obligated to pay the insurance company to maintain your coverage under the plan. Some or all of your premium could also be paid by your employer, union, or plan sponsor.
- A *deductible* is the amount you need to pay for your insured expenses before the insurance company will start to pay. Some basic and preventative services are covered before you meet your deductible, depending on your plan.
- A *copayment* ("copay") is a fixed dollar amount you must pay out of pocket each time medical service is received. Copayments vary by your plan and the type of care you are receiving.
- *Coinsurance* is the percentage you pay of your insured expenses, usually after you reach your deductible. The insurance company will cover the remaining cost.

When deciding which type of insurance is appropriate for you, you will need to do a fair amount of research and some important thinking about your personal health and financial situation and needs.

First, you need to understand the various types of policies available to you. Consider the following questions:

- Are you covered by some sort of group plan through your job or union? Or must you buy your own insurance?

- If you are covered by a group plan, is it sufficient for your needs? Can you afford to pay the deductible and copayments, and is there a maximum limit on the coverage?
- Does it cover any specific situation or condition that you or a member of your family may have? Verify that the policy does not exclude certain medical conditions or treatments, especially if you have a family history with these situations.
- Are the doctors you use and trust available under the plan?
- Is the plan flexible, allowing you to use out-of-network caregivers?
- What sort of ongoing health care needs do you anticipate, such as a future pregnancy or care for a chronic health problem, such as asthma, diabetes, arthritis, or high blood pressure?
- How much can you afford to pay in premiums? You can determine this after analyzing your statement of cash flow and eliminating some of your unnecessary wants, and replacing them with this basic need.
- How high a deductible can you afford? The higher your deductible, the lower your premium will be, so in general, if you can self-insure up to the amount of the deductible, then this would be a wise choice. This works best if you are in overall good health and are less likely to need the insurance unless a major medical situation occurs.
- If you choose a high-deductible plan, is it qualified for a Health Savings Account (HSA)? Are you eligible to make contributions? Using an HSA is a terrific way to help subsidize the cost of your health insurance and save your money. By doing so, you will not only get an upfront tax deduction, but the distributions from the account to cover your health costs would be tax-free. See the "Health Savings Accounts" section of this chapter for more information on eligibility.

For decades, most Americans got their health insurance through their employers, and this is still the case. These insurers are usually private companies (Cigna®, Aetna®, and UnitedHealthcare® are a few well-known companies), and corporations, unions, or other organizations can negotiate good rates for their employees and members because they are bringing so much business to the insurance company. Usually with these plans, the employer pays a portion of the cost of the plan and the employee pays a portion, often in pretax dollars.

Despite employer contributions toward employees' insurance plan premiums, most employees are still responsible for paying an average of 31% of the total cost for a family health insurance plan. This is up from 28% five years ago, and is still on the rise, according to a recent study from the Kaiser Family Foundation and the Health Research & Education Trust. This is further aggravated by the Commonwealth Fund's findings that salaries have not kept pace with drastically rising premium costs, causing most Americans with job-based insurance to pay over 10% of their salaries to health insurance premiums and deductibles, nearly double the rate 10 years earlier. For this reason, it is essential that you consider premium costs when choosing the best plan for you.

Indemnity Plans (Fee-for-Service)

Indemnity plans or *fee-for-service* plans were long the traditional form of health insurance plan – and many companies still offer this type of plan to their employees. With fee-for-service plans, the insurer either pays the service provider (the doctor) or you (the patient), directly, usually after you have already covered the full cost of the service. Most plans require you to pay an annual deductible, after which the insurance company pays a set percentage of the average rate that doctors charge in your area for the service claimed.

Managed-Care Health Plans

For the past 20 years or so, because of the high costs of both medical care and insurance, many employers have chosen to opt for *managed-care plans*. With this type of plan, the subscriber (or user) contracts with and makes monthly payments directly to the organization that provides the healthcare service. (In some cases, an insurance company is not involved; however, most major health insurance companies offer both indemnity plans as well as managed-care plans.)

With a managed-care plan, the insured pays a fee or copayment for office visits and medications, and most basic medical services and preventive care services are fully covered. To keep costs down, managed-care insurers control (i.e., *manage*) the costs of the medical care. For example, they may restrict access to a specific list of doctors; require patients to get a referral from a primary care physician in order to see a specialist (such as a heart surgeon or a dermatologist); and require that the specialist also accept the insurance company's fee schedule.

The four principal types of managed-care plans are HMOs, PPOs, EPOs, and POSs, described in the following paragraphs.

HMOs (Health Maintenance Organizations)   An HMO is a collection of hospitals, physicians, and other healthcare providers who have joined to provide healthcare services to its members. There are two types of HMOs:

1. *Group HMOs,* which provide a group of doctors who provide healthcare in a central facility (usually a hospital).
2. *Independent practice associations (IPAs),* the more popular type, where doctors practice from their own offices, as well as from community hospitals that are affiliated with the IPA.

Basic HMOs tend to be the least expensive form of health insurance. Copayments, when they are required at all, are usually small, and preventive care services are almost always completely covered. In exchange, patients must see only approved doctors and need to get permission from a primary care physician before seeing a specialist or getting any care outside the HMO. (IPAs can be a bit more flexible.)

PPOs (Preferred Provider Organizations)   A PPO is a plan that shares characteristics of both an IPA and a traditional fee-for-service plan. The insurance company or provider group contracts with physicians and hospitals that agree to accept a negotiated fee for services provided for the insured. In addition (unlike a conventional HMO), a PPO also provides coverage for services not provided by the PPO network, so you can go to other doctors and hospitals at your own discretion, although you will be required to pay a higher fee. Also, PPOs allow you to see other doctors and specialists without prior approval.

EPOs (Exclusive Provider Organizations)   Like an HMO, the insurance company contracts with various medical providers to offer services to members of the EPO at reduced costs, as it reimburses EPO members only when providers associated with the insurance company are used, except in case of emergencies. An EPO is a better plan if you want to see a specialist within your network without a primary care physician referral.

POS (Point-of Service) Plans   This plan encourages you to use network providers but allows you to choose others outside of the plan, usually at a higher copayment or deductible and with a doctor's referral for specialists. This is called a point-of-service plan because you decide (at the point-of-service) whether to use it more like an HMO (within the HMO network) or PPO (outside the HMO network).

Catastrophic Plans

Indemnity and managed-care plans cover most types of health care costs, but for some people, the cost of these health plans are just too high. If you are on a really tight budget, you might consider purchasing a catastrophic plan, which is a prepaid hospital and medical expense plan that only covers you for major medical and hospital expenses if you become seriously ill or injured. With a catastrophic health insurance plan, you are taking the chance that you will stay reasonably healthy and be able to pay for your basic preventive health services out of pocket. At the same time, however, you are protecting yourself from financial ruin if you should need substantial care or hospitalization. Premiums are lower on this type of coverage because you pay out-of-pocket for your common medical expenses, such as checkups and minor emergencies, and you will be charged a relatively high deductible if you require hospitalization. Look for a policy that is guaranteed renewable, has a maximum lifetime benefit of at least $1 million, and covers at least 70% of your doctor and hospital bills after you meet the high deductible.

Medicare

Medicare is the United States government's health insurance program. Administered under the Social Security Administration, it is funded from a portion of Social Security and self-employment taxes, as well as by Medicare premiums paid. It primarily provides medical insurance to citizens over age 65. It also covers Americans younger than age 65 who are collecting Social Security disability benefits for at least 24 months and people of any age with end-stage renal disease (ESRD) or permanent kidney failure requiring dialysis or a kidney transplant.

You are automatically eligible for Medicare when you turn 65, although you must apply one to three months before your 65th birthday; if you apply later, your coverage can be delayed. If you have applied, coverage begins on the first day of the month in which you turn 65. For more information, visit www.medicare.gov or call 1-800-MEDICARE (1-800-633-4227).

Medicare covers three basic health care components: hospital insurance, supplementary medical care, and prescriptions, as well as an optional plan run by private insurance companies. Medicare provides very limited coverage for only certain kinds of long-term care needs (discussed further in this chapter under the section on long-term care). Medicare Part A and B are also called *Original Medicare.*

Medicare Part A   Medicare Part A covers hospital care, rehabilitation facilities, nursing home care, hospice care, and home health services. These services are generally only covered for a set period of time and only when medically necessary.

Medicare Part A is free to anyone who has paid Medicare taxes for more than a decade (or is married to someone who has). If you are not eligible for premium-free Medicare Part A, you can still choose to buy it for a monthly premium, usually together with Medicare Part B.

As of 2018, Medicare Part A requires a $1,340 deductible for the benefit period. Also, for over 60 days of hospitalization in any benefit period, a daily coinsurance from $335 to $670 per day can apply.

Medicare Part B   Medicare Part B covers medically necessary and preventative services, such as clinical research, ambulance services, durable medical equipment, mental health services, getting a second opinion before surgery, and limited outpatient prescription drugs.

Unlike Part A, which is usually free, Part B charges a monthly premium that is usually deducted from your Social Security check. The standard Part B premium is $134 as of 2018, but can be as high as $429, depending on annual income. There is also a small deductible ($183 in 2018), followed by a 20% copay on Medicare approved services. Therefore, many people buy a Medicare supplemental insurance policy as well.

When you sign up for Medicare Part A, you will be asked if you want to be covered under Medicare Part B. You need not sign up for Part B if you are covered through insurance from your workplace or your spouse's current job; however, unless you or your spouse is actively employed and insured, you need Part B. If you fail to sign up right away (either when you turn 65, or when you stop working and are no longer covered by a private health insurance company) you may be charged an additional 10% of your premium for every year you could have signed up but did not.

Medicare Part C   Medicare Part C (also known as *Medicare Advantage* or *MA*) offers health plan options run by Medicare-approved *private insurance companies*, including HMOs and PPOs. These plans allow recipients to receive Medicare benefits and services covered under Part A and Part B, most cover Part D (prescription drugs), and some even offer additional benefits for an additional cost. When choosing a Medicare Advantage plan, be cautious not to be lured with low to zero copays until you are certain that all your physicians are in the plan and all your prescriptions are covered.

Medicare Part D   Medicare Part D covers the costs of both brand-name and generic prescription drugs at participating pharmacies. All Medicare recipients are eligible for this coverage, and like Parts B and C, it is a voluntary program.

Medicare Part D also incurs a monthly premium that varies from plan to plan. The Part D coverage may also be subject to an income-related monthly adjustment amount (IRMAA), a surcharge premium based on your prior period income, which ranges from $13 to $75 for 2018.

This coverage has an annual deductible of up to about $405 in 2018. Once again, it is important to compare plans to be sure that your prescriptions are covered without requiring high copays.

You may have to pay a late enrollment penalty if you go without Medicare recognized drug coverage for any continuous period of 63 days or more after your initial enrollment period is over. Recognized coverage includes a Medicare prescription drug plan, a Medicare Advantage Plan, another Medicare health plan that offers Medicare prescription drug coverage, or another creditable prescription drug coverage. Because of this, it is important to get drug coverage as soon as you are eligible, if you believe you will want or need drug coverage in the future. It may be a good idea to buy the most basic and inexpensive plan as a place holder. If you go more than 63 days without coverage after you are eligible, a penalty premium will be tacked on to your part D premium *every month*. That penalty is 1% of the average plan cost multiplied by the number of full months you did not have coverage. That can add up very quickly.

Medigap   Medigap (also called *Medicare Supplement Insurance*) is a private health insurance policy designed to fill in the gaps that exist in fundamental Medicare coverage, including copayments, coinsurance, and deductibles. If you have Medicare as well as a Medigap policy, Medicare will pay its share of the Medicare-approved amounts, and then the Medigap policy will pay its share.

A Medigap policy is different from a Medicare Advantage Plan because Advantage Plans replace your original Medicare A and B plans and may offer additional benefits, whereas a Medigap policy only supplements basic Medicare benefits. You cannot carry both a Medigap policy and a Medicare Advantage Plan.

There are many different types of Medigap policies that are regulated under various federal and state laws and that vary in quality and cost. For additional information you should visit www.medicare .gov or call 1-800-Medicare (1-800-633-4227).

Medicaid

Medicaid is a combined federal and state program that helps with the medical costs of nearly 70 million Americans in qualified categories with limited income (generally between 100% and 133% of the federal poverty level with some states at higher levels depending on the eligible category). For example, in 2017 for a family of four, the 100% federal poverty line was $24,600. In addition to being financially needy, other conditions may apply. You should check your state's Medicaid eligibility rules for more information.

Since its inception in 1965, Medicaid originally provided medical insurance to persons getting cash assistance from the government. Since 2014, those eligible for Medicaid coverage in most states now include all those under 65 whose income is 133% or less than the federal poverty line. This represents a significant increase in the number of people covered on Medicaid, which puts a tremendous strain on the system that is already on the brink of insolvency. In 2018, the Trump administration released guidance allowing states to impose certain work requirements on those who are receiving Medicaid based on poverty alone.

Most of the costs of Medicaid coverage is paid by the states and federal government. Under current regulations, states have the option to charge limited premiums, enrollment fees, copayments, coinsurance and deductibles. Depending on your state, Medicaid covers a variety of benefits, such as doctor visits, emergency care, hospital care, vaccinations, prescription drugs, vision, hearing, long-term care, and preventive care. For more information, visit www.medicaid.gov.

Children's Health Insurance Program (CHIP)

CHIP provides low-cost health insurance coverage for children (up to age 19) in families who earn too much to qualify for Medicaid, but can't afford private health insurance. Depending on your state, CHIP covers comprehensive services such as routine check-ups, immunizations, hospital care, dental care, and lab and X-ray services for children. Children receive free preventive care, but low fees may be required for certain services. Each state sets its own rules for CHIP; to find out more, visit www.medicaid.gov.

COBRA (Consolidated Omnibus Budget Reconciliation Act of 1985)

COBRA requires employers with 20 or more employees to give you the opportunity to continue your health insurance under the company's insured group for up to 18 months, at your *own* expense. You are eligible for COBRA after one of the following qualifying events:

- You leave your job voluntarily (or begin working part-time) or involuntarily.
- Your spouse, who was the primary insured member of your family, dies.
- You are getting divorced from a spouse who is the primary insured member.

The employee retains all benefits (except for disability income coverage), and pays the employer premiums, up to 102% of the company's cost. COBRA coverage can be extended for up to 36 months under certain extenuating circumstances, such as the divorce or death of the employee. If you become eligible for Medicare, but your spouse isn't yet eligible for Medicare, your spouse can extend his or her COBRA coverage for up to 36 months or until he or she becomes eligible for Medicare – whichever comes first.

Workers' Compensation Insurance

Workers' compensation insurance is designed to compensate workers who are injured on the job or who become ill through work-related causes and are therefore unable to draw a salary. Each state regulates its own workers' compensation insurance program, and details vary from state to state; however, normal benefits include medical and rehab expenses, disability income, and lump-sum payments for death and certain severe injuries. This is a benefit that must be provided by most or all employers, depending on the state.

The Patient Protection and Affordable Care Act

On March 23, 2010, President Barack Obama signed the Patient Protection and Affordable Care Act of 2010, the central piece of legislation that overhauled the American healthcare system.

A week later, on March 30, 2010, he also signed the Healthcare and Education Reconciliation Act of 2010, a shorter piece of legislation that amended several provisions in the initial Patient Protection Act. Taken together, these two pieces of legislation, nicknamed "Obamacare," provided for massive healthcare reform and include an estimated $437 billion in new taxes and fees. The expanded healthcare coverage provided by the legislation was expected to drastically reduce the number of uninsured Americans. The legislation also included several extra pieces that are only imaginatively related to healthcare. In July 2012, the Supreme Court generally upheld the constitutionality of the controversial 2010 healthcare law.

Here are some of the provisions (which include many non-health-related issues) in the health care reform laws that have gone into effect and include 2018 amounts when applicable:

- **Insurance for older children:** Children can remain on their parents' health insurance policies through age 26.
- **Insurance for preexisting conditions:** Insurance companies cannot deny coverage because of a preexisting condition. This went into effect January 1, 2014.
- **Adoption credits:** The credit for adoption expenses is increased to $13,840 for 2018 and is not refundable. This credit is adjusted annually for inflation and has been permanently extended.
- **Small business tax credits for providing healthcare:** Small businesses (as well as tax-exempt organizations) with up to 25 full-time equivalent employees may qualify for a tax credit for the cost of purchasing health insurance for their employees through the Small Business Health Insurance Program (SHOP) marketplace. In general, eligibility for the credit is based partially on the number of full-time equivalent employees and on the average annual wages per employee. To qualify for the credit, the employer must pay at least 50% of the cost of health coverage at the single rate. For 2014 and beyond, the maximum credit increased to 50% of premiums paid by businesses and 35% of premiums paid by tax-exempt organizations. The maximum credit goes to those employers who employ 10 or fewer full-time equivalent employees and who pay annual average wages of no more

than $25,000, adjusted for inflation. The credit gradually phases out for firms with average wages between $25,000 and $50,000 (adjusted annually for inflation), and between 10 and 25 full-time equivalent workers. The credit is available for two consecutive years.

- **Medicare drug coverage:** For those covered under Medicare Part D in the so-called donut hole, the law provides a 65% discount on brand-name drugs and a 56% discount for generic drugs. You are considered to be in the donut hole if your plan has paid up to a certain amount for covered drugs, but you have not yet spent up to the yearly limit out of pocket. During this gap in coverage, you would be forced to pay your drug expenses out of pocket until reaching the limit initiates coverage again. Under the current law, the amount you pay for generic drugs will decrease each year until it reaches 25% in 2020, when the donut hole will be eliminated.
- **Health insurance reporting requirement:** Starting in 2012, most employers must report the value of each employee's health insurance coverage on the employee's annual Form W-2. Under transitional rules and pending further guidance from the Internal Revenue Service, only employers filing 250 or more W-2 forms are required to report this coverage.
- **Medical savings accounts:** Unless prescribed by a medical professional, over-the-counter medications can no longer be paid for with funds from a health savings account (HSA), flexible spending account (FSA), or health reimbursement account (HRA).
- **Additional tax on nonqualified savings account distributions:** The additional tax on nonqualified distributions from HSAs increased from 10% to 20%. For nonqualified distributions from an Archer medical savings account (MSA), the additional tax increased from 15% to 20%. An exception to these penalties is nonqualified distributions after disability, death, or attaining age 65.
- **Drug industry fee:** An annual fee is assessed on drug manufacturers, starting at $2.5 billion in 2011 and increasing over the following years. The applicable amount for 2018 is $4.1 billion.
  - **FSA limits:** In 2018, the amount that can be contributed to a health flexible spending account (FSA) was limited to $2,650 per year, indexed annually for inflation.

- **Medical expense deduction:** Starting with tax year 2017, everyone, regardless of age, is subject to the 7.5% income threshold for deducting unreimbursed medical expenses. Then, starting in 2019, the 7.5% income threshold will increase to 10%.
- **Executive pay limit:** Starting in 2018, the compensation deduction for certain health insurance companies is limited to $1,000,000 per year for high-level executives.
- **Additional Medicare Tax on Earned Income:** Employees are subject to 1.45% Medicare tax withholding on their earnings. Self-employed individuals are subject to 2.9% Medicare tax on their self-employment earnings. An additional 0.9% Medicare tax is imposed on earned incomes amounts above $250,000 for married couples filing joint returns, $125,000 for married taxpayers filing separately, and $200,000 for other types of individual taxpayers. The income threshold levels will not be indexed for inflation.
- **Net Investment Income Tax:** A 3.8% Medicare tax is imposed on net investment income (interest, dividends, royalties, rental income, capital gains, etc.) on the lesser of net investment income or modified adjusted gross income (MAGI) above the threshold amount. The threshold amounts for U.S. citizens and resident individuals is $250,000 for married taxpayers filing jointly, $125,000 for married taxpayers filing separately, and $200,000 for single and head of household taxpayers.
- **Medical device tax:** The Affordable Care Act imposed a 2.3% excise tax on the sale of certain medical devices that presumably makes medical treatment for persons with chronic or critical conditions more expensive or not available at all. On January 22, 2018, H.R. 195 was signed into law, again postponing the implementation of this tax until 2020. It is unknown whether future legislation will further delay implementation of this provision of the Affordable Care Act.

The Healthcare Mandate and Other Issues

Starting in 2014, the so-called *mandate* – the heart of the healthcare act – went into effect. This mandate requires that all Americans carry some form of healthcare insurance. Individuals who are not covered by Medicare, Medicaid, or other government health insurance will be required to maintain health insurance coverage or pay a penalty. Penalties are calculated using a percentage of the taxpayer's income or a flat dollar amount. Subsidies and tax credits are available to help lower income taxpayers pay for coverage. In addition, other factors have slowly gone into effect, including these:

- **Health insurance exchanges:** Health insurance exchanges were established by many states to enable people to comparison shop for coverage. In other states, federally facilitated exchanges may be used for the same purpose.
- **Required coverage by large employers:** Large employers and big businesses (with 50 or more full time equivalent employees) must provide coverage for employees or face penalties.
- **Tax credits for small businesses:** Tax credits are at a maximum of 50% of premiums paid by qualifying small businesses that provide coverage for their workers. The credit available to nonprofit employees is as much as 35%.
- **Health industry fee:** An annual fee will be assessed on the health insurance industry. For 2018 the fee is $14.3 billion.
- **Tax on "Cadillac plans":** In 2022, insurance companies will be assessed a 40% excise tax on health insurance plans with annual premiums exceeding individual coverage and family coverage limits that will be determined after this book is published. It is unknown whether future legislation will further delay implementation of this provision of the Affordable Care Act.

With the Tax Cuts and Jobs Act of 2017, the individual mandate and related penalty are set to be eliminated in 2019. Exchanges will remain open, and subsidies will remain for lower income individuals. There is concern that people who do not qualify for subsidies and do not have employer sponsored plans will drop the coverage once the penalty is removed. The premium increases that came from adding significant numbers of previously uninsurable people to the market will likely drive healthy individuals in this segment to drop coverage, which would potentially cause premiums to rise even further. As the Trump administration brings this major blow to Obamacare, the future of the Affordable Care Act is uncertain. It would not be surprising to see a new version of health reform in the near future.

Health Savings Accounts

Created in 2003, *health savings accounts* (HSAs) are tax-free savings accounts – funded by employees, employers, or both – to spend on routine medical costs. Usually, HSAs are for individuals who are covered by high-deductible health plans (HDHPs) and have no other health coverage. Health savings accounts can provide excellent tax benefits, so it is strongly recommended that you determine whether you can qualify.

Not all high-deductible health plans are HSA eligible, so before choosing one, you should look for the special HSA designation on the name or details of the plan. An HDHP is generally eligible for an HSA if it has a higher deductible than the average individual health insurance plan and no insurance coverage payments until the plan deductible is met. Each year, the Internal Revenue Service determines the minimum and maximum deductibles for individual or family medical coverage for all qualifying plans.

Even if you have an HSA-qualified policy, there are limitations on whether you are actually allowed to contribute to your health savings account in a given year. You must have no other health coverage, although certain types of ancillary coverage are acceptable (accidents, disability, dental, vision or long-term care). You also may not contribute if you are covered by Medicare or if you were claimed as a dependent on someone else's tax return that year.

If you can contribute, there are limits on how much you can fund per year. In 2018, individuals can contribute $3,450 for a single policy and $6,900 for a family policy. If you are 55 or older, you can make an additional catch-up contribution of $1,000 each. Annual contribution limits may be affected by the number of months you had a qualifying high-deductible health plan in a given year. The deadline for funding HSAs is the same as IRA accounts and is normally April 15 of the following year. So the good news is, even if the year has passed, you can still make a prior-year tax-deductible contribution. You get the best of both worlds, since contributions are tax-deductible, and distributions for medical expenses are tax-free.

An Archer MSA (Medical Savings Account) is similar to a Health Savings Account in that participants must be covered by a qualifying high deductible health plan (HDHP). This can be offered by a small employer (generally less than 50 employees).

Long-Term Care Insurance

If you or someone in your family develops a prolonged physical illness, a disability, or a cognitive impairment, it is likely there will be a need for some form of long-term care. Many different care providers help people with chronic conditions overcome limitations that are keeping them from being independent. Long-term care is similar to traditional medical care, except that it relates to prolonged medical care treatment. Long-term care assists individuals by providing them with the best quality of life possible under the circumstances, but it typically does not improve or correct medical conditions. Long-term care services may include assistance with:

- Activities of daily living
- Home healthcare
- Respite care
- Hospice care
- Adult day care
- Care in a nursing home
- Care in an assisted-living facility

It is extremely important to note that these types of long-term medical care are *not* covered under health insurance policies, with the exception of Medicaid.

Don't Be a Victim of Long-Term Care Costs

Richard and Nicholas were two clients I had known for more than 20 years. They were twin brothers who lived next door to each other in a modest neighborhood in Brooklyn, New York. Although they were twins, their personalities were polar opposites. Richard was a hard-working, conservative guy who always *paid himself first*, paid his bills on time, and of course, had an excellent credit score. By the time he retired, he had managed to accumulate $1.5 million in investible assets and was able to retire at age 65 without changing the lifestyle he and his wife were accustomed to. They had two grown children, three grandchildren, and were settling into a comfortable retirement life.

In contrast, Richard's twin brother, Nicholas, always had difficulty maintaining a job. He lived his life in the proverbial fast lane, regardless of the consequences. He never saved any money; worse, he continuously accumulated debt throughout his life. By the time he turned 65, he owed more in liabilities than he had in assets; in other words, he was broke. He had no choice but to continue working until his age and physical condition made it impossible.

Eventually, Nicholas was no longer able to care for himself. Fortunately, Richard and his wife happily found him the care he needed in a nursing home on Staten Island. Because Nicholas was living off only a small Social Security retirement check, he was able to qualify for Medicaid. He received care in this nursing home, and it did not cost him or his family a dime. The nursing home took over Nicholas's monthly Social Security check, and Medicaid took care of the rest.

Six months after Nicholas entered the nursing home, Richard suffered a major stroke. Although he survived the initial stroke, he was unable to walk, feed himself, or dress himself without the help of his wife. His condition got worse, and it became impossible for his wife to continue caring for him on her own. As difficult as the decision was, his wife and children decided that Richard would need the help only a nursing home could provide.

Richard's family was able to get him into the same excellent nursing home as his brother Nicholas; in fact, they became roommates, and in a funny twist of fate, ended up living out the rest of their lives together. However, their respective financial fates could not have been more different.

As mentioned, because Nicholas had no assets, Medicaid paid for his nursing home care. However, Richard, who had always lived responsibly and was able to accumulate assets to secure his family's future and peace of mind, was therefore ineligible for Medicaid. As a result, his family needed to pay for the nursing home costs out-of-pocket, and the bill came to more than $120,000 per year. They thought they had no choice but to pay because there was no other way to care for Richard. He lived for another 11 years, which almost completely wiped out the assets that he had worked so hard to accumulate.

Unfortunately, sometimes the Medicaid system rewards bad behavior and penalizes good behavior, and this is a classic example. Richard's nursing home care used up his entire life savings. His wife and children were denied the fruits of his labor and the benefits of the sacrifices he made for them throughout his life. Meanwhile Nicholas, who lived at the same nursing home as Richard and received exactly the same care, did not have to pay a dime. This, in my opinion, is a very sad ending to what should have been a financial success story.

Perhaps one of the most important things to plan for once you become financially independent is how to protect the assets you have accumulated. Clearly, if you do not protect your financial indepen-dence once you have achieved it, it is almost as irresponsible as never taking the steps to achieve it in the first place. This is where meeting with a financial planner and elder care attorney is critical.

Richard could have taken the necessary steps early on to protect his family and the assets they were able to accumulate throughout their lifetime. This is one family health risk you cannot afford to take. *You must take preventive action to ensure that your life-long hard work and assets are protected in case a catastrophic long-term illness occurs.* There are numerous strategies you can employ to protect your assets; however, *obtaining an adequate long-term care insurance policy* is probably the eas-iest way you can accomplish this.

There are numerous other planning options available that fall under the umbrella of Medicaid planning, which include Medicaid trusts, retaining a life estate, and outright property transfers. The rules and regulations in this area are quite complex and differ from state to state. Therefore, my advice to every family is to seek out the proper help and guidance of a qualified elder care planning attor-ney. This planning must take place years in advance of developing the need for long-term care. If you or a family member require long-term care and have not already implemented a plan, you should immedi-ately meet with an elder care planning attorney to minimize the loss of your hard-earned money. Please refer to the "Asset Protection and Long-Term Care" section of Chapter 10, "Preserving Your Estate," for more guidance on this topic.

The Cost of Long-Term Care

The cost of long-term care is extremely expensive. The cost depends on the amount and type of care that you will need and where and how you get it. For example, of the 50 states, New York State has one of the highest costs for obtaining care in a long-term care facility. Accord-ing to a recent survey conducted in 2017 by Genworth Financial, the median cost of care for a private room in a New York nursing home is $140,416 per year, and the median cost to hire a home health aide is $54,340 per year. These costs not only vary state by state, but also county by county within each state. To find out the cost of the various options of long-term care treatments in your state, visit Genworth's website at www.genworth.com. Use this website to obtain a general guide of what your long-term care cost might be.

For most people, the cost of long-term care will wipe out their life savings within just a few short years. Being prepared for this type of family health management risk is critical to maintaining your family's financial independence.

You can pay for long-term care in a variety of ways. These include using your and your family's personal resources, obtaining long-term care insurance, and receiving some assistance from Medicaid (if you qualify).

As described earlier in this chapter, Medicaid is the government-funded program that pays nursing home care only for individuals who have low income and little or no assets. To get Medicaid help, you must meet federal and state guidelines for income and assets. Many people start paying for nursing home care out of their own funds and "spend down" their assets until they are eligible for Medicaid. Medicaid may then pay part or all of their nursing home costs. You may have to use up most of your assets on your healthcare before Medicaid will help. Basically, you need to be broke, because this is a form of public assistance.

State laws differ regarding how much money and assets you can keep and still be eligible for Medicaid. (Some assets, such as your home, may not count when deciding if you are eligible for Medicaid.) However, federal law requires your state to recover from your estate the cost of the Medicaid-paid benefits you receive. Contact your state Medicaid office or state department of social services to learn more about the rules in your state.

This is only the most general information. There are many other rules about what you can and cannot keep, but the bottom line is that if you are single or a widow(er), you must give up almost everything you have worked so hard to accumulate in order to qualify for Medicaid coverage in a nursing home. Whether you are married or unmarried, you should get legal advice regarding the options available to protect your assets. This is a very hot topic, and the law is in a constant state of flux.

Rules for married people vary from state to state. For example, in community-property states, all of your income from any source (no matter which spouse the checks are made out to) is considered to be divided equally between the spouses. In any other state, only checks that are made out to you count toward your Medicaid eligibility.

In most states, if the cost of a nursing home is higher than your income, you will qualify for the Medicaid nursing home funds. An elder-care attorney is best suited to help you figure this out, because each state has different formulas to determine your eligibility. Your elder-care specialist can help you estimate the amount that your stay-at-home spouse would be able to keep, or even have the amount increased according to his or her needs.

After qualifying on the income test, you also need to pass an asset eligibility test. Your home, car, and personal property are generally protected for your healthy spouse. Married couples can also keep some money in investments or cash. You may have to give up most of your other assets to qualify for Medicaid. Studies of individuals entering nursing homes have documented that half of the people in the study on Medicaid were not poor when they entered the facility. They had to "spend down" their assets until nothing was left before Medicaid took over.

While your spouse is living in the house, the state will not try to take it. Once your spouse dies, however, and the estate is left to your beneficiaries, the state could try to make a claim against the home by placing a Medicaid lien against it. Some 30 states actually have "filial responsibility laws," which allow care providers to come after the children of care recipients for the cost of their parents care. They are not often enforced, but do indeed exist.

Paying for Long-Term Care with Insurance

Long-term care insurance is one other way you may pay for long-term care. This type of insurance will pay for some or all of your long-term care.

The Health Insurance Portability and Accountability Act of 1996 (HIPAA) is a federal law that gives some federal income tax advantages to people who buy certain long-term care insurance policies. These policies are called *tax-qualified long-term care insurance contracts,* or simply *qualified contracts.* Numerous states also provide for special tax breaks for long-term care premiums. These include tax deductions and tax credits that would help you pay part of the cost of your premiums. If you are paying premiums for long-term care insurance, be sure to let your tax preparer know, and ask your tax preparer to find out what special tax deduction or credits may be available in your state.

For 2018, qualified long-term care insurance contract premiums can be deducted as medical expenses with limitations based on age ($420 if you are up to age 40, $780 if you are age 41 to 50, $1,560 if you are age 51 to 60, $4,160 if you are age 61 to 70, and $5,200 if you are over age 70).

Should You Buy Long-Term Care Insurance?

Whether you should buy a long-term care insurance policy will depend on your age, health status, overall retirement goals, income, and assets. For example, if your only source of income is a Social

Security benefit or Supplemental Security Income (SSI) and you have a minimal net worth, you probably should not buy long-term care insurance, because you may not be able to afford the premium and you may qualify for Medicaid.

Conversely, if you have a large amount of assets but do not want to use them to pay for long-term care, you may want to buy a long-term care insurance policy. Many people buy a policy because they want to stay independent of government aid or the help of family. They do not want to burden anyone with having to care for them.

Consider buying long-term care insurance if:

- You have significant assets and income,
- You want to protect some of your assets and income,
- You can pay premiums, including possible premium increases, without financial difficulty,
- You want to stay independent of the support of others, and
- You want to have the flexibility of choosing care in the setting you prefer or one in which you will be most comfortable.

Private insurance companies sell long-term care insurance policies. You can buy an individual policy from an agent or through the mail. You can also buy coverage under a group policy through an employer or through membership in an association. The federal government and several state governments offer long-term care insurance coverage to their employees, retirees, and their families. This program is voluntary, and premiums are paid by participants. You can also add a long-term care benefit rider through certain life insurance policies.

The following paragraphs describe some of the specific terms used in a long-term care policy that will determine your eligibility under the plan. When comparing policies, be sure to compare how each of the policies defines these terms.

Activities of Daily Living   The inability to cope with activities of daily living (ADLs) is the most common way insurance companies decide that you are eligible for benefits. The ADLs most companies use are: *bathing, continence, dressing, eating, toileting, and transferring.* Typically, a policy pays benefits when you cannot do a certain number of the ADLs, such as two of the six or three of the six.

Elimination Period   With many policies, your benefits will not start the first day you go to a nursing home or start using home care. Most policies have an *elimination period* (sometimes called a *deductible* or a *waiting period*). That means benefits can start 0, 20, 30, 60, 90, or 100 days after you start using long-term care or become disabled. How many days you have to wait for benefits to start will depend on the elimination period you pick when you buy your policy. You might be able to choose a policy with a zero-day elimination period, but expect it to cost significantly more.

Inflation Protection   Protecting against inflation can be one of the most important additions you can make to a long-term care insurance policy, although it will increase the premium you pay. If your benefits do not increase over time, years from now, you may find that they have not kept up with the rising cost of long-term care. The younger you are when you buy a policy, the more important it is for you to think about adding inflation protection; otherwise, you will be only partially covered when the need arises.

Underwriting   Companies that sell long-term care insurance medically *underwrite* their coverage. They look at your health and family history before they decide to issue a policy. You may be able to buy coverage through an employer or another type of group without any health underwriting or with more relaxed underwriting.

Guaranteed Renewable Insurance   In most states, long-term care insurance policies sold today must be *guaranteed renewable*, which means that an insurance company cannot cancel or fail to renew coverage because of a change in a person's health or age. As long as premiums are paid and benefits have not been exhausted, coverage will continue. However, it does *not* mean that it guarantees you a chance to renew at the same premium; your premium may increase over time. You should consult with an insurance agent or broker who specializes in long-term care insurance and would be able to secure a policy that will meet your specific needs.

Partnership Policies   Many states offer "partnership" long-term care policies. By buying a policy that meets the guidelines of your state's partnership program, you receive asset protection from Medicaid spend-down. This means that if you ever exhaust the benefits of your policy, you will not have to spend down all of your assets to qualify for Medicaid. The asset protection amount can differ by state. Some states offer asset protection up to the amount of the total benefit you purchased, and some offer total asset protection. Not all states honor partnership policies from other states. This is important to know if you plan to retire to a different state than where you currently reside.

Hybrid Policies According to Jonathan Dodd, CFP®, an insurance specialist at HD Vest Financial Services®, "The newest trend in the industry is 'hybrid' policies. These are usually a combination of life and long-term care benefits. The feature that makes these products attractive to many buyers is that the premiums on most are guaranteed, meaning the policy premiums cannot change as long as you pay the agreed-upon amounts at the agreed upon intervals. However, most do not qualify for the potential tax deductions or partnership qualification that a traditional long-term care policy can provide."

Do not let your long-term care needs wipe out your family's financial independence!

Disability Insurance

If you became disabled and couldn't work, would you have enough savings to cover your living expenses until you were able to work again? For most people, the answer to this question is unfortunately no, which means that they would not be adequately prepared.

A *disability* is generally defined as a limitation of your physical or mental ability to work resulting from sickness or injury. It may be *partial*, in which case you are unable to perform certain job tasks and functions, or *total*, in which case you are unable to work at all.

According to the Council for Disability Awareness (CDA), 3 in 10 people entering the workforce today will become disabled before retiring, and 1 in 7 people can expect to be disabled for five years or more before retirement. A major misconception about disability is that it is typically caused by an accident or an injury. Many people think because they don't have a hazardous job or participate in hazardous activities, that they do not need disability coverage. However, the CDA reports that accidents and injuries cause only 10% of disability claims. The remaining 90% of claims are the result of a major illness. These are startling statistics and make it very clear that short- and long-term disability is a necessity, especially if you are the primary wage earner in your family and your income is needed to cover your living expenses.

Most employers are required by law to provide some form of workers' compensation and short-term disability coverage for their employees. The extent of coverage under these employer-provided short-term disability plans is very limited and short in duration. Short-term disability insurance replaces part of your income while you are injured or ill for any reason for a short period of time. Workers' compensation only protects you if you are injured while performing your job at work. It is important to understand that very few employers provide *long-term* disability coverage, so this responsibility usually rests on your shoulders.

Depending on the state you live in and the policy you have through your employer, your benefits may be insufficient to meet your basic living expenses. Whether or not an employer is required to provide short-term disability will also vary based on your state of employment.

New York State is one of the states that actually requires employers to carry short-term disability coverage for workers who are injured off the job or who suffer a serious illness. Using New York State as an example, the short-term disability benefits pay only $170 per week or up to 50% of the employee's salary, whichever amount is smaller. Payments will continue while you are disabled, but they end after 26 weeks. If you cannot afford to live on this amount per week for six months, then you need to be prepared.

Social Security Disability Benefits

The disability qualification under Social Security is different from the general definition and most insurance companies' definition. Social Security pays only for *total disability*. No benefits are payable for partial disability or for short-term disability.

Disability under Social Security is based on your inability to work. They consider you disabled under Social Security rules only if:

- You cannot do work that you were able to do before;
- The Social Security Administration decides that you cannot adjust to other types of work because of your medical condition; and
- Your disability has lasted or is expected to last for at least one year or to result in death.

The SSA uses a much stricter definition in determining your eligibility for benefits. Under its program, the rules assume that working families have access to other resources to provide support during periods of short-term disabilities, including cash reserves from savings, workers' compensation, and short-term disability insurance.

To be eligible for Social Security disability benefits, you need to pass two tests. The first test is a "recent work" test based on the age when you become disabled. For example, if you are under 24 at that time, you need to have worked 1.5 years out of the 3 years ending with the calendar quarter you are disabled. If you are over 30, you need to have worked at least 5 out of the 10 years ending with the quarter you are disabled.

The second work-related test is called the "duration of work" test. This test measures the amount of work you have performed over your lifetime. Generally, if you are under the age of 42 and pass the recent work test, you are likely to pass the duration of work test. However, once you turn 42, you must add one quarter of work per year in order to pass the duration of work test. For example, a 46-year-old beneficiary must have worked for 6 years since turning 21 in order to pass the duration of work test and a 50-year-old beneficiary must have worked for 7 years. The beneficiary must have earned at least 5 of those years within 10 years of becoming disabled.

The Social Security Administration calculates time spent working based on a quarter system, and that measurement is based on the amount of money an individual makes during a calendar year. In 2018, you earn one credit for each $1,320 of wages or self-employment income. When you have earned $5,280, you have earned your four credits for the year.

It is entirely possible to be deemed disabled by a commercial insurance company and not by the Social Security Administration, because insurance companies set their own eligibility requirements. To receive benefits, the SSA requires that you be disabled from doing almost any sort of work, whereas commercial companies may require only that you be disabled from doing your own particular type of work or profession.

The Social Security Administration's benefits – for retirement, disability, survivors, or dependents – were initially intended to be a safety net that could be used to replace *some* of your lost income. You cannot rely on Social Security disability alone, and this is why it is so important that you obtain a long-term disability policy through an insurance company.

Long-Term Disability Insurance

If you become seriously ill or injured, long-term disability insurance would substitute a portion of your salary after a certain period of time. Being able to replace the salary you were making before you became disabled and unable to work is a necessity for most people. If you don't have the proper insurance coverage, a long-term disability could potentially wipe you out financially and prevent you from ever becoming financially independent. You need to consider whether you and your family could survive comfortably without your salary. If the answer is no, then you must seek out the proper coverage immediately. This is one family health risk management solution you should not do without; it is clearly a need and not a want.

Ideally, you want to secure coverage that would pay you the typical maximum benefit of 60% of your income after an event that leaves you unable to work at your current job. It should cover you in case of an illness or an accident.

You should have a policy that would cover you for what is known as *owner's occupation*, not *any occupation*. This is the option that clearly separates what is available on the market through insurance companies from what the Social Security Administration provides. If you become disabled and can no longer perform your current occupation, regardless of what other kinds of work you might be able to do, the insurance company will pay you this disability benefit. A policy that covers *any occupation* would pay you only if you could not perform any job at all.

Long-term disability insurance should be *guaranteed, noncancelable,* and *renewable.* If it is not, your insurance company can cancel your policy. By including these options, the only reason your policy can be canceled is if you stop paying your premiums. With these options, your insurance company cannot increase your premium or change any of your policy's provisions, even if there is a change in your health that may increase your probability of becoming disabled.

Your policy should have *residual benefits,* which means it will guarantee a certain percentage of your former job's income in comparison to your new job's income. It should also include cost-of-living adjustments (COLAs), via a rider that can be included in your policy, typically for an extra cost. This rider allows you to increase your coverage periodically so that you can factor in inflation to future benefits without having an additional physical examination.

The elimination period, which is the amount of time after your injury or the onset of your illness when you receive no benefits, varies from policy to policy. Ideally, a 60-day elimination period is preferable, but you can select a policy with a 90-day elimination period to reduce the cost of your premiums. I would recommend the 90-day period only if you can afford to live without a paycheck for 90 days. This is also why I recommended in Chapter 1 that you have three to six months' worth of liquid cash available in case of an emergency. In essence, you are self-insuring against the possibility of a short-term disability by maintaining this cash reserve. If you do not have this emergency cash available, make sure you are working toward establishing an emergency fund for yourself and your family.

Life Insurance

Life insurance was originally designed to protect people while they were relatively young, in case the family wage earner died prematurely. Later on in life, once the children had grown and the couple's retirement nest egg had already been established, there was no longer a need for life insurance, and the policy would be canceled. I believe that, for many people, this is actually the way their life insurance should be handled today. It is my opinion that most people should not be using life insurance as a savings strategy. If you're single and have no dependents, there is usually no need for you to have life insurance.

There are four basic questions to ask yourself when determining your life insurance needs:

1. Do I really need it?
2. What dollar amount do I need?
3. How many years will I need it?
4. What type of life insurance policy would best meet my needs?

Examine your statement of cash flow (described in Chapter 3). Now imagine what your family's statement of cash flow would look like in the event that one or both wage earners were no longer alive and that income was no longer available. Could the remaining family income cover the financial obligations and dreams you have set for the future, such as paying for your children's education? If your survivors would have enough money to maintain their standard of living, then you do not need life insurance. On the other hand, if there is a shortfall, you will need to make this up by securing the proper type and amount of life insurance.

Quite frankly, life insurance should really be called *income-replacement insurance*. After all, the policy cannot bring you back to life; it can only serve as a means to replace the income you would have earned if you had lived. As a general rule, many life insurance advisors recommend having at least 10 times your annual salary as a death benefit, to allow your family the ability to generate income with these funds that will partially replace the lost earnings when you are no longer around. How much life insurance you really need will depend on several factors, including these:

- What your current income is
- What percentage of this income your family will need when you are gone
- How many years your family will need this income to continue
- What inflation rate you expect during this time period
- What rate of return you expect your family will earn on the death benefit over this time period
- What lump-sum payments your family will need to make when you die

To help you determine what may be the right amount of life insurance for you and your family, consider the following example: Let us assume you currently earn $100,000 per year before taxes and that your family would need $75,000 per year to maintain their current standard of living after your death. Let us also assume that you would need this income stream for 15 years, because at that point, your home mortgage would be paid off and your children would be out of college and independent from your spouse. You assume that your family can expect to earn a 5% rate of return on this money. We will also assume you have sufficient assets set aside to cover your funeral costs, and to keep the example simple, we will not factor in any inflation. To factor in all of these other variables, I encourage you to use a financial calculator, such as the one I describe below.

This hypothetical situation can be analyzed by also saying how much money you will need at a particular point of time in order to ensure a $75,000-per-year income stream over a 15-year period while these funds are earning a 5% rate of return. This is a present-value-annuity factor, and you can use Exhibit 12.5 in Chapter 12 to assist you with this calculation.

In step 1, enter 5% and in step 2, enter 15 years. Then determine the proper present-value-annuity factor by looking at row 15 years and column 5% for a factor of 10.37966. In step 4 of this exhibit, insert $75,000 in annual cash receipts your family would need to receive. Then, multiply the $75,000 by the present-value-annuity factor of 10.37966.

Therefore, you would need approximately $778,475. I recommend rounding this off to $800,000, as this is really a rough estimate of your life insurance needs to replace the lost income from your unexpected death.

Please understand there are numerous ways to estimate the amount of life insurance your family would need and numerous other factors that may need to be taken into consideration. A financial calculator can assist you with this more complicated calculation. For example, you can use the financial calculator found at www.calcxml .com/calculators/life-insurance-calculator, which may include additional variables in your "what-if" scenarios. This online calculator will provide you with a reasonable estimate of the proper amount of life insurance to meet your needs. Securing the right life insurance will provide you and your family with a tremendous amount of security, and if you choose term insurance (described next), I think you will be surprised by how affordable a large policy can be.

Term Life Insurance

I strongly believe that *term life insurance* is the best type of life insurance for the vast majority of people, and it literally costs a fraction of the price when compared to permanent insurance. Term life insurance is an efficient way to protect your family, which will give you the highest coverage at the most affordable price.

One of your goals should be to make sure that you will have enough income from your retirement plans to support yourself and your loved ones after you are gone. Once you have enough to live on, there may be no need for life insurance. With that said, you should never cancel or attempt to change a policy without checking with your doctor and having a thorough physical, as medical issues may encourage you to keep insurance that you otherwise would not have needed. By the time you are financially independent and ready to retire, your need to have life insurance and pay the premiums may be gone.

Term life insurance protects you for a certain number of years (typically 1 to 20), and once the *term* of the policy is over, you can usually renew the policy and begin another term without providing evidence of your insurability, although often at a higher cost. If you die during the term of the policy, the insurance company pays out the death benefit to your beneficiaries. The older you get, the more expensive term insurance becomes, because it is more likely that the company will have to pay out the death benefit. By the time you are in your seventies, the premiums in term life insurance will be very high, but if you have planned properly, you should no longer need it. Depending on your particular situation and individual needs, you may want to select a level, annual guaranteed-renewable, decreasing, or increasing term life insurance policy.

With a *level term policy*, your premiums would stay the same for the term you have chosen, usually 5, 10, 15, or 20 years.

You can also buy *annual guaranteed-renewable term insurance*, where the premiums increase to reflect your new age at the end of each year that you renew the policy.

Decreasing term insurance reduces the amount of your death benefit over time. This is typically used if you want the peace of mind in knowing that, in the event of the breadwinner's death, your mortgage can be paid in full. It is sometimes referred to as *mortgage insurance*, but it is really a term life insurance policy. This kind of policy starts with a specific death benefit that decreases each year until your policy expires, which typically goes hand in hand with the payoff of your mortgage.

There is also *increasing term life insurance*, which provides a death benefit that rises steadily as the term continues. This may be an option if it meets your needs.

When selecting the number of years of coverage under your term policy, it must be long enough to protect your family financially after your death and the loss of your earned income.

Permanent Life Insurance

If you decide that you don't want term life insurance and that permanent life insurance will better meet your specific needs, there are three major types you can purchase: whole, universal, and variable life insurance. With whole and universal life policies, the insurance company will invest your cash value and give you a declared interest rate. In contrast, variable life policies give you mutual-fund type investment options for your cash value, and you have numerous investment options to choose from.

One of the major advantages to these policies is that the money you invest in a cash-value life insurance policy will grow on a tax-deferred basis, similar to a fixed or variable annuity.

Whole Life Insurance   A cash value policy, also known as a *whole life policy*, is a permanent policy in which you are guaranteed coverage for life. Your premiums are priced accordingly, because the insurance companies know that they will eventually have to pay out the death benefits (unless you let the policy lapse by not paying your premiums). These policies have a cash value, which means that the insurance company takes your annual premium, deducts some administrative fees and a profit margin plus the cost of death protection, and puts the rest into a savings account called your *cash value*. So you are actually buying term life insurance that will not expire, with a savings plan as an add-on. Whole life insurance is generally just a costly way to maintain a tax-deferred, and in some cases tax-free, savings account.

Universal Life Insurance   This is a variation of whole life insurance, except that the return on the investment portion of your insurance premiums is not guaranteed and grows at a variable rate. As with whole life insurance, the insurance company makes many of the investment decisions.

Because whole life insurance policies and universal life insurance policies have cash values, if you decide not to keep your policy, or if you suddenly need money while you are alive, you can cash out. However, if your goal in buying life insurance is to put money aside, there are far better ways to save.

Variable Life Insurance   Variable life insurance is a product that has evolved significantly over the past several years. My experience has been that this type of policy fits only a small number of clients. While it can certainly benefit the right client, you must use caution when dealing with a product that has as many moving parts as a variable life insurance policy. Make sure that you fully understand the costs and benefit features before using any of these products.[1]

Comparing Term Life Insurance and Permanent Life Insurance   In most cases, the most effective strategy is purchasing a term life insurance policy that will cover you until you are financially prepared to retire. If you do not opt into a more expensive permanent policy (whether whole, universal, or variable life), you can use the money that you save to accumulate wealth, which can be used while you are alive in retirement. If you also use this savings toward funding a qualified employer-provided retirement plan or an individual retirement account (IRA), you will be able to save in pretax dollars. This will

---

[1]Before investing, you should consider the costs and fees associated with a variable life insurance policy. Plans are subject to enrollment, maintenance, administration/management fees, surrender charges, mortality and expense risk charges, and charges for any optional benefits. As with any investment, it's important to fully consider the plan's objectives, risks, charges, and expenses before investing.

make a significant difference in the time it takes for you to reach *point X*, financial independence. (I cover this in more detail in Chapter 8, "Planning for Retirement.")

A Second-to-Die Life Insurance Policy

This type of policy is also referred to as a *survivorship life policy*: it insures two people (usually spouses), and it does not pay until both insured people have died. Such a policy is normally worth considering if you are going to leave a very large estate that will incur substantial estate taxes. The most common type of second-to-die policy is universal life, which is permanent insurance. You can also purchase 10-, 20-, or 30-year *convertible* second-to-die term life insurance, which is much more affordable. Keep in mind that the primary purpose for this type of insurance is for estate planning; therefore, you do not want to outlive the term of your policy. Ultimately, a permanent second-to-die life insurance policy will be needed for this purpose.

If you convert a term policy to a permanent policy, you will end up paying more than if you bought a no-frills permanent policy upfront. This strategy is less expensive upfront, but can be significantly more expensive once you exercise your option to convert. It is only less expensive if you end up not needing to convert. If you take this route, you must buy a policy that does not limit your conversion options. Many carriers allow you only to convert to their more expensive products, potentially compounding the greater expense of conversion. They do this because most people who choose to convert do so because of unexpected health problems.

Federal tax law allows you to leave an unlimited amount of money, tax-free, to your spouse. When your spouse dies, federal taxes will be due on both your estates, and they usually must be paid within nine months of the death of the second spouse. A second-to-die life insurance policy could theoretically be used to cover the payment of these estate taxes.

If you have a substantial net worth and believe your estate will be subject to significant estate taxes, a permanent life insurance policy may then be the right choice for you. Although most people need only term insurance, high-net-worth individuals can take advantage of the significant tax savings a permanent insurance policy can offer. When combining a permanent life insurance policy with an irrevocable life insurance trust (ILIT), you can significantly preserve your family's financial legacy. (Estate planning with life insurance is covered in more detail in Chapter 10, "Preserving your Estate.")

As you can see, having the right type of life insurance at different stages in your life is an essential part of any high-quality financial plan. Making the right choices will accelerate your progress toward achieving financial independence. You must always remember to distinguish between what you *need* and what you *want*. Life insurance is perhaps the most unselfish *need* in your life, because you will not personally benefit from it; it is a need you fulfill for the benefit of your loved ones.

Buying Insurance Policies

Make sure you have done your research before purchasing insurance. Compare policies and companies to be certain you are getting what you really need at the best possible price available. For detailed advice on comparison shopping as it relates to insurance, see the "Buying Insurance Policies" section toward the end of Chapter 6, "Protecting Your Property with Insurance."

If you do not pay attention to the tax consequences of insuring your health and life, you may be paying significantly more in taxes than the law requires. This is why you must include tax planning as part of your overall insurance strategy. Using a financial planning approach that takes advantage of these *Tax Alpha to the 2nd Power*^{SM} facts and strategies will maximize your wealth through proper risk management.

TAX ALPHA TO THE 2ND POWER^{SM} FACTS AND STRATEGIES FOR INSURING YOUR HEALTH AND LIFE

Here are several tax facts and strategies that will address your wealth accumulation goals at an exponential rate, which will help put you on the path to financial independence, *point X.*

- Take full advantage of medical insurance premiums paid by your employer on your behalf. This is considered a tax-free fringe benefit. These medical insurance premiums are 100% deductible by your employer and tax-free to you. All payments made by the medical insurance company to cover your medical expenses are also tax-free payments made for your benefit.
- **Under the Tax Cuts and Jobs Act, you have more opportunities to deduct medical costs in 2017 and 2018 for you and your family.** Starting in 2017, your deduction is limited to the amount that exceeds 7.5% of your adjusted gross income (AGI). Then, starting January 1, 2019, your deduction is limited to the

amount that exceeds 10% of your AGI. This is why having medical insurance through your employer and a Health Savings Account (HSA) is so important; it allows you to pay for these costs in pretax dollars.

- **The threshold for the medical expenses itemized deduction has been reduced from 10% of adjusted gross income (AGI) to 7.5% of AGI.** For example, if your AGI is $80,000, you can deduct any unreimbursed medical expenses over $6,000, and not $8,000 as was set under the old tax law. This is one of the few provisions in the tax law that is retroactive to 2017.

- **Obamacare penalties will be eliminated, effective January 1, 2019.** The tax reform act repeals the individual mandate requiring people to purchase health insurance or face paying a tax penalty. Unfortunately, the Obamacare penalty can still be assessed through the end of 2018, unless Obamacare is fully repealed sooner.

- If your health insurance is an HSA-qualified high-deductible plan, you should establish a health savings account and fully fund tax-deductible contributions to cover future medical expenses. In 2018, individuals can contribute and deduct $3,450 for a single policy and $6,900 for a family. If you and your spouse are 55 or older, you can make an additional tax-deductible, catch-up contribution of $1,000 each.

- Insurance premium costs for long-term care policies may be partly or fully deductible, depending on your age, as well as the limitations on your AGI. (The limitations are similar to those for medical costs.) Benefits from a qualified long-term care insurance contract are generally not included as income and are tax-free to the extent that they are reimbursements of qualified expenses. For 2018, qualified long-term care insurance contract premiums can be deducted as medical expenses with limitations based on age ($420 if you are up to age 40, $780 if you are age 41 to 50, $1,560 if you are age 51 to 60, $4,160 if you are age 61 to 70, and $5,200 if you are over age 70).

- The payments for personal injuries and sickness under a qualified long-term care insurance policy can be excluded up to $360 per diem in 2018.

- Workers' compensation payments for job-related injuries or illnesses are tax-free.

- Dividends on life insurance policies are generally treated as a refund of your premiums and are not taxed until they exceed the total premiums paid.

- You can exchange certain insurance policies on a tax-free basis (these are called tax-free exchanges under Code Section 1035) if they meet certain requirements. Generally, you can exchange a life insurance policy for another life insurance policy, endowment policy, or an annuity contract. You can also exchange an endowment policy for another endowment policy or annuity contract, and you can exchange annuity contracts for another annuity contract with identical annuitants. See your insurance advisor for more details.

(*continued*)

- Life insurance proceeds you receive upon the death of the insured are generally income-tax-free to the beneficiary. If not properly structured, however, the insurance proceeds may be subject to estate taxes (the 40% rate may apply), and the beneficiary may actually receive the reduced amount. This reduction may be eliminated by setting up an irrevocable life insurance trust (ILIT). (For more details, see Chapter 10, "Preserving Your Estate.")
- If you are terminally ill, you may be able to take a tax-free withdrawal from your life insurance policy to pay medical bills and other living expenses. If your policy does not have an accelerated benefit clause, you may be able to sell your policy to a viatical settlement company without paying taxes. A viatical settlement allows you to sell your life insurance policy to a third party and collect a portion of the death benefits while you are still alive. Upon your death, your death benefits are paid to the buyer.

AN ACTION PLAN FOR INSURING YOUR HEALTH AND LIFE

1. **If your employer offers health insurance, make sure you understand all facets of the plan.** If details of the plan are not crystal clear to you, make an appointment with your human resources representative, and make sure it is explained to you.
2. **If your employer offers health insurance benefits, make sure your plan adequately covers your healthcare needs** (and your family's). If it does not, buy supplemental insurance or another policy altogether.
3. **Familiarize yourself with various types of health insurance plans:** Indemnity plans, managed-care plans, health discount plans, government plans, and so forth.
4. **If you are approaching age 65, become familiar with current Medicare laws.** Apply for Medicare at least one month before you turn 65, so you will be covered on the first day of the month of your birthday. Although you are automatically covered under Medicare Part A once you apply, clarify whether or not you want to be covered under Medicare Part B or Medicare Part D.
5. **Check to see if your employer offers long-term disability insurance** as an employee benefit, because group rates are substantially lower than individual rates.

6. **If you must buy your own long-term disability insurance** (which is usually expensive), consider buying a small policy now with a rider to add more later.
7. **When considering a long-term disability insurance policy,** look for ways to cut down on the price of premiums, such as to age 65 (not lifetime), prepayment, or excluding chronic medical conditions that require treatment but will not cause permanent disability.
8. **Consider buying long-term care insurance,** especially if you are older than age 50 (or have parents who may require your help) or you have substantial assets to protect.
9. **Carefully analyze your needs for buying life insurance.**
10. **Understand the pros and cons of the basic types of life insurance** (permanent and cash value – also known as whole life – and term life insurance).
11. **If you feel unsure of your insurance choices and decisions,** consider securing the help of an insurance broker or insurance advisor.
12. **Always secure new insurance coverage before you drop an old policy.** Never leave yourself without proper coverage.

CHAPTER 6

Protecting Your Property with Insurance

The personal right to acquire property, which is a natural right, gives to property, when acquired, a right to protection, as a social right.

—James Madison,
fourth president of the United States

Insuring your home, its contents, and your automobile is not only a necessity, but, in some situations, a requirement by law. This chapter shows you how to analyze your property insurance needs and make sure you are sufficiently covered. Protecting your property by implementing the proper risk management strategies is critical to achieving and maintaining your financial independence. The type and extent of insurance you need will change throughout your lifetime, as will the types of assets and the extent of wealth you have accumulated.

The three major personal property risk management issues include the following:

1. Homeowners insurance
2. Automobile insurance
3. Umbrella liability insurance

Your particular situation will determine what type of insurance you need, what kind of policy will work best, and what amount of coverage you should have. You should consult with your property liability insurance agent or broker to fully evaluate your needs, so that you can determine proper coverage to meet those needs. It is critically important to remember that you should always secure your new insurance coverage before you drop your old policy. You never want to leave yourself unprotected without proper coverage in between policies.

Insurance helps protect you and your family from the unexpected. The premiums you pay will provide you with the peace of mind that comes with knowing that your assets and family will be financially protected if accidents or disasters occur.

I begin this chapter by sharing a client story that will underscore the importance of securing the necessary property and liability insurance. This is the most tragic story in this book, but I feel it is necessary to make you understand the importance of this topic.

Case Study: How a Lack of Insurance Wiped Out One Woman's Life Savings

One of my clients is a medical doctor who devoted her entire life to helping children with cancer. She is one of the most caring and loving people I know. She became a doctor to care for and nurture children in need, which became her life's work. At the age of 50, she felt something was missing in her life. She had never been married and had no children of her own. She made the bold and courageous decision to adopt a child. I refer to her as Dr. Bigheart.

Dr. Bigheart started the long, emotional, and costly process of adopting a child. After several disappointments, she finally found a three-year-old child named Tania, who was living in an orphanage in Russia. The child was a beautiful, blond-haired, blue-eyed little girl. She was very thin, wore old clothing, and was teary-eyed, but she still managed to smile when she first saw Dr. Bigheart, who also had tears of joy in her eyes, because she knew she had found her little girl.

She spoke with the social worker responsible for Tania, who told her it would be at least six months before the adoption process would be completed and approved. The same day, she noticed that little Tania was very attached to a two-year-old boy named Joshua, and she discovered that this was Tania's brother. By the next day, Dr. Bigheart decided there was no way she could separate the siblings and leave Joshua behind. So she completed the paperwork to adopt both children at the same time.

As expected, the process took just over six months to complete, and she made six separate trips to Russia during this time, each time hoping to return with the children. Finally, that day came and she got on the plane from Moscow with both children in her arms. To this day, she describes this as the single most important day of her life.

She watched her children grow and went through the usual joys and disappointments of parenting. She finally felt that her life was complete. Through her work as a children's cancer doctor and her family life, she felt there was a true purpose and meaning to her life.

On Tania's 17th birthday, her mother surprised her with a brand-new car. Tania had gotten her driver's license and was a good driver. Six months later, Tania got into an argument with her boyfriend, and he broke up with her. She was very upset and drove off, speeding down the road in her car. She spun out of control and killed a man who was getting out of his car. Her car then crashed and rolled over, killing Tania instantly.

When Dr. Bigheart got the news of the accident, she rushed to the hospital. When the emergency room doctor told her that Tania did not survive, Dr. Bigheart collapsed and fell to the ground and could not stop crying. She was overcome with grief, could not catch her breath, and needed to be admitted into the hospital. She had just experienced every parent's worst nightmare: the death of a child. The wake was heartbreaking; Joshua had lost his sister, and Dr. Bigheart had lost her daughter. The emotions she was feeling could not be described in words, but only through the expression in her face and eyes.

A month after her daughter's death, she was sued by the family of the innocent man who was struck and killed in the accident. The lawsuit was for wrongful death and the pain and suffering of his family, in the amount of $5 million. At this point, Dr. Bigheart came to me for advice, and I asked her to bring in her auto and other personal liability insurance policies. Just when it seemed like her life could not get worse, I had to tell her that she did not have enough coverage. She had only a basic auto liability policy, which provided only $300,000 in personal liability coverage. When I asked about her personal umbrella liability insurance, she said she never bothered to get that type of policy.

As I feared, after her auto insurance company reviewed the claim, it threw in the towel and said this claim was in excess of its policy limits. The insurance company informed Dr. Bigheart that it would pay the full $300,000 from the policy limits, but it refused to cover the legal defense costs. Dr. Bigheart was forced to retain a lawyer at her own expense to defend this case against her, seeking $5 million.

Along with the grief and depression that came with the loss of her daughter, she now had to deal with the fear that her life savings would be wiped out as a result of this lawsuit. The lawsuit dragged on for two years until it was eventually settled. She paid more than

$80,000 in legal fees and made a final settlement to the victim's family of $800,000, of which the insurance company covered only $300,000. At the age of 67, she was forced to pay this $580,000 from her investment savings (and she said that was not even the most difficult part of the trial: having to relive what happened that day over and over was unbearable). Dr. Bigheart is now in her mid-70s and is still working part time. She was not able to fully retire, because a big part of her retirement savings was wiped out.

I cannot overemphasize the importance of having the appropriate property and liability coverage. Speak to your property and liability agent or broker today. If you do not have the appropriate umbrella liability coverage, you must get it immediately. Property risk management is one of the keys to achieving and maintaining financial independence. The rest of this chapter describes what you need to know about the three major property risk management issues that are critical to getting to *point X.*

Homeowners Insurance

Homeowners insurance needs to cover the cost of rebuilding or repairing your home in the event of damage from a fire, storm, burglary, or other type of catastrophe. Standard policies typically cover the house (the structure) and its contents (furniture, clothing, etc.), the latter usually for 50% to 70% of the amount for which you insured the structure of the house. Therefore, if you have $300,000 in insurance coverage on the structure of your home, you would have between $150,000 and $210,000 worth of coverage for your personal belongings, above and beyond the coverage for the structure.

Homeowners policies also include liability coverage for damage or injury incurred inside or outside your house.

Property Coverage

An actual *cash-value policy* will compensate you for the cost of your belongings less their depreciation (used value), whereas a *replacement-cost policy* means that the insurance company must compensate you for the actual cost of replacing the lost or damaged items. For example, if you have a fire in one room of your house and all the furniture in that room is destroyed, and you have a cash-value policy, your insurance company will ask you how much you spent for that furniture. If you spent $5,000 and you owned that furniture for

10 years, the insurance company may decide that its *current* value is only $2,000 – because, after all, you used it for 10 years. And that is the amount the insurance company will pay you: $2,000.

In contrast, if you have a replacement-cost policy, the insurance company is likely to compensate you with at least $5,000 and probably even more, given that prices and inflation have increased and the cost of a new bedroom set may be more like $7,500 today. So which would you want to receive: $2,000 or $7,500?

Of course, you need to consider that the premiums on a replacement-cost policy will be more than for a cash-value policy, but the difference may be a small price to pay for the additional peace of mind you will have in knowing that you will be fully compensated should something catastrophic happen in your home. In my opinion, you should always opt for a replacement-cost policy, because it will provide you with a reimbursement sufficient to replace your loss.

If your home is damaged and uninhabitable, your insurer may also compensate you for the costs associated with maintaining a temporary residence (renting a hotel room or other home) elsewhere, while repairs are made on your home. Please note, flood insurance typically requires a separate policy, because it is not covered through standard policies.

The majority of homeowners policies are written under the HO-3 contract form. These form numbers are standardized throughout the insurance industry, so that if you purchase HO-3 insurance, you will be getting the identical coverage, regardless of your insurance provider. The HO-3 contract provides the following coverage:

- **Broad coverage for your dwelling:** Damage to your dwelling from most causes is covered unless it is specifically excluded.
- **Damage to your personal property for "named perils" only:** Your personal property is covered against only the perils specified in the contract. For example, if you do not live in an earthquake-prone area, but you are still concerned about fire, theft, flooding, and hail damage, you may elect to get a named perils policy and declare coverage only against fire, theft, flooding, and hail, while leaving the earthquake coverage off the policy.
- **Limited coverage for jewelry that is stolen:** Coverage is usually $500 to $2,000, depending on your resident state. The majority of policies do not cover jewelry that is lost. Often a basic burglar alarm that is monitored will pay for itself through a discount on your homeowner's insurance.

Endorsements Provide Additional Coverage   If you would like to increase the amount of your coverage for valuable items or want to protect yourself from identity theft, endorsements may provide the additional coverage you desire. You can increase your limits for items such as jewelry, furs, gold, silverware, or firearms.

Choosing the Right Deductible and Filing Claims   Homeowners insurance is for major disasters (as mentioned at the beginning of this section), not for filing small claims, such as a broken window from your neighbor's son playing hardball in his yard. You may be tempted to file small claims to get back the money you contributed to premiums. In most cases, if you merely file one claim, that will not raise your rates or cancel your policy. But if you file multiple claims – in fact, as few as two, with certain policies – that may cause your insurance company to raise your premiums or even cancel your homeowners insurance policy altogether. It is best to get a policy with a high deductible so that you have no reason to file lower-cost claims. The higher the deductible, the lower your premium; in essence, you are self-insuring for any damage up to the amount of the deductible. The standard flat dollar deductible is typically $1,000. I would recommend increasing this amount to $2,000, $5,000, or even more if you feel you can cover this cost on your own. Because you will not be filing small claims anyway, why not save the premium dollars? You can then use this savings to cover these deductibles in the event a situation occurs.

Liability Coverage

Liability coverage is intended to protect your assets in the event that you are sued by someone who is hurt or whose property is damaged because of your negligence. For example, you may be a fanatic about keeping your house clean and safe at all times, and when it snows you are always the first one out the door with a snow shovel and rock salt to keep the sidewalk safe for others. But suppose an unexpected blizzard hits your hometown during Thanksgiving week, when you are visiting with your family out of town. While you are away, you obviously are not able to care for your property and ensure the safety of others by shoveling and properly cleaning the walkway. If an elderly woman trips and falls, breaking her leg and hip, she may require major surgery and hospitalization. Without the proper liability insurance, you would be held liable for her injuries, which could cost you hundreds of thousands of dollars.

You must also have liability insurance and medical protection coverage for your visitors. Let us say your children decide to have a sleepover in your home with a few of their closest friends, and one of their friends falls and breaks his arm. You may need this coverage to help pay for the child's medical expenses, should you be sued by the child's parents.

You should consider increased limits if you have "attractive nuisance" features on your property, like swimming pools, hot tubs, or a pet that is capable of causing harm.

What Liability Insurance Covers and What It Doesn't Cover   Most homeowners insurance covers the following:

- **Accidental injuries to visitors that take place on your property, such as slips and falls:** If that person sues you, your insurance usually provides protection against judgments where you are found negligent and also offers medical payments to others who are hurt or injured on your property.
- **Injuries to people who are hurt by you, by your household members, or by your pets, even when you are away from home.**

On the other hand, your homeowners insurance probably does *not* cover the following:

- **Deliberate actions that result in a claim or loss:** These are typically not covered by any insurance policy. For example, one of your neighbors parks in your driveway and you want to teach him a lesson, so you hit him repeatedly with a baseball bat. Intentional acts of violence such as this would not be covered.
- **Known hazards and risks:** Failure to take reasonable precaution to repair, correct, or fix a situation that could result in injury or loss is typically not covered by insurance. Always keep your property in good condition and take care of potential hazards immediately. For example, if you have a defective sidewalk that is uneven and clearly a hazard, yet you simply choose to ignore it, your insurance company may deny coverage for a resulting injury to a third party.

For most people, their home is their castle, and it also represents one of their most significant personal use assets. Having the proper homeowners insurance is an important step to keep you on track to achieving financial independence. Without the proper insurance, one of your major assets can be lost and be impossible to replace. Furthermore, if you are sued for injuries sustained by others because of your negligence, you can be wiped out financially.

Automobile Insurance

Auto insurance is required by law, and the state you live in will dictate the extent and type of coverage required. An auto insurance policy is made up of seven different primary coverage types, each with its own premium: The cost for each of these protections will vary based on numerous factors such as where you live, the type of car you drive, your driving record (i.e., whether or not you have been in accidents before or have been ticketed by the police), and even your credit history. The only way to find out what your cost of coverage will be is to ask for a personalized price quote. When pricing auto insurance, it always pays to shop around, and you should always obtain a minimum of two price quotes from two separate insurance companies.

1. **Bodily injury liability** provides protection if you injure or kill someone while operating your car. It also provides for a legal defense if another party in the accident files a lawsuit against you. To protect your personal assets, you should have sufficient coverage against a judgment from a lawsuit as a result of a serious accident. Bodily injury liability covers injury to people, not the cost to repair or replace your vehicle. Generally, you would want the same amount of coverage for all of your cars.

2. **Medical payments, no-fault, or personal injury protection coverage** typically pays for the medical expenses of the injured driver and passengers in your car, regardless of who was at fault for the accident.

3. **Uninsured motorist coverage** pays for your injuries caused by an uninsured driver or, in some states, a hit-and-run driver, in a crash that is not your fault. Some states also offer uninsured motorist coverage for damage to your vehicle. Even if you live in a state with no-fault insurance, it is very important to have this coverage; you would be surprised by how many uninsured motorists are on the road. According to a recent report from the Insurance Research Council, about 13% of U.S. motorists

(or about one out of eight) are without insurance and operating their vehicles illegally.

4. **Comprehensive physical damage coverage** pays for losses resulting from damages to your car if it is stolen or damaged by flood, fire, or animals, but it does not cover collision. One strategy for keeping your insurance premium costs low is by selecting a high deductible. Self-insuring against these minor losses is wise as long as you have sufficient cash reserves to cover these costs when the need arises.

5. **Collision coverage** pays for damage to your car when your car hits, or is hit by, another vehicle or other objects. A rule of thumb is that your car value should be at least 10 times the cost of your annual premium. If it is not, consider dropping or reducing collision and physical damage coverage. Once again, self-insuring against certain losses can be wise as long as you have sufficient cash reserves to cover these costs when the need arises.

6. **Property damage liability** protects you in the event that your car damages someone else's property. It also provides you with the legal defense coverage if a lawsuit is filed against you. For example, if you are backing out of your driveway and accidentally step on the accelerator instead of the brake, causing you to crash into your neighbor's living room, the property damage liability protection can come in handy.

7. **Rental reimbursement** coverage pays for the cost of a rental vehicle when the insured person's vehicle cannot be used because of losses covered under comprehensive or collision coverage.

The insurance industry uses shorthand to describe how much coverage each policy provides. For example, *30/50/20* means you have:

- $30,000 in bodily injury coverage per person,
- $50,000 in bodily injury coverage per accident, and
- $20,000 in coverage for property damage.

However, the standard minimum recommendation for auto liability coverage is at least *100/300/50*:

- $100,000 in bodily injury coverage per person,
- $300,000 in bodily injury coverage per accident, and
- $50,000 in property damage liability.

Most states use a no-fault auto insurance system; the other states use a third-party system to settle claims. To determine whether your state is a no-fault auto insurance state, contact your auto insurance carrier or visit the insurance information institute website at www.iii.org. This website was established for improving public understanding of insurance, what it does, and how it works. No-fault states require drivers and their insurance companies to pay their own costs after a car accident, regardless of whether they were responsible: this is why it is referred to as *no-fault.*

Even with no-fault insurance, you may still need liability insurance, because if you cause an accident and the costs to the other injured people are above a certain amount, they can sue you to recover the difference. Without sufficient liability coverage, the shortfall would have to come out of your own pocket. In the case study discussed earlier in this chapter, the necessity of having sufficient liability coverage was underscored by the tragic real-life story of Dr. Bigheart.

If your child is going to drive, he or she has to have insurance. Insurance companies know that young drivers are risky drivers, so they will charge you high rates to protect against this added risk. The only way to determine what the added cost of insurance will be once your young driver gets a license is to ask your insurance provider for a price quote. Knowing the answer to this question early may encourage you to have your child wait until he or she is older to get a license.

If this does not go over well with your teenagers and you decide to have them apply for a driver's license, you can still save some money on your auto insurance by not purchasing another car. If you do purchase a car for your teenage driver, then you should also consider buying your child a used car, because it is more sensible to have your child drive the oldest and least-expensive car you own: This helps keep your cost of insurance lower than it would be otherwise. Of course, if you have an older car, make sure it is still safe to drive: Your family's safety is always more important than saving some money.

Make sure you are aware of all discounts available from your insurance carrier. Good grade discounts for younger drivers can be a handy motivator. Low mileage discounts are great for those who do not drive frequently, and drivers' education discounts may be available to both young people and adults.

An insurance company determines your premium based on certain statistics and facts about you and other drivers. These factors are based on your age, your gender, where you live, the type of car you drive, your driving record, your credit score, etc. Although some of these factors are out of our control, the ones that you can control should be carefully analyzed before purchasing a car.

For example, the cost of insuring a red Corvette is much higher than insuring a white Dodge minivan. Selecting an eight-cylinder vehicle will generally cost you more than a six-cylinder vehicle because the number of cylinders determines the speed of the car. When analyzing which car to purchase for yourself and family members, be sure to ask your insurance company for a price quote on each separate vehicle. This may make your vehicle choice a wiser one and a less costly one.

The basic rule from Chapter 1, "Committing to Living within Your Means," holds true with purchasing auto insurance or a new automobile. Always ask yourself, is the purchase of this vehicle a need or a want? If in fact it is a need, is there a less expensive alternative? And always remember, shop around and do comparisons to get the very best price possible.

Umbrella Liability Insurance

Homeowners, auto, and boat insurance policies do provide a limited amount of liability protection, but these policies may not provide you with enough coverage to protect your assets in the event of a major lawsuit. A major lawsuit can cost you significant dollars both in terms of legal defense costs and the ultimate settlement payments, beyond any amount you can reasonably expect to pay from your savings. Umbrella liability insurance policies provide you with a secondary layer of insurance protection that is over and above the normal coverage limits of your other policies; umbrella insurance protects you only after your homeowners, auto, or boat insurance policy has paid or is expected to pay its maximum benefit.

For example, in the tragic story involving Dr. Bigheart, her insurance company raised the white flag and surrendered. The lawsuit brought by the family of the man her daughter killed was seeking $5 million, yet Dr. Bigheart's auto insurance policy limit for liability was only $300,000. Because Dr. Bigheart did not have an umbrella liability insurance policy, she had no other resources to turn to for help.

Umbrella liability insurance is like having a secondary parachute to protect you in case your first parachute (standard policy) fails. An umbrella policy can offer coverage above and beyond the liability protection of your standard policies, into the millions of dollars, in case you are sued under any of your other insurance policies as a result of an accident or injury. The amount and type of coverage offered through an umbrella liability policy varies based on the policy and insurance provider. Be sure you know exactly what the policy you purchase covers and does not cover.

Your total combined insurance policies for homeowners, auto, boat, and umbrella must cover at least an amount equal to or greater than your personal net worth. In my opinion, a personal liability umbrella policy is something that no one who owns a car and a home should do without, and I recommend buying a policy that will fully protect you. Personal liability umbrella coverage typically ranges from $1 million to $5 million, and in some cases, you can obtain even more. Moreover, the cost of that insurance is very low: you can expect to pay only $100 to $300 per year for $1 million in coverage; each additional million dollars' worth of coverage typically costs only $50–75 per year.

Most insurance companies will require you to have a certain level of coverage (as described below) under your regular insurance before you can purchase an umbrella policy. Therefore, very often you will need to upgrade the coverage under your home, car, and boat insurance policy. Most personal umbrella policies will require you to maintain at least the following amount of coverage under your other policies in order to be eligible for this additional coverage.

- **Auto insurance policy:** $300,000 per person and $300,000 per occurrence (for bodily injury) and $100,000 (for property damage).
- **Homeowners insurance policy:** $300,000 liability.
- **Boat insurance policy (if applicable):**
  - $100,000 liability for boats under 26 feet long and under 50 horsepower.
  - $300,000 liability for boats 26 feet and longer, or 50 horsepower and up.

The following paragraphs describe some of the coverage you can typically find under a personal umbrella insurance policy. It is important to review and compare these policies carefully so you can determine exactly what you are and are not covered for.

Bodily Injury Liability   This covers the cost of damages to another person's body – for example, the cost of medical bills as well as liability claims resulting from:

- Injuries to other parties due to a severe auto accident where you were at fault.
- Injuries sustained by a guest in your home.

- Injuries sustained by your child's friend who falls and breaks a leg while playing in your yard.
- Injuries caused to others by your dog.

Property Damage Liability This covers the cost of damage or loss to another person's physical property – for example, the cost associated with claims resulting from:

- Damage to someone's vehicle as a result of an auto accident where you were at fault.
- Damages to public or private property accidentally caused by your family members.
- Damages incurred when your dog destroys a neighbor's couch with its paws.

Rental Property Insurance If you own rental property, you can protect yourself against liability that you, as the landlord, may be subject to – for example, the cost of liability claims from:

- Someone who slips on ice in front of your rental property, or
- Someone who has been bitten by your tenant's dog.

Umbrella extended coverage may also be provided in the event you are sued for:

- Slander, which is injurious spoken statements.
- Libel, which is injurious written statements.
- Malicious prosecution.
- False arrest or imprisonment.
- Various other personal liability situations.

One of the most frequently overlooked reasons to purchase umbrella insurance is because you have children. Just think back to the tragic story I shared with you about Dr. Bigheart and her daughter. As your child's parent, you are responsible for your minor child's actions, which could result in financial hardships if they are found responsible for a serious accident, injury, or death. The age of majority is the age at which a minor becomes an adult in the eyes of the law of your resident state. This age is 18 in most states, but a few states extend the age of majority to 19 or 21.

Millions of Americans are nearing retirement age: on average, 10,000 are turning age 65 every day. Some of them have lived their lives based on the principles in this book and are now financially independent. Yet, as we saw with Dr. Bigheart, the cost of a major lawsuit could easily wipe out their entire life savings.

As mentioned, the premiums for an umbrella insurance policy typically range from only $150 to $300 a year for $1 million in coverage, and about $50 to $75 a year for every additional million dollars in coverage thereafter. In my opinion, that is a very small price to pay for the added peace of mind that comes from the protection provided through these policies.

Buying Insurance Policies

Before you purchase insurance, make sure you have done the proper research. Always shop around and compare policies to make sure you are getting what you really need at the best possible price available. When doing your comparison shopping, be certain you are comparing the detailed coverage and limitations that may apply. Are these policies providing the same level of coverage? Are the deductibles the same for each policy? Does one policy exclude certain items and the other one include them? It is easy to obtain a less expensive policy by purchasing one that provides you with more limited coverage. Also, do not compare based on price alone, because the cheapest policy may not be the best policy to meet your needs. You must be sure to find out exactly what the policy will specifically cover and what is excluded from the coverage. Make sure you know specifically what is required for you to qualify for the benefits. Finally, reevaluate your needs each year and ensure that your policies are still meeting your requirements.

As a general rule, you always want to compare policies from two or more insurance companies. You may want to consider increasing your deductible, which will generally lower your premiums. Many insurance companies offer you a reduced premium if you are able and willing to pay on an annual basis instead of monthly or quarterly. You should find out about multiple policy discounts if you are purchasing a number of policies through the same insurance company (for example, your auto, home, and umbrella policy).

When shopping for a new policy, consider asking friends and family about their claims experience with the carriers you are considering. A less expensive policy may not be such a great deal if the provider is difficult to work with or is slow to pay claims.

When choosing an insurance company, you want to make sure it is financially sound and will be around to pay your claim when the time comes. All insurance companies are not created equal, and very often, you may be quoted a lower price from a company that is not as financially sound as the others you are comparing it to. There are four major rating services for insurance companies that can assist you in determining their financial strength; check with these rating agencies before entering into an insurance contract:

- AM Best (www.ambest.com)
- Moody's (www.moodys.com)
- Standard & Poor's (www.standardandpoors.com)
- Duff and Phelps (www.duffandphelps.com)

Before you buy an insurance policy from any company, please be sure the company carries at least a rating of "AA" or better from Moody's, Standard & Poor's, or Duff and Phelps; if you are evaluating an insurance company through AM Best, look for a rating of "A–" or better.

Throughout your journey to financial independence, you never know what unexpected property risk issues may arise. There are major family risk management issues that concern all of us. Obtaining the proper homeowners, auto, boat, and personal umbrella liability coverage can provide you with the peace of mind of knowing that you and your property will be protected. Being unprepared for the unexpected can rob you and your family of your pursuit of financial independence.

If you do not pay attention to the tax consequences of protecting your property with insurance, you may be paying significantly more in taxes than the law requires. This is why you must include tax planning as part of your overall insurance strategy. Using a financial planning approach that takes advantage of these *Tax Alpha to the 2nd Power*[SM] facts and strategies will help maximize your asset protection goals.

TAX ALPHA TO THE 2ND POWER[SM] FACTS AND STRATEGIES FOR PROTECTING YOUR PROPERTY

Here are several tax facts and strategies that will address your wealth accumulation goals at an exponential rate, which will help put you on the path to financial independence, *point X*.

- Generally, the cost of personal homeowners, automobile, boat, and umbrella liability insurance are not tax-deductible. Insurance reimbursements to the extent of your loss are generally not taxable. If you receive an insurance

(continued)

reimbursement in excess of your adjusted basis (i.e., what you paid for it), this will result in a gain you must report as income unless you acquire replacement property and elect to defer the gain.

- If you own a rental property, you can generally deduct most of the expenses associated with maintaining and managing the property, as well as the cost of property insurance, which includes premiums for fire and liability.
- Casualty and theft losses attributable to personal use property may be partly tax-deductible. **Under the Tax Cuts and Jobs Act, this deduction has been significantly limited, starting in 2018. Taxpayers can now take a deduction for casualty losses only if the loss is attributable to a presidentially declared disaster.** For example, if a major hurricane damaged your home and your property is located within a presidentially declared disaster zone, you may qualify for this deduction. This deduction would be included on Schedule A of your tax return but would only apply after the limitations set by the Internal Revenue Code. After the casualty or theft loss amount is determined (less insurance reimbursement), any applicable dollar floor will reduce the deductible loss.
- Casualty losses resulting from *presidentially declared disasters*, such as Hurricane Irma, may be deducted in the prior tax year by filing an amended return. This is done to expedite funds into the hands of disaster victims. For Hurricane Irma, the effect of deducting the casualty loss for 2016 on an amended return should be compared to the results of deducting the loss on your 2017 return so that the largest tax benefit can be chosen. The goal is a simple one: take the loss in the year that provides you with the most tax benefit. Hopefully you will not encounter such a casualty loss in the future, but in the event that you do, you may be able to use the same strategy to get you through it financially.
- Having the proper insurance coverage on your property will provide you with a tax-free reimbursement of your loss.
- Insurance reimbursements for the cost of added living expenses attributable to damage to your home do not reduce a casualty loss. The payments from the insurance company for these excess living costs are generally not taxable and are treated separately from the payments for property damage.
- As a matter of law, compensatory damage for physical injury or sickness is treated as tax-free. For example, if you are injured in a car accident and you sue the driver and are awarded $100,000 because of your back pain, you do not have to pay taxes on this settlement payment. In contrast, however, damages for nonphysical personal injuries are taxable, such as from discrimination, back pay, wrongful termination, or injury to your reputation. So if you sue a former employer for wrongful termination and the court rules that you were indeed wrongfully terminated, awarding you $1,000,000, you will have to pay taxes on that $1,000,000.

AN ACTION PLAN FOR PROTECTING YOUR PROPERTY

1. Consult with your property liability insurance agent or broker to fully evaluate your homeowners insurance needs so that you can determine proper coverage to meet those needs.
2. Always secure new insurance coverage before you drop your old policy. You never want to leave yourself unprotected without proper coverage in between policies.
3. When buying homeowners insurance, choose a replacement-cost policy (rather than the cash-value policy) because it will provide you with a reimbursement sufficient to replace your loss, in the event of fire or other damage specified in your policy.
4. Make sure your homeowners insurance includes both liability insurance and medical protection coverage for your visitors, to protect you in case someone is injured on your property and brings a lawsuit against you.
5. Remember that auto liability coverage is required in all states, and anyone who owns a home and has significant assets should strongly consider buying a minimum of 100/300/50 in coverage: $100,000 for bodily injury coverage per person, $300,000 for bodily injury coverage per accident, and $50,000 for property damage liability. Collision and comprehensive damage are both optional types of auto liability insurance coverage.
6. Make sure your children and other members of your household are insured under your auto insurance policy. (Check with your auto insurance company since these rules vary by state.) Also, keep in mind that you can probably lower your insurance premiums if your children drive an older car, rather than a brand-new, expensive model.
7. Consider buying an umbrella liability insurance policy, which provides a secondary layer of insurance protection that is over and above the normal coverage limits of your other insurance policies. This can cost as little as $150 per year, but can protect you up to $1 million if you are sued.
8. When choosing an insurance company, check with the major insurance rating services to determine the quality of the company. You want to be sure that your insurer will be in business and financially sound if something happens and you need the protection offered by that company.

CHAPTER

7

Paying for College

An investment in knowledge always pays the best interest.

—Benjamin Franklin,
Founding Father of the United States

Most parents struggle with the difficult decisions they need to make while juggling all of their competing financial needs. Throughout this book, I discuss many financial goals that we typically have throughout our lifetime. These include building a cash reserve, minimizing debt, paying for health and life insurance, protecting your property, and saving for retirement. Each time we focus on one of our goals, our limited resources require us to make sacrifices with the other goals. Therefore, parents need to make very important decisions when it comes to how to pay for education. The information I provide in this chapter will help you make an informed decision and prepare you to meet this challenge.

In fact, one of the most satisfying aspects of my work as a Certified Financial Planner™ is that I have the opportunity to meet with some amazing people and become an integral part of their lives. There is no more satisfying feeling than helping clients and their children achieve their financial goals and live out their dreams.

Is College the Best Choice for You and Your Child?

Before I address how best to plan, save, and pay for college, you first need to decide if college is in fact the best choice for you and your child. If your child is not in the top 25% of his or her class in high

175

school, chances are this will also be the case in college. Earning a four-year undergraduate degree will not guarantee a well-paying job, or any job for that matter. In fact, many college graduates are taking jobs that they could have actually gotten right out of high school. The main difference with many of these college graduates is that they, or their family, had to lay out $100,000 to $200,000, and they may now be in debt with student loans that can take decades to pay off. So quite frankly, you need to address the difficult decision and reality check of whether your child is college material before sending him or her off on this very expensive journey.

A college degree has now somehow become a *necessity* when, in fact, in many cases, it is just something else that you as a parent or your child may *want*. Colleges and universities across the country and abroad have terrific recruiting and marketing departments that promise you and your children the world. In reality, they should not be making any promise at all, since there are no guarantees that your child will graduate. Even if your child manages to graduate with straight As, this does not mean that all of his or her dreams will come true. Universities make extremely misleading claims, borderline lies, that your child will get a top-paying job and that it is impossible to get ahead without a college education. These statements are simply not true.

In fact, some of the most brilliant and successful people in our society are college dropouts. Quite frankly, they were bored and unchallenged with higher education, and they instead chose to pursue their passion. The following is an eye-opening list of just a few entrepreneurs who dropped out of college to then become billionaires:[1]

- Michael Dell, Dell founder, dropped out at the age of 19.
- Steve Jobs, Apple founder, dropped out at the age of 19.
- Bill Gates, Microsoft founder, dropped out at age 20.
- Mark Zuckerberg, Facebook founder, dropped out at age 20.

I know what you are thinking. These guys are all protégé geniuses, but my son or daughter is not. I must tell you that, in my 30 years of working with small businesses, many of the most successful people never set foot in college. In fact, some of them even dropped out of high school. What they did have was passion and drive, and they were

---

[1]Abigail Hess, "10 Ultra-Successful Millionaire and Billionaire College Dropouts," CNBC.com, 10 May 2017.

relentless in the pursuit of their business enterprise. Perhaps, instead of investing $100,000 or $200,000 and four or more years in a college education, it may be best to invest some time and money in a small business. See Chapter 11, "Starting Your Own Business."

So now you may be thinking that your children might not be passionate enough or have the skillset necessary to be an entrepreneur and start their own business. If that is the case, then they should consider pursuing some of the very high-paying jobs available to high school graduates. These are blue-collar jobs that are equally important to our society. Without the butchers, bakers, plumbers, carpenters, electricians, and civil servants, our economy and society could not survive.

An article published in *MarketWatch* identified the following five blue-collar jobs that can pay $100,000 or more per year.[2]

1. **Bartenders:** According to the Bureau of Labor statistics, bartenders in upmarket bars in major cities earn between $45,000 and $73,000 a year on average with tips. Depending on the location of the bar and restaurant, some may bring home more than $100,000 a year.
2. **Contractors and construction managers:** According to the Bureau of Labor Statistics (BLS), salaries can range from $82,790 to $144,520.
3. **Farmers and ranchers:** According to the BLS, farmers in California have the highest annual average wage of all states at approximately $93,630 a year. Farmers can earn nearly $120,000 a year, depending on their state and area of expertise.
4. **Oil rig foremen/managers and directional drillers:** Some of these jobs that don't require a college degree can earn over $100,000 a year, depending on their specialty.
5. **Police officers:** New York Police Department salaries, depending on their rank and years on the job, can reach up to $131,000 per year, not to mention the amazing benefit packages (need only 60 college credits or two years full-time active military service).

Not every young adult will go down the same path to achieving financial independence. For many of them, they need to fall down,

---

[2]Quentin Fottrell, "5 Blue-Collar Jobs that Pay $100,000 a Year," *MarketWatch*, 18 November 2017.

pick themselves up, and perhaps even redefine themselves before they can reach their full potential. Perhaps the best way for me to make this point is to share my own struggles as a young adult.

As you know, my parents emigrated here from Italy after World War II with only an eighth-grade education and barely spoke English. My parents had an extremely strong work ethic and always encouraged their children to work hard and get a solid education. It is fair to say that I did not always do what my parents had asked of me.

By the time I was 16 years old I had already worked as a newspaper delivery boy, an apprentice butcher, and a grocery store clerk. All I was concerned with was making money, hanging out with my friends, and having enough cash to pay for the gas for my seven-year-old 1972 Cadillac Coup de Ville. The things I was interested in at this age definitely did not include college. Although I considered myself to be smart, I had absolutely no interest in reading books and studying for exams at this point in my life. In fact, I dropped out of high school and took on a full-time job working as a truck driver earning $100 a day, which at the time, felt like a small fortune.

My parents, as well as my siblings, were not very happy with my decision and continued to encourage me to go back to school. Although I consider being a truck driver a very respectable job, I eventually came to realize that this was not the type of work I wanted to do for the rest of my life.

With the continued encouragement and persistence of my sister Rose, I took the General Educational Development (GED) exam and earned my high school equivalency diploma by the time I was 19. I enrolled in a two-year associate program at Kingsborough Community College in Brooklyn. This is where I turned my life around and was given the opportunity for *a second chance in life*. I took this strong work ethic that was instilled in me by my parents and put it into my college studies. I transformed myself into a straight-A student and to this day have not stopped studying and furthering my education. You can read the "About the Author" section of this book to find out a little bit more about my accomplishments since then.

Not everyone will go down the same path in their pursuit of financial independence. No matter what paths your children take, you should never give up hope or stop encouraging them to be the best that they can be. Taking a two-year break between high school and college was the right choice for me. Had I gone straight to college from high school, I am not sure I would have had the same level of enthusiasm and passion with my studies, and I may have never gone into business for myself by starting my own practice. I am not encouraging anyone to go down the same path I did, but my point is that everyone needs to create their own path in life to success.

No one knows your son or daughter better than you, so you need to be honest with yourself and listen to what your children have to say. If you think college isn't the right choice for them and do not want to burden yourself or your children with the cost and time spent, then you have no need to read the rest of this chapter. If you still believe pursuing a college degree is the right choice for your child, please read on.

The Cost of College and What You Can Expect to Pay

If you are like most parents, one of your biggest concerns is *How am I going to pay for my children's education when the time comes to send them off to college?* Some parents hope their children will receive academic or athletic scholarships or grants. But for most parents, the reality is that they will have to pay most of the cost of college from their savings – or even worse, they may have to go into debt.

Moreover, the cost of college is skyrocketing. According to the College Board, from 2007 to 2017, published in-state tuition and fees at public four-year institutions increased at an average rate of 3.2% per year *beyond* the rate of general inflation, compared with 4.4% between 1997 and 2007. Although it is somewhat encouraging that the rate of increase has declined by 1.2% over the past decade when compared to the prior decade, it is still increasing at a rate greater than the general inflation rate. The College Board also cited the tuition and fees at a private four-year college or university (for the 2017–2018 school year) as an average $34,740 – which is a whopping $138,960 for four years! When you include room and board, that is $46,950 per year – or $187,800 for four years. (For more information about the cost of college, I encourage you to visit their website at www .collegeboard.org.)

Exhibit 7.1 shows how four-year college costs are projected to increase, from 2011 to 2035 – which is when parents of babies born in 2017 will be sending those kids to college. As you can see, college costs are projected to rise at an alarming rate that far exceeds the rate of inflation, so if you are a parent, you need to find ways to save for your child's education that will have a reasonable chance of keeping pace with these increasing costs.

To have a fighting chance to succeed with this financial goal, you need to avoid the financial mistakes that are made by many parents. The key to accomplishing this is to have a good understanding

Exhibit 7.1   Projected Annual Four-Year College Costs 2011–2035 (in 2017 constant dollars)

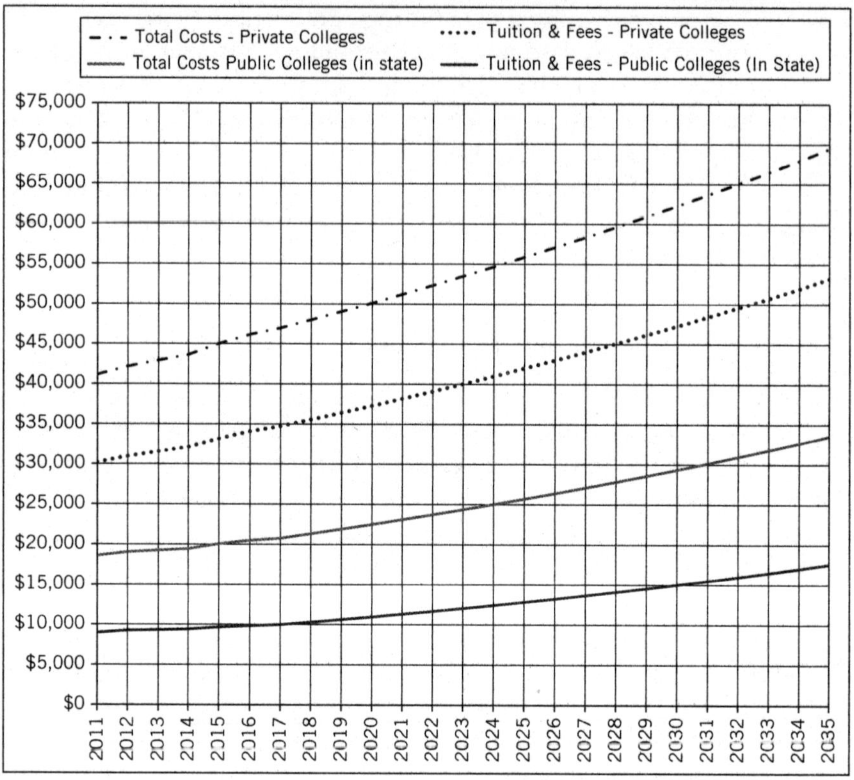

of the key components of paying for a college education. These components usually include some combination of personal savings, Section 529 plans,[3] Coverdell education plans, savings bonds, financial aid (such as federal grants, loans, and scholarships), and education tax credits. I will cover each of these in this chapter after sharing the following client story with you. Please note that I have

[3]529 Plans are subject to certain restrictions. By investing in a plan outside your state residence, you may lose available state tax benefits. 529 plans are subject to enrollment, maintenance, administration/management fees, and expenses. If you make a withdrawal for any other reason, the earnings portion of the withdrawal will be subject to both state and federal income tax and a 10% federal tax penalty. As with any investment, it's important to fully consider the plan's objectives, risks, charges, and expenses before investing. Units of the 529 plan investment options are municipal securities and may be subject to market value fluctuation. Before investing in a state-specific 529 plan, you should compare your own state's qualified tuition program and any state tax or other advantages it may provide.

used, for the purpose of this example, tax laws as they would apply in 2018 and not necessarily the tax laws that would have applied at the time period of the story. I have done this to simplify the facts and to make it more relevant to you under the current tax system.

Case Study: How *Not* Saving for Your Child's Education Can Ruin Your Finances – and Your Child's

About 30 years ago, a young couple named Kathy and Bill came to my office to have their income tax return prepared. During the interview, I asked whether they had any dependents that we could claim on their tax return. They both looked at each other and smiled and then turned to me at the same time and said "we have a dependent on the way." Kathy was four months pregnant. I immediately congratulated them, and then I told them they needed to start saving now for their child's college education. They both laughed at my suggestion; they thought I was joking. I replied that it is never too early to start saving for a child's education, and I recommended that they establish a Section 529 plan before the end of the year.

They both lived and worked in New York City and qualified to contribute to a New York State 529 Educational Savings Program. New York State allowed them both a $5,000 deduction against their New York State taxable income, which would have given them the added advantage of a $10,000 New York State and City tax deduction. This would translate into at least a $1,200 state and city income tax savings (based on 12% tax rate). Therefore, they could have set aside $10,000 for their child's education, which would have cost them only $8,800 after the tax savings. The contribution to a 529 Plan for federal purposes is always made in after-tax dollars. I further explained to them that the entire distribution, including any gain they earn from this 529 Plan over the next 18 years or longer, would be distributed *tax-free* if they used it to pay for qualified higher education expenses. That is right: there can be both a tax break for putting money into the plan up front *and* tax-free income when you take it out to pay for college. However, although they appreciated my advice, they felt it was too early to start saving: they said they needed the money to pay for their child's new bedroom set, clothing, and other items. In sum, they said they could not afford to do it this year, but they would start next year.

Kathy was a school teacher and earned a modest salary, but she had great benefits with a lot of vacation time. Bill was an electronics salesman and his salary was based mostly on commissions from his sales. His income varied widely from year to year, and he did not have much in terms of employee benefits from this job.

Every year during tax season, I met with them and again reminded them of the advantages of planning and preparing for their child's college education costs. But every year, they always had an excuse for why they were not able to set the money aside, even though they were losing out on the many tax benefits available. They had to set their priorities based on what was most important to them at that time. They always chose to satisfy their *immediate wants* and not set aside money for their *future needs*. Every year that Bill earned a nice bonus, this money went toward things like vacations, new cars, furniture, remodeling their home, and a new built-in pool in the backyard. They always justified their spending with the pleasure of immediate gratification they experienced.

The days, the months, and the years went by, and then it was time for their son Billy to start looking at colleges. Billy had just turned 16, started studying for his SAT exam, and was very excited about starting his junior year of high school. Billy was interested in medicine and told his parents he wanted to become a doctor. Kathy and Bill were very excited and had never seen their son more motivated and eager about school. The three of them spent the afternoon doing Google searches about what colleges would be best to attend to prepare him for becoming a doctor. When they saw what the average cost was, they were in shock: $32,000 to $52,000 per year seemed to be the price range for a private college, and $15,000 to $25,000 a year for a public in-state college. Although this troubled Kathy and Bill, they did not want to let Billy know they were concerned.

For the next two years, Billy hit the books and brought his grade point average from 82 to 87. He studied long and hard for the SAT exam and was able to score a 1900. He applied to a dozen schools that he believed had a reasonable chance of accepting him. Some were private and some were public. He was also committed to going away to school and did not want to apply to any local colleges. From November through April, Billy rushed to the mailbox after school each day to see if he had received any college acceptance letters.

Of the twelve schools he applied to, he was rejected from six of his choices, accepted to four, and wait-listed at two. Of all the schools he visited, he fell in love with Quinnipiac University in Connecticut, but this was one of the two schools at which he was wait-listed. He and his parents visited the schools and did further research on the six college choices that were still a possibility for him. Two of the schools were public. One was in New Jersey, and the tuition with room and board would have been about $25,000. The other was a New York state school (SUNY) that would have cost about $7,000 per year.

Although both of these schools would have provided Billy with a top-rate education, he and his parents were not completely satisfied. They felt more comfortable with a private education with small class sizes, a beautiful campus, and comfortable dorms. The other two private schools he was accepted to would have cost $40,000, and he had been awarded a $15,000 merit scholarship; still, this would have cost approximately $25,000 per year.

It was April 28 and there were only two days left before the big decision needed to be made. It was on this date that the letter came from Quinnipiac that notified Billy he had moved from the wait list to the acceptance list. Billy was extremely excited, and he could not wait to tell his parents the great news. The only problem was that this school cost more than $50,000 per year, and there was no mention of a scholarship in the letter.

His parents were overjoyed when they saw how excited their son was. When Billy said "I am going to Quinnipiac: this was always my first choice," his parents showed their excitement and acceptance, but inside their heads they were thinking, *How in the world are we going to pay for this?*

Later that evening, Kathy and Bill were lying in bed, discussing their concern about how they were going to pay for this education. Bill realized they would never qualify for financial aid, because their combined income was just over $100,000. Kathy looked at their savings and realized that they did not even have enough money available to cover the first semester. They both agreed that they should have listened to my advice 18 years ago, before Billy was even born. But now it was too late, and they had to make a difficult choice: *Do we take away our son's first-choice college and send him to a public college, which will cost a fraction of the price?* Of course, they made the decision to give Billy what he wanted and not what they could afford.

Kathy said she would be able to get a $50,000 loan from her 401(k) plan at work. Bill agreed that would get them through the first year; they would figure out a plan for the second year later.

By the time the second year came, they had to max out their credit cards to get the money needed to pay that year's tuition. They were having a very difficult time paying their bills and making the minimum payments on their credit cards, as well as the 401(k) loan. They did not want Billy to take out any student loans of his own, and they did not apply for any government-based student loan programs. They were confused about how these loans worked, so they simply chose to ignore any of the options available.

When they looked over their finances, they realized that their main asset was their home and that they had more than $250,000 in equity just sitting there, which they could access. They immediately applied for a home-equity loan and were approved for a $150,000 loan. They used these funds to get through the next two years of college and to catch up with some other bills on which they had fallen behind. To make matters worse, during Billy's fourth year of college, Kathy had a nervous breakdown and made the decision that she could not go back to her full-time job.

Kathy was notified by her personnel department that she was required to pay back the $50,000 401(k) loan within 30 days of her last day of employment or it would be deemed an early distribution. They simply had no funds available and nowhere else they could borrow from. When tax time came, they owed $20,000 in taxes plus a $5,000 early withdrawal penalty to the IRS. What made matters worse was that this happened in 2009, when the real estate market crashed.

Billy graduated college, but he was not able to go to medical school, because his grades were not high enough for him to even consider applying. After six months of interviewing, he was able to get an entry-level job working in the administrative department of a local hospital.

In the meantime, the recession continued to cause financial strain to the family, since Bill did not get his usual bonus for two years due to low sales volume. Bill and Kathy were in a financial mess, and they knew they needed to do something drastic to straighten out their finances and minimize the stress in their lives. So they made the difficult but necessary decision to sell their house. Even with the drop in real estate values, they were able to sell their home, eliminate all of their debt, and still have about $20,000 in cash left over.

They moved into a small rental apartment and were able to significantly minimize their monthly expenses. They were able to live off Bill's salary and Kathy's new part-time job.

This story could have had a much happier ending if they had simply started a college savings plan early on and consulted with me before making so many other financial mistakes in the process. They made almost every financial mistake possible throughout Billy's first 22 years of life. To be financially responsible and achieve and maintain financial independence, you need to *forego your short-term wants,* and then *plan and prepare for your family's long-term needs.*

Do not make the same mistakes these parents made. Start planning for your child's education as soon as possible. Be open to your children about financial decisions and what consequences these decisions will have on the family's future. Your family's financial situation is not a topic that needs to be kept private; instead, it should be shared and understood by all of your family members. Understanding the difference between your family's needs and your family's wants involves the participation of you, your spouse, and your children. Making the right choices and fully understanding the consequence of these actions is a must. Taking advantage of college savings programs will help you get there more easily. Understanding how scholarships, government grants, and student loans can help is essential. Taking advantage of all the special tax breaks and credits that may help subsidize the cost of college is a must. This chapter will provide you with what it takes to get not only your children, but you and your spouse through the burden and stress of paying for a college education.

Conducting a "Needs Analysis" for Your Children's College Educations

The starting point for planning to pay for education is performing an education "needs analysis." Before creating an educational funding plan, you must first determine your estimated needs. For each of your children that you expect will be attending college, you will need to estimate his or her total cost for higher education. This estimate should include their tuition, fees, books, supplies, equipment, tutoring, transportation, and possible extracurricular activities. If you believe your child will be going away to school, you will also need to estimate the added room and board, meal plans, and travel costs. Once you have estimated what this cost may be per year in today's dollars, you will need to adjust this for the expected education inflation rate and determine this for each year they will be attending college.

If you are like most parents, saving for your child's education is a major financial concern. Given the fact that the current cost of a four-year college education could be well into the six figures for certain colleges and universities, this will most likely cost you a lot more than you have anticipated. I would recommend utilizing the various college funding calculators provided at http://calcxml.com/english.htm.

For the purpose of this example, you want to click on "How much should I be saving for college?" and you will need to answer the following questions.

- What is the current age of your child?
- What age do you expect your child to start college?
- How many years do you expect your child will be attending college?
- What is the current annual cost for attending the college of your child's choice?
- What is the expected rate of inflation for college costs?
- How much money do you currently have saved and earmarked for this purpose?
- What is your expected before-tax return on your investments during this time frame?
- What is your marginal tax bracket?
- What is your expected annual percentage increase in income?

After inputting your own personal information into the college funding calculator, you will be able to determine how much money you will need to save each month (or the lump sum you need now) to cover the total cost of your child's future college education needs.

Let us walk through an example together, answering each of the questions above as follows:

- What is the current age of your child? (6 years old)
- What age do you expect your child to start college? (18 years old)
- How many years do you expect your child will be attending college? (4 years)
- What is the current annual cost for attending the college of your child's choice? ($17,000)
- What is the expected rate of inflation for college costs? (5%)
- How much money do you currently have saved and earmarked for this purpose? ($10,000)
- What is your expected before-tax return on your investments during this time frame? (8%)[4]
- What is your marginal tax bracket? (24%)

---

[4]The rates of return shown above are purely hypothetical and do not represent the performance of any individual investment or portfolio of investments. They are for

- What is your expected annual percentage increase in income? (0%)

After you input all of the information above, click calculate to get the following results:

- You will need to save $131,586 by the time your child goes to college.
- To meet this goal, you will need to either invest a lump sum now of $49,230 or you will need to save and invest $385 per month.

And that is for only *one* child.

Fortunately, the sooner you start to save, the more manageable this financial goal becomes. For most people, this calculation becomes a reality check and a rude awakening. Unfortunately, most parents are not prepared when this day comes, and they put their children and themselves into debt (as Kathy and Bill did, in the case study at the beginning of this chapter). This does not have to be the case for you and your family. If you apply the powerful education planning strategies discussed in this chapter, you can and will be prepared.

By taking full advantage of the tax savings offered through Section 529 "qualified tuition plans," Coverdell Education Savings Accounts, and savings bonds, you can accumulate the money you will need much more rapidly and possibly on a tax-free basis. Understanding all of the government grants and loans available and how to qualify for them may go a long way in reducing your costs. If you encourage your children to do well in high school, they may qualify for merit scholarships and other awards. Lastly, if you qualify, you may be eligible for special tax breaks and credits in the years that your children are attending college and you are paying for their college costs.

Therefore, there are numerous strategies you can use to make this process much more affordable. You should seriously consider state and city colleges and universities that provide a top-rated

illustrative purposes only and should not be used to predict future product performance. Specific rates of return, especially for extended time periods, will vary over time. There is also a higher degree of risk associated with investments that offer the potential for higher rates of return. You should consult with your representative before making any investment decision.

Exhibit 7.2   Comparison of Education Savings: Tax-Deferred, Tax-Exempt, and Taxable Plans

Attribute	Section 529 Plan[5]	UGMA/UTMA	Coverdell Education Savings Account	US Savings Bonds
Federal taxation of account earnings	Tax-deferred and then tax-exempt when used for qualified education expenses (including elementary or secondary education with a cap of $10,000 per child per year)	Taxable each year	Tax-deferred and then tax-exempt when used for qualified education expenses (including elementary or secondary education)	Tax-exempt when used for qualified higher education expenses
Income limits	None	None	Phases out at $95,000 to $110,000 for single filers, head of households, and married filing separately, and $190,000 to $220,000 for married filing jointly	Inflation adjusted income limits apply. Phases out at $79,700 to $94,700 for single and head of households filers and $119,550 to $149,550 for married filing jointly filers
Control of assets	The account owner retains control of assets and can choose to change the beneficiary or revoke the account through a nonqualified withdrawal	Custodian controls the assets until the beneficiary reaches the age of majority	The responsible individual named on the account controls assets, which must be used for the benefit of the named minor. Assets will be transferred to the beneficiary at age 30	The account owner retains control of assets and can choose to change the beneficiary or redeem the bond
Ability to change beneficiary	Can be changed to a qualified family member of the current beneficiary without adverse federal tax consequences	No	Can be changed to a member of the family of the current beneficiary if the right to do so is established when the account is opened	Can be changed to a qualified family member of the current beneficiary without adverse federal tax consequences
Penalty for nonqualified withdrawals	Subject to federal and possibly state income tax and a 10% penalty on earnings	Subject to federal income tax each year, no penalty applies. Withdrawals can be for any purpose if used by the child.	Subject to federal and possibly state income tax and a 10% penalty on earnings	Subject to federal income tax on earnings, no penalty applies
Gift tax treatment (2018 amounts)	Gifts of up to $75,000 ($150,000 for married couples) qualify for federal gift tax exclusion, provided no other gifts are given to the beneficiary over the following five years.	Qualified for the annual $15,000 gift tax exclusion	Qualified for the annual $15,000 gift tax exclusion	Qualified for the annual $15,000 gift tax exclusion

[5]See footnote 3.

at much more affordable prices. A college education is extremely valuable, but you must fully weigh the benefits and compare them to the cost. As I have said throughout this book, you must always be able to distinguish between your *needs* and your *wants*. Since a college education can be considered a *need* for many people, you then must ask yourself if there is a less costly college-selection alternative. Appropriately planning how to pay for your child's education is one of the keys to achieving and maintaining financial independence.

Strategies for Saving Money for College Education

Here are four of the most commonly used strategies for saving money for a college education:

1. Section 529 educational savings programs
2. Uniform Gifts/Transfers to Minors Act (UGMA/UTMA) account
3. Coverdell Education Savings Accounts
4. US savings bonds

Each has distinct advantages, as well as some drawbacks. Understanding how each of these education savings techniques works will go a long way to helping you decide which approach (or combination of approaches) would work best for your individual circumstances. Exhibit 7.2 provides a detailed comparison of these four options, based on 2018 tax rules, followed by a detailed discussion of each of these four strategies, plus a few more you might consider.

Section 529 Plans (Qualified Tuition Programs)[6]

IRS Code Section 529 was created in 1996 with the passage of the Small Business Job Protection Act. This was the birth of *qualified tuition programs (QTPs)*, commonly referred to as *529 plans*, which were specifically designed to help people save and ultimately pay for college education on a federal tax-free basis. Investment assets held within a 529 plan account accumulate on a tax-deferred basis. Contributions are made with after-tax dollars at the federal level. Withdrawals of principal and accumulated earnings are free from federal income tax, if you use them for qualified education expenses at any eligible postsecondary educational or vocational institution

---

[6]See footnote 3.

in the United States. Some states also allow you a tax-deductible contribution for state income tax purposes, if you establish your 529 plan in that state's sponsored program.

Qualified expenses generally include:

- Tuition
- Room and board
- Books and supplies
- Special needs services relating to enrollment at a qualified institution

As of January 1, 2018, a significant change in the tax law expanded availability for the use of 529 educational savings plans to include levels of education other than college. *These education savings plans can now be used for private schools, including kindergarten through high school.* A $10,000 limit applies annually on a per-student basis, rather than on a per-account basis. This limit does not apply to undergraduate and graduate tuition.

If utilizing a 529 plan to pay for K–12, you must check with your state to ensure that these distributions will also be tax-free at the state level. Many states that provide a state tax deduction for the contribution are currently not following the same rules as the federal government on these distributions. For example, petitions have been filed with New York State, urging it to conform to the federal tax law on this issue. When this book went to print, the federal distributions would be tax-free, but the full amount would be subject to New York State income tax. Therefore, you should not use qualified New York State approved plans to cover K–12, until New York State agrees to conform to federal tax law. You can, of course, continue to use these plans to pay for higher education.

You can open a 529 qualified tuition program account for your children, your grandchildren, or anyone who is a US citizen or legal US resident. There are no age or family relationship limitations on 529 plan beneficiaries. In fact, you can even open an account naming yourself as the beneficiary to help with your own education expenses.

Exhibit 7.3 shows how your earnings can grow on a tax-free basis. First, Exhibit 7.3 shows the difference between investing $10,000 in a taxable account and a tax-exempt account, with subsequent investments of $10,000 at the beginning of each year for 18 years. This example also assumes an 8% annual rate of return with a 40% marginal tax rate.[7] This illustration demonstrates the possible

---

[7]See footnote 4.

Exhibit 7.3 Growth of Savings Invested in a Tax-Free 529 Plan Versus a Taxable Savings Account[8]

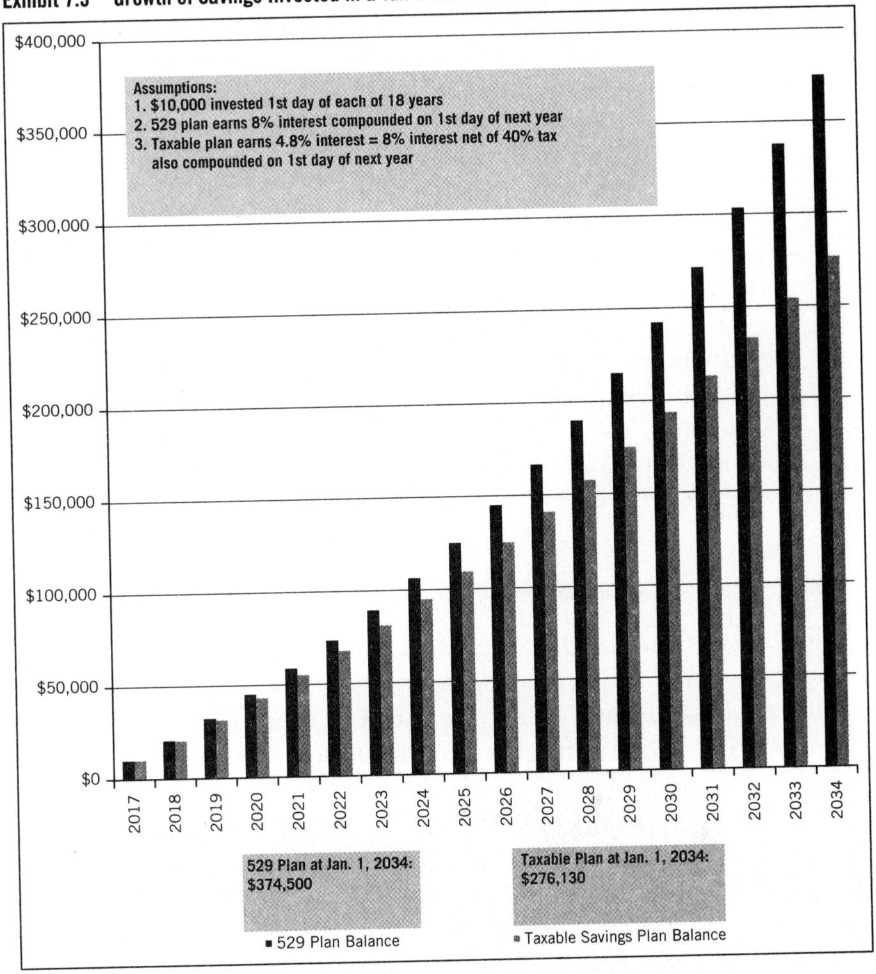
$400,000
$350,000
$300,000
$250,000
$200,000
$150,000
$100,000
$50,000
$0
Assumptions:
1. $10,000 invested 1st day of each of 18 years
2. 529 plan earns 8% interest compounded on 1st day of next year
3. Taxable plan earns 4.8% interest = 8% interest net of 40% tax also compounded on 1st day of next year
2017
2018
2019
2020
2021
2022
2023
2024
2025
2026
2027
2028
2029
2030
2031
2032
2033
2034
529 Plan at Jan. 1, 2034: $374,500
Taxable Plan at Jan. 1, 2034: $276,130
529 Plan Balance
Taxable Savings Plan Balance

value of tax-exempt earnings over time through a 529 education savings plan. As you can see, for the same amount of money invested, *you could earn almost $100,000 more* over 18 years when you invest in the tax-free 529 plan.

As you evaluate various college savings options, you should consider the control and tax advantages you have with each type of plan; for example:

- **Control:** With a section 529 plan, you are able to exercise control over who the ultimate beneficiary of these funds will be,

[8]See footnote 4.

and you can even terminate the account if you wish. There-fore, if your firstborn decides not to go to college and you have invested in a 529 plan in his name, you can transfer the funds to your second child, or you can simply terminate the plan. If you do not want your beneficiary to have the ultimate con-trol of these funds, then a 529 plan may be the right choice for you, as it clearly gives you flexibility.

- **Tax advantages:** A 529 plan offers a variety of noteworthy tax advantages, such as no income tax on earnings, tax-free with-drawals for qualified educational purposes, accelerated federal gifting and estate tax benefits, and, in some cases, state tax deductions. This is perhaps one of the most tax-effective strate-gies for saving and paying for education. There are no income limitations as to who can establish an account. High-income earners can take full advantage of these tax benefits. *This is my number-one recommended strategy for an education savings plan.*[9]

Uniform Gifts to Minors Act and Uniform Transfers to Minors Act[10] *(UGMA/UTMA)*

The Uniform Gifts to Minors Act (UGMA) and Uniform Transfers to Minors Act (UTMA) accounts allow your children to invest for their college education by holding the funds in their own accounts. Any income generated from this account will now be subject to the new "kiddie tax" rules.

These accounts provide you with a method to transfer assets out of your name and into that of a minor, without having to establish a trust (which can be expensive). Please note that these transfers are considered completed gifts and may require the donor (the person that gave the gift) to file a gift tax return.

UGMA and UTMA accounts were not created specifically as sav-ings vehicles for college, but many parents use them for this purpose because these assets typically become available to the minor when they are in the early years of college.

The accounts are managed by a custodian – usually a parent, grandparent, relative, or friend. Individuals can make an irrevocable transfer for any amount to these accounts as a gift to the minor. In the event that the custodian passes away before the child reaches major-ity (i.e., is considered an adult by state law, which varies from state to

---

[9]See footnote 3.

[10]See footnote 3.

state between ages 18 and 21), the account may then be includable in the taxable estate of the donor (i.e., the custodian).

The key difference between UGMA and UTMA accounts is that UTMA law allows more flexibility with the type of investments that can be included in the account. The UGMA law limits the type of investments that can be held in these accounts to bank deposits, securities (stocks, bonds, mutual funds), and insurance policies.

The main income-tax advantage to transferring these assets to a child used to be that all the income earned on these investments would be subject to tax at the child's significantly lower marginal tax rate. However, the IRS created a "kiddie tax" that significantly reduced the tax advantage of establishing these accounts. It was specifically created to close this tax loophole and to discourage this type of tax-saving strategy. This tax may apply to your child if he or she has investment income (such as interest, dividends, and capital gains).

The Tax Cuts and Jobs Act of 2017 *simplifies the "kiddie tax" by effectively applying ordinary and capital gains rates applicable to trusts and estates to the net unearned income of a child. Thus, as under present law, taxable income attributable to earned income is taxed according to an unmarried taxpayers' brackets and rates. Taxable income attributable to net unearned income is taxed according to the brackets applicable to trusts and estates, with respect to both ordinary income and income taxed at preferential rates. Thus, under the provision, the child's tax is unaffected by the tax situation of the child's parent or the unearned income of any siblings.* This will make UGMA/UTMA accounts even more undesirable as a tool for saving for education.

The kiddie tax applies not only to children younger than age 19, but also to children who are full-time students ages 19 to 23 and do not have earned income exceeding half of their own support.

Another major disadvantage to these types of accounts is that all assets transferred under UGMA and UTMA laws represent an irrevocable gift (transfer). Upon reaching the age of majority under the state UGMA/UTMA laws, the child gains control of the assets and may use them any way he or she wants. For example, if little Suzie decides to jump on the back of her boyfriend's motorcycle on her eighteenth birthday and head to California to start a new life, she can take the money with her, because she is no longer considered a minor.

Yet another major potential disadvantage of UGMA or UTMA accounts is that they may affect the amount of financial aid your child receives. This is discussed further in the government grants and loans section of this chapter.

As a general rule, I discourage people from using UGMA or UTMA accounts as a method of saving for a child's education. The minimal tax savings you may achieve is usually not worth the potential pitfalls. If you want to retain control of the assets, take advantage of tax-deferred savings and qualified tax-free withdrawals, and avoid jeopardizing any potential financial aid, you should avoid these types of accounts. Instead, use one or more of the other education-saving vehicles covered in this chapter.

If you do use either a UGMA or UTMA account, you should seriously consider spending down the account (instead of using your own money) for the benefit of your children for such expenses as their high school tuition, computers, and whatever else they may ask for. You will then have extra funds of your own available to fund a Section 529 plan.

Coverdell Education Savings Accounts

A Coverdell Education Savings Account (ESA, formerly known as an Education Individual Retirement Account) is a tax-advantaged educational savings account designed specifically to encourage savings to cover future education costs. These accounts can be used to pay for elementary education, secondary education, and college costs, such as tuition, books, uniforms, and other education-related expenses.

The tax treatment of a Coverdell ESA is similar to the Section 529 plan with some differences. Similar to a 529 plan, Coverdell ESAs allow your investments to grow tax-deferred, and the distributions can be tax-free for qualified education expenses at a qualified institution.

A Coverdell ESA compliments a 529 plan when saving for a private elementary, high school, or college education.

The key features of a Coverdell Education Savings Account include the following:

- There are income limitations for the donor, which may affect the ability to make contributions into a Coverdell ESA. If you are a single individual, head of household, or married taxpayer filing separately, you can make the full contribution if your income is below $95,000, and then it is phased out through $110,000. A married couple filing jointly can make a full contribution if their income level is below $190,000 and then it is phased out through $220,000. The money held in a Coverdell ESA account is not considered part of your child's assets when applying for federal financial aid, as long as your child is listed as the *beneficiary* and not as the *account owner.*

- The custodian of a Coverdell ESA account (i.e., you, the parent) can *change the named beneficiary without incurring taxes or penalties,* as long as the new beneficiary is an eligible family member of the previous beneficiary.
- Coverdell ESAs have an annual contribution limit of $2,000 per child; therefore, the use of a Coverdell is limited. This $2,000 annual contribution limit has been extended permanently under the American Taxpayer Relief Act of 2012.
- Coverdell ESAs allow almost any type of investment to be held, including stocks, bonds, and mutual funds.
- The funds in a Coverdell ESA must be used for qualified education expenses by the time the designated beneficiary is 30 years old. Alternatively, you can change beneficiaries to another family member younger than the age of 30 in order to avoid taxes and penalties before that time comes.
- Coverdell ESAs allow distributions on a tax-free basis for qualified elementary and secondary school expenses and colleges and universities.
- If distributions are taken from a Coverdell ESA, and they are not used for qualified education expenses, then any gain from these distributions would be subject to federal and state taxes, as well as a 10% IRS penalty.

Try to fit a Coverdell ESA into your overall education savings strategy. If you do not qualify to contribute to an ESA account because of the income limits, encourage other family members to do so, assuming they qualify. For example, if your child gets a summer job, you can invest the extra cash he or she earns into an ESA account (based on your child's income level). Although this education tax saving break is limited, everything you do in the aggregate will make a difference in the long run.

Savings Bonds

US savings bonds are yet another popular way of saving for college. They offer a low rate of return on your investment, but they are also low risk. For example, if you purchased $1,000 in series EE bonds or series I bonds between May 1 and October 31, 2017, the rate would have been 0.10% and 1.96% respectively. The series EE bonds would have earned only $1 and the series I bonds would have earned only $19.60 over a one-year period, which is not an attractive rate of return, especially when you consider the loss of purchasing power due to inflation.

However, savings bonds are considered a safe investment, because they are backed by the full faith and credit of the US government. Both the principal and earned interest is safe, which means you cannot *lose* money due to market changes, because US savings bonds are not considered marketable securities. US savings bonds are registered with the US Treasury Department; therefore, you can easily replace them if you lose them or they are stolen or destroyed. This is in contrast to bearer bonds, which are almost equivalent to having cash in that they are not registered to anyone; possessing them means you own them. Anyone who presents bearer bonds to a bank, even if they were stolen, can convert them to cash at any time. You would be out of luck if you lost your bearer bonds.

Through a special Education Savings Bond Program, interest on certain savings bonds is tax-free when you use them to pay for qualified higher education expenses. The US savings bonds that qualify for this tax-free treatment include series EE bonds issued after December 31, 1989, and all series I bonds.

You must also be very careful and make sure you meet the following requirements for this tax-free treatment.

- The bond owner (you) must be at least 24 years old on the bond issue date (the first day of the month in which the bonds were purchased).
- Parents can purchase bonds for their children, but the bonds must be registered in the parents' name.
- The child cannot be listed as a co-owner, but the child can be listed as a beneficiary.
- You can also purchase bonds for your own education, in which case the bonds must be registered in your own name.

Currently, there is an annual purchase limit of $10,000 per Social Security Number for Series EE Bonds and $10,000 for Series I Bonds. The purchase limit for Series I Bonds is not affected by purchases of series EE Bonds; these purchase limits are independent of one another.

There are, of course, some major advantages and disadvantages to purchasing qualified Series EE and I US Savings Bonds. First, let us look at the advantages:

- You don't need to open an account with a financial institution, because US savings bonds are registered and issued by the US Treasury Department. You can walk into almost any bank, credit union, or savings and loan to buy US savings bonds. You can now also get savings bonds online, directly from the US Treasury, at treasurydirect.gov.
- You can buy savings bonds for as little as $25, which makes them easily affordable for most people.
- The interest on these bonds is always exempt from state and local income tax and may be fully exempt from federal income taxes when the bonds are used for qualified college expenses.

Now for the disadvantages:

- You are locking yourself into a very low rate of return, which most likely will not keep pace with inflation; this is especially true with Series EE Bonds. With interest rates at historical lows, the rate of return currently offered by these bonds does not make them an attractive choice. This is the biggest disadvantage; therefore, you need to weigh this low return against the safety and security of knowing they are government-guaranteed obligations.
- The exemption from paying federal income taxes when you use savings bonds to pay for college expenses is more restricted than some of the other alternatives: Series EE and I Bonds are only exempt from taxation when they are used for tuition, not room, board, or books.
- There is a phase-out for excluding a US Savings Bond from taxes for qualified education purposes. For 2018, if you (as the taxpayer holding the bonds) file your taxes as single or head of household, there is an income phase-out for adjusted gross income between $79,700 and $94,700; if you are married and filing jointly, the income phase out for adjusted gross income is between $119,550 and $149,550. It may completely eliminate the tax advantage of using US savings bonds as a vehicle for saving for college if your income reaches these levels in the year you need the funds.

For all the above reasons, although savings bonds are a popular way of saving for college, it is not one of my favorites, especially for potentially high-income earners.

Roth Individual Retirement Accounts

I know what you are thinking: why are Roth IRAs included in this chapter as a strategy for saving money to pay for college? The simple answer to this question is that although Roth IRAs were not established as an education savings vehicle, they can serve that purpose if you use it in the right way.

Let us assume your son or daughter has been working at a part-time job and has earned $7,500 or more over the year. What would be the best use for this money? I am sure your child is thinking video games or designer jeans, but that is not the correct answer, of course.

The best use for this money is to fund a Roth IRA for $5,500 and a Coverdell Education Savings Account for $2,000. The argument for doing this is even stronger if your income level does not allow *you* to contribute to these accounts on your own, but your child would qualify based on his or her level of income. I have already covered the many benefits of establishing a Coverdell Education Savings Account, so now I am going to focus on the Roth IRA.

Let us also assume your child managed to save $5,500 per year from his earned income for five years in a Roth IRA and now is in his third or fourth year of college. Let us also assume that this (5 years × $5,500) $27,500 is now worth $45,000 because of some good investment choices.[11] Your child would be able to take a distribution from this account to cover the cost of undergraduate or graduate school. Assuming he took the full $45,000 out in one year, only $17,500 ($45,000 less $27,500) of this amount would be subject to tax. Moreover, this income is subject to tax *at your child's low tax rate*, which could be as low as 0%, if it is structured properly (the child must provide more than 50% of his or her own support).

Although the IRS levies a 10% penalty if you withdraw money from a retirement account before you are 59 1/2 years old, there is an exception to this penalty if you use that distribution to pay for qualified higher education costs. Therefore, this amount would not be subject to this penalty. Once again, Roth accounts were not designed

---

[11] See footnote 4.

to cover higher education expenses, but you can clearly use them as an additional strategy for saving for college.

Furthermore, if your child does not need the funds to cover higher education expenses, it is still a benefit for your child to have this money invested in a tax-free retirement account before he even graduates from college. This would give your child an amazing start and advantage to achieving and reaching his or her own financial independence. I always encourage children and their parents to start saving for retirement as soon as possible.

Government Grants and Loans

When you consider the multitude of options and opportunities available for saving and paying for college education, the subject of government grants and loans probably has the most ambiguity associated with it. The US Department of Education's National Center for Education Statistics conducts a study each year that reveals selected findings regarding student financial aid. You can download the full report at nces.ed.gov/programs/coe. These findings should give you some idea of the type and sources of financial aid that may be available.

Many families expect much more from financial aid than they will receive. It is important to note that less than half of all students receive grants and scholarships. Less than 0.3% receive enough for a "free ride," so do not expect to go to college without paying for it.

According to a Sallie Mae report, for the 2016/17 school year, only 47% of families received *needs-based grants*, which averaged $7,722. On average, these grants covered 15% of costs for a private school, 13% of a four-year public school, and 23% of a two-year public school.

This same report indicated that 49% of families received *merit-based scholarships*, which averaged $9,712. On average, these scholarships covered 25% of private school, 18% of four-year public school, and 12% of two-year public school.

A very exciting development occurred in New York State recently, which may now make it possible for New Yorkers to attend college free of charge. This in fact may become a trend in the future that will expand free public school education to include colleges and universities. On April 8, 2017, it was announced that Governor Andrew M. Cuomo's Excelsior Scholarship, a program that is the first of its kind in the nation, will provide tuition-free college at New York's public colleges and universities to families making up to $125,000 a year. The plan will be phased in over three years, which began for New Yorkers making up to $100,000 annually in the fall of 2017, $110,000 in 2018, and $125,000 in 2019. The benefit is only available to students who are New York residents, and they are obligated to remain New York residents after graduation for the same number of years the Excelsior Scholarship award applied. The Budget additionally includes $8 million to provide open educational resources, including e-books, to students at SUNY and CUNY colleges to help defray the prohibitive cost of textbooks. For more details on this program, please visit www.suny.edu. You should also check your own resident state's educational website to see if they have any plans to introduce a similar program in the future.

It is also very important to understand how the federal government and institutions calculate how much aid they provide students, whether in the form of grants, federal loans, or work study. For the most part, the formula to determine the amount of need for financial aid will factor in your family's ability to pay over time. This is expressed as an *expected family contribution*. If there is a gap between the cost of attendance at a school and the expected family contribution, a financial aid offer may be made by the school.

According to the US Department of Education, the Expected Family Contribution (EFC) is *not* the amount of money your family will have to pay for college, nor is it the amount of federal student aid you will receive. It is a number used by the student's school to calculate how much financial aid the student is eligible to receive by law.

For a dependent student, the 2018–2019 EFC Formula Guide includes the following essential factors in the expected family contribution calculation:

- What you (the parents) currently earn
- What your child (the student) currently earns
- What the parent owns
- What the student owns directly

The Studentaid.ed.gov website further advises the Expected Family Contribution is calculated according to a formula established by law. Your family's taxed and untaxed income, assets, and benefits (such as unemployment or Social Security) all are considered as well as family size and number of family members who will be attending college or career school during the year.

The most heavily weighed factors in evaluating eligibility for financial aid is current income received by the parent or child and then whether the parent or the child has control over financial assets. It is vital to understand the significance and importance that these key factors play in determining financial aid. You should consider these factors when you are selecting the college savings vehicles you plan to use, as well as how you plan to hold ownership to these assets.

Understanding what effect your overall savings will have on your chances of receiving financial aid is critical to assessing your additional needs. There are several types of financial aid including federal, state, and institutional. Federal aid is the most widely used form of assistance available to college students. To be considered for federal aid, a student must complete the financial aid Free Application for Federal Student Aid (FAFSA) forms.

Exhibit 7.4 provides the ranges of parental and student income and assets that are used to calculate the annual expected family contribution for any given student. Once the expected family contribution has been determined, a college's or university's financial aid officer subtracts it from that institution's cost for attending their college or university, in order to determine the annual financial need. Exhibit 7.4 reveals that *income* is more heavily factored in the calculation than *assets,* and that *student* income and assets are factored in more heavily than his or her parents' income and assets. Exhibit 7.4 also highlights the impact that some of the most common college saving vehicles will have on your child's ability to qualify for financial aid.

Exhibit 7.4   Factors Used in Calculating the Annual Expected Family Contribution for Financial Aid Purposes

	Parents	Students
Income	22% to 47% of Adjusted Available Income (AAI) above the protected amount*	50% of Available Income (AI) over protected amount of $6,570
Assets	0% to 5.64% of assets above the protected amount:	20% of assets held in student's name, including:
	• Mutual funds • Securities • Bank accounts, CDs • 529 savings plans where the account owner is the parent(s)	• UGMA/UTMA accounts not held in a 529 plan • Minor trusts not held in a 529 plan • Savings bonds (in student's name)

*Protected amount for parents is dependent upon a number of factors, including household size and number of students in college.

Source: This information is based on the US Department of Education's Federal Student Aid Expected Family Contribution Formula Guide, 2018–2019.

The following assets are not considered when determining the child's financial needs:

- All retirement accounts
- Home equity in a primary residence
- Annuities
- Cash value of life insurance

Many parents believe that investing for college will hurt their children's chances for financial aid. In reality, family income counts much more than assets in the formula that determines the financial aid awarded.

However, Exhibit 7.4 does not take into consideration withdrawals from a 529 plan, which can have a direct effect on a student's financial profile for the purpose of determining expected family contribution and therefore can affect the extent of that student's financial aid package. **The significant differences in determining the effect of a 529 plan withdrawal is whether the 529 plan is a *prepaid tuition plan* or a *college savings plan.***

529 prepaid tuition plans commonly allow you to purchase units or credits at a participating college or university, which can then be applied toward future tuition payments. In some situations, they can be used to cover the cost of room and board. The majority of these plans sponsored by the state have residency requirements. Investments in prepaid tuition plans are also sometimes guaranteed by the sponsoring state government.

529 college savings plans generally allow you to establish an account for a beneficiary for the purpose of paying the beneficiary's qualified educational costs. As the account holder, you typically have several investment choices for your contributions in the 529 savings plan, which typically include stock and bond mutual funds as well as money market funds. Some also offer age-based portfolios. You can usually use the distributions from 529 savings plans at any US college or university and effective January 1, 2018, this has now been expanded to include private kindergarten through high school (with limitations). Your beneficiary has the flexibility of choosing any college or university he or she gets accepted to, in any state. It is important to note that the investments in these 529 savings plans are not guaranteed by state governments.

Prepaid 529 plans are treated differently than 529 savings plans, because *prepaid 529 plans are considered resources* and *529 savings plans are considered assets.* This distinction is significant and extremely important to understand. Although assets held in prepaid 529 plans are not considered in the federal student financial aid calculation, the *withdrawals* from these plans will reduce your financial aid eligibility dollar-for-dollar. This means that withdrawals are direct reductions in the amount of financial aid that would have otherwise been available. *This is why you should avoid 529 prepaid plans at all costs if you believe there is a possibility that your child may qualify for financial aid. In this situation, the 529 savings plan would be a much better alternative.* A prepaid 529 Plan might be more suitable if you are a wealthier family and want to lock in today's tuition prices for the future cost of a college education where you may have a legacy and you are confident that your child will be able to attend.

With a 529 savings plan, the portion of the withdrawal that represents a return of your principal contribution is not included as income and therefore would not have a negative effect on eligibility for federal financial aid. Furthermore, the portion of the withdrawal that represents earnings is not included as income to the beneficiary (i.e., your child) or the college saver (i.e., you) as long as you use it to pay for qualified higher education expenses. The key issue to remember is that these withdrawals will not result in a dollar-for-dollar reduction in the amount of financial aid that your child would have otherwise received.

The information in this section provides a basic understanding of the calculations used in determining eligibility for federal student financial aid. For more detailed information regarding the financial aid process, the many different types of financial aid available, and how your particular facts and circumstances may affect the chances of qualifying, visit the following websites:

- www.finaid.org: one of the most comprehensive sources of information about student financial aid
- www.ed.gov: the website for the US Department of Education
- www.fafsa.ed.gov: the Department of Education's website for FAFSA, which provides comprehensive information on federal student aid and allows users to apply online for such aid
- www.studentaid.ed.gov: the website for the Department of Education's Federal Student Aid programs

- www.collegeboard.org: the website for the College Board, a national nonprofit membership association composed of more than 6,000 schools, colleges, universities, and other educational organizations

There are numerous government grant and loan programs. It is important for you to do your research and become thoroughly familiar with these options early when planning for your college funding needs. If you believe you will qualify for some of these programs, you can factor these funds into your college-funding plan. On the other hand, if you believe you will not be entitled to any of these programs because of your income and assets, you will clearly need to focus more on the other college savings programs described in this chapter.

Athletic Scholarships

For those proud parents who may be counting on little Johnny's football skill or Christine's gymnastic abilities to pay their way through college, take a hard look at what your actual chances are of receiving athletic scholarships.

According to the National Collegiate Athletic Association, very few high school athletes earn athletic scholarships. In fact, only about 2% of high school athletes are awarded some form of an athletic scholarship to compete in college. For more information, you can download the NCAA Recruiting Facts Sheet from the NCAA website.

Education Tax Breaks and Credits

During the years your child is attending college, you may qualify for significant tax savings through education tax breaks and credits. Because tax credits can be a dollar-for-dollar reduction in your taxes, I cover this in great detail. The two major education tax credits for higher education are the American Opportunity Tax Credit and the Lifetime Learning Credit.

American Opportunity Tax Credit

To qualify for the American opportunity tax credit in 2018, your family member (student) must be taking at least one-half of the normal course load of a full-time student for the first four years of postsecondary education. This is available under the following circumstances:

- You can qualify for full credit if your tax filing status is married filing jointly with a modified adjusted gross income under $160,000.
- You can qualify for partial credit if your tax filing status is married filing jointly with a modified adjusted gross income over $160,000 but less than $180,000.
- If you are married as of the last day of the year, you must file jointly to claim this credit; married persons filing separately are not eligible.
- All other filing statuses can qualify for full credit if your adjusted gross income is under $80,000.
- All other filing statuses can qualify for *partial credit* for adjusted gross income over $80,000 but less than $90,000.
- This tax credit is available for qualified tuition and related fees incurred and paid in the first four years of postsecondary education for the taxpayer, spouse, and/or dependents.

The American opportunity tax credit is equal to 100% of the first $2,000 of qualified expenses paid in the tax year, plus 25% of the next $2,000. Therefore, the maximum tax credit allowed in any given year is $2,500 per student, if there is at least $4,000 in qualifying expenses. It is important to note that this $2,500 credit is available for each eligible student in your household. In other words, if you qualify for this tax credit, it would be the same as receiving a $2,500 tax-free scholarship for each of your children who qualifies. In essence, the federal government is subsidizing the cost of sending your child (or other family member) to college. Up to 40% ($1,000) of this tax credit can be refundable, even if it exceeds your tax liability for the year. *It is extremely important to note that you should not make this $4,000 payment from a 529 Plan or Coverdell Educational Savings Account.* This $4,000 must come from your other savings or loans, since you cannot combine this tax credit with the funds and benefits received from qualified education plans. Any amount above the $4,000 can come from one of your qualified education savings plans.

The Protecting Americans from Tax Hikes Act of 2015 (PATH Act) made the American Opportunity Credit permanent.

Lifetime Learning Credit

The Lifetime Learning Credit does not call for your child (or any other family member) to have a certain degree or workload requirement. This credit may be claimed for one or more courses at an eligible education institution that is either part of a postsecondary degree program or part of a nondegree program taken to acquire or improve job skills. The Lifetime Learning Credit can be claimed for an unlimited number of years. For 2018, here are the requirements:

- You can qualify for full credit if your tax filing status is married filing jointly with a modified adjusted gross income under $114,000.
- You can qualify for partial credit if your tax-filing status is married filing jointly with a modified adjusted gross income up to $134,000.
- If you are married as of the last day of the year, you must file jointly to claim this credit; married persons filing separately are not eligible.
- All other filing statuses can qualify for full credit if your modified adjusted gross income is under $57,000.
- All other filing statuses can qualify for partial credit if your modified adjusted gross income is up to $67,000.
- This tax credit is available for tuition and enrollment fees for undergraduate, graduate, or professional degree programs for you, your spouse, or your dependents.

The Lifetime Learning Credit provides an annual per taxpayer reimbursement for qualified tuition and related expenses per family in the amount of $2,000 per year. This means that if you pay qualifying expenses for more than one eligible student, the overall credit you may claim remains $2,000, regardless of the number of children who are students in your household. This credit is based on a 20% factor of qualified expenses. Therefore, to obtain the full $2,000 credit, you must have at least $10,000 of qualified education expenses for all eligible children who are students in your family. This tax credit is nonrefundable; therefore, you will not be entitled to receive it if it exceeds your regular tax plus Alternative Minimum Tax (AMT) liability.

It is extremely important to note that you should not make this $10,000 payment from a 529 Plan or Coverdell Educational Savings Account. This $10,000 must come from your other savings or loans, since you cannot combine this tax credit with the funds and benefits received from qualified education savings plans. Any amount above the $10,000 can come from one of your qualified education savings plans.

If you have more than one qualifying child in college during the same year, you may have the option of using both the American Opportunity Tax Credit and the Lifetime Learning Credit in the same year; however, you cannot claim both in the same year for the same person in college.

Employee Educational Assistance Programs

Under the Employee Educational Assistance Program, an employer can reimburse an employee's tuition, enrollment fees, books, supplies, and equipment for undergraduate and graduate studies. This tax-free treatment applies, provided that the courses do not satisfy the employer's minimum education standards and do not qualify you for a new profession. Both undergraduate and graduate courses qualify for this exclusion.

These working-condition fringe benefits can be excluded from the employee's income, up to $5,250 per year. This is a tax-free benefit to the employee (i.e., you or your spouse); at the same time, your employer receives a full business tax deduction.

It is important to note that neither the employer nor the employee can claim an education tax credit for the same expense. If the employee has expenses that exceed the $5,250 employer reimbursement, the employee will be permitted to claim the American Opportunity Tax Credit or the Lifetime Learning Credit for those expenses paid over this amount. Of course, the employee needs to meet the qualifications for these credits. Under the American Taxpayer Relief Act of 2012 the employer-provided education assistance has been made permanent.

If you do not pay attention to the tax consequences when paying for college, you may be paying significantly more in taxes than the law requires. Therefore, you must include tax planning as part of your overall strategy for saving and paying for college. Using a financial planning approach that takes advantage of these *Tax Alpha to the 2nd Power*[SM] facts and strategies will maximize your college saving goals.

TAX ALPHA TO THE 2ND POWER^{SM} **FACTS AND STRATEGIES FOR PAYING FOR EDUCATION**

Here are several tax facts and strategies that will address your wealth accumulation goals at an exponential rate, which will help put you on the path to financial independence, *point X*.

- Establish and fund the maximum annual contribution of $2,000 per year to a Coverdell Savings Account for each of your children under the age of 18, if you or your child qualifies. Although there is no upfront tax deduction, all future earnings and principal will be paid out tax-free if you use it to cover private school costs from kindergarten through graduate school.
- Consider transferring appreciated property (such as stocks, bonds, and mutual funds) that you plan to sell (to cover education costs), to your children age 19 and older or children who are full-time students ages 19 to 23, if their earned income is more than half of the amount of their support. They can then sell this appreciated property and have the capital gain taxed at a rate as low as 0%, as long as their overall taxable income is below $38,600. They can use this money to pay for their education, and you can avoid paying tax on any gain.
- Keep in mind that if you buy US EE savings bonds or I bonds to pay for educational expenses and you defer reporting the interest, you may be eligible to exclude the accumulated interests from income when you redeem the bonds.
- Also keep in mind that if you receive a scholarship and fellowship as a degree candidate, these payments are tax-free to the extent that they pay for tuition, cost-related fees, books, supplies, and equipment that are required for your courses. Any amounts paid for room and board, as well as other incidentals, are taxable.
- Consider establishing a Code Section 529 savings plan. Although you do not receive any federal tax deduction for the contributions you make to these plans, the distributions are generally tax-free to the extent that you use them to pay for qualified education expenses.
- **A major change with 529 educational savings plans is that starting January 1, 2018, it now includes levels of education other than college**. If you have children in private school, including kindergarten through the 12th grade, you can use the funds in your account for these expenses. There is a $10,000 limit that applies annually on a per-student basis, rather than on a per-account basis. This limit does not apply to undergraduate and graduate tuition.
- If your state has its own sponsored 529 educational savings plan, you may get the added benefit of a state tax deduction for any contributions you make before the end of the year. Each state has different rules, however, so be sure to check with your tax advisor.

- **If utilizing a 529 plan to pay for K–12, you must check with your state to ensure that these distributions will also be tax-free at the state level.** Many states that provide a state tax deduction for the contribution are currently not following the same rules as the federal government on these distributions.
- If you paid qualified tuition and fees for an eligible student in the first four years of college or postsecondary institution, you may qualify for the American opportunity tax credit of up to $2,500 for each eligible student. Special rules apply, and this credit starts to phase out for married couples filing jointly with incomes over $160,000 and $80,000 for people filing as single, head of household, or qualifying widows and widowers.
- If you paid qualified expenses for yourself, your spouse, or your dependents who are enrolled in eligible educational institutions during the year, you may be able to claim the Lifetime Learning Credit of up to $2,000. This credit does not have a degree or workload requirement. The credit may be claimed for one or more courses that are either part of a postsecondary degree program or a part of a nondegree program to acquire or improve job skills. This credit is not limited to the first four years of postsecondary education, and there is no limit on the number of years it can be claimed. The credit is 20% of the first $10,000 paid in 2018, and the maximum credit per family is $2,000 per year. Special rules apply, and for 2018 this credit starts to phase out for married couples filing jointly with incomes over $114,000 and at $57,000 for people filing as single or head of household.
- If you are not getting the benefit of this educational tax credit because of your high income level on your tax return and your child has his or her own tax liability against which the credit may be claimed, you can forego claiming your child as a dependent exemption on your tax return. This allows the education tax credit to be claimed on your child's tax return. Calculate your tax bill as well as your children's, and take advantage of the method that provides your family with the greatest tax savings.
- If you paid interest on a qualified student loan, you may be able to claim an above-the-line deduction of up to $2,500 on your 2018 tax return. This amount is phased out in 2018 for married couples filing jointly starting at $135,000, and $65,000 for individuals filing as single or head of household. If you are married and filing separately, however, you may not claim this deduction, no matter what your income level.

AN ACTION PLAN FOR PAYING FOR EDUCATION

1. **Decide if college is the right choice for your child** or if they are better suited to pursue their passions in setting up a business (see Chapter 11, "Starting Your Own Business") or taking a high-paying blue-collar job.

2. **Find out – today – what your child's college expenses might be,** even if college is still 18 years away. Do not wait until your child is in high school, because by then, it may be too late for you to save enough to help your child, and you will regret not having started planning sooner.

3. **Do not spend money on what you want to buy now** – your *immediate wants* – without first setting aside money for your *future needs*. No matter what it is you think you "need" now – furniture for your child's nursery, tennis or piano lessons for your budding prodigy, or a bigger home so your kids can each have their own room – none of that is really as important as saving for your child's education. Do not make the same mistake so many parents make by not starting to save now.

4. **Determine your family's "needs analysis"** by using the college cost calculator at http://www.calcxml.com/calculators/when-to-start-saving-for-college; This helps you calculate *your* specific needs by plugging in your child's age, how much you have saved already, and other factors.

5. **Understand the differences among the four most commonly used approaches to saving for college:** Section 529 educational savings programs, UGMA/UTMA accounts, the Coverdell Education Savings Accounts, and US savings bonds. Each has different tax implications, income restrictions, and factors affecting who controls the money in the account, as well as other differences, so discuss them with your tax advisor to determine which of these is best for your family's needs.

6. **Keep in mind that you have the most control and the greatest tax benefits if you save money via a 529 plan:** The example in this chapter showed a difference of almost $100,000 more if you save via a tax-exempt 529 than if you save via a taxable account. Find out how much more *you* could earn by doing a similar comparison using your specific savings plan.

7. **Be sure to know the difference between a prepaid 529 plan and an educational savings plan.** Although assets held in ***prepaid 529*** plans are not considered in the federal student financial aid calculation, the withdrawals from these plans will reduce your financial aid eligibility dollar-for-dollar. This means that withdrawals are direct reductions in the amount of financial aid that would have otherwise been available. This is an important distinction and why you should avoid 529 prepaid plans at all costs if you believe there is a possibility that your child may qualify for financial aid. In this situation, the ***529 savings plan would be a much better alternative***.

8. **Understand that if you use a** Uniform Gift/Transfer to Minor Act to transfer assets to your child for him or her to use for college, your child will have total control over that money – and may decide not to use it for college after all. Look for other ways to help your child save for college. And under the new tax law, this would be a tax disadvantaged strategy.

9. **Consider saving via a Coverdell Education Savings Account** for your child's primary or secondary education expenses, in addition to college, if you plan to send your child or children to private schools.

10. **Recognize that although investing in US savings bonds is safe,** they offer a very low return, which may make it very difficult for you to reach your child's financial needs for college expenses.

11. **If your child has a part-time paying job, consider establishing a Roth IRA in your child's name.** Although this is a retirement account, your child can withdraw money from it to pay for college, and that withdrawal will be taxed at your child's tax rate, which could be as low as 0%, if structured properly. And if your child decides not to go to college, or does not use the money to pay for college, he or she will have already begun saving for retirement!

12. **Learn as much as you can about what financial aid your child might qualify for,** based on your and your spouse's income and assets, as well as that of your child. See Exhibit 7.4 for 2018–2019 guidelines.

13. **Find out if you qualify for either of the two major education tax credits** – the American opportunity tax credit and the Lifetime Learning Credit: These depend on the number of courses your child is taking in college, your and your spouse's income, and your tax filing status. If you are unsure whether you qualify, talk to your tax advisor or financial advisor.

CHAPTER

8

Planning for Retirement

If you don't want to work, you have to work to earn enough money so that you won't have to work.

—Ogden Nash, American poet

Everyone should be planning financially for retirement, regardless of how old or young they are. Many employers no longer guarantee employee pensions, so your financial needs during your retirement may rest completely on your shoulders. People reaching retirement age are facing concerns that retirees did not face 20 or 30 years ago. They must plan for their retirement funds to support them for a longer expected lifespan, and they must seriously question whether they can count on Social Security benefits when the time comes.

This chapter helps you determine your financial needs for retirement and how to properly fund them. I show you how to determine your own individual *point X*, financial independence. I also describe tax implications and other risks that might jeopardize your retirement plans, and what steps you need to take to secure the peace of mind that comes from a financially secure retirement.

Case Study: Saving Versus Not Saving for Retirement: The $1.7 Million Difference

When it comes to being prepared for retirement, I have seen two scenarios that most people tend to follow. One is *not having* any plan at all, and the other is *having* a well-thought-out retirement planning strategy. Unfortunately, the majority of people are in the former category and do not have any plan to achieve their retirement goals of becoming financially independent. After reading through this chapter, ask yourself whether or not you will follow the example set by my clients Mr. and Mrs. Poorman or Mr. and Mrs. Richman. Please note that I have used, for the purpose of this example, tax laws as they would apply in 2018 and not necessarily the tax laws that would have applied at the time period of the story. I have done this to simplify the facts and to make it more relevant to you under the current tax system.

Before telling you their specific stories, I would like to highlight four critical issues that will control and significantly affect your success or failure in reaching your retirement goals:

1. How much of your income will you save and invest each year?
2. How many years will you be setting aside money for your retirement?
3. What type of investments will you use to meet your goals?
4. Will you be disciplined and stay on track?

Let us start by considering the story of two clients of mine, who I will call Mr. and Mrs. Poorman. About 25 years ago, the Poormans came into my office for the first time to have their income tax return prepared. They were recently married and had started their first jobs out of college about four years earlier. When I prepared their income tax return, I noticed they had not participated in their company's 401(k) plans and had not taken any steps in saving for retirement. I discussed the advantages of starting to save at an early age. I also went through the tax calculations to determine their refund both with and without an $11,000 Individual Retirement Account (IRA) contribution. With this IRA contribution, their refund increased by $3,850. I further explained to them that for every $1,000 they put into a traditional IRA, they would get back an extra $350 (35% for every $1). They were quite impressed with the tax saving incentives that would be made available by setting money aside for their retirement, either through their 401(k) or an IRA.

Although they agreed that funding a retirement plan was the smart thing to do, they said they had no money available to do so. They had just finished paying for their wedding and honeymoon, and they had no money left for savings. Although they were concerned about the future, they said they would definitely do this next year when they had some extra cash. Over the next three years, they set money aside for a down payment for their home and were not able to fund their retirement. Over the next two years, once again, they said they were unable to fund their retirement because they needed to furnish their new home. This story continued throughout their lives, with the birth of their first and then second child. Before they knew it, it was time for their two sons to go to college, and they were still not able to set money aside for their retirement.

Throughout their lives, they always had what appeared to be valid excuses for not saving for their future. They failed to understand that they must first set money aside (pay themselves first) each year and *then* determine their standard of living based on what was left over. Each year, they came in to see me and talked about all the new events and projects that were going on in their lives, and each year, they swore as soon as they were done, they would start putting money away for retirement. Although they seemed to understand the importance of saving for the future, their attitude was always *we will start next year, after all, it is no big deal if we wait another year.*

Moreover, in the years that they did manage to set aside some money, they turned a deaf ear to my suggestions of investing in a well-diversified stock and bond mutual fund portfolio. Instead, they decided to keep their savings in a nonretirement account, which earned little or no interest on their savings. Because *they* did not understand the stock and bond market, they felt it would be best for them not to get involved. They were fearful of the stock market, because their parents had lost quite a bit of money in the crash of 1987. Also, even though they did not understand the basics of investing, they were not willing to work with an advisor to guide them through this process. The Poormans did not have a disciplined approach to saving for retirement and acted like they had no choice other than ignoring and avoiding the decisions that needed to be made to ensure their financial future. In fact, the Poormans had no plan to reach financial independence – their own *point X* – at any point in their lives.

Twenty-five years later, they are in their early 50s and still living paycheck to paycheck to maintain their current standard of living. In fact, they recently borrowed all of the equity in their home to pay for their two sons' first two years of college at private universities.

Are you living your life in a manner similar to the Poormans? If so, you can and must change the pattern of this vicious cycle immediately. This is a matter of financial life and death, with no way to get around it unless you are willing to make the necessary changes.

The same year I met the Poormans, I also met the Richmans. Their story was amazingly similar to the Poormans, but with significantly different results based on the decisions the Richmans made. The Richmans were also recently married when I met them, but they decided early on to be conservative with their spending, and they understood the importance of saving for tomorrow. They had a modest wedding and only invited their closest friends and family members. They had a weeklong honeymoon and were able to get a great deal on an all-inclusive trip to the Bahamas. When they first met with me, they not only had no debt, they had a combined savings of more than $18,000! As I prepared their tax return, I noticed they had started funding their retirement accounts during their first full year of employment after college.

Even though they did not qualify for an IRA tax-deductible contribution, they both agreed that they would make an annual nondeductible IRA contribution. The Richmans clearly had a vision of what was truly important to them. When they found out the following year that they had twins on the way, they became even more disciplined and focused on their finances. Financial security for their family was now their number-one priority, not the materialistic goods and services that measure a person's standard of living throughout their lifetime. They always came in and joked about the fact that they will "pay themselves first," and then determine what they can afford after they set aside their savings. They knew that what they saved and set aside was not meant to be spent on nonessential items.

They also realized the value of the tax savings the government offered them through fully funding their retirement accounts. They were able to save significantly more money because they were doing it with pretax dollars. This 35% tax savings (from their 401(k) contributions) meant they would have 35% more set aside each year.

The Richmans understood the power of the time value of money. They started saving from their very first paycheck and understood early on that their young age was one of their most valuable investment assets. They knew that the longer they saved, the greater their chance of achieving financial independence. They appreciated the fact that the amount of time they had to save and invest was more important than a strategy of trying to time the entry point to investing in the market. They took a dollar-cost-averaging approach to saving and investing for their future, by having a payroll deduction come out of each and every one of their paychecks to fund retirement savings.

Although the Richmans were not in the financial service industry and did not fully understand investing, they did seek out my advice. They kept a large portion of their money invested in stock and bond mutual funds; they were not overly concerned about the ups and downs of the market because they saw themselves as long-term investors. Their investment approach was simple: they were well diversified in a balanced portfolio and viewed themselves as owners of many quality businesses as both shareholders and bondholders. Each year when I spoke to them and prepared their tax return, we also took a look at their asset allocation and made the appropriate changes to rebalance their portfolio. They stayed very disciplined throughout the past 25 years and focused on buying quality investments, were properly diversified, patiently held on to their investments even during down markets, and rebalanced their portfolio annually.[1]

Today, the Richmans have more than $1.7 million in retirement savings, have paid off their home mortgage five years early after taking advantage of falling interest rates, and have also set aside sufficient funds to get their son and daughter through four years of state college.

From early on in their relationship, even before they were married, they had a clear plan for a comfortable retirement and a strategy for achieving financial independence. If you are an able-bodied individual with a job, you can also achieve financial independence, by simply paying yourself first, and then living within a budget of whatever is left over. It really is that simple. If my parents were able to do it as Italian immigrants working for modest wages and raising four children, so can you!

So, would you consider yourself like Mr. and Mrs. Poorman or Mr. and Mrs. Richman? Are you willing to do what it takes to live your life like the Richmans? If so, congratulations! You have just made your commitment to planning for a comfortable retirement and for achieving financial independence for you and your family.

Retirement Equation: Calculating Your Personal *Point X*

Most people have the desire and dream to become financially independent. Wanting to achieve this goal requires planning; you cannot leave this to chance. I define financial independence as the point where your money can start working for you instead of

---

[1] Asset allocation does not assure or guarantee better performance and cannot eliminate the risk of investment losses. Diversification does not assure or guarantee better performance and cannot eliminate the risk of investment losses.

you working for your money, while still maintaining your desired standard of living.

This number is different for everyone because there are so many variables that need to be taken into consideration. The starting point is estimating how much income you will need in retirement and then determining whether your current savings and investment plan will be able to provide you with that desired amount. This is the centerpiece of planning for retirement, and going through the necessary calculations will show you what you need to do to get there.

The 12 key questions in determining your own *point X* are shown in Exhibit 8.1. Although there are many other variables you need to consider, these are the fundamental questions you need to analyze and answer when determining your retirement planning strategy.

The answers to these questions will enable you to calculate how much money you will need when you retire. The math used in this calculation is quite complicated because there are so many variables (including present value and future value calculations). Therefore, it is best to use an online retirement planning calculator. Keep in mind, there are numerous financial calculators that you could use online, all of which may have a different variation on these questions. Always remember, these are just rough estimates based on a set of assumptions you will need to make. You can access one of

Exhibit 8.1   Twelve Questions to Analyze Your Retirement Needs

1. What is your current age?

2. What is your current income?

3. What is your spouse's income (if applicable)?

4. What is your current retirement savings?

5. What is your desired retirement age?

6. How many years of retirement income do you expect to need?

7. What is the expected inflation rate?

8. What percentage of your current combined income will you need at retirement?

9. What do you expect your preretirement return on investments to be?

10. What do you expect your postretirement return on investments to be?

11. Would you like to assume that you will be receiving Social Security benefits in retirement?

12. If you do expect to receive Social Security, what is the monthly dollar amount in today's dollars?

these calculators by simply going to www.calcxml.com/calculators/retirement-calculator. You will be able to run through an unlimited number of "what if?" scenarios to try to answer the question, "How much will I need to save for retirement?"

This exercise will give you a reality check, and you may need to alter some of your assumptions. But remember, it is best to be conservative and realistic. If the amount you will need to save does not appear achievable, you will need to go back and make some adjustments in your standard of living not only now but in retirement. Never forget the lesson of Chapter 1, "Committing to Living Within Your Means."

The High Cost of Waiting to Save for Retirement

Should I start saving now or later? That is the question. Procrastination is never the answer in life. The best time to start is always *right now*!

Almost everyone has the desire to save for retirement. But all too many people delay this process, believing that next year it will be easier. As shown in the story about the Poormans, there will always be an excuse not to save this year. Falling into this trap can have financially devastating consequences to your financial security. Most people do not know when they should start and how much they should save each year. Quite simply, you need to start immediately, and my general rule of thumb is putting away 10% or more of your gross annual paycheck each year.

The easy way out of making the right decision is to justify it by saying you will wait until your income level increases. Unfortunately, with every salary increase most people simply increase their standard of living and not their retirement savings. The longer you wait, the harder it will be to accumulate the amount you need to be financially independent. Remember one of the most valuable investment assets you have is time: the more years you save, the greater your chance of financial success.

The financial rewards of starting to save at an early age for retirement far outweigh the costly mistake of waiting and spending your money on your wants. By starting with even small amounts each month, you may be able to accumulate a great deal of retirement savings over time. By far the easiest way to do this is by contributing to your employer's retirement plan or, if that is not available, to an individual retirement account (IRA). Implement a retirement saving strategy that allocates a specific dollar amount or percentage

(I recommend at least 10%) of your salary every pay period. Therefore, you are paying yourself first, as though saving for retirement is your number-one required expense. In fact, saving for retirement is not an expense because it adds to your investable assets, but treating it as such is of utmost importance to your success.

If you are not convinced of the old saying *time is money*, I want you to spend some time thinking about the following example, which compares two individuals with different views on the value of time as it relates to saving.

Melanie started saving at the age of 25, setting aside $2,000 per year for 10 years, which then continued to grow for an additional 30 years. Over the 40-year period, her tax-deferred account grew at a rate of 8% per year, bringing the value of her account to *$291,565*.[2]

Brian delayed saving for retirement until the age of 35, when he also began to save $2,000 per year for 10 years, which then continued to grow for an additional 20 years. Over the 30-year period, his tax-deferred account grew at a rate of 8% per year,[3] bringing the value of his account to *$135,042*.

Exhibit 8.2 shows the difference in how their savings grew.

Both Melanie and Brian set aside $2,000 per year over a 10-year savings time span. They both managed to save $20,000, but they ended up with significantly different results when they reached the age of 65: Because Brian started 10 years later than Melanie, his savings were $156,523 less than Melanie's! This example verifies that time is money and that one of your most valuable financial assets is time. By getting off to an early start with your retirement savings program, you can take advantage of the power of compounding.

Your annual savings have the potential of earning a rate of return, and so does your reinvested earnings. Look at the Rule of 72 in Exhibit 12.1 to see just how powerful compounding can be. This is the secret to financial independence: By letting your money work for you, eventually, you will no longer have to work to maintain your desired standard of living.

---

[2]The rates of return shown above are purely hypothetical and do not represent the performance of any individual investment or portfolio of investments. They are for illustrative purposes only and should not be used to predict future product performance. Specific rates of return, especially for extended time periods, will vary over time. There is also a higher degree of risk associated with investments that offer the potential for higher rates of return. You should consult with your representative before making any investment decision.

[3]See footnote 2.

Exhibit 8.2   The High Cost of Waiting to Save for Retirement[4]

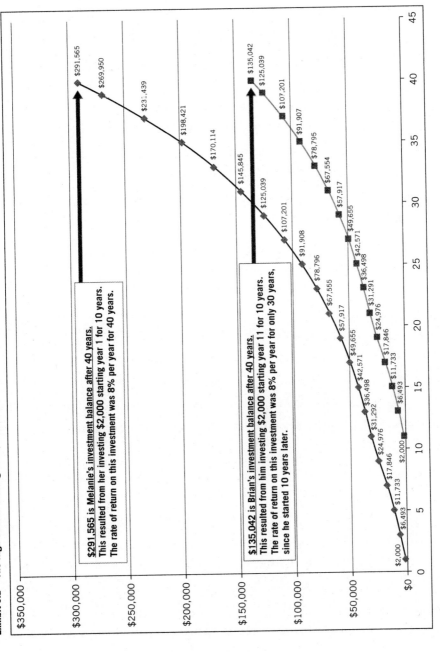

[4]See footnote 2.

If you have been finding it difficult to save money on a regular basis, implement the following savings strategies that will take money directly from your paycheck on a pretax basis. By utilizing employer-sponsored retirement plans, you will establish a systematic strategy that will force you to pay yourself first in a tax-efficient manner, implementing a dollar-cost-averaging investment plan.

No matter what method you use, it is extremely important that you start saving now!

What You Can Expect to Receive from Social Security

Social Security benefits are viewed by many of us as the building blocks of our retirement planning strategy. However, advances in medicine have increased life expectancies beyond any actuarial assumptions used when the program was originally established. These longer life spans have dramatically increased the number of people collecting Social Security benefits. The current Social Security system is under a great deal of stress, and many people fear that it will no longer be around when they are ready to retire.

On January 1, 2011, the very first Baby Boomers – people born between 1946 and 1964 – turned 65. Millions of them are rushing toward retirement age, and the government has promised to take care of them through Social Security. Currently, an average of 10,000 Americans turn 65 every single day. The US Census Bureau estimates that 22.1% of the population will be 65 or older by the year 2050, as compared to only 14.9% in 2015. This has caused and will continue to cause a strain on the Social Security and Medicare systems. This all comes at a really bad time for the federal government, which is already flat broke, and for a national economy that was recently on the brink of financial disaster. Exhibit 8.3 demonstrates the historical and projected downward trend of covered workers to beneficiaries, as reported by the Social Security Administration. A covered worker represents someone that is employed and paying Social Security taxes into the system. A beneficiary is anyone who is receiving Social Security benefits and therefore taking money out of the system.

In 1945, when the system was first established, there were 41.9 people paying Social Security taxes for every beneficiary taking money out of the system. There is now an astonishing projection that by 2035, there will only be 2.1 people paying Social Security taxes for every beneficiary taking money out of the system. The cause of this is very simple to understand. Baby Boomers have started to enter into their retirement age and the population is living significantly longer than anyone could have ever anticipated.

Exhibit 8.3   Ratio of Social Security–Covered Workers to Beneficiaries over Time

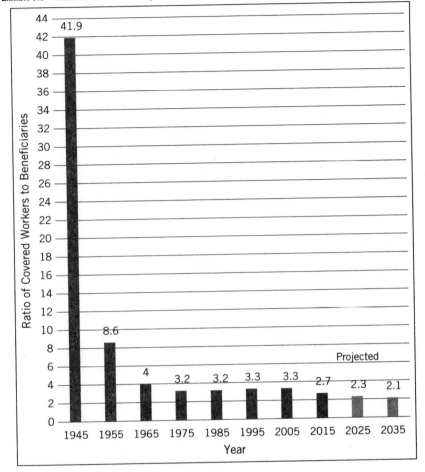

Unless there is some major change in the system, its future is going to be very uncertain.

Before 2003, you could receive full Social Security retirement benefits on reaching age 65. The age to qualify for full retirement benefits began to increase on a graduated scale for those born prior to 1960. By 2027, the age to qualify for full Social Security retirement benefits will have increased to age 67 for all retirees, where it is scheduled to remain. It is my belief that this retirement age for full benefits will continue to increase in order to avoid the insolvency of the Social Security system.

In a 2011 Social Security Trustees Report, a warning was issued about the serious problems facing Social Security in the future. The trustees indicated that program costs (benefits paid) were more than noninterest income (Social Security payroll taxes) for the first time in 2010, and they expect this situation to continue. As of the 2017 report, the Social Security Trust Fund is expected to be exhausted by 2034, when there will only be enough money to pay about 77 cents for each dollar of scheduled benefits.

Chances are that most people will probably have to wait longer to qualify for full Social Security benefits and these benefits will be replacing a *smaller* percentage of their preretirement income. For higher-income earners, the percentage of retirement benefits that Social Security replaces is proportionally even smaller. Therefore, it is critically important to understand that your long-term retirement planning strategy should factor in a more limited role for your Social Security benefits when calculating required income in retirement.

Many people fear that Social Security benefits may no longer be there at all when they are ready to retire. I believe that future benefits will be delayed by further extending the age to qualify for retirement. In addition, I believe that the level of benefits to both new and existing retirees will be reduced. On top of this, the Social Security tax rate will be increased, and the dollar limit on which the tax is imposed will be increased. The combination of these changes will be the only way to ensure the continued sustainability of the system and the continued payment of these benefits.

One of the first steps in developing a retirement planning strategy is estimating your Social Security benefits in retirement. The Social Security Administration (SSA) no longer mails the annual estimated benefit statements. Instead, to obtain this information, you must go online to www.ssa.gov/estimator. This retirement calculator will give you an estimate based on your actual Social Security earnings record. This SSA website and calculator will ask you for the following information:

- Your name
- Social Security number
- Date and place of birth
- Your mother's maiden name
- Additional information you provide about future earnings
- Age at which you expect to stop working

Based on this information and your actual earnings history as maintained by the SSA, the retirement calculator generates an estimate of the amount you would receive under three scenarios:

1. If you retire at age 62 (the earliest date you can receive benefits).

2. If you wait until full retirement age (which currently ranges from 65 to 67, based on year of birth).

3. If you continue working until age 70 before claiming retirement benefits.

You cannot use the retirement estimator if you have blocked access to your personal information; in that case, you need to request that a statement be mailed to you. In the meantime, if you want a rough benefit estimate, you can use the "quick calculator" at www.socialsecurity.gov/OACT/quickcalc/index.html. Most likely, however, *this rough estimate will not match the information provided by your Social Security statement.* Therefore, I recommend using the SSA's quick calculator only to get a rough estimate of your Social Security benefits, both in today's dollars as well as inflation-adjusted future dollars.

The quick calculator asks you three simple questions that helps calculate your Social Security benefits. Be sure to do this in both current and future dollars, because you will need this information later when calculating the retirement equation to your personal *point X*. Please note that these benefit estimates depend on your date of birth and on your *estimated* earnings history. For security, the quick calculator cannot access your earnings record (i.e., the information that you have provided to the US government every year that you file a tax return). Instead, it estimates your earnings based on the information you provide.

Qualified Retirement Plans

If the government had a program that would provide you with an interest-free loan so that you could take this money and invest it for the long term to secure your retirement, would you take advantage of such an offer? What if this program also included a provision that if you lost some of this money through your investments, you would not have to pay back that portion of the loan to the government? What if this program also allowed you to start paying back the loan gradually (also interest-free) over your life expectancy, starting at the age of 70 1/2?

Although this program sounds too good to be true, it is, in fact, available to every working individual in the United States, and far too few are taking advantage of it. Quite simply, this is precisely what happens when you contribute money to a retirement account and take advantage of the tax-deferral option.

Tax deferral is a method of postponing the payment of income tax on income earned in the current year until you withdraw the funds from the tax-deferred account. The government uses the Internal Revenue code to influence taxpayers' behavior. The government wants individuals to save money for the long term and specifically to allow them a secure, comfortable, and sustainable retirement. With that said, the Internal Revenue code allows individuals to take advantage of tax deferral in many different ways to help encourage and accelerate an individual's retirement savings. There is no single better strategy for achieving financial independence than by doing it in a tax-advantaged way.

For example, Individual Retirement Accounts and 401(k)s allow taxes to be deferred. Various insurance products, such as fixed and variable annuities and certain life insurance contracts, also allow taxes to be deferred.

There is a significant benefit to deferring taxes as long as possible, because it allows the entire principal and earnings to compound on a tax-deferred basis, which can have a dramatic effect on your retirement savings over an extended period of time. The benefit of this tax-deferred compounding was highlighted in the section on "The High Cost of Waiting to Save for Retirement" (Exhibit 8.2), where Melanie accumulated $156,523 more than Brian simply by starting 10 years earlier (even though the total amount each of them set aside was the same $20,000). Clearly the combined effects of tax deferral with compounding are significant over long periods of time.

For many people, the initial tax-deferral period is during their higher-income earning years when their tax bracket is much higher. The added benefit to this is that you are deferring income during years that would require you to pay a higher tax rate and possibly picking up this income in years where you will be subject to a lower tax rate. Although there is no guarantee that you will be in a lower tax bracket in retirement (tax rates can increase in the future with new presidential administrations), tax deferral is still one of the most powerful tools available in retirement planning.

Now that you are convinced that tax-deferred compounding is the most effective way to achieve financial independence, let us look at a summary of some of the most popular plans available. There are numerous options available for funding your retirement on a tax-deferred basis, depending on your particular facts and circumstances. These options are also limited to what may be available through your employer: Some plans are fully funded by your employer, some are partially funded by you, and some are fully funded by you. To clarify this even further, employer contributions come directly from your employer's funds whereas employee contributions come from a direct reduction in your gross paycheck.

A *qualified retirement plan* is a plan that meets requirements of the Internal Revenue Code and, as a result, is eligible to receive certain tax benefits, primarily a tax deduction to your employer and tax deferral to you. These plans must be for the exclusive benefit of employees or their beneficiaries. There are two kinds of qualified plans: defined-benefit plans and defined-contribution plans. Keep in mind that, in most cases, withdrawals made before age 59 1/2 are subject to a 10% penalty, unless you qualify for one of the exceptions. Withdrawals must begin no later than April 1 of the year after you turn age 70 1/2 and are subject to income taxes in most cases.

The following sections describe various types of qualified retirement plans. Once you have a good understanding of the various qualified retirement plan options available, you will be in a much better position to achieve financial independence. These retirement plans are by far the most tax-efficient weapons available to you in your pursuit of accumulating wealth. Think about this for a minute. You are allowed to defer the payment of significant tax dollars, which amounts to an interest-free loan from the government. At the same time, you have the potential to earn a rate of return with these funds. You cannot afford to *not* take advantage of this.

Defined Benefit Pension Plans

With this type of plan, an employer commits to paying you (the employee) a specific benefit for life, beginning when you retire. The amount of the benefit is known in advance and is usually based on factors such as your age, your earnings, and your years of service. Defined benefit plans do not have contribution limits, because they are based on a specific benefit to be paid in retirement. Today, very few large private-sector employers provide defined benefit plans because they have turned out to be very costly, given the low rates of return from the equity markets in the past decade and the longevity that employees are experiencing in their retirement years. These plans are now primarily offered through government employers, as well as smaller businesses with 100 or fewer employees.

Defined Contribution Plans

In contrast to a defined-benefit plan, a defined contribution plan does not promise to pay you a specific amount when you retire. Instead, your employer generally allocates contributions to your account, many times in the form of matching contributions. As an employee, you may be able to make contributions to your account within the plan. Therefore, the retirement benefit you receive from a defined contribution plan depends solely on the value of your account balance when you retire. The most common defined contribution plan provided through employers is a 401(k) plan.

401(k) Plan

This is a qualified plan established by employers to which eligible employees may make contributions (in the form of deductions from your salary) on a post-tax or pretax basis. Employers offering a 401(k) plan may make matching or non-elective (safe harbor) employer contributions to the plan on behalf of eligible employees. Those plans that allow you to contribute money on an after-tax basis are known as Roth 401(k) plans.

403(b) Plan

These plans differ from 401(k) plans in that they are offered to employees of tax-exempt entities, which typically are non-profits, churches, or schools. At retirement, employees have a choice of a lump sum or a series of monthly payments. Similar to 401(k) plans, 403(b) plans can be funded by pre- or post-tax salary deferrals by employees. These plans are commonly funded by employee deferrals, however employer contributions could be made as a match or as a lump sum. Employer contributions are not common.

Profit-Sharing Plans

Profit-sharing plans are funded by your employer, who has the responsibility of determining when and how much the company will contribute to the plan. The company's contributions may depend on the company's profits and therefore, so will your retirement benefit. When you retire, you can either receive your benefit as a lump sum or over a period of time. A 401(k) is a feature that is adopted under the profit-sharing plan document. If the profit-sharing plan offers the 401(k) feature, you can make additional contributions from your paycheck.

Employee Stock Ownership Plan (ESOP)

With this type of plan, your employer periodically contributes company stock toward an employee's retirement plan. When you retire, the ESOP may provide a single payment of stock shares. At age 55, with 10 or more years of plan participation, you must be given the option by your employer to diversify up to 25% of your ESOP account value. This diversification enables you to invest in other stocks, bonds, and so forth, so that you are not solely invested in the success of your company. This diversification option continues up to age 60, at which time you have a one-time opportunity to diversify up to 50% of your account.

Simplified Employee Pension (SEP)

These plans were designed to benefit owners and employees of small businesses. Like IRAs, they can provide either a lump-sum payment or periodic withdrawals when you retire. They are principally funded by the employer, although some SEPs established prior to 1997 do allow employee contributions. SEPs are usually invested in the same types of accounts that hold IRAs.

Savings Incentive Match Plans for Employees (SIMPLE)

These plans were also designed for small businesses. They can be set up either as IRAs or as 401(k)s. The employee funds them on a pretax basis, and employers are required to make matching contributions.

For more information on this subject, see Chapter 11, "Starting Your Own Business," in the section titled, "Choosing the Right Retirement Plan for Your Business."

The Difference Between Traditional IRAs and Roth IRAs

Individual Retirement Accounts (IRAs) are available to all wage earners at any salary level, as well as to nonworking spouses. You and your spouse cannot contribute more than your combined earned income to an IRA. IRAs are funded completely by the individual's contributions and not by an employer. This is why they are referred to as "individual" retirement accounts. These specially designated retirement accounts are required to be held with a bank, brokerage firm, mutual fund company, insurance company, or other financial institutions. Once you set up an IRA, you have several investing options. You can choose to invest in stocks, bonds, mutual funds, exchange-traded funds (ETFs), cash equivalents, real estate, and other investments. You have total control over these accounts, and you can elect a lump-sum payment or periodic withdrawals when you retire.

You can choose from two different types of IRAs, either a traditional or a Roth. Please understand that these are simply titles placed on the accounts so that you can distinguish them from nonretirement accounts. These account titles do not represent an investment. The decision on whether to open an IRA and which type is completely independent of how the funds will be invested once the account is established. See Chapter 9, "Managing Your Investments," for more details on investment options.

Contributions to traditional IRAs may be tax-deductible if you meet the requirements; your withdrawals will be taxable in the year that you make those withdrawals. Therefore, a traditional IRA gives you a tax deduction in the current year and a tax deferral for any earnings, but ultimately you will pay tax when you withdraw from your account. In contrast, contributions to a Roth IRA are *not* tax-deductible, but qualified withdrawals are tax-free. Therefore, Roth IRAs do not give you a tax deduction in the current year, but ultimately your qualified withdrawals including earnings will be paid out to you tax-free.

So the real question to ask yourself when deciding between a traditional and a Roth IRA is whether you prefer getting the tax benefit in the current year or tax-free income in retirement.

Both a traditional IRA and Roth IRA are subject to the same contribution limits, which are $5,500 in 2018. Although you can contribute to both within the same year, this $5,500 limit applies to the maximum combined contribution. The maximum *total* annual contribution an individual can make to a traditional and Roth IRA at the same time is $5,500 (as of 2018). There is a special "catch-up" provision that allows individuals age 50 and older to save even more by allowing them to contribute an additional $1,000, for a total limit of $6,500 per year. See Exhibit 8.4 for details.

Traditional Individual Retirement Accounts (IRAs)

Traditional IRAs can be an excellent way to save for retirement. If you do not participate in an employer-sponsored retirement plan, or if you would like to save more money than that plan allows, then a traditional IRA could be a great choice for you. A traditional IRA is simply a tax-deferred savings account that you can establish through a financial institution.

One of the greatest advantages of a traditional IRA is the potential for tax-deductible contributions. If your income is below the threshold or if you and/or your spouse are not covered through an employer plan at any income level, you can qualify for a tax-deductible contribution. For example, if your marginal

Exhibit 8.4   Table 1: 2018 Effect of Modified AGI on Traditional IRA Contribution *If You Are Covered by a Retirement Plan at Work*

Filing Status	Single or Head of Household or Married Filing Separately and did not live with spouse any time during the year	Married Filing Jointly or Qualifying Widow(er)	Married Filing Separately and lived with spouse any time during the year
MAXIMUM TRADITIONAL IRA **contribution** is the lesser of actual taxable compensation or the amount below:			
Under Age 50	$5,500	$5,500	$5,500
Age 50 or Over	$6,500	$6,500	$6,500
Maximum Modified Adjusted Gross Income for above Full TRADITIONAL IRA **deductions**:			
	$63,000	$101,000	$ZERO
The TRADITIONAL IRA contribution is phased out for higher incomes and reduced to $ZERO at the following Modified Adjusted Gross Income level of:			
	$73,000	$121,000	$10,000

Exhibit 8.4   Table 2: 2018 Effect of Modified AGI on Traditional IRA Contribution *If You Are Not Covered by a Retirement Plan at Work*

Filing Status	Single, Head of Household or Qualifying Widow(er)	Married Filing Jointly or Separately with a spouse who is not covered by a plan at work	Married Filing Jointly with a spouse who is covered by a plan at work	Married Filing Separately with a spouse who is covered by a plan at work
MAXIMUM TRADITIONAL IRA **contribution** is the lesser of actual taxable compensation or the amount below:				
Under Age 50	$5,500	$5,500	$5,500	$5,500
Age 50 or Over	$6,500	$6,500	$6,500	$6,500
Maximum Modified Adjusted Gross Income for above TRADITIONAL IRA **deductions**:				
	No Modified AGI Limit for Full Deduction	No Modified AGI Limit for Full Deduction	$189,000	$ZERO
The Maximum TRADITIONAL IRA contribution is phased out for higher incomes and reduced to $ZERO at the following Modified Adjusted Gross Income level of:				
			$199,000	$10,000

Exhibit 8.4   Table 3: 2018 Effect of Modified Adjusted Gross Income on Roth IRA contributions

Filing Status	Single, Head of Household, or Married Filing Separately and did not live with spouse any time during the year	Married Filing Jointly and **Qualifying Widow(er)**	Married Filing **Separately** and lived with spouse any time during the year
MAXIMUM ROTH IRA **contribution** is the lesser of actual taxable compensation or the amount below:			
Under Age 50	$5,500	$5,500	$5,500
Age 50 or Over	$6,500	$6,500	$6,500
Maximum Modified Adjusted Gross Income for above ROTH IRA contributions:			
	$120,000	$189,000	$ZERO
The Maximum ROTH IRA contribution is phased out for higher incomes and reduced to $ZERO at the following Modified Adjusted Gross Income level of:			
	$135,000	$199,000	$10,000

income tax rate is 40% and you qualify for the deduction, then a $5,500 traditional IRA contribution could save you $2,200 in income tax. Would you not rather put that $2,200 aside for your own retirement than pay it in taxes to the government?

Your contributions to a traditional IRA must come from a nonretirement account in order for it to be treated as a current-year contribution, which may then be tax-deductible. You can also roll over money from a qualified employer-sponsored plan, such as a 401(k) or 403(b), after you change jobs or retire. It is important to note that these rollovers are not considered current-year contributions but are simply transfers from retirement accounts that came from prior-year contributions. Doing a tax-free rollover from one qualified plan to another will not affect your ability to make a current-year contribution to an IRA.

Not every person contributing to a traditional IRA is entitled to a tax deduction. If you *are an active participant in a qualified retirement plan through your employer* [such as a 401(k) plan], your IRA deduction may be reduced or eliminated, based on your modified adjusted gross income. If you are below the phase-out range, you will qualify for a full deduction. If you are within the range, you will qualify for a partial deduction. If you are at or above the top part of the range, you will receive no tax deduction. The following are the phase-out ranges based on your 2018 modified adjusted gross income:

- For single tax payers covered by a workplace retirement plan, the phase-out range for income is $63,000 to $73,000.

- For married couples filing jointly, where the spouse making the IRA contribution is covered by a workplace retirement plan, the phase-out range is $101,000 to $121,000.
- For an IRA contributor who is not covered by a workplace retirement plan and is married to someone who is covered, the deduction is phased out if the couple's income is between $189,000 and $199,000.
- For a married individual filing a separate return who is covered by a workplace retirement plan, the phase-out range is not subject to an annual cost-of-living adjustment and remains at $0 to $10,000.

If you do not qualify for a tax-deductible contribution, you can always make a full *nondeductible* contribution, to the extent of earned income. This will require you to keep track of your basis in the IRA with the IRS by completing Form 8606, which must be included with your personal tax return. Once you start making distributions, you will not be taxed on the portion of the distribution that is considered a return of your basis (nondeductible contribution). I would only recommend making nondeductible contributions if you do not qualify for a Roth IRA contribution.

The money in a traditional IRA grows and compounds on a tax-deferred basis – which means you will not pay taxes until you start receiving distributions after you retire. Many retirees are in a lower tax bracket during this stage of their lives. Therefore, your tax rate and the overall amount of taxes you save when making these contributions may be much greater than the amount of taxes you will pay on the distributions in retirement. Although withdrawals are taxed as ordinary income, many states have special exclusions which may result in little or no tax paid at the state level on these distributions.

The IRS gives you all of these significant tax-advantaged savings in order to encourage you to be responsible and save for your retirement. However, the IRS will also penalize you if you take distributions from your retirement account before you reach age 59 1/2 – once again to encourage responsible savings for retirement (because obviously, if you are withdrawing from your retirement account before you are retired, that will deplete the money that is supposed to be there for you when you retire). In addition to paying income tax on these withdrawals, you may also be subject to a 10% federal income tax penalty.

There are some exceptions to the early withdrawal penalty:

- If you withdraw money as a result of a disability,
- If you use that money to pay for medical insurance while you are unemployed, or
- If you use that money to pay for higher-education expenses.

Once you reach age $70\frac{1}{2}$, you must begin taking annual required minimum distributions (RMDs) from a traditional IRA, starting no later than April 1 of the year after the year you reach age $70\frac{1}{2}$. If you do not take your RMD, you will be subject to a 50% income tax penalty on the amount that you should have withdrawn. Required minimum distributions (RMDs) are the minimum amount that you are required to withdraw on an annual basis, which is based on your IRA account values at December 31 of the previous year, as well as IRS actuarial tables, which estimate life expectancies.

Roth IRAs

Roth IRAs are another type of specially designated account that allows individuals to save money for retirement in a tax-efficient manner. You cannot deduct the contributions you make to a Roth IRA. However, qualified Roth IRA distributions are free of federal, state, and city income tax and are not included as part of your AGI once you retire. If you expect to be in a higher tax bracket in retirement, a Roth IRA could be a great choice.

An added benefit, even if you expect to be in a lower tax bracket, is that, unlike traditional IRA distributions, Roth IRA distributions are not added to your AGI. When your AGI reaches a certain level, up to 85% of your Social Security benefits can also become taxable. Many retirees who must take their required minimum distribution (RMD) from their traditional IRAs are forced to pay taxes on their Social Security income; a Roth IRA could possibly avoid this additional tax.

Roth IRAs can be valuable in that you can contribute to a Roth after age $70\frac{1}{2}$, provided you are still working and have earned income. There is no RMD requirement with Roth IRAs, and therefore you will have no mandatory distributions regardless of your age. After you pass away and leave your Roth IRA to your beneficiaries, the RMD rules will apply to them.

Also, you can withdraw contributions – but not the earnings on those contributions – from your Roth IRA, at any time and for any reason without paying tax, and those withdrawals are not subject to the 10% federal income tax penalty. However, the *earnings* are subject to income tax and the IRS 10% penalty if you withdraw them before age 59 1/2. In order to make a qualified tax-free and penalty-free distribution of earnings, your account must meet the five-year holding requirement and you must be age 59 1/2 or older. The exceptions to this penalty are the same as under the traditional IRA.

The eligibility to contribute to a Roth IRA phases out for taxpayers with higher incomes. The rules regarding eligibility for traditional and Roth IRAs are confusing (to say the least). Therefore, I encourage you to visit www.calcxml.com/calculators/ira-calculator. This calculator will assist you in determining your eligibility for either IRA.

I believe every individual should take full advantage of the tax benefits that are available through employer-sponsored retirement plans and should fully fund their IRA accounts each year based on eligibility. There is no more efficient way to save for your retirement than to do it through a tax-advantaged account. The government is giving you a gift that will allow you to accelerate your savings over time.

Because of the strict annual contribution limits, many higher-income individuals may not be able to save sufficient funds for retirement through conventional retirement accounts. Moreover, many individuals have delayed the process of saving for retirement and will not have sufficient funds set aside when the time comes. Establishing an annuity may be one solution to addressing these problems.

Fixed and Variable Annuities

By far annuities, in particular variable annuities, are some of the most controversial financial planning strategies in planning for retirement. Many financial advisors are dead set against annuities and do not believe they are appropriate for their clients. Others are strong advocates for annuities and believe they should be part of an individual's overall retirement strategy. I believe that both sides of this argument have some merit, but the true answer lies with the needs of the individual. In my opinion, annuities are not right for everyone, but depending on your specific circumstances, they may be exactly what you need. Before you consider whether annuities are appropriate for you or not, however, you need to understand what annuities are.

An annuity is an investment product created by a life insurance company that promises to provide a series of payments over time. An *annuity contract* is not a qualified retirement plan. However, it does provide tax-deferred growth like a qualified retirement plan. One of the biggest advantages to establishing an annuity is that there are no contribution limits, which gives you the opportunity to save substantially more for retirement. After fully funding your employer-provided retirement plans and your IRA accounts, an annuity is a potential option to complement your overall retirement savings strategy.

One of the biggest arguments against annuities is that they have contract limitations, fees, and charges, which can include mortality and expense charges, account fees, underlying investment management fees, administrative fees, and charges for various other optional benefits. The majority of annuities have backloads (surrender charges) that are assessed if you (as the contract owner) surrender the contract before a certain period of time. All withdrawals of earnings are taxed as ordinary income, and the tax advantage of long-term capital gain and qualified dividends does not apply to earnings from annuities. Withdrawals of the income portion of the annuity prior to age 59½ may also be subject to a 10% federal income tax penalty.

All guarantees are made by the insurance company issuing the contract and are based on their claims-paying ability. Annuities are not guaranteed by the FDIC or any other government agency.

Some annuity contracts allow you to purchase an insurance option that could pay an income for a specified period of time, such as your lifetime or the lifetimes of you and your spouse. The guaranteed retirement income or income for life option may help with your fears of outliving your money.

With both a fixed and variable annuity, you have the option of either an immediate or deferred annuity. Deciding on which is the most appropriate for you is a function of when you anticipate starting the distribution process:

- With an *immediate annuity,* you typically fund it with a lump-sum premium up front. Payments usually start immediately after the contract is funded and continue for the life of the contract. This type of annuity is often purchased at the beginning of retirement and is usually more suitable if you are nearing or already in retirement.

- A *deferred annuity* can be funded with either a lump-sum or a series of contributions over time during the accumulation period. The accumulation period is the time during which premiums are paid for a purchase of an annuity. The payments are typically deferred for a certain number of years and are based on the account value after the accumulation period. The income payment amount will depend on several factors, such as the initial investment amount, the contract's actual rate of return, the contract holder's age, and the number of years payments will be received.

Fixed Annuities

A fixed annuity is a contract with an insurance company that guarantees a fixed and guaranteed rate of interest on your money during the life of the contract. In essence, you give your money to an insurance company, and it promises to pay you back with a predetermined rate of interest. Fixed annuities are typically viewed as conservative investments; the biggest risk associated with them is the claims-paying ability of the insurance company making the guarantee.

In the current low-interest-rate environment, most fixed annuities do not offer an attractive rate of return. Therefore, if you are seeking growth and the potential of your investment returns beating inflation, then a fixed annuity may not be appropriate for you.

Variable Annuities

A variable annuity is a long-term investment vehicle designed specifically for retirement. It is a contract, where you (as the contract holder) agree to make a single payment or a series of payments to an insurance company in exchange for a future income. The insurance company usually makes these income payments to you in retirement, and they can be planned to last for your lifetime or the lifetimes of you and your spouse (individual or joint).

Throughout the accumulation period, you invest in an assortment of investment subaccounts based on your risk tolerance, time horizons, and long-term goals. If you have purchased an annuity with income-for-life guarantees or with a guaranteed death benefit, you may be willing to take on some additional risk, because of the downside protection. You can take part in the growth potential of the stock market or other investment choices. The future value of the annuity and the amount of income available in retirement depend on the performance of these investments. This may provide you the opportunity for greater growth and increase your chances of outpacing inflation.

The actual account value of a variable annuity (which includes the investment principal and income) is not guaranteed. Instead, the value of your account will depend on the performance of your investment choices within the subaccounts of the variable annuity. Therefore, the account value may be worth more or less than your original purchase if you ultimately choose to surrender it. The additional guarantees you may be able to purchase typically do not guarantee the actual account value, but they may guarantee an income stream for life or a death benefit.

A variable annuity may also offer you the option to purchase guarantees for an additional cost. These guarantees can help protect against the downside risks of investing in the stock market, through guaranteed lifetime payout options. Some contracts provide guaranteed death benefits, regardless of the actual account value. In my opinion, some of these guarantees are exactly what make variable annuities so valuable to many individuals.

Some financial analysts believe that retirees may get more financial security by combining insurance products and mutual funds.[5] Most people would agree that insuring ourselves against the risk of the unknown is the prudent thing to do. Risk management is an everyday part of our lives. We have health insurance, life insurance, long-term disability insurance, long-term care insurance, auto insurance, homeowner's insurance, and so on to protect many aspects of our life and secure our family. Therefore, it is only natural that we take steps to guarantee the long-term security of our retirement. With the proper riders, a variable annuity contract with an insurance company can help provide this added peace of mind. This form of insurance may not be necessary or appropriate for everyone, but in many cases, I believe it should be one of the tools used as part of your overall retirement planning strategy.

Please see an Investor Education Series published for FINRA for even more information at finra.org/sites/default/files/InvestorDocument/p125846.pdf.

---

[5]Based on an article from the *Wall Street Journal* dated 8 March 2011, "Making the Case to Buy an Annuity."

Retirement Funding: "Needs Analysis"

The starting point for planning for retirement is performing a "needs analysis." In other words, you must first estimate how much money you will need after you retire, for *the rest of your life*. You will also need to estimate the benefits you will receive from your defined-benefit retirement plan and Social Security. Then, you need to determine what investment assets you currently have that you can use during your retirement. Finally, you must identify the amount of retirement investment assets you will need to generate sufficient income to support your anticipated cost of living in retirement.

To do this, let us revisit Chapter 3 and analyze James and Patricia Loomis's retirement planning needs, as an example. We have already worked through the most difficult part of this retirement planning needs analysis because we already have the Loomises' statement of financial position (shown in Exhibit 3.1) and their statement of cash flow (shown in Exhibit 3.3).

We start by analyzing their statement of financial position and specifically focusing on their investment assets, because these are the assets that will help generate the necessary income when they retire. The total value of their investment assets as of December 31, 2017, was $951,850. Then we will look at their statement of cash flow (after recommendations) to determine their total cash outflow to sustain their current standard of living. The Loomises' total cash outflow was $189,976.

To complete this analysis, we have included the Loomises' answers to the 12 key questions and assumptions from Exhibit 8.1, shown here in Exhibit 8.5.

James is currently 37 years old and his wife Patricia is 36. Their combined family income is $216,876, as outlined on their statement of cash flow as of December 31, 2017 (see Exhibit 3.3). Based on their statement of financial position (shown in Exhibit 3.1), their total investment assets are $951,850. However, from this amount, we will exclude the $4,000 currently in the educational savings plan, because this will not be available during their retirement. Their total investment assets currently include a building valued at $750,000, which has a mortgage of $740,000. Therefore, this mortgage would be a reduction in their net investment assets. That leaves them with a net of $207,850 in investable retirement savings assets ($951,850 less $4,000, less $740,000).

Exhibit 8.5   Sample Answers to Analyze Your Retirement Needs

1. What is your current age? 37

2. What is your current income? $191,876

3. What is your spouse's income (if applicable)? $25,000

4. What is your current retirement savings? $207,850

5. What is your desired retirement age? 67

6. How many years of retirement income do you expect to need? 29

7. What is the expected inflation rate? 3%

8. What percentage of your current combined income will you need at retirement? 62%

9. What do you expect your pre-retirement return on investments to be? 7%

10. What do you expect your postretirement return on investments to be? 5%

11. Would you like to assume that you will be receiving Social Security benefits in retirement? Yes

12. If you do expect to receive Social Security, what is the monthly dollar amount in today's dollars? $3,902

Although it is impossible for anyone to accurately predict the actual rate of inflation before and during their retirement, the Loomises have decided to estimate a 3% inflation rate, which is above the historical average. James will reach his full Social Security retirement age at 67 and will also be entitled to Medicare at the age of 65. Therefore, the Loomises are using this age as their realistic retirement age.

Based on James's family history, he does not believe he will live past age 90; based on Patricia's family history, she expects to live until age 95. Because they are both in relatively good health, they would like to use age 95 for Patricia and therefore expect to live 29 years in retirement.

James went to the Social Security website and used the retirement estimator calculator: He expects to receive $31,212 per year in Social Security benefits and his wife expects to collect $15,606 per year, for a total of $46,818. This would be $3,902 per month of combined benefits and represents approximately 21% of their current income.

Based on the detailed needs analysis of their cash flow statement, they believe they will need 62% of the current year's income to maintain their standard of living in retirement. Here's how they calculated this:

- They took their total cash outflow for the 12 months ending December 31, 2017, which was $189,976, and they subtracted the $7,620 of outflows being added to their investment assets.
- They subtracted the $34,049 per year from their annual home mortgage payment, because this mortgage would be paid off a few months before James turns 67.
- They further analyzed their cash flow statement and realized they would no longer need to make the $1,400 per year payment for term life insurance or the $1,200 per year payment for James's long-term disability.
- They subtracted the $3,328 in student loan payments currently being paid, because they anticipate this loan will be paid off in the next five years.
- They subtracted the $19,125 in Social Security tax, because this will no longer be applicable in their retirement years.
- They prepared a tax projection based on their expected retirement income and determined that their overall federal and state income tax would be reduced from the current $47,400 to $40,400, which reduced their cash outflows by $7,000.
- They also would have been able to eliminate their entire child-care-related expenses of $6,090, but they chose not to do so, because they factored in helping their future grandchildren.

Based on these calculations, they realized they will need $116,254 ($189,976 less $7,620, less $34,049, less $1,400, less $1,200, less $3,328, less $19,125, less $7,000). In addition, the Loomises plan on being very active and fully enjoying their retirement; therefore, they wanted to budget an additional $18,000 per year for travel and entertainment.

This brings their total cash flow needs in today's dollars to $134,254, which represents about 62% ($134,254/$216,876) of their current cash inflows. Therefore, they will have to have sufficient investable retirement assets to be able to cover this shortfall by the time James reaches his expected retirement age of 67.

Based on the answers to the above questions, along with the assumptions made, we are ready to determine James and Patricia Loomis's *point X* – the amount of investable assets they will need in order to secure a comfortable retirement and maintain their current standard of living. We utilized a retirement calculator and input all the above facts and assumptions, and we determined that, in order to achieve their inflation adjusted income in retirement:

- The total amount they will need for retirement when James reaches age 67, which includes the amount they already saved, is $4,546,756.
- They should save 10.5% of their yearly income, less any employer match.

A big assumption we made in this "Retirement Needs Analysis" is that Social Security will still be around to make good on its promised benefit to the Loomises. If we changed that one variable and indicated to not include Social Security benefits, the following would have been the results of our analysis:

- The total amount they will need for retirement when James reaches age 67, which includes the amount they already saved, is $6,976,006.
- They should save 19.2% of their yearly income, less any employer match.

This further comparison and analysis highlights the potential impact on the Loomises if in fact Social Security will not be around when they are ready to retire. If this is a major concern for them, they will need to increase their annual savings to 19.2% of their yearly income or make major changes in their standard of living once they reach their retirement years.

You can conduct a similar analysis of your own financial situation by going to www.calcxml.com/calculators/retirement-calculator. This will give you an opportunity to do numerous what-if scenarios utilizing your particular facts and circumstances.

Based on the analysis we conducted for the Loomises in Chapter 3, they are on a clear path to achieving financial independence. They were saving $7,620 per year before implementing the cash flow recommendations we made. They were also able to free up an additional $26,900 after implementing the cash flow savings strategies outlined in Chapter 3. They had already committed to funding James's SIMPLE plan with an additional $7,500 (bringing him up to the maximum $12,500 for 2017) and Patricia's traditional IRA with an additional $4,000 (bringing her up to the maximum $5,500 for 2017). After their retirement needs analysis, they have further agreed to fund James's maximum $5,500 nondeductible IRA for 2017, since he had already made the maximum contribution to the SIMPLE plan. This will bring their total savings to $24,620 starting this year, which is more than they need to achieve financial independence in retirement.[6] They were able to fund these retirement accounts for 2017, since they completed this analysis before the tax filing deadline.

If you do not pay attention to the tax consequences when planning for retirement, you may be paying significantly more in taxes than the law requires. This is why you must include tax planning as part of your overall retirement planning strategy. Using a financial planning approach that takes advantage of these *Tax Alpha to the 2nd Power*[SM] facts and strategies will maximize your wealth accumulation goals.

TAX ALPHA TO THE 2ND POWER[SM] FACTS AND STRATEGIES FOR PLANNING FOR RETIREMENT

Here are several tax facts and strategies that will address your retirement planning goals at an exponential rate, which will help put you on the path for financial independence, *point X*.

- Compare the benefits of a traditional IRA to a Roth IRA and choose the one that is best for your particular situation. With a traditional IRA, you may get a current year tax deduction for your contribution and tax-deferred growth. With the Roth IRA contribution, you do not receive any upfront tax deduction, but your qualified withdrawals are completely tax-free.
- With a Roth IRA, you do not have to take a required minimum distribution (RMD) at age 70½. This may have the added benefit of keeping your AGI low enough to also avoid paying taxes on your Social Security benefits during your retirement years.

(continued)

---

[6]For more information on the costs/fees and risks associated with investments, see Chapter 9.

- The deadline for making a traditional or Roth IRA contribution is April 15, the regular due date for filing your income tax return, even if you are filing an extension.
- Fully fund your employer-provided retirement plan before the end of the year. The deferral limit for a 401(k) is $18,500 for 2018; the deferral limit for a SIMPLE plan is $12,500 for 2018.
- Take advantage of the additional deferral limit "catch-up" contribution to a 401(k) of $6,000 and to a SIMPLE plan of $3,000 for each participant age 50 or older.
- Make a Roth contribution of $5,500 for 2018 per spouse ($6,500 if age 50 or older), if you qualify. In order to qualify as a married couple your AGI must be under $189,000 or partial contribution up to $199,000. In order to make a Roth contribution as a single taxpayer, your AGI must be under $120,000 or partial contribution up to $135,000. If your income exceeds these levels, establish these as traditional nondeductible IRA contributions. You can then convert these to a Roth IRA, regardless of your income level, but special rules apply.
- There is no income limitation for converting a traditional IRA to a Roth IRA. Consider converting part or all of your traditional IRAs into a Roth IRA so that all your future earnings can grow tax-free. This can be very beneficial, especially in years where you are in very low tax brackets and in years where your IRA accounts have decreased in value. Keep in mind, however, that a conversion is a taxable transfer, and you must report the conversion amount as income on your tax return in the same year.
- If you made a contribution to a retirement plan (including an IRA or Roth IRA), you may be eligible for a nonrefundable saver's credit. The income limit of the saver's credit for low and moderate income workers is $63,000 for married couples filing jointly, $47,250 for head of household, and $31,500 for single. This credit can be as much as 50% of the first $2,000 of eligible retirement contributions made in 2018. This means you could receive a saver's credit of $1,000 by simply making a $2,000 retirement plan contribution. Talk about great incentives to save for your retirement!
- If you are separated from your employment for any reason, such as getting laid off, quitting, or retiring, you may be entitled to a distribution from a qualified employer retirement plan, which would be fully taxable if not properly handled. You must set this up as a tax-free rollover, which allows you to make a tax-free transfer of a distribution from one qualified employer retirement plan to another qualified plan or to a traditional IRA. You should instruct your employer to directly roll over the funds either to a traditional IRA you designate or to the plan of your new employer. If you elect the distribution to be paid directly to you, you still have 60 days to make a tax-free rollover yourself. If you do not meet these requirements, the full amount may be subject to tax and an additional 10% penalty.

- Generally, there is a 10% penalty that applies to taxable distributions made to you before age 59½ from qualified plans. You may avoid the 10% penalty if you meet one of the following exceptions: rollover, disability, separation from service if age 55 or older, medical costs, substantially equal payments for at least five years, beneficiary of a deceased plan participant, IRS levy, or part of a qualified domestic relations court order. For more details on the exceptions to the early withdrawal penalty, see IRS Form 5329 and instructions.
- In addition to the above penalty exceptions, with a traditional IRA, you may avoid the 10% penalty if you use the distribution to pay for qualified higher education expenses or if the distribution is used for qualified first-time home-buyer expenses of up to $10,000.
- You should avoid borrowing money against your retirement plan because that can have dire consequences. For example, if you leave your employer before you pay off the loan, your employer will reduce your vested account balance by the amount of the outstanding loan and will report this loan amount as a taxable distribution in the year you separated from service. This amount may be subject to tax and the 10% penalty.
- **Effective January 1, 2018, if you had a qualified retirement plan loan that has been deemed taxable, you are now given more than 60 days to roll it over tax-free into another qualified plan. In the tax year the offset is treated as a distribution from your plan, you now have until the due date (including extension) of filing your federal income tax return to complete the tax-free rollover.** If you realize you have to pay tax and a penalty before the filing due date of your return, you can still complete the rollover and avoid paying both the tax and the 10% penalty.
- Making elective salary deferrals to your company's retirement plan allows you to defer tax on your salary and get a tax-free buildup of earnings within your plan until you start making withdrawals when you retire. You must take full advantage of these plans by taking the maximum deferral allowed by your employer's plan. If you cannot manage to do the maximum, then you must at least contribute the minimum amount that will maximize your employer's match.
- Many employer-sponsored 401(k) plans allow employees to contribute as after-tax Roth contributions. If you take advantage of a Roth 401(k), you can make significantly higher contributions than what would be available in a Roth IRA. Keep in mind, Roth contributions are made in after-tax dollars, so you will not receive any upfront tax savings.
- Where employer plans include a qualified Roth contribution program, conversions can also be made from a pre-tax contribution 401(k) account to the Roth 401(k) account. However, you must remember that a conversion is a taxable transfer, and you must report it on your tax return for the year of the conversion.

(*continued*)

- When rolling over retirement plan distributions, your employer must withhold 20% if the check is first paid to you. To avoid the 20% withholding, you should have your employer make a direct rollover to your new employer's qualified plan or an individual IRA.
- If you are collecting Social Security benefits, up to 85% of these benefits could be subject to federal income tax. You can avoid paying income tax on your Social Security benefits if your provisional income is $25,000 or less if you are single, or $32,000 or less if you are married and filing jointly. Planning your retirement income to include tax-free withdrawals, such as from a Roth IRA account, may allow you to keep your income under these thresholds and ultimately avoid paying tax on your Social Security benefits.
- If you are 70½ or older, you can take up to a $100,000 tax-free distribution to the charity or charities of your choice from an individual retirement account (IRA). This will allow you to meet your RMD (required minimum distribution) without increasing your adjusted gross income. This can be used as a strategy to avoid paying taxes on Social Security benefits for lower income taxpayers, and it can avoid the 3.8% Medicare tax on net investment income for higher income taxpayers.
- For 2018, the maximum annual retirement *distribution* (benefit to be paid out in retirement years) that can be paid to a retired employee by a defined benefit plan is $220,000 (indexed for inflation annually) with an equivalent annual *contribution limit* (amount to be funded by your employer into the plan in the current year) of up to $270,000 or more. The retirement plan actuary makes these calculations as the contribution amounts vary depending on the age of the plan participant. These contributions are deductible to the business entity and never subject to Social Security and Medicare taxes when contributed on behalf of an employee. Earnings on investments and subsequent withdrawals are also not subject to Social Security and Medicare taxes. Starting 2013, this became even more important, since the 0.9% increase in Medicare tax for high income salaries and self-employed earnings may apply, as well as the additional 3.8% Medicare surtax on net investment income.
- For 2018, an employee may make up to an $18,500 salary deferral (withholding) contribution from pretax dollars to a defined contribution plan such as a 401(k) or 403(b). An additional $6,000 contribution can be made if the taxpayer is 50 years old or older. The maximum combined employer and employee contribution for 2018 is $55,000 ($61,000 if age 50 or older). It should be noted that the employer portion of contributions is not subject to Social Security or Medicare taxes.
- For 2018, an employee may make a pretax salary deferral up to $12,500 to their SIMPLE (Savings Incentive Match Plans for Employees) retirement plan. If 50 or older, the employee can make an additional $3,000 catch-up salary deferral. In a matching SIMPLE plan, the employer's contribution is the lesser

of 3% of the employees taxable compensation or actual salary deferral (there are some exceptions to this rule).

- According to Carol Ventura, CFP®, CLU®, ChFC®, Retirement Services Manager with HD Vest Financial Services, "For 2018, the maximum compensation to be considered for a SEP IRA and a Solo 401(k) contribution is $275,000. The SEP and Solo 401(k) contributions are further limited by a maximum contribution and deduction limit. Generally, the maximum contribution is limited to 25% of compensation, which typically is W-2. In the case of the self-employed, the 25% of compensation limit is reduced to 20%, because the contribution is based on earnings from self-employment. The SEP is limited to $55,000. The Solo 401(k) is limited to $55,000 or $61,000 if the business owner is age 50 or older."

AN ACTION PLAN FOR PLANNING FOR RETIREMENT

1. **Calculate how much money you will need when you retire.** There are many retirement calculators available online, including one at www.calcxml.com/calculators/retirement-calculator. You will be able to run through an unlimited number of "what if?" scenarios.

   Once you know how much you will need, you can start planning to reach that goal – your personal *point X*.

2. **Start saving and investing for your retirement as soon as you finish school and start working.** You may not believe it, but you *can* live on 90% of what you earn, no matter how little you think that is. So set aside at least 10% of your earnings, because the earlier you start, the better off you will be. You have the benefit of time on your side, to help that money grow. Do not continue to put off saving for your retirement until "later," whether that is next year, or when you get a raise, or a promotion, or a new job – start saving *now*.

3. **Learn the difference between various types of retirement plans.** Then find out what the maximum is that you can contribute to the plans that apply to you. If you are not sure about this, meet with a financial advisor who can review your specific financial situation and help you plan better for your future.

   (continued)

4. **Invest as much as your company will allow you to contribute into your employer's 401(k) plan.** You do not have to pay income taxes on that money now, because you are not receiving it currently as income. Plus, most employers still match at least some percentage of what you contribute. Getting a 3% employer match is like getting a 3% raise. If not contributing makes you ineligible for the match, that would be like turning down a raise your employer is willing to give you.

5. **Do not worry about the day-to-day ups and downs of the stock market; keep in mind that you are saving for *the long haul*** – for your retirement. So if you are in your twenties, that is at least 40 years away. Even if you are in your fifties and hope to retire at 65, but accept that you may be working until you are 70, you still have at least 10 years before retirement. So what happened to the stock market today is not important to the money you will need and hopefully have when you retire. Just keep saving, and keep investing, with your long-term goal in mind.

CHAPTER 9

Managing Your Investments

In the twentieth century, the United States endured two world wars and other traumatic and expensive military conflicts; the Depression; a dozen or so recessions and financial panics; oil shocks; a flu epidemic; and the resignation of a disgraced president. Yet the Dow rose from 66 to 11,497.

—Warren Buffett,
the most successful investor of the twentieth century

This chapter provides information and guidance for dealing with investments, beginning with basic definitions of various investment vehicles: stocks, bonds, hybrid securities, mutual funds, and exchange-traded funds (ETFs). I then give general information on the process of creating an investment portfolio that considers your financial goals, comfort levels, expectations, and the effects of inflation and taxes on these investments. I will also discuss how to adjust a portfolio as your financial goals change.

The purpose of this chapter is to provide you with an understanding of investing, which normally takes people many years to learn on their own. Unfortunately, many investors learn this lesson the hard way and never recover from their financial losses. It is important that we learn from our past and do our best not to repeat the mistakes history has taught us. The rewards of proper investing have been very generous when investors have adopted an investment discipline that allows them to purchase quality investments and then allow those investments to take their course. This may have been best said by Warren Buffett, the primary shareholder, chairman, and CEO of

Berkshire Hathaway, who is also considered by many to be the most successful investor of the twentieth century:

> Put together a portfolio of companies whose aggregate earnings march upward over the years, and so also will the portfolio's market value.

The information and guidance on investments that I provide in this chapter are designed to help you stay the course toward financial independence and your *point X.*

Analyzing Your Ability and Willingness to Take Risk

Understanding your ability to take risk is one of the most fundamental first steps you must take before implementing any investment strategy. Keep in mind that your *ability* to take risk could be different from your *willingness* to take risk, and that is why we need to analyze both.

In a practical sense, your biggest risk as an investor is the failure to achieve your goal. For example, if you know you need to achieve 8% annual return on average over the next ten years to retire, if you invest in fixed income paying 4% because you are afraid of market risk, you have set yourself up for failure.

That being said, you should take no more than is necessary to achieve your investment goal. For example, if you are closing on a house next month, the best course of action is to just keep the down payment in your bank or money-market fund. The downside risk of failing to close on the house far outweighs making a few extra bucks with a more aggressive investment strategy.

Besides investment goals, from an investment standpoint, when we talk about risk, we are thinking about probability and magnitude of loss, particularly in the short term.

Your *ability* to take on risk can be quantified primarily through your net worth (see Exhibit 3.2 to calculate this) and the composition of your assets and liabilities reflected on your statement of financial position. In addition to this, you must consider other factors such as your time horizon (number of years you will be invested), human capital (income from employment), and expected income from investing.

When evaluating your *ability* to take risk, you must also take into consideration what your ultimate financial goals will be and the downside risk of failure to achieve the goal. This will help you frame the minimum market risk you need to take to achieve your goal. The shorter your time horizon, the less risk you should be able to take. For example, an 18-year-old investor who has 49 years ahead of her before retirement can tolerate a much greater level of risk than a 60-year-old who is only 7 years away from retirement.

With regard to *willingness* to take risk, every investor has his or her own unique view and can tolerate only a certain number of losses before becoming emotional, which may lead to bad investment decisions. Of course, a higher level of risk corresponds to the potential for a higher rate of return on your investments. If your investing risk tolerance was as simple as stating you want the highest rate of return in the long run, then you would simply invest in the most speculative types of investments. But it is not that simple; instead, you need to examine your own personal tolerance to risk, so that the ultimate investment portfolio you choose will have staying power in both good and bad times. Staying power means that no matter how bad things appear, emotionally you will not make the bad decision to sell at market lows, sell too early, or chase investments. It is important to remember that it is you, the individual investor, who must have the staying power.

In a perfect world, willingness to take risk would be framed by the targeted return to achieve the desired investment goal. Unfortunately, people's willingness to take on risk at an emotional level sometimes undermines their investment discipline, as shown in the following examples of common emotional mistakes.

- **Selling at the bottom:** The best time to be in the market is at the bottom, because stocks and bonds are poised to rise. This obviously results in gains as long as you, the investor, have staying power. Unfortunately, we human beings bring our emotions into the investment decision-making process, and emotions cost money. When the economy is booming and the stock market reaches new highs, people are more likely to invest their money because of all the positive news and emotions surrounding the market. Naturally, the opposite is true when the economy is doing poorly and the world is filled with negative news. Most investors are not willing to invest then; in fact, many sell their investments at lower prices at this time. If Macy's department store ran a 50% off sale on every item in the store, most people would rush to Macy's and buy everything they could. On the other hand, if Macy's increased its prices by 50% from the original price, very few people would shop in their store.

However, when it comes to investing, human nature causes us to react very differently than this, and many people tend to buy high and sell low. It is a very expensive portfolio decision to miss the rebound.

- **Selling early:** When the investment has gone up, undisciplined investors sell too early to "capture most of the gain." This means they miss any additional growth, incur trading costs, and potentially have tax consequences.

- **Buying late to chase returns:** Too often, investors pile into last year's best investment strategies to chase returns. Unfortunately, this is often the worst time to invest. An asset class that has had a significant run-up may be fully valued and may underperform next year. Worst case, the run-up has created a bubble, and there will be severe losses. Reference Exhibit 9.3 to see why chasing returns typically does not pay off.

Therefore, it is critically important that you select an investment model that you are willing to stay with, even in the worst of markets. The appropriate investment plan for you should be the one that provides you with the highest potential rate of return in the long run that is within your risk tolerance.

Part of determining your risk tolerance goes back to analyzing your personal behavior and how you deal with your other life issues. For example, if you typically are a nervous individual and tend to go down the straight-and-narrow path in life, then you most likely will choose a more conservative investment risk model. On the other hand, if you are fearless and like to live life in the fast lane, then you would most likely choose a more aggressive investment risk model.

Because the question of your personal risk tolerance revolves around human behavior and emotions, it is important to understand your own investment psychology. I consider this the investor's psychological evaluation of his or her risk tolerance. There are many ways to measure your risk tolerance and numerous questionnaires are provided on many investment websites. Exhibit 9.1 provides a simplified questionnaire. Please take a few moments to answer these questions to determine your own investor risk tolerance profile and score.

The answers to the questions in Exhibit 9.1 provide you with a numerical score that measures your tolerance to investment risk. This risk tolerance measurement is the gauge by which we determine your *willingness* (psychological) to take risk. The higher your score, the more risk you would be willing to tolerate. Understanding your

Exhibit 9.1   Six Questions to Assess Your Investor Risk Tolerance Profile and Score

1. How many years will you stay invested for?
   1. ___ 5 years or less
   2. ___ 5–10 years
   3. ___ 10 years or more

2. What would you typically consider most important when investing?
   1. ___ Preserving your capital
   2. ___ Conservative growth with income
   3. ___ Maximum growth

3. A year after making a $50,000 investment, your account value drops to $40,000 and the Dow Jones Industrial Average is also down by 20%. How would this make you feel and what would you do about it?
   1. ___ Extremely uncomfortable: I would sell my investments immediately.
   2. ___ Uncomfortable, but I would be willing to listen to my financial advisor's recommendation.
   3. ___ I would view this as a buying opportunity and would be willing to invest more money at these lower prices.

4. Which of the following phrases matches your view of taking on risk with your investments?
   1. ___ Not willing to take on risk
   2. ___ Willing to take a limited amount of risk
   3. ___ Willing to take a high level of risk

5. If you invested $50,000, which range of possible outcomes would you be most comfortable with within a year?
   1. ___ Value fluctuating from $48,500 and $51,500 (3% increase or decrease)
   2. ___ Value fluctuating from $46,500 and $53,500 (7% increase or decrease)
   3. ___ Value fluctuating from $45,000 and $55,000 (10% increase or decrease)

6. Which of the following statements best describes your attitude toward life?
   1. ___ Slow and steady wins the race.
   2. ___ Live a balanced life, everything in moderation.
   3. ___ The greater the risk, the greater the reward.

Now that you have answered these six questions, you are ready to determine your risk profile score. Simply add up the numbers next to each question you check off in the questionnaire. For example, if you checked off item number 2 for each question, your risk profile score would be a 12. This would place you in the conservative growth investor profile as outlined below.

Investor Risk Tolerance "Profile"	"Score"
___ Conservative Income	6–7
___ Income	8–10
___ Conservative Growth	11–13
___ Growth	14–16
___ Maximum Growth	17–18

risk tolerance is the second step you must take before implementing any investment strategy.

If your *ability* and *willingness* to take risk bring you to the same result, then you have accurately determined the proper investment strategy for you. Very often, the results from this analysis could vary significantly. Consequently, investors who have high *ability* to take risk may not be *willing* to take on that level of risk; conversely, the opposite is true as well. You may need to make a compromise between both results, but ultimately you must decide for yourself what level of risk makes you comfortable.

Understanding Investment Risk

Now that you have evaluated your own risk tolerance, it is important to understand exactly what the investment risks are. This will help you to be better prepared to make more informed investing decisions, put together an investment portfolio that includes various asset classes, and manage your investments. Based upon my experience, I have identified and defined a number of investment risks; the most common include inflation risk, interest rate risk, default risk, market risk, economic risk, and company- or industry-specific risk.

> *Inflation risk* is the threat that your investment returns will not keep pace with the rate of inflation. For example, if inflation increases each year by 3%, but your investments are only growing by 1%, you are effectively losing money. This is because the general price of goods and services is rising faster than your investment, so each year you effectively can buy less. In order for your portfolio to have a reasonable chance of beating inflation, it should include growth-oriented stocks, growth and income stock mutual funds, and other growth-related investment vehicles. These types of investments have historically outpaced the rate of inflation over the long term, although there is no guarantee that they will do so in the future.

> *Interest rate risk* is typically associated with bonds and other fixed-income investment vehicles, which tend to be sensitive to changes in interest rates. When interest rates rise, the value of these investments falls. Of course, the opposite is true as well: As interest rates drop in our economy, the value of these investments increases. One way to protect against interest rate risk when you believe interest rates will be rising

is to shorten the duration of your bond holdings (closer maturity dates).

Default risk is typically associated with bonds and other fixed-income investment vehicles, where credit is extended. This is the risk that a company or other issuers of debt will be unable to make the required payments on their obligations.

Market rate risk is the risk of the overall market experiencing a decline. It typically drags down the value of all securities at the same time. Market rate risk is a result of the aggregate movement in the market and may not relate specifically to your investments. Market risk can affect almost any type of investments, including stocks, bonds, commodities, real estate, and many others.

Economic risk occurs when the overall economy experiences a downturn, such as when a recession occurs. These economic downturns can result in a decrease in earnings and profits from the underlying companies you may be invested in. This can diminish a company's ability to pay a dividend or even the interest on its bonds. It is important to note that certain companies and industries may be more sensitive to economic changes than others. For example, companies that produce luxury items will be much more sensitive to economic downturns than companies that produce necessities.

Company- or industry-specific risk occurs when an event affects only a specific company or industry – for example, if accounting irregularities are discovered during a particular company's financial statement audit, the value of investment in that company is likely to decrease. These types of events can have a significant effect on a company's value, as well as the confidence investors can place with its management. By far, this is the strongest argument for a well-diversified portfolio and why you should never keep all your eggs in one basket.

Stocks, Bonds, Hybrid Securities, Mutual Funds, and Exchange-Traded Funds

Based on my years of experience, the most efficient and popular way to invest is by purchasing individual stocks, bonds, hybrid securities, mutual funds, and exchange-traded funds (ETFs). Therefore, I believe that it is essential that I provide you with a description of each of these investment vehicles.

Stocks[1]

A stock represents a fractional ownership interest in a corporation. When you invest in a corporation, you become a partial owner in the company's business and can participate in the company's profits or losses. As a shareholder in a corporation, you have the benefit of limited liability protection, which minimizes your downside to no more than your investment in the company.

When the corporation makes a profit, you may be rewarded with a dividend. Furthermore, if the corporation continues to grow its revenues and profits, the value of the stock you own will grow as well. You can also realize these gains in the stock's value by selling your shares of a company.

If the company does not do well, you may never see the payment of a dividend, and in fact, the value of your stock could decline. The risk and potential reward associated with investing in stocks are generally much higher than with the other investment vehicles. Therefore, you should be prepared to experience high volatility when investing in stocks.

Bonds[2]

A bond represents a loan that you make to a corporation or government entity, which then in return promises to pay you back with interest over time. In essence, you act as the banker (lender), and the bond issuer is the borrower. This indebtedness to you is documented through a bond certificate, which is issued to you by the entity.

The bond issuer typically needs to raise money to meet other obligations or to facilitate certain projects. If you decide to invest in that issuer's bond, you are willing to lend your money in exchange for the promise to be paid back with a specific rate of interest. The bond investor usually will receive regular interest payments every six months. The interest payments on a bond are usually fixed and stated as a percentage of its "face" value.

---

[1]As with other investments, there are fees and expenses associated with buying and selling securities. Fees may include taxes, commission costs, markup, account transfer and maintenance fees, and custody fees.

[2]See footnote 1.

It is important to understand that bonds come with interest-rate risk (described previously): As noted, the values of bonds have an inverse relationship with the direction of interest rates in our economy. The longer the time frame to maturity, the more sensitive the fluctuation in market price will be.

When you own individual bonds purchased at face value and hold them to maturity, you will receive the interest payments plus your original principal. Of course, this assumes that the bond issuer does not default on its promise and ultimately pays you back.

Not all bond issuers are created equal. The stronger their balance sheet and the higher their credit rating, the lower the risk involved. The opposite is also true. Therefore, it is logical that the higher the risk associated with purchasing the bond, the higher the rate of return that will be offered by the bond issuer. Bonds are typically considered safe investments, but keep in mind that a higher rate of return being offered is typically associated with a higher potential for default risk.

Bonds can be divided into three major categories: US Treasury bonds, municipal bonds, and corporate bonds. Each category has its own unique features, which you should take into consideration when selecting and evaluating the components of your bond holdings.

U.S. Treasury Securities   Bonds, bills, and notes issued by the US government are also known as *Treasuries* and typically represent the highest-quality bonds available to investors. However, in August 2011, credit-rating agency Standard and Poor's (S&P) announced that it had downgraded the US credit rating for the first time in history. This sent shock waves throughout the credit markets. S&P said, "Political brinksmanship in the debate over the debt had made the US government's ability to manage its finances less stable, less effective, and less predictable." On June 6, 2017, S&P Global Ratings affirmed its AA+ (excellent) long-term and A-1+ short-term unsolicited sovereign credit ratings on the United States of America, and that the outlook on the long-term rating remains stable. With the current political divide in the United States and the federal debt at nearly $20.5 trillion as of December 31, 2017, it does not appear that this rating will be increased back to AAA (outstanding) anytime soon.

In spite of this, many people continue to invest in US Treasury securities, clearly for their known safety and peace of mind. I would be very cautious here because US Treasury yields are currently at historical lows (but rising) and below the expected inflation rate. What may seem like a very safe and conservative investment could still result in losses.

US government bonds are issued by the US Department of the Treasury. They are extremely liquid and traded on the secondary market. Treasury securities are backed by the full faith and credit of the US government. They are considered to have less risk than other bonds and are considered a safe haven, especially during turbulent economic times. The interest earned on Treasury bonds is exempt from state and local taxes. There are four major categories of US Treasury securities:

1. *Treasury bills* (T-bills) are short-term bonds that mature in less than one year. They are sold at a discount from their face value and do not pay interest until their maturity.
2. *Treasury notes* (T-notes) earn a fixed rate of interest every six months and have maturities ranging anywhere from 1 year to 10 years.
3. *Treasury bonds* (T-bonds) have maturities ranging from 10 to 30 years. Similar to treasury notes, T-bonds also have a coupon payment every six months.
4. *Treasury Inflation-Protected Securities* (TIPS) are inflation-indexed bonds. The principal of TIPS is adjusted by changes in the Consumer Price Index. They are typically offered in maturities ranging from 5 to 20 years.

Municipal Bonds Municipal bonds are issued by state and local governments. The money raised by the issuance of these bonds is typically used to pay for public service projects, such as the construction of public schools, highways, low-income housing, sewer systems, and other municipality projects. Municipal bonds are exempt from federal, state, and local income taxes for investors who live in the jurisdiction where the bond is issued: This "triple tax-free" treatment can make them very attractive investments to high-income taxpayers. Exhibit 9.2 shows the equivalent corporate bond rates of return to municipal bonds: For example, if you have a marginal tax rate of 40%, you would have to earn 10% on a corporate bond to equal a 6% rate of return on a municipal bond.

Exhibit 9.2   Municipal Versus Corporate Bonds

In-State Municipal Bonds Rate	Corporate Bond Equivalent Rate at Marginal Federal, State, and Local Tax Rate of:			
	10%	20%	30%	40%
1.00%	1.11%	1.25%	1.43%	1.67%
2.00%	2.22%	2.50%	2.86%	3.33%
3.00%	3.33%	3.75%	4.29%	5.00%
4.00%	4.44%	5.00%	5.71%	6.67%
5.00%	5.56%	6.25%	7.14%	8.33%
6.00%	6.67%	7.50%	8.57%	10.00%
7.00%	7.78%	8.75%	10.00%	11.67%
8.00%	8.89%	10.00%	11.43%	13.33%
9.00%	10.00%	11.25%	12.86%	15.00%
10.00%	11.11%	12.50%	14.29%	16.67%

If $10,000 investment – the annual amount of return based on the above table

$100	$111	$125	$143	$167
$200	$222	$250	$286	$333
$300	$333	$375	$429	$500
$400	$444	$500	$571	$667
$500	$556	$625	$714	$833
$600	$667	$750	$857	$1,000
$700	$778	$875	$1,000	$1,167
$800	$889	$1,000	$1,143	$1,333
$900	$1,000	$1,125	$1,286	$1,500
$1,000	$1,111	$1,250	$1,429	$1,667

This exhibit shows the equivalent full taxable interest rate at different marginal tax rates to result in the same after tax rate for in-state municipal bonds.

There are two major categories of municipal bonds issued by state and local government:

1. *General obligation bonds* are secured by the full faith and credit of the issuer and are supported by the issuer's taxing authority.
2. *Revenue bonds,* unlike general obligation bonds, are secured by the revenues specified in the legal contract between the bond holder and bond issuer. They are required to use these revenues for repayment of the principal and interest on the bonds. They are not backed by the full faith and credit or taxing authority of the municipality; instead, they are backed solely by the revenue-generating ability of the municipal project, such as a bridge toll and other user fees. Under certain circumstances revenue bonds can be subject to federal, state, or local alternative minimum tax.

Corporate Bonds   These bonds are issued by corporations and other for-profit business entities, which issue bonds to raise capital for their expansion and other operating needs. Corporate bonds pay a higher level of interest than government bonds, because they are not backed by the government. A business that has a strong balance sheet, strong earnings, and an excellent credit rating will pay a much lower rate of interest than a business that is not as financially stable. It is important to understand that, when a corporation provides a higher interest rate on their bonds, these bonds come with greater risk. Lastly, it is essential to note that interest earned on corporate bonds is subject to ordinary income tax rates.

Corporate bonds are broken into two categories: investment grade and high yield. *Investment grade bonds* indicate that there is a low risk of default and that the company has a strong capability to repay the debt. *High-yield bonds* have a lower credit rating because of the higher risk of default. To compensate investors for this risk, high-yield bonds pay a significantly higher yield to investors (2% to 4+% annually).

Hybrid Securities

Over the past 20 years, there has been a rise in the popularity of investing in hybrid securities that contain features of both equities and bonds. Among the more notable securities which you should consider for your portfolio are the following:

- **Real estate investment trust (REIT):** A REIT is an investment vehicle to invest in real estate. REITs can own income-producing property and mortgages. What makes REITs unique is that, as long as they distribute at least 90% of their income, they are not taxed at the company level. This means that you as the investor get high dividends.
- **Master limited partnership (MLP):** An MLP is a limited partnership that is publicly traded. The MLP structure is heavily used for gas pipelines.
- **Business development corporation (BDC):** A BDC is a closed-end investment company that provides loans to small and mid-sized companies.
- **Preferred equity:** Preferred equity is a class of ownership with a higher claim on assets and earning than common stock. The investment allure of preferred equity is that they have dividend seniority to common stock. The dividend yield is normally higher than the company's fixed-income interest payment.

- **Convertible debt:** Convertible debt is a type of bond that can be converted into common stock of the company. The allure of convertible debt is that investors benefit from fixed income payments and have the ability to convert to equity if the equity appreciates.

Under the Tax Cuts and Jobs Act, the new law provides a deduction of up to 20% of "domestic qualified business income" from the taxable income of pass-through entity owners, who are individuals, estates, or trusts. This Section 199A deduction is allowed for a taxpayer's aggregate amount of qualified REIT dividends, qualified publicly traded partnership income, and qualified cooperative dividends for the taxable year.

Mutual Funds[3] and Exchange-Traded Funds (ETFs)

According to James Hickey, CFA, the chief investment strategist at HD Vest Financial Services, "Mutual funds and ETFs have become the two most popular ways to gain exposure to individual stocks and bonds. This is because it is a more efficient way to create a diversified portfolio than individually selecting stocks and bonds. As a general rule, I encourage investors to focus on investing in mutual funds and ETFs over individual securities selection. The benefits of professional management and diversification outweigh the incremental costs."

Technically speaking, a mutual fund is an investment security where individual investors pool their money together into a professionally managed fund. Mutual funds also offer investors easy access to investing your money at all levels – that is, regardless of how much or how little money you invest.

When you invest in a mutual fund, you become a shareholder of that mutual fund. As a shareholder, you will participate in the profits and losses of the mutual fund. Keep in mind that investing in mutual funds is similar to investing directly in an individual corporation, in that your liability is limited to the amount you invested.

The mutual fund itself is professionally managed by one or more investment managers, who are assisted by a team of investment analysts in deciding what and when to buy within the framework defined

---

[3]As with other investments, there are fees and expenses associated with buying mutual funds. Some of these fees may include shareholder transaction costs, investment advisory fees, and marketing and distribution expenses.

in the mutual fund's prospectus. These investment decisions involve trading securities, recognizing capital gains and losses, and generating interest and dividends, all on behalf of the mutual fund and its investors. As one of the mutual fund's investors, you participate in these results in proportion to your holdings.

Like a stock, you make your money from dividends and capital appreciation of the underlying securities. The price is set at the end of the day based on the net asset value (NAV) of the underlying securities. The NAV is set by the total value of securities owned divided by the number of mutual fund shares. You have yet another way to participate in the success or failure of your mutual fund investment by selling the shares you own. If you sell your mutual fund shares at a price higher than you originally paid, you may realize capital gains and conversely, if you sell them for less, you may realize capital losses. As a result, mutual funds provide you with three opportunities for growth of your investments: through dividends, capital gains distributions (from the sale of investments within the fund), and possibly capital gains on the sale of your investment in the fund.

When you invest in a mutual fund, you are pooling your money together with many other investors under the common control and management of an investment company. A mutual fund company is an investment company that professionally manages your investment portfolio.

Every mutual fund company has a list of various mutual fund's investment options with varying objectives as stated in their prospectus. You can pick and choose the mutual fund type that is best aligned with your own long-term objectives.

One of the drawbacks to mutual funds is that they cannot be traded throughout the day; although the order may be placed at any time, it will not be executed until the end of the day once the closing value has been determined.

A popular alternative to a mutual fund is the exchange-traded fund (ETF). Like a mutual fund, an ETF holds assets such as stocks, bonds, or commodities. However, unlike a mutual fund, but similar to a stock, an ETF's value fluctuates throughout the day, and there is immediate transparency into the underlying holdings. Many ETFs are based on a particular index, such as the S&P 500, the Dow Jones Industrial Average, gold index, corporate bond index, or health care index. Keep in mind that you cannot invest directly in an index. Most ETFs are not actively managed; instead, they simply hold investments that represent a particular index. This makes ETFs with passive strategies more attractive to certain investors because they typically have lower costs, and most mutual fund managers cannot consistently outperform the indexes.

As a clarification, in the investment world, an index is a passive benchmark for the asset class. It is the baseline measure for determining manager expertise. Popular indexes include:

- **Dow Jones Industrial Average (Dow):** a price-weighted stock market index, which includes a price-weighted (price per share) average of 30 actively traded blue chip stocks
- **S&P 500:** the index computed by the weighted average of the market capitalization (market cap) of the value of the 500 underlying stocks
- **Russell 2000:** a popular measure of small-cap companies that consists of the smallest 2,000 companies in the Russell 3000 index and is a capitalization-weighted (market cap) index

The expectation is that good fund managers should outperform a passive index for their asset class. Otherwise, it makes more sense to just invest in a fund replicating the index at low cost.

When picking a mutual fund or ETFs, below are the major considerations:

- **Investment strategy:** Does the fund/ETF strategy and asset class focus fit within your portfolio?
- **Investment track record:** Does the mutual fund consistently beat its index?
- **Expense ratio:** All else being equal, you should choose a fund/ETF with lower costs.
- **Risk tolerance:** Do the asset class and manager approach fit your risk tolerance?

If you prefer investing in asset classes and do not put much weight on the value of active investment management, then ETFs may be better suited for you than investing in mutual funds. Conversely, if you do value the decision-making abilities of professional investment managers, then mutual funds may be the better choice for you.

Finally, it is worth touching on the major asset classes that you might want to include in your portfolio:

- *Fixed income (bond funds),* which invest primarily in bonds and other debt instruments.

- *Tax-exempt bond funds (muni bond funds),* which invest in municipal bonds (debt securities issued by a state, municipality, county, or special-purpose district).
- *Money market funds,* which earn interest while trying to maintain a net asset value of one dollar per share, typically invested in short-term securities representing high-quality, liquid debt, and monetary instruments.
- *US equities,* which are typically further divided into *large-cap funds, mid-cap funds, and small-cap funds.* These divisions are based on the market capitalization of the companies.
- *International funds,* which invest in securities in nations besides the United States. This is typically further divided into *developed nations* and *emerging nations.*
- *Real asset funds,* which invest in real assets like real estate, infrastructure, and energy/MLPs.

Within each of these broad categories, there are many subcategories, with new ones being created every year; therefore, you should always consult with your investment advisor and read the prospectuses before investing in any fund or ETF.

As with any decision in life, you must weigh the advantages and disadvantages of investing in stocks, bonds, hybrid securities, mutual funds, or ETFs. For many people, the right choice may be a combination of all of the above.

Diversification, Asset Allocation, and Rebalancing

The most important tool to manage risk is diversification.[4] As can be seen with Exhibit 9.3, the returns of various asset classes can fluctuate significantly from year to year. You need to have multiple asset classes within your portfolio to mitigate the financial impact if any one asset class falls short of expectations – and to capture the upside when an individual asset class has a strong year. For example, in 2006, REITs were the top performer of all asset classes that year, and in 2007, they were the worst asset performer. This is verifiable proof that you cannot chase returns.

---

[4]Diversification does not assure or guarantee better performance and cannot eliminate the risk of investment losses.

Exhibit 9.3 also illustrates the best, the worst, and the average over the past 12 years for each of the eight asset classes listed. This highlights the importance of having staying power with your portfolio. When an asset class performs very poorly one year, it is often followed by a very good year.

Therefore, the first step to constructing a portfolio is asset class allocation. Asset allocation is an investment strategy that provides a systematic approach to diversification that may help you establish the most efficient blend of assets based on your particular risk tolerance level and investing time horizon. Asset allocation seeks to control investment risk by diversifying a portfolio among the major asset classes.

Each asset class has a different level of risk as well as potential rate of return. The basic idea is that, while one asset class may be increasing in value, one or more of the others may be decreasing. Therefore, asset allocation and diversification may help you ride out market fluctuations and protect your portfolio from a major loss in any one asset class. They may also provide you with the staying power and control over your emotions even after a big downturn in the market. Further, it is smart to diversify within an asset class to minimize the risk of any individual security. This is one major reason to invest in mutual funds and ETFs – because it is the most efficient way to diversify within an asset class.

However, it is important to understand that asset allocation and diversification do not guarantee against loss. They are simply strategies that may help smooth the ride to your financial independence, *point X.*

It is fundamental to find a mixture of asset classes with the highest potential return within your risk profile. Exhibit 9.4 shows six sample asset allocation models that can be used as a theoretical guide to fit into your own risk tolerance level. Please understand that these are hypothetical models and do not represent actual recommendations to be used. There are, of course, an unlimited number of variations to these sample models.

For our portfolio construction, we will focus on the following asset classes. For now, we will assume you are investing in a nontaxable account. If you were investing from a taxable account, you might want to switch some (or all) of your fixed income exposure to muni bond funds.

Exhibit 9.3   Annual Returns for Eight Major Asset Classes over the Past 12 Years, from Best to Worst[5]

2006	2007	2008	2009	2010	2011
REITs 35.1%	Emerging Market Stocks 39.8%	High Grade Bonds 5.2%	Emerging Market Stocks 79.0%	REITs 28.0%	REITs 8.3%
Emerging Market Stocks 32.6%	Int'l Developed Stocks 11.6%	Cash 1.4%	High Yield Bonds 57.5%	Small Cap Stocks 26.9%	High Grade Bonds 7.8%
Int'l Developed Stocks 26.9%	High Grade Bonds 7.0%	High Yield Bonds −26.4%	Int'l Developed Stocks 32.5%	Emerging Market Stocks 19.2%	High Yield Bonds 4.4%
Small Cap Stocks 18.4%	Large Cap Stocks 5.5%	Small Cap Stocks −33.8%	REITs 28.0%	High Yield Bonds 15.2%	Large Cap Stocks 2.1%
Large Cap Stocks 15.8%	Cash 4.4%	Large Cap Stocks −37.0%	Small Cap Stocks 27.2%	Large Cap Stocks 15.1%	Cash 0.1%
High Yield Bonds 11.8%	High Yield Bonds 2.2%	REITs −37.7%	Large Cap Stocks 26.5%	Int'l Developed Stocks 8.2%	Small Cap Stocks −4.2%
Cash 4.7%	Small Cap Stocks −1.6%	Int'l Developed Stocks −43.1%	High Grade Bonds 5.9%	High Grade Bonds 6.5%	Int'l Developed Stocks −11.7%
High Grade Bonds 4.3%	REITs −15.7%	Emerging Market Stocks −53.2%	Cash 0.2%	Cash 0.2%	Emerging Market Stocks −18.2%

---

[5]This chart's data was adapted from novelinvestor.com.

2012	2013	2014	2015	2016	2017
REITs 19.7%	Small Cap Stocks 38.8%	REITs 28.0%	REITs 2.8%	Small Cap Stocks 21.3%	Emerging Market Stocks 37.8%
Emerging Market Stocks 18.6%	Large Cap Stocks 32.4%	Large Cap Stocks 13.7%	Large Cap Stocks 1.4%	High Yield Bonds 17.5%	Int'l Developed Stocks 25.6%
Int'l Developed Stocks 17.9%	Int'l Developed Stocks 23.3%	High Grade Bonds 6.0%	High Grade Bonds 0.6%	Large Cap Stocks 12.0%	Large Cap Stocks 21.8%
Small Cap Stocks 16.4%	High Yield Bonds 7.4%	Small Cap Stocks 4.9%	Cash 0.1%	Emerging Market Stocks 11.6%	Small Cap Stocks 14.7%
Large Cap Stocks 16.0%	REITs 2.9%	High Yield Bonds 2.5%	Int'l Developed Stocks −0.4%	REITs 8.6%	REITs 8.7%
High Yield Bonds 15.6%	Cash 0.1%	Cash 0.0%	Small Cap Stocks −4.4%	High Grade Bonds 2.7%	High Yield Bonds 7.5%
High Grade Bonds 4.2%	High Grade Bonds −2.0%	Emerging Market Stocks −1.8%	High Yield Bonds −4.6%	Int'l Developed Stocks 1.5%	High Grade Bonds 3.5%
Cash 0.1%	Emerging Market Stocks −2.3%	Int'l Developed Stocks −4.5%	Emerging Market Stocks −14.6%	Cash 0.3%	Cash 1.0%

Asset Class	Index	12-Year		
		Average	Best	Worst
REITs	FTSE NAREIT All Equity Index	9.7%	35.1%	−37.7%
Emerging Market Stocks	MSCI Emerging Markets Index	12.4%	79.0%	−53.2%
International Developed Stocks	MSCI EAFE Index	7.3%	32.5%	−43.1%
Small Cap Stocks	Russell 2000 Index	10.4%	38.8%	−33.8%
Large Cap Stocks	S&P 500 Index	10.4%	32.4%	−37.0%
High Yield Bonds	BofAML US High Yield Master II Index	9.2%	57.5%	−26.4%
Cash	3 Month Treasury Bill Rate	1.1%	4.7%	0.0%
High Grade Bonds	Barclay's U.S. Aggregate Bond Index	4.3%	7.8%	−2.0%

- **Cash and cash equivalents** includes currency, coins, checking accounts, savings accounts, money market accounts, and certificates of deposit.
- **Fixed income (bond funds)** invest primarily in bonds and other debt instruments.
- **US equities** represent an ownership interest in a business entity by investing in a US company's stock.
  - **Large-cap funds, or large-market capitalization funds** generally invest in securities of companies with a market capitalization of $10 billion or more.
  - **Mid-cap funds, or middle-market capitalization funds** generally invest in securities of companies with a market capitalization of $2 billion to $10 billion.
  - **Small cap funds, or small-market capitalization funds** generally invest in securities of companies with a market capitalization of $300 million to $2 billion.
- **International**
  - **Developed markets funds** invest in securities in developed nations in terms of economy and capital markets (besides the US).
  - **Emerging markets funds** invest in securities in a single developing country or a group of countries, typically in Eastern Europe, Africa, Latin America, and Asia.
- **Real assets** invest in real assets like:
  - **Real estate**
  - **Master limited partnerships (MLPs)**

It is worth highlighting an implicit assumption in these models: that fixed income is less risky than other asset classes. In some economic and market scenarios, such as rapidly rising interest rates, this assumption is false. Additionally, it is important to remember that less risky does not mean there is not still a risk of loss. For example, in times of extreme negative swings, like 2008, virtually all assets decline except cash, although short-duration investment-grade debt suffer a less severe drop.

The second key assumption in these models is that the projected returns meet your long-term goals. If the model selected based upon your risk tolerance cannot achieve your long-term goals, either your goal must be modified, or you must accept additional risk.

The third key assumption in these models is that we have no insights into the returns of asset classes for next year. In the real world, at any given time, an asset class might be over or undervalued relative to other assets, and we might choose to opportunistically tweak allocations.

Finally, before we dive into the models, a key component to effective portfolio management is rebalancing.[5] As Exhibit 9.3 illustrates, asset class returns widely fluctuate. Rebalancing allows us to take advantage of these fluctuations. Rebalancing is the act of selling out of our "winner" asset classes and buying our "loser" asset classes to bring the portfolio back to its original allocations. Effectively, by selling out of our winners and buying our losers, we are shifting our investments from overvalued to under-valued asset classes. Over time, this enhances returns.

Depending on your risk tolerance and time horizon, you can select anywhere from model 1 to model 6; for example:

- If you need money in the near future, you should consider a model that involves less risk, such as model 1 or 2.
- If you are saving for retirement and have 10 or more years until you will need access to these funds, you may be able to take on more risk to increase your potential for growth. In this case, model 3, 4, 5, or 6 may be more suitable.
- If your time horizon is less than a few years, you should probably not be investing at all; instead, you should keep your cash in a savings account for easy access. Investing should always be viewed as a long-term commitment.

It is very important to keep in mind that there is no one approach that will fit every individual investor.

Now that you have selected your ideal asset allocation model based on your acceptable risk tolerance, it is important to monitor and maintain this allocation. Rebalancing your portfolio is one of the essential aspects of maintaining a successful investment strategy over time. Rebalancing requires you to analyze the changes in your asset allocation model periodically and make changes in an attempt to bring you back to your original allocation. You do this by selling and buying various investments within each of the asset classes to maintain your established asset allocation.

---

[5]Before you rebalance your portfolio, you should consider whether the method of rebalancing you decide to use will trigger transaction fees or tax consequences. Your financial professional or tax adviser can help you identify ways that you can minimize these potential costs.

Exhibit 9.4   Six Sample Asset Allocation Models (1 = Most risk-adverse investor; 6 = Most aggressive investor)

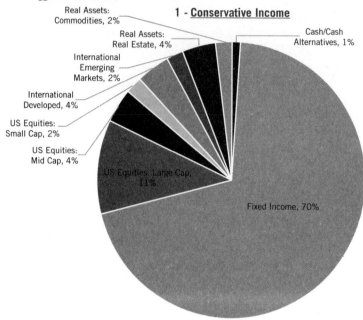

1 - <u>Conservative Income</u>

Real Assets: Commodities, 2%
Real Assets: Real Estate, 4%
International Emerging Markets, 2%
International Developed, 4%
US Equities: Small Cap, 2%
US Equities: Mid Cap, 4%
US Equities: Large Cap, 11%
Cash/Cash Alternatives, 1%
Fixed Income, 70%

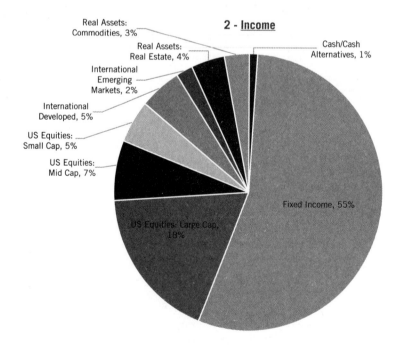

2 - <u>Income</u>

Real Assets: Commodities, 3%
Real Assets: Real Estate, 4%
International Emerging Markets, 2%
International Developed, 5%
US Equities: Small Cap, 5%
US Equities: Mid Cap, 7%
US Equities: Large Cap, 18%
Cash/Cash Alternatives, 1%
Fixed Income, 55%

Exhibit 9.4   (*Continued*)

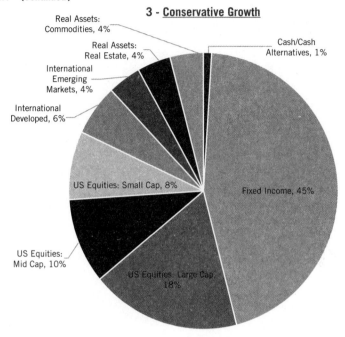

3 - <u>Conservative Growth</u>

Real Assets:
Commodities, 4%

Real Assets:
Real Estate, 4%

International
Emerging
Markets, 4%

International
Developed, 6%

Cash/Cash
Alternatives, 1%

US Equities: Small Cap, 8%

Fixed Income, 45%

US Equities:
Mid Cap, 10%

US Equities: Large Cap,
18%

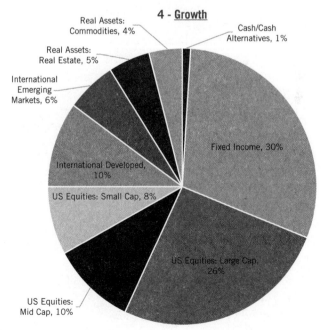

4 - <u>Growth</u>

Real Assets:
Commodities, 4%

Real Assets:
Real Estate, 5%

International
Emerging
Markets, 6%

Cash/Cash
Alternatives, 1%

International Developed,
10%

US Equities: Small Cap, 8%

Fixed Income, 30%

US Equities: Large Cap,
26%

US Equities:
Mid Cap, 10%

Exhibit 9.4   (*Continued*)

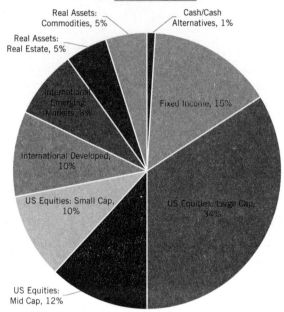

5 - <u>Maximum Growth</u>

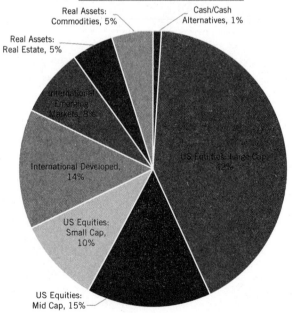

6 - <u>Maximum Growth No Fixed Income</u>

Suppose the original asset allocation model you established included 1% cash, 28% stock, and 71% bonds. During a period of falling interest rates, your bond values increased to represent 76% of your portfolio, and your stock values now only represent 23% of your overall portfolio. Rebalancing will require you to sell off part of your bond portfolio and to purchase additional stock holdings to bring you back to your original model. This also forces you to sell some of the bond holdings that have done well at a higher price and allows you to purchase stocks that have not done well at a lower price. This is a systematic approach to buying low and selling high for at least some portion of your overall investment holdings. It is also important to note that by maintaining your asset allocation, you will keep your risk tolerance level within your comfort zone.

To further highlight how the rebalancing would work, refer to Exhibit 9.5, "Investment Rebalancing." Here, we start with an example bond-only investment model, conservative bond income, with 15% allocated to fixed high-yield bonds, 35% allocated to fixed-income investment-grade bonds, and 50% to fixed-income short-term and money-market. After year 1, the initial asset allocation percentages have changed because of the performance of each asset class. To rebalance and put your model back to its original allocation, you would be required to purchase $1,875 of fixed-income short-term bond mutual funds and money market, and you would have to sell $788 of fixed-income investment-grade bond mutual funds and $1,088 of fixed-income high-yield bond mutual funds. This would take you back to your original percentage allocation.

In the example provided, rebalancing is being done once a year, always taking you back to your original asset-allocation model investment percentages. Once again, this is a systematic approach that allows you to not only stay within your risk tolerance profile but also allows you to sell a portion of your holdings after they have increased in value and to purchase a portion of your holdings that have decreased in value. The added benefit to this is that you are using a disciplined approach to buying low and selling high for at least a portion of your portfolio.

For many investors, rebalancing once a year is usually sufficient. However, in recent years, because of the high volatility in the markets, rebalancing more frequently has become more appropriate. Rather than using a specific date or time frame, I think it is best to use a percentage change in your allocation as the trigger point for rebalancing. For example, if any one asset class percentage within your

Exhibit 9.5   Investment Rebalancing

Example Bond-Only Investment Model – Conservative Bond Income

| | Market Value of Portfolio | | | | | % of Portfolio | | |
	Total	Fixed Income High Yield	Fixed Income Investment Grade	Fixed Income Short Term and Money Market	Total	Fixed Income High Yield	Fixed Income Investment Grade	Fixed Income Short Term and Money Market
Initial Investment	$100,000	$15,000	$35,000	$50,000	100.00%	15.00%	35.00%	50.00%
% Change Year 1		10%	5%	-1%				
Change During Year 1	$2,750	$1,500	$1,750	$(500)				
Year 1 Before Rebalance	$102,750	$16,500	$36,750	$49,500	100.00%	16.06%	35.77%	48.18%
REBALANCE – Year 1	$-	$(1,088)	$(788)	$1,875				
Year-1 After Rebalance	$102,750	$15,413	$35,963	$51,375	100.00%	15.00%	35.00%	50.00%
% Change Year 2		4%	6%	0%				
Change During Year 2	$2,774	$617	$2,158	$-				
Year 2 Before Rebalance	$105,524	$16,029	$38,120	$51,375	100.00%	15.19%	36.12%	48.69%
REBALANCE – Year 2	$-	$(200)	$(1,187)	$1,387				
Year 2 After Rebalance	$105,524	$15,829	$36,933	$52,762	100.00%	15.00%	35.00%	50.00%
% Change Year 3		2%	3%	5%				
Change During Year 3	$4,063	$317	$1,108	$2,638				
Year 3 Before Rebalance	$109,587	$16,145	$38,041	$55,400	100.00%	14.73%	34.71%	50.55%
REBALANCE - Year 3	$-	$293	$314	$(607)				
Year 3 After Rebalance	$109,587	$16,438	$38,355	$54,793	100.00%	15.00%	35.00%	50.00%

model changes by more than 5% of its original value, that would be a trigger point for rebalancing.

One of the major advantages of using rebalancing as one of your investment strategies is that it provides you with a disciplined approach to taking profits from some of your winners, allowing you to cash in on these gains. Another advantage to rebalancing is that it allows you to pay close attention to your portfolio; because you are examining the changes in your investment allocation, you can reevaluate your individual investment choices within each asset class. Finally, rebalancing may smooth out your overall investment rate of return.

Dollar-Cost Averaging

The simple fact of investing is that if you could always buy at market lows and always sell at market highs, then you would guarantee yourself a profit and never have a financial worry. Unfortunately, after 30 years of working with thousands of individuals, I have yet to meet any investor or financial advisor who has figured out a system to accomplish this. One basic principle to investing is that you must be realistic as to what is possible and what is not.

Far too many investors try to predict the market along with their entry and exit points. This strategy typically results in a disappointing overall rate of return. To participate in market gains, you need to be invested in the market during its profitable days. Trying to time the market is a very risky game. Instead, focus on the amount of time you will be invested in the market and not on the timing of your investments. An investment strategy that may help you find the way around these investing pitfalls is *dollar-cost averaging*.

With a dollar-cost averaging investing strategy, you put a certain amount of money into your investment portfolio every month over an extended period. Regardless of market conditions and the ups and downs in the value of your particular investments, you will be committed to purchasing a certain dollar amount each month. When the individual share price of your investment increases, you buy fewer shares, and when the individual share price of your investment decreases, you will buy more shares with the same monetary investment. Therefore, your average cost per share will reflect both the low prices and high prices you paid. This system averages out the overall price per share you ultimately will pay.

One of the main advantages of dollar-cost averaging is that you are *not* trying to predict the entry or exit point of your investments.

This approach simply puts you into a routine of investing on a regular basis, regardless of market conditions. This investment strategy may also reduce your risk of investing a large sum of money in one investment when the share price may be overvalued.

Another big advantage to utilizing a dollar-cost averaging investment strategy along with a rebalancing strategy is that it may help smooth your investment ride, especially during volatile markets. You will not experience the largest possible gains during a bull market, but you may minimize your losses during a bear market. The simple idea is the more you do to take the emotions out of investing, the more likely you are to stick to your investment strategy. The ultimate goal, of course, is to come back to your original asset allocation model, periodically rebalancing and consistently adding funds to your investment portfolio on a regular basis so that you can pursue your targeted rate of return on your investments over time.

Most people do not realize that when they are contributing to their 401(k) plan at work through each paycheck, they are actually implementing the dollar-cost averaging investment strategy. As I have repeatedly mentioned throughout this book, there is no better way to achieve financial independence than to do it in a tax-efficient manner. Combine these investment strategies with a systematic savings plan that includes paying yourself first, and you will be well on your way to becoming financially independent.

Inflation and Taxes: The Biggest Drains on Investment Return

Inflation and taxes are perhaps the two biggest drains on your investment returns. Taking these factors into consideration is very important in your journey to achieving financial independence.

The technical definition of inflation is the rise in consumer prices over time. *It is vital to your savings that your investment returns keep pace with the rate of inflation to avoid a true loss of purchasing power.* If the average inflation rate has been 2% and your adjusted after-tax rate of return on your investments is below 2%, you are in fact losing purchasing power and diminishing your wealth.

In order to accumulate wealth, your investment objective should be to earn a rate of return after taxes that will exceed the prevailing inflation rate. Looking back to the history of the investment markets, the one way to beat inflation is to have some of your money invested in growth-oriented investments. This includes growth stocks, growth mutual funds, growth ETFs, and alternative growth investments. These investment vehicles may provide the potential for returns

Exhibit 9.6   Long-Term Capital Gain and Qualified Dividend Maximum Taxable Income Thresholds

Long-Term Capital Gains Rate	Single Taxpayers	Married Filing Jointly	Head of Household	Married Filing Separately
0%	Up to $38,600	Up to $77,200	Up to $51,700	Up to $38,600
15%	$38,600–$425,800	$77,200–$479,000	$51,700–$452,400	$38,600–$239,500
20%	Over $425,800	Over $479,000	Over $452,400	Over $239,500

that could exceed inflation over the long term. Of course, these growth-oriented investment vehicles also come with a greater risk than other types of investments.

As you select your asset allocation model based on your risk tolerance level, never forget that smart investors always focus on a well-diversified portfolio. Taking on too much risk or taking on too little risk can both be equally damaging to your financial success. You must find your own perfect balance in determining your risk-reward ratio.

You must always consider the tax consequences of your investment when determining your true rate of return. See Exhibit 9.6 and "Medicaid Surtax on Net Investment Income" in the next section for information on how taxes affect investments.

Under the new tax law, the three capital gains and qualified dividend income thresholds do not match up perfectly with the ordinary income tax brackets. These preferential tax rate income thresholds are similar to where they would have been under the pre-2018 tax law. For 2018, they are applied to maximum taxable income thresholds as shown in Exhibit 9.6.

Please note that if the only thing causing your income to be greater than these amounts is the capital gains or qualified dividends, then only the excess amount of capital gains or qualified dividends are taxed at the next higher capital gains tax rate.

Medicare Surtax on Net Investment Income

- Starting in 2013, a new 3.8% Medicare tax was imposed on net investment income for single or head of household taxpayers with income over $200,000, married couples filing jointly or a qualifying widow(er) with income over $250,000, and married taxpayers filing separately with income over $125,000.

- The combined federal maximum tax rate on short-term capital gains could be as high as 40.8% (37% + 3.8%).
- The combined federal maximum tax rate on long-term capital gains for those in the 20% capital gains tax bracket could be as high as 23.8% (20% + 3.8%).
- The combined federal maximum tax rate on long-term capital gains for those in the 15% capital gains tax bracket could be as high as 18.8% (15% + 3.8%).
- The combined federal maximum tax rate on long-term capital gains for those in the 0% capital gains tax bracket would still be 0% since they are not subject to the 3.8% Medicare tax.

Cryptocurrency and Its Tax Treatment

Cryptocurrency was introduced into the market a few years ago, and, more recently, investors have flocked in droves to capitalize on its highly speculative value. Cryptocurrency, such as Bitcoin, is a form of digital currency that is exchanged over the internet for goods and services, through secure transactions. Unlike regular currency, cryptocurrency is not backed by the good faith of any government or precious metal. This means it is only worth what people will pay for it, and it is difficult to regulate. While some believe cryptocurrency is the future of the economy, critics argue that its dubious nature could cause it to collapse at any time.

The IRS issued guidance in 2014, stating that virtual currency is treated as property. The IRS does not view virtual currencies as money because they are not legal tender in any jurisdiction. The character of the gain or loss generally depends on whether the virtual currency is a capital asset in the hands of the taxpayer. If held for investments like stocks and bonds, virtual currency can be treated as a capital asset whose sale results in short-term and long-term gains and losses. However, if it is used as inventory or other property held mainly for sale to customers in a trade or business, this is not a capital asset, and transactions result in ordinary income gains and losses.

There is no requirement for third-party reporting from brokers or other investment entities, so you will not be issued a Form 1099-B or equivalent when it comes to your virtual currency, as of the date of this printing. Since using cryptocurrency to pay for goods and services is treating it as cash, you must consider each of these transactions as a sale or exchange of property. Cryptocurrency trading is a taxable event, whether or not you formally cash out. You can view this as another form of bartering.

Payments for employee or independent contractor services with cryptocurrency is subject to the same reporting requirements as if it was paid in US dollars, including the issuance of W-2 and 1099 forms. Payments may even be subject to backup withholding.

Cryptocurrency is at risk of virtual theft and is not FDIC insured. In my opinion, this is not really a currency, since it is not backed by precious metals or any government guarantee. In addition, currency should be a stable and secure way to transact business. Clearly, cryptocurrency does not have any stability in its pricing.

To better take control of this newly exploded facet of our economy, the US government is paying particular attention to the reporting of cryptocurrency transactions. The IRS has taken steps to force these privatized cryptocurrency companies to turn over customer records, so that unreported transactions can be properly investigated. In late 2017, the IRS won a case against a major virtual currency storage company, Coinbase, in *United States v. Coinbase, Inc.* This allowed them to access records of more than 14,000 customers, giving them the ability to assess back-taxes where these transactions were not recorded. By law, you must report all financial transactions, including bartering. If substantial underreporting of income is discovered, the IRS could pursue these cases as criminal charges. The bottom line here is that, if you are performing any transactions with cryptocurrency, you must be sure you are reporting it on your income tax return.

If you do not pay attention to the tax consequences of your investments, you may be paying significantly more in taxes than the law requires. This is why you must include tax planning as part of your overall investment strategy. Using an investment approach that takes advantage of these *Tax Alpha to the 2nd Power*^{SM} facts and strategies will potentially help maximize your after-tax return on your investments.

TAX ALPHA TO THE 2ND POWER^{SM} FACTS AND STRATEGIES FOR MANAGING YOUR INVESTMENTS

Here are several tax facts and strategies that will address your wealth accumulation goals at an exponential rate, which will help put you on the path to financial independence, *point X*.

(*continued*)

- If you are planning to sell investment real estate and plan on replacing it with other like-kind investment real estate, take advantage of Internal Revenue Code Section 1031 Exchange Rules. With a qualified exchange, you can postpone the current tax liability until you dispose of the newly acquired investment real estate. **It is important to note that starting in 2018, the new law limits the 1031 exchange to real property only, which is not treated as inventory in the hands of dealers**.
- Consider selling some of your investments in stocks, bonds, or mutual funds that have declined in value from when you originally purchased them. To realize these capital losses, you must complete the transaction before December 31. Capital gains can be offset to capital losses to the extent of gains, and an additional $3,000 in capital losses can be used to offset your ordinary income. Any excess loss above this amount can be carried forward to future years.
- You can then buy back these investments after 30 days to avoid the wash sale rules, which would otherwise disallow these losses. The *wash sale rules* prevent you from claiming a loss on a sale of stock if you buy replacement stock within 30 days before or after the sale.
- Stock dividends and stock splits on common stock are usually not taxable, but dividends paid out of current or accumulated earnings of a corporation are, in fact, taxable. Be sure to include only *taxable* dividends on your income tax return.
- Short-term capital gains are still taxed at your ordinary income level, but since the ordinary income tax rates have been lowered straight across the board as a result of the Tax Cut and Jobs Act, your short-term capital gains rate has also been reduced.
- Net long-term capital gains are taxed at a preferential federal rate that does not exceed 20%. If you hold an investment for more than a year, you will have the added advantage of long-term capital gains treatment. Long-term capital gains tax rates still remain as they were under the previous tax law, which includes a 0% tax rate, a 15% tax rate, and a 20% tax rate. **These rates will apply based on the new long-term capital gain and qualified dividend maximum taxable income thresholds. See Exhibit 9.6**.
- Dividends from most domestic corporations and many foreign corporations are usually treated as qualified dividends. For 2018, qualified dividends will continue to receive favorable tax-rate treatment which includes a 0% tax rate, a 15% tax rate, and a 20% tax rate. These rates will apply based on the new long-term capital gain and qualified dividend maximum taxable income thresholds. See Exhibit 9.6.
- **Under the Tax Cuts and Jobs Act, the new law provides a deduction of up to 20% of "domestic qualified business income" from the taxable income of pass-through entity owners, who are individuals, estates, or trusts.** This Section 199A deduction is allowed for a taxpayer's aggregate amount of

qualified REIT dividends, qualified publicly traded partnership income, and qualified cooperative dividends for the taxable year.

- Under the Patient Protection and Affordable Care Act, starting in 2013 there is a 3.8% Medicare tax on net investment income if your modified adjusted gross income is above $250,000 for married filing jointly and qualifying widow(er), above $125,000 for married filing separately, and $200,000 for single and head of household. If the current administration is successful in repealing the Affordable Care Act, it is possible that this tax could be eliminated in the future.

- Interest from municipal bonds and municipal bond funds are generally triple tax-free if the underlying bonds are from the state or local government where you reside. If the municipal bonds are not from the state where you reside, they will be free of federal tax and may be subject to your state and local tax. If part of your investment objective is to generate tax-free income, you should consider buying municipal bonds. Since 2013, with the Medicare surtax of 3.8% on net investment income, municipal bonds have become even more attractive since they are also exempt from this tax.

- Interest on securities issued by the federal government (such as Treasury bonds, notes, and bills) is fully taxable at the federal level, but it is not subject to state or local income tax.

- **Now that state and local income taxes are part of the new cap set at $10,000 on itemized deductions, both federal as well as instate municipal bonds are even more attractive.** Under the past law, any state or local income taxes paid on taxable bonds were fully deductible. Since they no longer are, they will be less attractive than bonds that are free of state and local taxes.

- If you take an early withdrawal from a certificate of deposit, you will be able to deduct the full amount of the early withdrawal penalty from your income tax return.

- Capital losses on the sale of property held for personal use, such as your home, are not tax-deductible.

- When evaluating investment and financial decisions, you should consider the after-tax effects (create tax alpha) of a transaction so that you truly understand your real rate of return when compared to other investment choices.

- Keep an accurate record of all stock transactions, along with when you bought it, especially if you purchased stock from the same company at different times. By using specific identification, you may be able to control the amount of gain or loss on the sale or part of your investment holdings. You are required to make an adequate identification, typically by giving your broker specific instructions of which shares are to be sold. This must be communicated to you in writing through the brokerage firm.

ACTION PLAN FOR MANAGING YOUR INVESTMENTS

1. **Know how tolerant of risk you are, and properly determine your ability and willingness to take risk, before investing.** Your financial net worth, sources of income, and your age play an important role in determining your ability to take risk. If you know you are the type of person who prefers to "play it safe," then you may need to invest accordingly; conversely, if you are the type of person who won't lose sleep at night if you lose money in the market, then you are more likely to be comfortable with taking risk. Ultimately, the decision on the proper level of risk to take will be some combination of both your ability and willingness to take risk.

2. **Understand the different types of risk that can affect your investments.** Learn as much as you can about inflation risk, interest rate risk, default risk, market-rate risk, economic risk, and company-specific or industry-specific risk – all of which may influence how well or how poorly your investments perform.

3. **Diversify your investments so that you do not have "all your eggs in one basket."** If you spread your investment dollars among several different asset classes, you may be able to lower your volatility on your overall investment portfolio without sacrificing your return on investment. For example, you might invest some of your money in specific company stocks, some in bonds, some in hybrid securities, some in mutual funds, and some in exchange-traded funds (ETFs).

4. **Do not try to predict when it is best to invest; instead, invest regularly with the same amount of money,** whether the market you are investing in is up or down. This is called *dollar-cost averaging,* and this approach helps you develop a routine or habit of investing. It also helps you not get emotional about your investing. When you combine this investment approach with the appropriate rebalancing as needed, you are also getting the added benefit of selling a portion of your investments high and buying others at their lows.

5. **Know the tax and inflation implications of the return on your investments.** At a minimum you must exceed the rate of inflation after implementing the tax strategies outlined above. Consider hiring a financial adviser who understands these *Tax Alpha to the 2nd Power* facts and strategies to help you gain the most from your investments.

CHAPTER 10

Preserving Your Estate

In this world nothing can be said to be certain, except death and taxes.
—Benjamin Franklin, Founding Father of the United States

So you have worked hard, lived within your means, followed the guidance provided in this book, and reached your very own *point X,* financial independence. Congratulations!

For your whole life, you dreamed of becoming financially independent for the benefit of yourself and your family. Now it is time to turn your attention to preserving your estate, so that your loved ones can benefit from your life's hard work and sacrifices. If you do not take the necessary steps to preserve your estate, unintended beneficiaries may take a significant amount of your estate instead. These unintended beneficiaries include the federal and state governments, the state administrator, attorneys, and perhaps even relatives you have not spoken to in decades. The money you may spend today on a qualified estate attorney may save your estate significant dollars in both estate taxes and administrative costs down the road and will ensure that the beneficiaries of your assets are those you intend.

Estate planning can give you peace of mind by ensuring that your family's financial security will continue even after your death. It allows you to dispose of your assets as you see fit, with consideration given to your heirs' individual needs. It is important to understand that estate planning is not just for the wealthy. Every adult person should have estate planning in place, some of which will be of assistance during life and some of which will come into play after death.

The Federal Gift and Estate Tax System

The federal gift and estate tax system is a unified system that works hand-in-hand with virtually the same rules and tax rates. The main difference between the two is that the gift tax is imposed on the donor for gifts made throughout his or her lifetime, whereas the estate tax is imposed on the donor based on the value of his or her net estate upon death.

As of January 1, 2018, the Tax Cuts and Jobs Act permanently extends the estate, gift, and generation-skipping tax exemptions to $11.2 million for individuals and $22.4 million for married couples, which will be adjusted each year for inflation. This means that the Internal Revenue Service will be taxing fewer people for dying. The estate tax rate remains at 40% of the amount above these lifetime exemption amounts. *Lifetime exemption represents the amount you can transfer in total while you are alive (by gift) or after death (through your estate) that will not be subject to estate or gift tax under this unified system.* Depending on your state of residence, there may also be state gift and estate taxes to consider.

In order to ensure that you preserve your estate for your intended beneficiaries, it is important to stay on top of the ever-changing rules of the game. Working closely with a trusted tax advisor is perhaps one of the best ways to ensure that you can take advantage of these tax law changes when they arise.

Legal Documents to Consider for Estate Planning

Regardless of the size of your estate, you should consider addressing your own individual planning issues in order to preserve your estate and make your wishes known, preferably in writing. I recommend meeting with a qualified estate planning attorney to determine exactly what estate planning documents you should have prepared, based on your particular facts and circumstances. If you have no minor children, if all of your assets are held jointly with your spouse, or if you have no assets to speak of, then your estate may not need to go through probate. If this is the case, or if you are willing to have your assets administered and distributed according to the rules of your particular state, you may not need a will.

If you need a will, it must be prepared in accordance with the laws of your resident state. Although your will may still be valid after you move to a new state, certain parts of it may become invalid or may require changes due to the unique laws of your new state of residence. It is always best to update it and to use an attorney who is familiar with the laws of your current state.

In my opinion, you should consider your own particular needs; then you should determine what legal documents are most appropriate for you. These documents may include a health care proxy and living will, as well as a durable power of attorney, all to assist you during your lifetime. To ensure that your assets are distributed to your intended beneficiaries after your death, you may utilize a Last Will and Testament or Trust, or some combination of both. These documents will be explained in more detail in this chapter. Please note that the names of some of these documents vary from state to state.

Before I discuss the details of estate planning techniques, it is important to understand some of the key legal documents that may be needed in this planning process. An effective estate plan may need to include one or more of these documents that may cover all three phases of your life. Phase I is while you are alive and well, Phase II is in the event that you become disabled, and Phase III is after your death.

To preserve your estate and allow your loved ones to share in your success of reaching *point X*, you will need to address numerous legal forms so that your legacy can be transferred with ease. All of the legal forms described in the next sections must be appropriate to your particular state of residence and may even be modeled after particular statutes existing in your state of residence. The advantage to using a "statutory form" is that it must be accepted, and it will ensure compliance with your wishes, even in an emergency situation.

If you already have an estate plan that includes some of these documents, pull them out and review them. You will be surprised how quickly they can become out of date with changes that take place throughout your life. You (and your spouse, if you are married) should have your estate plan reviewed at least once every five years by an attorney well-versed in estate planning, or sooner if you experience a life-changing event such as a birth or death in your family, marriage, or retirement. This is necessary to ensure that it is up to date with both your wishes and the laws that apply in your current state of residence. You should also consider reviewing and updating these documents more frequently in the event of legislation changes. Your financial advisor or estate attorney should bring any legislative changes to your attention so that you can take the necessary steps to ensure your estate plan is still fulfilling your wishes and minimizing your estate-tax exposure.

All of the following documents should be drafted by and executed in front of an attorney. Online legal services such as Legal Zoom or Nolo may be tempting to use, but even if they save you some money up front, I still believe that, in most cases, the legal advice and associated cost of working directly with an attorney should more than pay for itself in the long run.

Preparing Your Will to Distribute Your Assets After Your Death

A will, also called a *Last Will and Testament,* is a written document that provides, among other things, instructions on how you would like to distribute your assets after death. It is perhaps the most popular and basic estate planning document, and it also addresses many of your wishes and desires after death, such as the designation of your executor, the naming of a guardian of minor children, and the distribution of tangible personal property.

It is extremely important to understand that a will only covers only assets held solely in your name. Assets that already have named beneficiaries, jointly held property with rights of survivorship, and transfer on death accounts (TOD) are examples that pass to another automatically upon your death as a matter of law. These different types of ownership are discussed later in this chapter. Also, you should be aware that a will becomes effective only upon your death and after it is probated, that is, goes through the court process and is validated by a judge. You can change your will at any time prior to your death, assuming that you still possess the legal capacity to execute the document.

Creating a Trust for a Specific Beneficiary(ies)

A trust is a legal document that creates an arrangement where one person (named the *trustee*) manages property given by another person (named the *grantor, settlor,* or *trustor*) for the benefit of a third person, (named the *beneficiary*). There are many different types of trusts used for different purposes. Some trusts, called inter vivos trusts, are created during one's life and are valid during life. These trusts are separate legal entities that can contain provisions relevant during your life and, like a will, spell out how you want your property distributed upon your death. Others, called testamentary trusts, are contained within wills and only take effect upon death. If used properly, a trust can be a very effective estate planning tool that can accomplish such things as avoiding probate, minimizing taxes and post mortem legal fees, protecting assets, and simplifying the distribution of your assets to your intended beneficiaries. Trusts can also hold assets and provide a distribution scheme for minors and disabled persons. Trusts let you customize the distribution of your estate with the added advantages of property management. They are covered in more detail later in this chapter.

Designating a Health Care Proxy

A *health care proxy* is a document where you designate an individual to make decisions regarding your health care treatment in the event that you are incapacitated and unable to provide informed consent. This is also known as a *durable power of attorney for health care.* The person you designate can generally make decisions regarding medical facilities, medical treatments, surgery, and a variety of other health care issues. Much like a durable power of attorney, the health care proxy involves important decisions; therefore, you should take extreme care when choosing who will make them on your behalf. This is solely used for health care decisions and should not be confused with a general power of attorney.

A health care proxy provides an individual with control over the type and level of health care the individual will receive, after he or she is not capable of making the decision personally because of his or her mental and/or physical state. This proxy provides the most flexibility for a health care agent to make decisions based on the day-to-day conditions of a patient.

The cost of medical treatment is significant, especially when there are prolonged serious medical conditions involved. Making your wishes clear through a health care proxy can save your estate significant dollars on unwanted medical treatments.

Establishing a Living Will

A *living will,* which is also known as a *directive to physicians* or an *advanced health care directive,* spells out the kinds of life-sustaining treatment you desire in the event you are determined to be at an end-of-life stage or incurably ill with no hope of recovery. It gives doctors and hospitals your instructions regarding the nature and extent of the care you want should you suffer permanent incapacity, such as an irreversible coma or brain damage, or are deemed to be in a persistent vegetative state. This concerns life-support services of various kinds, from respiratory assistance to feeding tubes.

Unlike a health care proxy, a living will does not appoint an individual to make decisions for you and does not require actions on anyone's part. Instead, the directive provides written instructions from you for the attending physician. The decision for or against life support is one that only you should make. That makes the living will a valuable estate planning document. When I have this difficult but necessary discussion with clients, they almost always tell me they would choose to not prolong their lives if they are suffering from a terminal and painful illness. This is especially true if prolonging their lives will wipe them out financially and not allow them to provide for their loved ones. This is a difficult and sensitive topic, and I believe that every individual should have the right to make his or her choices known through a living will. A living will may be used in conjunction with a durable power of attorney for health care. Bear in mind that laws governing the recognition and treatment of living wills may vary from state to state. Nonetheless, it is important that you make your wishes known in writing and do not burden loved ones by leaving these decisions to them.

Designating Durable Power of Attorney

Durable power of attorney is a legal agreement that enables you to designate who will make your legal and financial decisions. This document may be necessary in order to avoid the need for a guardianship or conservatorship. Unlike the standard power of attorney, durable powers remain valid even after you become incapacitated. Obviously, in order for this power to be valid, you need to have capacity when you execute the document.

A durable power of attorney appoints a person you designate to act for you by handling financial matters, should you be unable or perhaps unavailable to do so. This power of attorney may include delegating control over all of your assets and belongings, including real estate, bank accounts, brokerage accounts, and so on. It can be as broad or as restrictive as you desire. It can be valid either when you execute it or at a specific time or event, such as if you become incapacitated.

A power of attorney that is not valid on its execution is called a *springing power of attorney*, because the powers spring out at some time in the future. Usually, this is prepared for an individual who does not trust giving someone full power of attorney at the time of its execution. The problem with a springing power of attorney is that, in the event that you want the powers to start upon your incapacity, no one will accept the power of attorney until you secure a court order or medical attestation to certify that you are incapacitated. This is a very long and costly process, and the power of attorney may not be legally valid at the time you need to use it, thus defeating the purpose of executing the power of attorney in the first place.

Any power of attorney should be used only if you absolutely trust the person you are granting the powers to. That individual has the ability to misappropriate your assets at any time without your knowledge. Therefore, your decision on which type of power of attorney to execute requires very careful consideration. You should exercise extreme caution when providing someone with this level of control.

The Probate and Administration Process and Why You May Want to Avoid It

Surrogate courts or probate courts are special courts of law that have specific jurisdiction over proceedings incident to the settlement of a decedent's estate. If you die and have a will, your will must be probated in order to have it legally recognized. The legal definition of *probate* is "the act of proving that an instrument purporting to be a Last Will and Testament was executed in accordance with legal requirements and of determining its validity thereby." Your estate will go through the *administration process* if you die without a valid will. In this instance, you are considered to have died *intestate*, and the intestacy laws of your state of residence will determine who will receive your assets.

The major problems associated with both probate and administration include high administrative costs, lengthy delays, retention of assets, and court involvement and supervision, not to mention all the added legal and accounting fees. Disgruntled family members can also pose a problem to probate by instituting will contests. The probate and administrative fees can consume between 6% and 10% of your gross estate, according to the American Bar Association. In my opinion, these are the major reasons you would want to avoid going through probate or administration, and applying some of the strategies outlined in this chapter can accomplish this.

If you are a private person and do not look favorably on disclosing your personal finances to others, you should be aware that the proceedings of the probate courts are a matter of public record open to anyone interested in knowing your personal financial affairs. Moreover, if you own real estate in more than one state, more than one probate proceeding may be necessary.

Properly titling your property, naming beneficiaries, and establishing trusts may facilitate your estate passing to your heirs without having to go through the probate or administration processes. Spending a few thousand dollars on estate planning while you are alive can ultimately save your beneficiaries a significant amount of money, headaches, and delays. Also, this process may allow you to be in complete control over the distribution of your estate after your death.

Estate Planning Strategies That Keep You in Control After Your Death

If you would like to have continued control of the distribution of your estate after your death, there are several planning strategies you may want to implement while you are alive. Each of these provides a different degree of control over distribution, and each has different pros and cons. Essentially, you need to understand how your property will be distributed when you die with or without a will, some form of joint ownership, beneficiary-designated contractual agreements, or a trust.

Understanding how each of these estate planning strategies works and interacts with one another is essential to properly controlling the distribution of your estate after your death. If you do not take all of these facts into consideration during the estate planning process, the results could be dramatically different from what you had intended.

What Happens to Your Estate When You Have a Will – and When You Do Not

As mentioned, when someone dies without a will, that is called dying *intestate*. When that happens, the laws of your state will determine who your assets are distributed to. These laws are always based on your family tree. When a blood relative cannot be located, the state may then be entitled to take over ownership of all of your estate; this is the common law doctrine known as *escheat*. If you have not implemented any estate tax planning strategies and you do not have a will, you are going to have the least control over the distribution of your assets and the fulfillment of your last wishes.

I encourage you to have a will as the most basic estate planning strategy, especially if you are not willing to implement any other strategies. Another essential reason to have a will is if you have minor children. If both you and your spouse die at the same time (for example, in a car accident or plane crash), it is best if you have already directed in advance who will care for your children. You would not want any of your family members fighting over legal custody of your children. Avoiding potential family conflicts over child custody will not only eliminate the expensive legal process, but it will be more likely that family members will work in harmony in looking out for your children's best interests.

With the exception of individuals with minor children, the following represents situations where a will may not be necessary:

- If you have no assets in your individual name (for example, if all your assets are either jointly held or are in the name of a trust for others) or if all the assets in your name have designated beneficiaries other than your estate (for example, if you have a named beneficiary for your life insurance or IRA account), then all of your assets will be transferred by operation of law. Therefore, you do not need a will to designate anything to anyone. I realize that even the poorest of people have some assets such as clothing, furniture, and other personal belongings, but this level of assets is not worth the costly probate process. Therefore, even if a will exists in these cases, it would still not be financially justified to go through this process.

- If you want to leave your assets to your beneficiaries in the same proportion as predetermined by your state's laws, you do not need a will to accomplish this. In this case, if you die with or without a will, your individual beneficiaries will receive the same inheritance. Note, however, that without a will, you will not have a say in who your legal representative will be. Therefore, a will is necessary when your wishes are different from your state's predetermined (default) allocations or when you want complete control over the settling of your estate.

By having a properly drafted will, you can decide who will ultimately inherit your assets. You can also choose your executor and set up any trusts that you may want to have in force after death. The *executor* is someone you appoint in your will to carry out your last wishes, as outlined in your testament.

The only people who can contest (dispute) a will are people who would be entitled to receive a certain percentage of your estate if you die without a will. For example, if you are a widow or widower and you have three living children, your three children would equally receive your estate, under all state intestacy laws (provided you do not have a trust naming someone else to receive some or all of your assets). However, suppose you execute a will and decide to exclude one of your children. When you pass away and the will is offered for probate, the excluded child has standing to contest the will because he will be receiving less than he would have received under the intestacy laws (namely one-third of the estate).

However, it is important to remember that someone who has standing to contest a will cannot contest the will on the grounds that he or she does not like its terms; instead, that person must allege and prove in court that the will was not properly executed in accordance with the formal requirements of the state, or that the person (e.g., you) did not have the requisite capacity to make the will at the time of its execution. If someone contests the will and is successful, then the will is declared void and the estate will be distributed in accordance with the state intestacy laws or in accordance with the provisions of an earlier will, if you had one.

What Happens to Your Estate When You Have Beneficiary-Designated Contractual Agreements

Yet another estate planning strategy to control your assets after death is through a *contractual agreement by beneficiary designation.* For example, if you have a retirement plan through your employer, an IRA, life insurance, or an annuity contract, you can and should designate a beneficiary. The rights to the proceeds from these contracts will automatically pass to the individual(s) you designate as your beneficiary. Using a designated beneficiary on these contracts typically has the added benefit of avoiding probate on those specific assets.

Alternatively, you can also designate your estate as the beneficiary, if you want the asset to be transferred in accordance with your will. Unfortunately, this makes these assets subject to probate; therefore, I recommend avoiding this choice, if possible. It is extremely important to review these contracts to make sure your beneficiary designations reflect your current wishes, because these contractual agreements supersede the intentions you state in your will.

What Happens to Your Estate When You Have a Trust

Perhaps the most flexible estate planning strategy that allows you to control your assets before and after your death is creating a trust. A trust can be created while you are alive (called an *inter vivos trust*) or after your death through your will (called *a testamentary trust*).

A trust can give you the maximum control over the distribution of your estate after your death, because the terms of a trust provide the trustee with your specific instructions.

A trust can have the added advantage of using the services of professional asset managers, who can protect your assets in the event of your incapacity. When a trust is set up properly, you can use it as a mechanism to significantly reduce your gift and estate tax liabilities. Later in this chapter, we will cover in great detail the many estate planning strategies that can be implemented with a trust. When evaluating whether a trust strategy is appropriate for you, you need to consider the upfront costs and ongoing administrative and professional fees to maintain it.

Using a Planned Gifting Strategy

For 2018, the gift tax exclusion is $15,000 per year. What this means is that you can make a gift in this amount to anyone – and to as many people as you like – every calendar year, and that money will not be subject to gift tax or included in your taxable estate. Furthermore, it will not be subtracted from your lifetime exemption of $11.2 million for 2018. This amount can be increased to $30,000 per year if a non-donor spouse agrees to split the gift. This can be a great way to transfer assets to children, grandchildren, and other intended heirs while you are still alive. Ultimately, this will reduce the taxable value of your estate and your ultimate estate tax liability at the same time.

In theory, if you and your spouse want to gift $30,000 to 10 people this year, you could reduce your estate by $300,000. Based on the 2018 federal estate flat tax rate of 40%, you would save your estate $120,000, assuming you would have a taxable estate upon death. With a properly structured lifetime gifting program, you could significantly reduce and in some cases completely eliminate any potential estate tax liability.

Two of the most overlooked exceptions to the gift tax exclusion limitation have to do with tuition and medical payments – specifically:

1. Any qualified tuition payments made on behalf of a donee beneficiary (for example, your child or grandchild) are not considered a gift if you make the payment directly to the educational institution.
2. Any medical payments made on behalf of a donee beneficiary are also not considered a gift if you make the payment directly to the medical provider.

Therefore, you can pay an unlimited amount of someone's college tuition directly to the school and still be permitted to give an additional $15,000 directly to the donee beneficiary without affecting your lifetime exemption. Thus, you may want to consider paying your children's and grandchildren's tuition directly to the institution, as one of your valuable estate planning tools.

Ownership of Property and How It Is Transferred

A critical part of the estate planning process revolves around how the ownership of property (including real estate and any other assets you hold title to) is treated and ultimately how it is transferred to your beneficiaries. In fact, the manner in which you hold title to your property will supersede provisions contained in other documents, such as your will. Many times people may execute a will with the intention of leaving some of their property to particular individuals, yet those individuals do not receive what was intended by the decedent because all their property was jointly held with other individuals.

For example, here is a very common scenario where a decedent's wishes may be denied because of operation of law. A parent (typically a widow or widower) may have joint bank accounts with only one of his or her children, for convenience purposes only. This is usually done with a child who is the primary caregiver for that parent or who simply does the parent's banking. The parent makes a will leaving all of his or her assets equally to his or her children. When the parent passes away, those bank accounts become the legal property of the child that had joint ownership over them. Therefore, the legal title of the account passes by operation of law and supersedes the intention of the parent as stated in the will.

For this reason, it is extremely important for you to verify the ownership of property and how it is held. You can either gain or lose significant tax benefits, depending on how you structure the ownership of your property. The following are the four basic forms of legal ownership to property. Understanding the differences between them can have a considerable impact on how your estate assets are eventually transferred.

Individual Ownership

Individual ownership occurs when one person owns a 100% interest in a property. For example, if you own a piece of real estate, a bank account, or a brokerage account and your name is designated as the only owner, this would be considered individual ownership. Through an estate, ownership is passed in accordance with a will or by the laws of intestacy. The complete value is included in the gross taxable estate of the decedent.

When two or more persons own property, it is said to be held *concurrently*. There are several types of concurrent ownership, including *tenancy in common, joint tenancy,* and *tenancy by the entirety.*

Tenancy in Common

Tenancy in common is the most common type of concurrent ownership in property. In this context, *tenant* means *owner* (not *renter*, as it does in everyday language). Each tenant (*owner*) has the right to convey his or her interest in the property. When one of the tenants (*co-owners*) dies, that tenant's interest passes to his or her heirs or by will to someone else. With this type of property ownership, each owner has an undivided fractional share of the property.

In other words, suppose you own a house with your husband, and the deed to your house is held by *tenancy in common*. What that means is that, if your husband dies, his ownership of the house passes to his heirs, not to you, even though you "co-own" the property. For you to receive the house, you would have to own the property as "joint tenants," described in the next section.

Joint Tenancy

Joint tenancy exists when two or more persons share equal, undivided whole interests in the property. The key feature of joint tenancy is the right of survivorship, whereby, upon the death of one of the joint tenants, his interest is automatically passed to the others by operation of law and cannot be transferred in accordance with a will or trust document.

An added benefit of joint tenancy is that it avoids probate with respect to this asset. Anyone can share joint interests, but there are additional tax benefits when this arrangement is shared between a husband and wife, which is known as a *qualified joint tenancy*. Under qualified joint tenancy, half of the property is included in the first decedent's estate. Because of this, the surviving spouse obtains a stepped-up basis on the first decedent's half of the property. A *stepped-up basis* allows the beneficiary to value the property at the decedent's date of death for tax purposes, and this value is used to determine gain or loss upon the eventual sale of the asset. Quite simply, the cost for determining gain or loss is based on the property's value after death, rather than on what the decedent actually paid for it. If any nonspouses participate in joint ownership, the entire value of the property is includable in the decedent's estate, reduced only to the extent that the estate can prove that the surviving tenant contributed to the cost of the property in proportion to his share.

The tax code provides a unique benefit to the surviving spouse who holds community property and resides in a community property state. On the death of the first spouse, community property may be stepped up to its *full fair market value* as of the date of death. If the community property has increased in value, a federal income tax on the realized gain upon sale will be avoided. The following are community property states: Arizona, California, Idaho, Louisiana, Nevada, New Mexico, Texas, Washington, and Wisconsin.

Tenancy by the Entirety

Tenancy by the entirety is another form of concurrent ownership, similar to joint tenancy, but it can be created only between a husband and wife. In states recognizing tenancy by the entirety, when a married couple owns real property, the presumption is that it is held as a tenancy by the entirety. To own property as tenants in common, the married couple would have to specifically state their wishes as such. Neither spouse can convey his or her interest without the express consent of the other. One of the main advantages to this type of joint ownership is that it offers protection from creditors. A creditor cannot put a lien against property held under tenancy by the entirety in a state where spouses must act together. Therefore, this property may be exempt under bankruptcy proceedings if only one of the spouses is the debtor of the creditor. Neither party can alienate or encumber the property, so that upon the death of one, it is inherited by the surviving spouse. In the event of a divorce, it becomes a tenancy in common, since tenancy by the entirety could only be between a husband and wife. However, tenancy by the entirety is recognized in only 25 states. Check with your attorney to see if your state allows this form of joint ownership; it may be vital to maintaining your financial independence in the event creditors try to put a claim against your property.

Amount Includable in the Estate and the Stepped-Up Basis

The amount includable in the estate of a decedent is based on his or her percentage of ownership. It is important to remember that the beneficiary can be chosen by the decedent, except in the case of joint tenancy or tenancy by the entirety, under which the surviving tenants automatically inherit the interest of the decedent.

There are major tax benefits to the beneficiary of property from an estate. The beneficiary of the property interest receives a stepped-up basis, as of the date-of-death value or the alternative valuation date (six months later). The beneficiary may be able to avoid or minimize capital gains tax on the sale of this asset, because their cost basis is increased to this estate valuation.

Here is a common scenario of the benefit from this stepped-up basis: A widow or widower passes away while owning real property. The children inherit the property either through a will or through administration (if there is no will, as described at the beginning of this chapter). The house is valued at $750,000, and the children sell it within a year for $750,000, with closing fees of $30,000. In this example, the children will collectively realize a $30,000 loss on their personal tax returns. If this asset is the only asset in the estate, it will not be subject to estate taxes, and the beneficiaries still receive the stepped-up basis. They not only receive the property free of estate tax, but may also be able to get an income tax deduction from the costs of selling the property.

Reasons for Creating a Trust

As mentioned earlier, perhaps the most flexible estate planning strategy that allows you to control your estate before and after death is creating a trust. A trust can take effect while you are alive (an *inter vivos* trust) or after death through your will (a *testamentary* trust). A trust can give you the maximum control over the distribution of your estate after death because the terms of a trust will provide the trustee with your specific instructions.

A trust is a device of protection and control of someone's assets that is also used to protect current and future beneficiaries. There are three key parties involved in the creation of a trust.

- The first party is the *trustor*, sometimes called the *settler* or *grantor* of the trust, which is the individual who establishes and funds the trust.
- The second party is the *trustee*, which can be a person or an institution. The trustee is entrusted to hold a legal title to property in order to administer it for the benefit of the beneficiary in accordance with the trust document.

- The third party is the *beneficiary* (or beneficiaries), who must eventually receive 100% distribution of the trust corpus. (The trust corpus refers to all property transferred to a trust. For example, if a trust is funded with $100,000 in cash, that money is considered the trust corpus.)

All trusts can be specifically defined and classified after asking the following questions.

1. Was the trust created during an individual's lifetime or upon his death?
   - If the trust was created to be effective during an individual's lifetime through a separate legal document (a trust document), it is considered an inter vivos trust.
   - If the trust was created to take effect after death within a Last Will and Testament, it is considered a testamentary trust.
2. Can the trust be changed, altered, amended, or revoked by the trustor?
   - If the answer to this question is yes, then this is considered a revocable trust.
   - If the answer to this question is no, then this is considered an irrevocable trust.
3. For federal income tax purposes, how is the trust classified and taxed?
   - Grantor trust
   - Simple trust
   - Complex trust
4. How does the trust define income?
   - It is important to note that a trust document's definition of income is considered its accounting income and this can be different from the tax law definition of income. These definitions can have a significant impact on distributions and taxation to both the trust and the beneficiaries.

A *living trust (inter vivos)* is a trust that is set up during your lifetime and takes effect when you transfer assets into the trust. It can be either revocable or irrevocable. A living trust can be used to transfer legal titles to property, including cash, stocks, real estate, and so forth, and can provide a means to manage these assets during your lifetime. Although these asset transfers change the legal title, you (as the creator or grantor) can retain income from the assets throughout your lifetime. Therefore, dependent on whether the living trust is revocable or irrevocable, you maintain control and the decision-making authority over the assets. These types of trusts are frequently used as a substitute for a will, because the trust usually terminates upon the death of the grantor and the trust documents dictate who the beneficiaries of the assets will be. You can also select the person you want as the trustee, which could include yourself in a revocable living trust, to carry out the instructions set out in the trust document. You can name successor trustees to take over if and when you can no longer act as the trustee. Last but not least, a living trust helps you avoid and minimize the administrative expenses, delays, and publicity involved with probate, because these trust assets transfer by operation of law.

In contrast, a *testamentary trust* is a trust created through a will and only takes effect when you die. With these trusts, the legal title to the assets does not transfer until your death. There is no separate legal trust document; it is created by a clause in your will. One of the pitfalls of a testamentary trust is that it will *not* avoid probate because the trust can be created only through the probate of a will.

According to Chad Smith, CFP®, ChFC®, CLU®, Director of National Sales at HD Vest Financial Services, "Family dynamics plays an ever more important role in estate planning in today's society. Unfortunately, most families have concerns with their heirs' ability to receive and manage money with an inheritance. These include: drug and alcohol addiction, spendthrift concerns, stability of marriages, and concerns over your children's spouse. These are just a few examples of the applicability of trust planning. When trust assets are left to a beneficiary, the terms of the trust can dictate how and when the beneficiary receives those assets. Many people establish trust so that they can influence the behavior of their heirs long after they have passed away. Family dynamics is a topic that should be discussed with your financial advisor and estate planning attorney."

Revocable and Irrevocable Trusts

Most trusts are revocable (in other words, you retain full control); if you create a revocable trust, you can be the trustee, make future changes, and even terminate the trust. On the other hand, if the trust is irrevocable, you give up a certain degree of control; therefore, changes and termination are dependent on the terms of the trust and sometimes can be very difficult to make.

When you transfer assets into a revocable trust, they are not considered a completed gift; therefore, you do not have to file a gift tax return, which is required when a gift exceeds $15,000 in any given year (as of 2018). However, upon the death of the trustor (i.e., you, as the creator of the trust), the assets of a revocable trust are included in your taxable estate. These assets are considered part of your estate because you retained beneficial ownership and control of those assets. Therefore, revocable trusts are not useful in minimizing estate taxes, but they do serve the purpose of avoiding probate or administration because the trust assets pass to your beneficiaries, in accordance with the trust document you created.

Living trusts allow you to control the distribution of your estate, and certain trusts may enable you to reduce or avoid some of the taxes and fees that will be imposed on your estate after your death. When you establish a revocable living trust, you are permitted to be the trustor, the trustee, and the beneficiary of that trust. By setting up a living trust, you transfer ownership of certain assets from yourself to the trust. You are no longer the legal owner of the assets you placed in your trust. Your trust is now the legal owner, even though as the trustee, you maintain complete control of these assets during your lifetime.

A-B Trusts

One of the most popular living trusts is an A-B trust, which is also known as a *bypass trust* or a *credit shelter trust*. This allows the surviving spouse to possibly double the amount of his or her estate tax exemption when the surviving spouse dies. When you use an A-B trust, two trusts are created upon the death of the first spouse. The decedent's assets will be separated between the survivor's trust ("A" trust) and the decedent's trust ("B" trust). This will create two separate legal entities, both of which are permitted to use the full amount of the federal and state estate tax exemption.

The surviving spouse still maintains full control of his or her own trust ("A" trust). He or she can also receive income from the deceased spouse's trust ("B" trust) and can even make withdrawals of principal for health, support, or maintenance when needed. Upon the death of the second spouse, the assets of both trusts pass directly to the heirs, and will avoid probate.

With the enactment of the 2010 Tax Relief Act, some couples may not obtain the same level of benefit from implementing an A-B trust in maximizing the federal estate tax exemption, because of the new portability rules. The Tax Cuts and Jobs Act of 2017 diminished the usefulness of these trusts from a tax benefit perspective, due to the increase in federal estate tax exemption to $11.2M. See the section towards the end of this chapter that goes into further detail about the spousal portability of this exclusion.

It is critically important to note that many states have their own estate or inheritance tax laws you will need to consider. Currently, none of the states have adopted the federal concept of portability. Therefore, if you are married and leave all your assets to your surviving spouse, he or she will only be able to use his or her own state exemption, and your exemption will forever be lost. Although A-B trusts may not be as beneficial as they were in the past, they should still be fully utilized by married couples, especially if they live in states that impose their own estate tax. Furthermore, a trust provides you with the ability to shelter the appreciation of assets placed in the trust. It may also protect these assets from creditors and allow you to preserve the state estate tax exemptions for both you and your spouse.

How a Trust Is Taxed

How a trust is classified and taxed for federal income tax purposes depends on the type of trust involved. When determining which type of trust would be most suitable to meet your financial objectives, it is important to understand how different trusts are taxed.

There are three types:

1. With a ***grantor trust***, for income tax purposes, the trust is treated as if it does not exist. All income in a grantor trust is reported on the trustor's personal income tax return, as if the trust was never created. All revocable trusts are considered grantor trusts and are taxed in this manner. Some irrevocable trusts are treated as grantor trusts when the terms of the irrevocable trust creates a grantor trust for income tax purposes.
2. With a ***simple trust***, all income must be distributed and is taxed at the income beneficiary level. Even if the income is not properly distributed, it can be deemed distributed for tax purposes.

3. With a **complex trust,** the trustee has certain discretion and can either distribute or not distribute the income to the beneficiaries. Any income not distributed to the beneficiaries is taxed at the trust level and at the trust's tax rate. The trustee has up to 65 days after the close of the trust year to make a distribution, which would be considered made during the previous tax year.

A complex trust is taxed in a manner similar to personal individual income taxation, except the tax rates are compressed and the trust is subject to the maximum tax rate at a much lower threshold. Income earned by a trust will either be taxed at the trust level or at the income beneficiary level. A trust is permitted to take an income distribution deduction against the trust income for all income that is properly distributed from the trust.

Under the Tax Cuts and Jobs Act of 2017, the following are the tax brackets on income taxable to the trust and estates in 2018:

- 10% on taxable income up to $2,550
- 24% on taxable income over $2,550 but not over $9,150
- 35% on taxable income over $9,150 but not over $12,500
- 37% on taxable income over $12,500

   In addition to the above income tax, a trust or estate has to pay a 3.8% Medicare tax on net investment income under the Patient Protection and Affordable Care Act. The tax is imposed on the lesser of "undistributed net investment income" or excess of adjusted gross income over the dollar amount at which the highest tax bracket begins, which would be the excess of $12,500 for 2018.

Transfers with Retained Life Interests

When assets are transferred and the transferor retains the use and enjoyment of the transferred asset for the remainder of his or her life, the rules of Internal Revenue Code Section 2036 apply. This is most common when individuals transfer real property to their children and retain a "life estate" interest in the property for themselves. This simple transfer is fairly common, as it accomplishes the following benefits to estate planning:

- This asset avoids probate or administration of your will when you die, as the property is already in your children's name.

- By retaining the "life estate," the IRS still considers the assets owned by you, and your children are therefore entitled to a stepped-up basis. Without the "life estate," the transfer may be considered an outright gift, and your children would not be entitled to a stepped-up basis.
- The life estate also protects you in case of a dispute between you and your children, because it keeps you from being disturbed or evicted from the property. Even in the best families, children may get divorced, predecease their parents, or have family arguments that may impact their decision to try to remove you from your house.

Caution should be exercised, however, in transferring real property to children, even when reserving a life estate interest. First, the transfer would be deemed irrevocable, meaning you would need the consent of the transferee(s) should you decide that you want the property back. Secondly, by titling your property in another's name, it will become vulnerable to things that may happen in that person's life, such as divorce, bankruptcy, lawsuits, and even death. This is another reason why some people are choosing to title real estate in an irrevocable trust. Since, with this type of transfer, ownership does not vest in the transferee until your death, the property is not subject to the above vulnerabilities.

Split-Interest Trusts

Certain trusts are established with the stipulation that there will be an *income beneficiary* as well as a *remainder beneficiary* for the assets transferred into the trust. A remainder beneficiary of a trust is entitled to the principal of the trust outright after the interest of the prior beneficiary has been terminated. These types of trusts are referred to as *split-interest trusts* and include the following:

- Grantor-retained income trust (GRIT)
- Grantor-retained annuity trust (GRAT)
- Grantor-retained unitrust (GRUT)
- Qualified personal residence trust (QPRT)

The major advantage of establishing these split-interest trusts include the following:

- You (as the trustor) continue to control the income for a set period of time.

- There is an objective discount in the value of the gifted asset, at the time the gift is made.
- All future growth of the asset remains outside of the living estate of the trustor (transferor).

These three points are critical components of several sophisticated estate-planning techniques. The value of the gift can be significantly reduced based on the value of the retained interest by the transferor. Because the value of the gift is significantly reduced by implementing this strategy, you can minimize and, in certain cases, eliminate the gift tax consequence of the transfer. If someone makes a gift of a future interest in a property and retains the right to use that property during a period of time, they are deemed to have given only a partial interest.

For example, let us assume you gave a gift of stock with a current fair-market value of $500,000 to a trust, but you retained the right to all income generated by this gift for a set time period of 20 years. You will need to determine the present value of this future gift to be completed 20 years from now. The IRS allows you to use the present value of this future gift of $500,000, 20 years from now, which is discounted based on the applicable IRS long-term interest rate. For the purpose of our example, we will assume that the IRS long-term interest rate has been set at 5% at the time of the gift.

Therefore, the future value (FV) of the gift is set at $500,000, the applicable long-term interest rate (i) is equal to 5%, and the number of periods (n) is equal to 20. At this point, you would turn to Chapter 12, Exhibit 12.4 "Present Value (PV) Factor of a Sum Certain," go to the 5% column, and then go down the row for 20 years, to find the factor of 0.37689. In other words, based on the present value factor table, the IRS will allow you to objectively discount the value of this gift from $500,000 to $188,445 ($500,000 × 0.37689). This technique will allow you to transfer $500,000 to the trust for the benefit of your beneficiaries and will use up only $188,445 of your lifetime exclusion. Therefore, if you ultimately have a taxable estate upon death, you have reduced your taxable estate by $311,555 ($500,000 − $188,445). Assuming the estate tax rate upon your death is 40%, this will result in a reduction of your estate tax liability by $124,622 ($311,555 × 40%). In addition, any future appreciation in the value of this $500,000 stock will not be included in your estate. The only catch is that you (the transferor) must live beyond the 20-year period established by this trust. If you die before the completion of this gift (which, in this example, is 20 years), the full value of the stock as of your date of death will be included in your estate. That defeats the whole purpose of establishing the split-interest trust. Therefore, the biggest pitfall in using this technique is that the trust must terminate before you die. If it does not, the trust assets are valued as a part of your estate, and these assets will be included as of the date of death value.

To highlight the significance of this estate planning technique, let us assume that the $500,000 is worth $2 million on your date of death, which is 21 years after the stock was transferred into the trust. One of the major advantages of transferring property out of your estate while you are alive is that all future capital appreciation will avoid being included in your estate valuation upon your death. Once again, this is a powerful technique for minimizing your estate tax liability and maximizing the amount passed on to your heirs. Let us also assume that your estate would have been subject to the estate tax rate of 40%; this technique would have reduced the ultimate federal estate tax liability by $724,622 ($2 million less $188,445 = $1,811,555 × 40%). This is a somewhat complex estate tax planning technique, but a very effective one for preserving your estate and ultimately maximizing the amount you pass on to your loved ones. Please note that the tax planning technique known as a split-interest has been significantly limited by the creation of Internal Revenue Code Section 2702.

You should consult with an experienced estate tax attorney and financial planner to determine whether using a split-interest trust would be beneficial to you. These are clearly advanced estate tax planning techniques and can only be properly used with the guidance of an estate tax attorney that specializes in these matters.

The "Charitable" Trust

Charitable trusts are created when you have a charitable intent and would also like to accomplish the following:

- Have continued control of income
- Potentially get an immediate charitable deduction while you are alive
- Potentially eliminate capital gains tax
- Potentially eliminate or reduce estate taxes

These types of trust include the following:

- Charitable lead annuity trust (CLAT)
- Charitable lead unitrust (CLUT)
- Charitable remainder unitrust (CRUT)
- Charitable remainder annuity trust (CRAT)

In theory, these charitable remainder trusts work the same as the split-interest trusts discussed above, except that the remainder beneficiary is a qualified charitable organization under 501(c)(3) of the Internal Revenue Code. The present value calculations and the benefit of removing assets from your estate would be the same, with the added benefits of getting a charitable deduction. A charitable remainder trust allows your spouse or children to access the earnings from assets in the trust for a time, with the asset eventually going to charity.

The vast majority of people simply give donations to charity by cash or check. Such donations entitle you to take a tax deduction in the year of your contribution, but you must be prepared to prove it with a receipt from the charity.

You can use several more sophisticated gifting techniques that will not only benefit your charity but, if structured properly, can significantly lower your income and estate taxes. Both you and the charity can significantly increase the benefit from your charitable gift if it is made from highly appreciated property of almost any kind. When you own property that has increased in value and have a charitable intent, you can get the best of both worlds. By gifting the property to the charity, you may be entitled to an income tax deduction for the fair market value of the gift; the charity could then sell the appreciated property, if it chooses to do so, and the charity will not be subject to capital gains tax. Therefore, you not only lower your taxable income by avoiding the capital gains tax, but you also benefit from a higher charitable deduction, since the gift is being made in pretax dollars.

To obtain the tax advantages associated with charitable giving, the gift must be made to a qualified charitable organization, which means the charitable organization must:

- Have been organized in the United States
- Be operated on a nonprofit basis
- Not be involved with political activities
- Be a qualified charitable organization recognized by the IRS as a 501(c)(3)

In addition to these qualified charitable organizations, you may give to veterans' posts, certain fraternal orders, volunteer fire departments, and civil defense organizations.

Using a Trust to Further Increase the Benefits of Charitable Gifting

There are several different gifting strategies available for planned giving, which include giving an outright gift to charity or setting up a charitable trust. Each has its own pros and cons, summarized in Exhibit 10.1.

Charitable lead trusts are designed for individuals who would like to see their charity benefit immediately from their gift. With a charitable lead trust, your gift can have an immediate benefit to your charity, and it may entitle you to benefit at the same time. If you usually make outright contributions to your charity, and you generally sell an appreciated investment and give all or some of the money to charity, you may be a perfect candidate to benefit from using a charitable trust.

With a charitable lead trust, you are actually gifting the asset's income to the charity and not gifting the actual asset. Your deduction will be based on the rate of return the charity can reasonably expect

Exhibit 10.1   The Pros and Cons of Various Gifting Strategies

Gifting Strategy	Pros	Cons
Outright Gift	Income tax-deductible in year of gift	No retained interest or control after gifted
Charitable Lead Trust	A current gift to charity	Charitable gift is irrevocable
	Current income tax deduction	With current income tax deduction, future income is taxable to the donor
	Transfers assets at a future discounted value	
		Donor gives up the use of income generated throughout the life of the trust
Charitable Remainder Unitrust	Current income tax deduction	Charitable gift is irrevocable
	Avoids capital gains tax on appreciated property and reduces estate taxes	Qualified appraisal commonly required
		Complex administration and setup
Charitable Remainder Annuity Trust	Current income tax deduction	Fixed payment is not limited to the net amount of trust income
	Avoids capital gains tax on appreciated property	Qualified appraisal commonly required
	Fixed income stream	Complex administration and setup

to receive, the duration of the trust, and the IRS valuation tables used in calculating the value of the gift. After the income from the gifted assets goes to the charity, the charity will then continue to receive distributions throughout the life of the trust. You can establish the life of the trust for a set number of years or for an individual's lifetime, including your own. Once this time period has expired, the trust will terminate, and the remaining assets will be paid to you or your beneficiaries. If during your lifetime, you are interested in increasing your gifts to charity as well as your tax benefits, a charitable lead trust may enable you to accomplish your goals. With a charitable lead trust, you can also pass an appreciated asset on to your heirs with little or no estate taxes.

Charitable remainder trusts allow you or your beneficiaries to receive payment of a specified amount annually, and, at the end of the trust period, the designated charity receives the remainder assets. You can receive either a percentage (*charitable remainder unitrust*) of the value of the trust or a fixed amount (*charitable remainder annuity trust*). The trustee can sell off the highly appreciated assets gifted to the trust and then reinvest the proceeds to generate income and avoid capital gains tax. This strategy may allow you to both rebalance your investment portfolio without the typical tax consequences and shift your investments to high income-generating assets, which will improve your cash flow. Furthermore, you may also be eligible for a current year income tax deduction on the calculated present value of the remainder interest that will ultimately go to the charity at a future date. Although the gift to the trust is irrevocable, you do have control over which charity will eventually receive this gift.

Summing Up What You Need to Know About Trusts

You must choose a trustee wisely and clearly state your intentions in the trust document. The beneficiary will ultimately assume ownership of the trust assets, even if this does not happen for decades. During the period in between, the trustee is in charge of controlling the assets in the trust and complying with the instructions in the trust document. Choosing someone who knows how to handle financial matters and will carry out your intentions is critically important to the successful utilization of these trust strategies. Trusts are highly complicated instruments that must strictly conform to tax rules and regulations, so you must consult with an experienced estate tax attorney and a financial planner before implementing these strategies.

Benefit from a Family Limited Partnership

If you own a family business, rental property, or a farm, you may have some additional estate planning hurdles to deal with down the road. If you are "hard asset rich" but cash poor, your family may be faced with liquidity problems upon your death, when it comes time to pay estate taxes. The federal government requires your executor or administrator to pay your estate tax liability within nine months of your date of death. Your family members may have no intention to sell any of the property you left behind for them, but they may be forced to do so to pay the estate taxes. The key goal of any estate planning strategy is to minimize estate taxes and to provide the necessary liquidity when the time comes. The main objective is to preserve the estate and to allow your family to continue to own and operate the family business, rental property, or farm.

The formation of a family limited partnership is another estate planning strategy to use in these situations. A family limited partnership is typically established as a separate legal entity to hold and manage a family business or investment property; it may also open up the opportunity to use various other estate and income tax planning strategies.

The family limited partnership agreement provides control to the parent and divides the right to the income, including future appreciation in value, among family members, in an attempt to provide financial and tax benefits to the overall family. These family partnerships typically commence by creating and transferring assets into a general limited partnership. As the parent, you can then start the process of gifting limited partnership interests (noncontrolling interests) to your children. You would continue to hold the general partnership interest (controlling interest), which makes the parent the partner with full control. The children would have no control as limited partners. You would continue to maintain and exercise complete control, even after your children become majority partners, as long as they are the only limited partners. As limited partners, your children would share in the income of the family limited partnership in proportion to their ownership interests, which have been established through your gifts.

This estate tax planning strategy allows you to provide your children with an ownership interest while you are alive, while also allowing you to reduce your future estate tax liability with the added benefit of a succession plan for your family-owned business, property, or farm. You will be able to gift limited partnership interests to your children over time, which will allow you to take full advantage of the $15,000 (possibly $30,000 if you are married) annual gift tax exclusion without giving them control of the money or property. If that was not reason enough, your children may also benefit by having their share of the income from this family limited partnership taxed at their potentially lower income tax rate.

The full value of the partnership interests transferred to your children while you are alive will escape inclusion in your taxable estate, including any appreciation in value after the date of transfer. This is a very powerful estate planning strategy if you are able to take advantage of it.

Estate Tax Planning and Life Insurance

An irrevocable life insurance trust (ILIT) is another estate planning strategy, which can be set up to hold life insurance policies, preventing the proceeds from being included in your taxable estate.

One of the key features of an ILIT is that it allows you to keep the life insurance death benefit out of the value of your estate. You (as the trustor) can make annual gifts to the trust in order for the trustee to pay for the life insurance premiums on your life that are owned by the trust. These gifts are made annually, up to $15,000 (2018) per beneficiary, which will also serve the purpose of further lowering the estate value and estate tax liability. Therefore, not only is the value of the estate reduced by the gifts you make each year, but ultimately the entire death benefit will escape estate taxes on your death.

It is very important to note that you never want to own life insurance in your own name if the possibility exists that your estate may be subject to estate taxes. The death benefit from life insurance held in your name will be included in your taxable estate. Based on the current estate tax rate, the federal government may be entitled to 40% of your death benefit. Although life insurance proceeds are generally not subject to income tax, they can and will be subject to estate taxes if they are owned by you and you have a taxable estate. The death benefit of a life insurance policy is included in the taxable estate if the policy is transferred to another individual or trust by a decedent within three years before his or her death.

A second-to-die insurance policy insures two people and pays a benefit after the death of the second person. (See Chapter 5, "Insuring Your Health and Life," for more details.) These premiums are typically much less expensive than premiums for a single life insurance policy, because they are based on the life expectancies of the two insured spouses. Because the unlimited marital deduction allows assets to pass to the surviving spouse without federal estate taxes, the estate taxes generally do not become an issue until the death of the second spouse. When the estate assets pass out of the marriage to the heirs, this is when you normally incur the estate tax liability. Thus, a second-to-die survivorship life insurance policy could pay a benefit at the time when your family really needs it, to pay estate taxes.

Once again, you must seek out a qualified estate attorney and financial advisor to not only set this up properly, but also to administer the trust, because there are strict guidelines that must be followed each year. The cost and availability of life insurance depends on a number of factors such as your age, health, and the type and amount of insurance coverage you want to purchase. Before implementing a planning strategy involving life insurance, it would be sensible to make sure that you are insurable.

Spousal "Portability" of the Exclusion

The 2010 Tax Relief Act revived the estate tax after it was eliminated at the end of 2009. Perhaps one of the most significant changes created by this act is spousal "portability" of the lifetime exclusion, which was made permanent with the American Taxpayer Relief Act of 2012. If the first spouse to die does not fully use his or her exclusion, then the surviving spouse may inherit the decedent spouse's unused exclusion and may therefore be entitled up to an inflation adjusted $22.4 million lifetime exclusion (as of 2018) upon his or her death.

The spousal portability is generally only available if an election is made by the executor or administrator on a timely filed IRS Form 706 for the first spouse to die. If this form is not filed, and the election is not made, the surviving spouse will be limited to only his or her $11.2 million exclusion. Therefore, even if an estate tax return is not required to be filed upon the death of the first spouse, the surviving spouse and the executor should consider filing and making this election to preserve the full amount of the exclusion made available under spousal portability rules. Although the election must generally be made on a timely filed 706, a late election can be made up to two years after the date of death. A 706 must be filed within this time frame, and "Filed pursuant to Rev Proc 2017-34" must be written on the top of the form. If the surviving spouse remarries, he or she can take advantage of portability rules only once. This rule prevents an estate from taking advantage of the spousal portability exclusion more than once because of multiple marriages.

Estate taxes are an important concern in distributing your estate because the money your estate pays in taxes will not be available to your heirs. Each estate is allowed a federal estate tax exemption and a certain amount that can pass tax-free, either through lifetime gifts or after death. By implementing some of the strategies covered in this chapter, you should be able to preserve more of your estate for the benefit of your loved ones. If the total value of your estate is less than the applicable exemption amount at the time of your death, no federal estate taxes will be due. Always remember to check the rules for your state of residence, because the exclusion can be much lower at the state level. I would recommend going to your resident's state department of taxation website and checking out what the exclusion would be at the state level for you. You can, of course, also ask your attorney and financial planner to provide you with further guidance on the state estate tax rules, since they do vary.

I would encourage you to go to www.calcxml.com/calculators/what-is-my-potential-estate-tax-liability to calculate the amount of estate taxes you may owe based on today's estate tax exemption and rates. Be sure to use your statement of financial position (as discussed in Chapter 3), and do not forget to add the death benefit of any life insurance held in your name when determining your net worth for this calculation. You should use this calculator to estimate the approximate amount of federal estate taxes that would be required to be paid based on the current tax laws.

Estate planning requires you to know strategies to minimize taxes and to plan how your family will pay them when the time comes. As mentioned, estate taxes are generally due nine months after the date of death and are to be paid with cash. There are just a few options when it comes to how your executor will pay the estate taxes upon your death, including:

- Using your current savings and liquid investments
- Borrowing the money
- Liquidating hard assets, such as selling real estate
- Using life insurance proceeds

If the first three options are not appealing or practical, then you should consider implementing the strategies discussed earlier regarding estate tax planning and life insurance. Paying estate taxes could present a challenge to the executor and your survivors. It is therefore essential to put a plan in place that will include how the ultimate estate taxes will be paid. You must put this plan of action in place while you are still alive; otherwise, your executor and survivors may be forced to liquidate your assets at bargain prices in order to meet this time-sensitive estate tax obligation.

State Inheritance and Estate Taxes

An inheritance tax is imposed on all beneficiaries who receive an inheritance from a deceased person. This tax is imposed by some states at the state level and is separate and distinct from the estate tax that the federal government or the state can impose on the assets of a decedent. Each beneficiary will need to report his or her share of the inheritance on their state's inheritance tax return. States that impose an inheritance tax would have their own tax rates, thresholds, and exemptions. As a result, some beneficiaries may be exempt from paying this inheritance tax, depending on the amount inherited and the rules for their particular resident state.

The following states impose their own estate tax, in addition to federal estate tax: Washington, DC; Maine; New York; Rhode Island; Connecticut; Illinois; Minnesota; Washington; Oregon; Maryland; Vermont; Massachusetts; and Hawaii. Please note that, as of January 1, 2018, both New Jersey and Delaware have now eliminated their state imposed estate tax.

The states of Pennsylvania, Kentucky, Iowa, Nebraska, New Jersey, and Maryland impose an inheritance tax on beneficiaries that receive an inheritance from a deceased person. The state of Maryland is the only state that imposes both a state estate tax and inheritance tax. You should check with your state tax department for more details if you live in one of the jurisdictions listed above.

Asset Protection and Long-Term Care

Throughout Chapter 10, we have been discussing various strategies available to you to preserve your estate for the benefit of those you intend as beneficiaries. While the steps you decide to take in this regard are largely within your control, one thing that is not is whether you or your spouse will ultimately require long-term care. With our statistical life expectancy increasing from year to year, the need for assistance with activities of daily living as we age is almost inevitable. The type of long-term care an individual may need, whether it be institutional care in a nursing home, assisted living, or home care may be unknown, but what is certain is that the cost of care in any of these settings could wipe out your savings, no matter how well you are prepared.

The good news is that, by seeking the advice of an estate planning attorney and financial planner knowledgeable in the area of long-term care, you can take the steps necessary to minimize the out-of-pocket expense to you (and, therefore, to your estate), should you ever need long-term care.

It is important to understand that there is a drastic difference between short-term rehabilitative care and long-term care. Private health insurance or Medicare typically provide coverage (of varying degrees depending on your plan) for short-term rehabilitation after an accident, surgical procedure, or prolonged hospitalization. If, however, your need for rehabilitative care extends beyond the short term, most health insurance coverage and Medicare benefits will cease. Not only would this negate the preservation of your estate for your heirs, it could deplete your assets during your lifetime.

One method of minimizing out-of-pocket expenses for long-term care is to purchase long-term care insurance. For more details regarding long-term care insurance, please refer to the "Long-Term Care Insurance" section of Chapter 5, "Insuring Your Health and Life."

For those who may not qualify for long-term care insurance, or if the premiums required are cost-prohibitive, another option is to consult an elder law attorney to discuss what steps may be taken to qualify you or your spouse for having long-term care paid for through state-administered Medicaid. Since Medicaid is a combined federal and state program, the specific rules of eligibility for Medicaid for long-term care purposes and the particular programs available vary greatly from state to state. Despite these variations, however, with the guidance of an elder law attorney, you may be able to create potential eligibility for Medicaid by making transfers of your assets, including your home and other real estate, as well as financial assets, out of your name five years or more prior to facing the need for long-term care. What is more important to know is that, depending on your state of residence, there are a variety of transfers and techniques that can be utilized, even within a five-year period of having to apply for Medicaid, for long-term care to eliminate or decrease your loss of assets while still qualifying you for Medicaid.

Earlier in this chapter, we referred to a legal entity known as an irrevocable trust. Use of this kind of trust is quite common in

Medicaid eligibility planning, because it allows for the transfer of assets into the trust to gain protected status from future long-term care expenses. The trustor (you) can continue to benefit from the use and occupancy of real estate titled in an irrevocable trust during life and can even receive income generated from trust assets. After five years, however, the assets titled in the irrevocable trust will not be counted in Medicaid eligibility, nor will they be reachable to pay for the cost of long term care.

According to Annamarie Gulino Gentile, Esq., who specializes in estate and elder law and is a partner of Angiuli & Gentile, LLP, "Utilizing an irrevocable Medicaid Asset Protection Trust is frequently preferable to transferring assets to children or other individuals because it eliminates vulnerability of these assets during the trustor's life, insures handling of the assets in accordance with the trustor's wishes (as opposed to decisions made by children) and mandates that any ownership interest in the assets does not vest in the trustor's beneficiaries until his or her death."

Another little-known source of benefits to assist with the cost of long-term care is the Veteran's Aid and Attendance benefit. For individuals who served in the military for at least 90 days of active duty, with at least one of these days being during a period of war, benefits are available to assist with the cost of long-term care. Surviving spouses of these veterans may also be eligible for benefits. Since individuals applying for Aid and Attendance benefits must qualify both medically and financially, it is important to consult with a VA accredited attorney as part of your long-term care planning if you are a veteran. There you can obtain assistance in taking the necessary steps you need to qualify for maximum benefits. To find an accredited attorney, go to the US Department of Veterans Affairs website.

Estate planning, including that for the purpose of long-term care, must be tailored to your individual needs. Inaction can be a costly and burdensome mistake. As discussed throughout this chapter, it is important to develop your estate plan as soon as possible with your attorney and financial advisor to make sure your goals are met for your lifetime and for your family.

If you do not pay attention to the tax consequences of preserving your estate, your estate may have to pay significantly more in taxes than the law requires, thereby reducing the amount your loved ones will ultimately inherit. This is why you must include estate tax planning as part of your overall estate preservation strategy.

TAX ALPHA TO THE 2ND POWER℠ FACTS AND STRATEGIES FOR PRESERVING YOUR ESTATE

Here are several tax facts and strategies that will address your estate preservation goals at an exponential rate, which will help maximize the legacy you leave behind.

- **The estate tax exemption has been increased under the Tax Cuts and Jobs Act of 2017 to $11.2 million for individuals and $22.4 million for married couples starting January 1, 2018.** The estate tax rate remains at 40% of the amount above these lifetime exemption amounts.
- If you give your child or any other individual an interest-free or below-market interest loan, you can limit or even completely avoid imputed interest by the IRS, as long as the total outstanding loan balance owed to you by this individual does not exceed $100,000 and tax avoidance is not the principal purpose of this loan.
- When you sell property that you inherited, you are automatically given a holding period of more than one year (long-term capital gain treatment). Generally, you will also receive a step-up in basis to the fair market value of the property as of the date of death. This step-up in basis completely eliminates the income tax on the sale of most inherited properties. With a step-up in basis, the cost for determining gain or loss is based on the property's value at death and not based on what the decedent actually paid for it.
- When determining the gain or loss from the sale of property that was gifted to you, your cost basis is generally determined by the donor's cost basis, plus all or part of any gift tax paid. If you sell the gifted property for less than the donor's cost basis, you cannot report a loss.
- Before an anticipated sale, making gifts of appreciated property to a family member who is in a lower tax bracket can reduce the overall income tax to be paid by the family as a whole.
- You can give gifts throughout your lifetime and receive an exemption for the first $11.2 million of taxable gifts starting in 2018; this is in addition to the $15,000 annual gift to any number of persons per year. These gifts will not be subject to gift tax to you and can be received on a tax-free basis by the recipient.
- **You can make annual gifts of $15,000 (2018) to any number of persons, typically children or grandchildren, without incurring a gift tax.** If a husband and wife both engage in gifting, they can jointly give away $30,000 per year per recipient without incurring a gift tax. Over several years, the amount of money that can be transferred to beneficiaries can be substantial, thereby reducing the size of the taxable estate and the ultimate estate tax liability.
- You can pay an unlimited amount of someone's college tuition directly to the school and still be permitted to give an additional $15,000 directly to the donee beneficiary without affecting your lifetime exemption. Therefore,

you may want to consider paying your children's and grandchildren's tuition directly to the institution as one of your valuable estate planning tools.

- You can pay an unlimited amount of someone's medical expenses directly to the hospital and still be permitted to give an additional $15,000 directly to the donee beneficiary without affecting your lifetime exemption.
- Gifts and inheritances you receive are not taxable at the federal level, but distributions taken from an inherited IRA or qualified plan are taxable. In addition, with an inherited nonqualified annuity, a portion (earnings above original basis) of the distributions may be taxable.
- A gift or inheritance will be subject to income tax if, in fact, it is a payment for services rendered.
- By establishing an irrevocable life insurance trust (ILIT), you can reduce the size of your taxable estate each year, while providing your beneficiaries with a larger inheritance. Each year, you make a gift to the ILIT, which lowers your taxable estate. The trust then buys life insurance for the benefit of your beneficiaries. When you die, the life insurance proceeds are kept outside of the estate (owned by the trust). Then, these proceeds are not subject to estate tax and are income-tax-free to your beneficiaries. This is a must-do for large estates that will be subject to estate taxes.
- As a married person, you may be able to use the marital deduction that allows the passing spouse to transfer an unlimited amount of assets to the surviving spouse free from estate and gift tax.
- Under the American Taxpayer Relief Act of 2012, the portability (originally established in 2010) between spouses of the lifetime estate tax exemption was made permanent, and the exclusion is $11.2 million for 2018. Any unused portion of the deceased spouse's exemption is available and added to the estate tax exemption of the second spouse. This will preserve the full $22.4 million estate tax exemption for the married couple.
- The spousal "portability" is only available if an election is made by the executor or administrator on a timely filed IRS Form 706, for the *first spouse to die*. If this form is not filed and the election is not made, the surviving spouse will be limited to only his or her $11.2 million exclusion. Therefore, even if an estate tax return is not required to be filed upon the death of the first spouse, the surviving spouse and the executor should consider filing and making this election to preserve the full amount of the exclusion that was made available under spousal "portability" rules.
- **Although the portability election must generally be made on a timely filed 706, a late election can be made up to two years after date of death.** A 706 must be filed within this time frame, and "Filed pursuant to Rev Proc 2017-34" must be written on the top of the form.

AN ACTION PLAN FOR PRESERVING YOUR ESTATE

1. **Decide which legal documents you need to ensure that you and your estate are taken care of properly.** Most people should have a will. You may also want to have a living will, a health care proxy, or a durable power of attorney. You may want to set up one or more trusts, in addition to your will. These documents ensure that your wishes are followed, should you become incapacitated and unable to make decisions for yourself. Your will ensures that the assets you have accumulated during your lifetime will be distributed the way you want them to be, to whomever you choose, on your death.

2. **Keep in mind that if you die without a will, your estate will be distributed according to the relevant laws in the state where you lived.** Generally, these laws follow your family tree, but distributions may be made in a proportion that is not what you would have wanted. Keep in mind that these distribution rules vary state by state.

3. **Take advantage of gifting strategies that can help you prevent losing some of the value of your estate to taxes.** For example, in 2018, you can gift up to $15,000 (to as many people as you want) each year, which achieves two benefits. First, you can give money or other property up to $15,000 per year directly to your family or friends and an unlimited amount to charities while you are alive. Second, by lowering the value of your estate, your estate taxes will be lower, assuming you have a taxable estate.

4. **Make sure you understand the difference between various types of property ownership** – individual ownership, tenancy in common, joint tenancy, and tenancy by the entirety – as each has a different effect on what happens to that property upon your death.

5. **If you have a significant estate, you must meet with an experienced estate attorney and implement some of the advanced tax planning techniques mentioned in this chapter.**

6. **You should determine if you currently live in a state that imposes a state level estate or inheritance tax.** If so, you may want to consider moving to a more tax-friendly state while you are among the living.

11

Starting Your Own Business

Your business, and your brand, must first let people know what you care about, and that you care about them.

—Donald J. Trump,
45th president of the United States

How Starting Your Own Business Can Lead to Financial Independence

Over the past 30 years, I have helped thousands of small businesses achieve financial independence, and in this chapter, I will share the secrets to their success. So many people are under the impression that starting their own business will give them freedom and flexibility like they have never had before. Not having to answer to someone you call a boss does have its appeal.

The truth of the matter is that nothing could be further from the truth than these statements. Not everyone is cut out to be an entrepreneur. The characteristics of a successful business owner are not something you can learn in school or by reading a book, not even this one. You need to have a skillset that includes being relentless, driven, and passionate about the product or service you are providing. Owning your own business means that you are working 24 hours a day, 7 days a week, 365 days a year. I am not saying you physically need to be at your place of business all the time, but mentally you will be. As a small business owner, you are always planning the next day, week, month, and year. You are always trying to stay ahead of your competition and trying to find ways to satisfy your customers, while juggling the needs of your employees. Some of my best ideas in running my own business came to me while commuting to work or while tossing and turning in bed all night trying to solve a problem. And by the way, when you own your own business, you don't have just one boss. Everyone you provide a product or service to is your boss, since they are the ones who ultimately pay you and determine your success or failure.

Anyone who is driven strictly by the money will eventually fail in business. You must truly believe in the product or service you are providing and understand why it's the best. When you truly care about people, this passion comes through, not just to your customers, but to everyone you meet. This is the true secret to success in any business.

In this chapter, I will cover the essential aspects of establishing and maintaining a successful business. Many of the most financially independent individuals I have met throughout my career have reached *point X* by owning their own business. If you have what it takes to be an entrepreneur, then this chapter will help you get there too.

The Three Pillars of Establishing a Successful Business

There are three pillars of establishing a successful business and without them, you will not have the proper foundation to support your success. The three pillars are *specialized, interpersonal,* and *business management skills,* each of which are equally important to your survival.

Your *specialized skills* would come from your education and training. Your specialized education could come from high school, college, or trade schools. Training comes from years of work experience in your particular field or profession. Before you venture into business, you must first master the specialized skills and training required in your desired enterprise.

Your *interpersonal skills* are imbedded in your DNA and help make up your personality. They can also come from your upbringing and how you were raised to behave when interacting with other people. You may be a natural salesperson, with the gift of gab and the ability to convince people of almost anything. You may have the gift of nurturing, often putting people at ease by comforting them. Some of us are introverts and prefer minimal interaction with our fellow human beings. Before you venture into a business, you must also ask yourself, "Do I possess the personality traits and interpersonal skills required to succeed in my desired enterprise?" If the answer to this question is "no," then this may not be the right business for you.

Your *business management skills* come from specialized training and experience in managing businesses like the one you are interested in starting. If you do not have the required high-level management experience, then you will need to rely more heavily on others who possess this skillset. You must develop a business management team that has expertise in all of the areas of operating a successful business.

Sobering Statistics on Business Success Rates

Before I get into what it takes to establish a successful business, I think that it is important to understand its risks and benefits by providing you with some sobering statistics. According to the Bureau of Labor Statistics, the survival rate of business establishments started since 1994 is just over 50% after 5 years. After 10 years, the survival rate is just over 35%. After 15 years, it drops to just over 26%. And after 20 years, it is just over 21%. Clearly, based on these numbers, it is fair to say that going into business for yourself is a very risky proposition. As you know from Chapter 9, "Managing Your Investments," the greater the risk, the greater the reward. Unlike investing in publicly traded companies on major stock exchanges, owning your own business puts you in the driver's seat and in control. Your success or failure will depend on you and you alone. If you follow the guidance I provide in this chapter, it may dramatically increase your chances of success in being part of the 21% statistic 20 years from now.

The starting point to accomplishing anything in life begins with a well-thought-out plan. In fact, it is my belief that planning is the single most important step in establishing a successful business. You must have a clear vision and goal on *why* you are starting your business. If your answer to this question is because you want to make a lot of money, then your chances of success are almost zero. Money can never be the primary goal for going into business for yourself. Money is the byproduct of providing a product or service that you are passionate about.

Business Plan

Once you have clearly defined why you are going into business, then you can move forward on *how* to start your own business by creating a written business plan. The seven key components that must be included in a business plan are as follows:

1. Executive Summary
2. Business Description

3. Market Analysis
4. Organization and Management
5. Sales Strategies
6. Funding Requirements
7. Financial Projections

There are many books on this subject and software programs that could assist you with writing a business plan, but this ultimately must be in your own words. Only you can describe your passion (mission statement), which you will need to incorporate into your executive summary. This is the first part of your business plan, but should always be written last. The *executive summary* is an overview of your business plan and should summarize the main points of each section of the plan.

Your *business description* will talk about your actual business operation and how you are going to provide your product or service. It is extremely important that this is written in a way that can be understood by those outside of your trade or industry.

You will also need to do your homework and include a detailed *market analysis* that describes where this product or service will be provided and why there is a need for it.

You will need to describe your *organization and management* structure, what makes you qualified to own and operate this business, and who will be part of your business management team.

The next section of your business plan has to do with your *sales strategies*. This section must provide an overview of your marketing plan, which should be tied into the results of your market analysis.

The *funding requirements* section should lay out all startup costs, including costs of furniture, equipment, marketing, and how you plan on staying afloat during the startup stages of your business. From my years of experience, the number-one cause of failure for a startup business is underestimating the budget to establish the business. This budget must include the hard costs, such as furniture, fixtures, and leasehold improvements. It must also include operating costs and the ability to sustain losses, not only throughout the startup stage, but also for the many months and sometimes years it takes to become profitable. This funding must provide for a sufficient cushion for the unanticipated setbacks. The truth is that these unexpected setbacks will happen. In fact, they should be *expected*.

You will need to prepare *financial projections* that include a statement of financial position, a statement of profit and loss, and a statement of cash flow. These statements should cover one-year, two-year, and five-year time periods. This will be covered in more detail later in this chapter. Keep in mind that you will be preparing these for your business entity, and they are not based on your own personal finances. I would strongly suggest that, once you go through these numbers on your own, you have a certified public accountant who specializes in your industry go through them with you to make sure they make sense and tie into your underlying assumptions.

You should have the funds for this business operation available from your savings. This does not mean that you will be tapping into your personal cash reserves, because those are for your personal survival. Since you will still need to live and support yourself and your family while you are trying to get your new business started, the funds for your business must come from your investment assets. You should never use short-term debt to finance long-term projects. Some of the biggest mistakes I have seen new entrepreneurs make are cashing out 401(k) plans, maxing out credit cards, and taking out short-term loans from banks, friends, and family members. Using any of these as a source to finance a long-term investment project like a small business is a disaster waiting to happen. If you are going to be borrowing funds for your startup business, then this funding must be long-term, typically 10 years or longer. When your business becomes profitable, you can always pay down these loans earlier. If your business is struggling, having only short-term financing can be the surest way to failure.

Establishing and Operating a Successful Business

We have all heard the phrase "location, location, location." Nowhere does this hold truer than in establishing a successful small business. If your business enterprise is in a location where your customers cannot get to you because there is no parking or easy access by public transportation, then chances are that they are not coming. If you are starting a pizzeria, you do not want to be on the same block as three other pizzerias that are barely surviving. Your market analysis should include the appropriate demographics of your expected business location, as well as the need and demand for your product or service. Your rent will most likely be one of your largest expenses and will remain the same whether you sell one product per day or a thousand. Determining the proper balance between your cost of rent and the quality of your location will be extremely important to your success.

If you are in a financial position to buy the building where your business is located, this could be an ideal situation. Rather than paying rent to a landlord, you could have your business pay rent to you and, at the same time, get the tax benefits of a rental property, primarily the ability to take a deduction for depreciation. Depreciation is a phantom deduction (you get to reduce your profit without paying for this expense) so that your property can generate a positive cash flow and you would possibly be in a position to pay little or no tax on this rental income. This, on top of the fact that the property value may appreciate over time, can make purchasing your business's real estate a terrific investment in the long run.

You should consult with industry experts in your trade or business to ensure that you are obtaining all of the appropriate permits and licenses necessary to legally operate your enterprise. I would strongly recommend working with an attorney who has expertise in your line of business. Whether you are establishing an Italian restaurant or a dental practice, you must work with a financial advisor who understands your business. Please refer to Appendix A, "Selecting a Trusted Advisor," for more details.

You will also need to speak with your insurance advisor. In addition to many of the types of insurance we covered in Chapter 5, "Ensuring Your Health and Life," and Chapter 6, "Protecting Your Property with Insurance," you will need to obtain the necessary business risk management coverage. This would include such things as workers' compensation insurance, short-term disability insurance, unemployment insurance, business overhead insurance, errors and omissions insurance, and the list goes on and on. Once again, work with an insurance advisor who understands your business or profession.

Another important consideration is whether to buy or lease your furniture and equipment. This decision in part has to do with how well funded you are. If you have more than enough funds to set up and support your business, then purchasing your furniture and equipment could be a better choice. You will be able to take depreciation deductions on these items and continue to use them until they become obsolete. In the long run, purchasing these items outright will be more cost effective. In the short term, this would result in a significant financial outlay. Leasing, on the other hand, will require the least amount of money up front during the critical stage of your business when you are making little or no profit. Leasing is in fact just another form of creative financing.

Suppliers are the life-blood of many businesses. After all, if you can't obtain the product from your vendor, then you will have nothing to sell to your customers. You should treat your suppliers with respect, and pay them on time, all the time. If they provide you with discounts for paying their invoices within 10 days, you should do so. Not only will this make you a better customer for them, but it will also save you a significant amount of money throughout the year. When you establish a good working relationship with your suppliers, they will become an asset to you and your business by helping you resolve problems and helping you get speedy delivery of merchandise when the need arises.

You should consider the most appropriate pricing for your product and service. If you simply price yourself lower than all of your competitors, you may get more business, but you may sacrifice profitability. Without a comfortable profit margin, you will then need to cut costs in other areas and may not be able to provide the same level of customer service. For many businesses where customer service and attention to detail are extremely important, pricing should not be as significant a factor. Many customers are willing to pay a slightly higher price if they are getting better service and attention. No matter what business or service you provide, understanding your customer, as well as their needs, is extremely important.

You will need to establish a credit policy when providing goods and services to your clients. Generally, you should receive payment in advance or at the point of sale. With some businesses, issuing credit terms is the norm, and you will be forced to do so unless you are willing to lose customers. With that said, it is better not to have a customer than to have a customer who is not going to pay you for the goods and services you provided. Having an easy credit policy is the surest way to lose money, as well as the time and effort in trying to collect.

The easiest way to generate higher profits without increasing revenues is by controlling your costs. Sometimes the difference between your needs and wants in operating your business is very difficult to distinguish. Every time you purchase something to be used in your business, you must ask yourself first, "Is this something I truly need? Will it increase or decrease my profitability in the long run? Is there a less expensive way to get this done without sacrificing quality?" In essence, your business must live by the same rules laid out in Chapter 1, "Committing to Living within Your Means."

The most profitable way for any business to gain new customers is not through marketing, but instead, through providing outstanding customer service. I think that the quote from Donald Trump at the beginning of this chapter says it best: "Your business, and your brand, must first let people know what you care about, and that you care about them." This message must be communicated, not only by you, but by every one of your employees every minute of every single day. This will not only ensure repeat business, but your customers will become the unpaid marketing team that will lead your business to success.

Entity Choices

One of the first decisions you will need to make when establishing your business is what entity form would be best for you and your business. The business entity form that you choose when establishing your business can have a significant effect on your liability as the owner, the amount of tax you will pay, the flexibility of obtaining financing, and the ultimate sale or transfer of part or all of your business. This decision will also affect the amount of paperwork you will need to maintain, as well as the type of tax forms you will have to file. Are you going to operate as a sole proprietorship, partnership, C corporation, S corporation, or limited liability company (LLC)?

The following is a summary of some of the major considerations you need to think about before deciding which entity will suit your needs.

Sole Proprietorship

A sole proprietorship by definition is owned by one individual. It is the least expensive way to set up a business and requires very little paperwork to get started. Typically, all you need to do is file for a DBA (Doing Business As) at your local county clerk's office and obtain an employer identification number (EIN) (as described in the following section), and you are ready to go. You will not be required to file a separate income tax return for your business. Instead, all of your business income and expenses are reported on your personal income tax return through a federal tax form referred to as a Schedule C. Once you are generating a profit, you will be required to pay taxes on that profit on a quarterly basis (April 15, June 15, September 15, and January 15) through personal estimated tax payments. Once you hire employees, you will be required to pay payroll taxes for those employees and withhold the appropriate taxes from their paycheck. You, as a sole proprietor, will also pay both the employer and employee share of Social Security tax and Medicare tax on your profit. These taxes will be included as part of your quarterly personal estimated tax payments.

The main drawback to being in business as a sole proprietorship is that you, as the business owner, have unlimited liability. This means that creditors, as well as lawsuits brought against your business, can attach to your personal assets. In essence, there is no difference between you and your business. If your business fails, you will go down with it. Another obstacle with this business entity choice is that the only way to raise capital is to secure it personally. Bottom line, you will be personally guaranteeing everything your business does. Sole proprietorships also draw a much higher risk of audit compared to other entity choices. This is because you would be viewed as a big fish in a small lake, instead of a small fish in a large ocean. All of your business income and expenses are reported directly on your personal income tax return, which can draw attention, especially to certain deductions that are red flags to the government.

Sole proprietorships also have a finite life. When it comes time to sell your business, the transfer of ownership can be more complicated and the acquiring company will need to create a separate business entity. When you pass away, so does your sole proprietorship, and it may be more difficult to sell your business assets.

With regards to funding retirement plans such as a SEP plan, SIMPLE plan, 401(k), and defined benefit plan, the employer contributions are still subject to Social Security and Medicare tax. Therefore, the Social Security and Medicare taxes paid as a sole proprietorship will be much higher than under a corporate entity.

The bottom line is that, for many individuals on a limited budget, starting out as a sole proprietorship may seem like the easiest way to get started, and it is. The problem is that if you have substantial assets or plan to have them in the near future, you will be leaving yourself exposed to unnecessary risks.

Partnership

In order to establish a partnership, by definition, you must have at least one partner in your business. The costs of establishing a partnership will be much higher than a sole proprietorship and should always include the drafting of a partnership agreement. The advantage of having partners is that you can bring into the business the combined creativity, skills, capital, and expertise of all the partners. This is especially important if you believe that you lack one or more of these critical skills. As a partnership, your business entity will be required to file an informational income tax return called Form 1065. Any income or losses, special tax deductions, or tax credits from this partnership pass through to the partners (reported to you through a Schedule K-1), who will be responsible for paying taxes on their share of any business income on their personal income tax return. Partnerships are referred to as flow-through entities, since no business income taxes are paid at the partnership level. Unique to partnerships is that each partner does not necessarily pay tax based on his or her percentage ownership in the partnership. Partnerships can be structured so that ownership interest and sharing of profits or losses do not have to be in proportion with each other. These allocations are determined as part of the partnership agreement when the entity is originally formed. Each partner will be responsible for paying the federal, state, and city income tax, as well as self-employment tax on his or her share of the profits. Similar to a sole proprietorship, these taxes are due on a quarterly basis (April 15, June 15, September 15, and January 15) through personal estimated tax payments.

One of the main drawbacks to being in business as a partnership is that each partner has unlimited liability. To make matters worse, each general partner can be held liable for the actions of their business partners. In most respects, partners in a partnership receive the same tax treatment as a sole proprietorship for tax purposes when it comes to fringe benefits.

Partnerships are also similar to sole proprietorships with regards to funding retirement plans such as a SEP plan, SIMPLE plan, 401(k), and defined benefit plan. The employer contributions are still subject to Social Security and Medicare tax, making those taxes paid as a partner much higher than they would be under a corporate entity.

Generally, when one partner dies, the partnership must be terminated, unless there is a provision in the partnership agreement that allows it to continue with another partner. The transfer of interest in a partnership can be restricted, since you generally will need the permission of your partners unless the partnership agreement contains a special provision. Obtaining additional funding may be easier than for a sole proprietorship, assuming your partner(s) has good credit, since the lender will now be holding more people than only you responsible.

Corporation (C Corp)

A corporation, also referred to as a C corporation, has the most complex business structure. It is a separate and distinct legal entity from its owners. Corporations are formed under the requirements of the states in which they are established. Perhaps the most significant distinction is that corporations provide limited liability protection, which is not available to sole proprietorships and general partnerships. Therefore, as a shareholder in a corporation, your losses are limited to your investment in the corporation. For example, if you invest $10,000 in IBM stock and the company goes out of business, its creditors cannot go after your personal assets since your liability is limited to your $10,000 investment. The same is true if you establish your own corporation to operate your business, but be careful not to sign or guarantee any loans personally. If you do, then your limited liability protection will be lost as it relates to that obligation. It is important to note that the corporate form does not provide complete limited liability protection when it comes to personal service corporations (PSC), such as medical doctors, dentists, lawyers, and CPAs. You must still have malpractice insurance to cover these types of potential lawsuits.

As an employee of your own corporation, you will be treated the same as any other employee regarding your payroll taxes on your wages. The applicable federal, state, city, Social Security, and Medicare tax will be withheld from each paycheck. Your corporation will then be required to pay these payroll taxes directly to the government after each payroll period (or at least monthly). You will not be required to make personal estimated tax payments on your earned income from your business, since these taxes will be covered through payroll taxes.

As a separate legal entity, your corporation will be required to file its own business income tax return through federal Form 1120. The corporation will be required to pay corporate income tax on any profits reported by the business at a flat rate of 21% (effective 2018). You will also be required to pay quarterly corporate estimated income taxes. By far, this is the biggest disadvantage to being incorporated as a C corporation; the profits of the business are subject to double taxation. That's right, you will pay taxes at the corporate level for any profits, and if these profits, after taxes, are then distributed to you as a dividend (or liquidating distribution), you will then pay taxes at the personal level. Most people do not like being taxed once, let alone twice. For this reason, being a C corporation is not the entity of choice for most small business owners. The fact is that corporations are not separate living entities. They are simply a business entity structure created by the government to encourage people to take risk without jeopardizing their own personal assets. In fact, when a corporation pays tax at the corporate level, this is just another way of levying a tax on you as the individual shareholder. Then, for the right of limited liability protection, the government taxes the same income twice. We have all heard the story of how Warren Buffet's secretary pays a higher tax rate than her billionaire employer. This is simply not true, because they are not factoring in the corporate tax as an indirect tax being levied on the business owner, in this case, Warren Buffet. The truth is, this income is taxed at the corporate tax rate of 21%, and then taxed at the qualified dividend tax rate of 20%, plus an additional 3.8% Medicare tax. If you do the simple math, you will see that corporate shareholders are paying more than their fair share of taxes.

Another drawback to being incorporated is that there are many more filing and record keeping requirements, such as keeping corporate minutes. Prior to January 1, 2018, a C corporation that was a personal service corporation (PSC) had a disadvantage when compared to other C corporations, since it was not taxed at a graduated tax rate. Under the Tax Cuts and Jobs Act of 2017, all C corps, including PSCs, are now taxed at a lower federal flat tax rate of 21%.

Corporate entities are allowed some additional fringe benefits that are tax-deductible by the corporation and tax-free to not only employees, but to employee shareholders. Employer contributions to retirement plans such as a SEP plan, SIMPLE plan, 401(k), and defined benefit plan, are not subject to Social Security and Medicare tax. Therefore, these taxes paid by the corporation, as well as the shareholder, will be much lower than under a sole proprietorship or partnership. This would result in a significant tax savings and is why I would almost always recommend a corporate structure when the owner anticipates making large pension contributions, especially at the level that can be made under cash balance defined benefit plans.

Another benefit to corporate entities is that they have an unlimited lifespan. Even if all current shareholders were to pass away, the corporate entity will continue to exist. The transfer and sale of a shareholder's ownership interest is relatively simple compared to other entities. The transfer of ownership could be structured simply as a sale or transfer of stock in the corporation from one party to another. Furthermore, raising capital through a corporate structure could be accomplished simply by issuing additional shares of stocks or even corporate bonds.

S Corporation

A C corporation can make an election to be treated as a Subchapter S corporation by filing IRS Form 2553. Many states also require that you file a separate Subchapter S election form with them to receive the same tax treatment at the state level. The primary benefit of making a Subchapter S election is that you can get the best of both worlds. You will be able to benefit from the limited liability protection and, at the same time, avoid the biggest negative of C corporations, which is double taxation. Because of this, for many small business corporations, making a Subchapter S corporation election is very often the best choice.

Not all corporations are permitted to take advantage of the benefits of making a Subchapter S election. The "S" in S corporation stands for "small business" corporation. To make this election, a corporation must meet certain requirements. These requirements include that the entity must be a domestic corporation, domestic partnership, or domestic limited liability company. An S corporation cannot have more than 100 shareholders, and shareholders can only be individuals, estates, tax-exempt organizations, or certain trusts. Shareholders cannot be nonresident aliens, partnerships, or corporations, and there can be only one class of stock.

Generally, an S corporation does not pay income tax at the entity level, although there are some exceptions to this rule. S corporations are flow-through entities, similar to partnerships in many ways. Corporations file Form 1120S, and the shareholders will receive a Schedule K-1 so that they can report their share of flow-through items on their personal income tax returns. Shareholders will report their share of income, losses, special tax deductions, and tax credits on their individual income tax returns. This is where the major benefit of avoiding double taxation comes in. Unlike partnerships, corporate profits must be allocated according to the percentage ownership of the individual shareholders.

Some of the disadvantages associated with S corporations is that some of the fringe benefits that are available to C corporations are restricted to owner-employees of S corporations. Similar to C corporations, S corporations have an unlimited life and the transfer of ownership interest can be accomplished by simply selling the stock to a new or existing shareholder. S corporations can also raise capital by issuing additional shares of stock to new investors or by issuing bonds. Keep in mind, issuing stock would be limited to no more than 100 shareholders, and therefore, going public would not be possible, unless converted back to a C corporation. Administrative costs are the same as for C corporations and they would be required to keep corporate minutes as well.

The benefits with regards to funding retirement plans for S corporations are the same as they are for C corporations. Employer contributions are not subject to social security and Medicare tax. Therefore, the social security and Medicare taxes paid by the corporation, as well as the shareholder, will be much lower than under a sole proprietorship or partnership. This would result in a significant tax savings and why I would almost always recommend a corporate structure when the owner anticipates making large pension contributions, especially at the level that can be made under cash balance defined benefit plans.

Limited Liability Company

A limited liability company (LLC) generally combines the flexibility and income tax treatment of a partnership with the limited liability protection offered through a corporation. An LLC can be treated as a single-member LLC (for tax purposes, the same as a sole proprietorship) by filing a Schedule C on the personal income tax return. It can be treated as a partnership (if there are two or more owners) by filing an IRS Form 1065. It can be treated as a corporation if an "Entity Classification Election" Form 8832 is filed, then requiring the filing of an IRS Form 1120. It can be treated as a Subchapter S corporation if a Subchapter S election is made and approved by the IRS. In short, the LLC will give you limited liability protection, and, if the entity qualifies, it can be treated as any one of the four other entity choices for tax purposes. Depending on your choice of tax treatment, the rules stated above will generally apply to your LLC. A major drawback to being an LLC is that there can be some inconsistencies with the tax treatment of certain items at the state and local level.

By the way, if you are a professional service organization that requires licensing through the state education department, such as a medical doctor, dentist, or CPA, your corporation will be designated as a professional corporation (PC). A professional service organization can be a C corporation, an S corporation, or a professional limited liability company (PLLC), which is the same as an LLC.

I realize that this seems very complicated and confusing, so you should definitely consult with your tax advisor to ensure you are making the proper entity choice that is best for you and your business. Once you have set up your entity, you will need to apply for a tax identification number before you can make any of the special tax elections described above.

Tax Identification Number

Now that you have selected and established your business entity, your next step is to obtain a Federal Tax Identification Number for your business, also known as an Employer Identification Number (EIN). This Employer Identification Number is like a Social Security number, but it specifically identifies your business. You do not want to provide customers, vendors, and your employees with your personal Social Security number, since this is clearly something you should keep confidential. You will use your Employer Identification Number (EIN) when you open up the business bank account, apply for a business credit card, and file your business and payroll tax returns. Obtaining this ID number is very easy. You can apply directly at www.irs.gov/businesses/small-businesses-self-employed/apply-for-an-employer-identification-number-ein-online. Be sure to click "provide pdf copy" so that the IRS will automatically generate and provide you with your EIN online. Otherwise, it will take approximately 21 days to receive a hard copy of your EIN by mail. If you prefer, you can ask your corporate attorney or certified public accountant to obtain it for you.

Accounting Methods

Generally, for tax reporting purposes, the Internal Revenue Service (IRS) allows you one of two methods of accounting. For individual taxpayers who are not in business for themselves, the cash method of accounting is used. For businesses, you are permitted to use either the accrual method of accounting or the cash method of accounting, subject to some special rules. Both methods are subject to the same Internal Revenue Code, with the major difference being how income and expenses are reported.

Generally, publicly traded companies are required to use the accrual method of accounting, since it is considered the most accurate method of reporting income and expenses. Under the accrual method of accounting, you must recognize income when it is earned, and expenses are recorded when they are incurred. For example, if you are a self-employed dentist and you just treated a patient, you have earned that income and are required to report it as income in the current year. This is true even if the patient or patient's insurance company has not yet paid you. For example, if you are owed $50,000 at the end of the year from your patients, you will be taxed on this income, even though you may not receive it until the following year. *It is fair to say that most people do not want to pay taxes on income that they have not yet received, but this is exactly what is required under the accrual method of accounting.*

The other side to the story is that you can deduct expenses when they are incurred and not necessarily when you pay for them. The advantage here is that you get a tax deduction even if you have not yet paid for these expenses. For example, if it is December 31, and you forgot to pay your December rent, you can still deduct it in determining your profit, even if it is not paid until the following year. The accrual method of accounting determines your profitability based on certain events and the passage of time, not necessarily when money exchanges hands.

Under the cash method of accounting, you are required to report income when it is actually or constructively received, and you can deduct expenses when they are actually paid. The major advantage to this is that you can have significantly more control over determining your profitability and ultimately the amount of tax you pay each year. For example, you can delay billing and collection efforts in December so that income can be shifted from the current year to the following year. You can also pay some of your January expenses in December to squeeze in these added tax deductions in the current year, which will lower your profitability and also lower the tax you will be required to pay in the current year.

For tax purposes, the cash method of accounting is almost always superior to the accrual method of accounting. If your small business is permitted to use the cash method of accounting, it will most often be your best choice.

Under the Tax Cuts and Jobs Act of 2017, the requirements to qualify to use the cash method of accounting have been expanded to include businesses with gross receipts that do not exceed $25 million (indexed for inflation after 2018) for the three prior taxable years.

The following is an excerpt from the conference report:

> The provision expands the universe of taxpayers that may use the cash method of accounting. Under the provision, the cash method of accounting may be used by taxpayers, other than tax shelters, that satisfy the gross receipts test, regardless of whether the purchase, production, or sale of merchandise is an income-producing factor. The gross receipts test allows taxpayers with annual average gross receipts that do not exceed $25 million for the three prior taxable-year period (the "$25 million gross receipts test") to use the cash method. The $25 million amount is indexed for inflation for taxable years beginning after 2018.

This represents a monumental change in the accounting reporting requirement, since the majority of small businesses will now be permitted to use the cash method of accounting. This also includes businesses engaged in manufacturing and those that have inventory for resale. It is important to note here that inventory must still be accounted for as inventory and is not deductible until sold. The accrual method is of course still allowed, but many businesses may now want to consider converting to the cash method, since this can result in significant tax savings to them. This is especially true if a company's accounts receivable are significantly higher than its accounts payable. Since the effect of such an adjustment will result in less profit under the cash method, it could therefore significantly reduce tax liability. In addition, IRC Section 263A inventory capitalization rules no longer apply until revenues exceed the $25 million prior three-year average. In order to make the election to change your accounting method from accrual to cash, you will be required to file IRS Form 3115.

Another important point here is that professional service corporations (PSCs) are allowed to use the cash method without limit to the $25 million average revenue test. Other service-based businesses are allowed to use the cash method without limit by the $25 million average revenue test, unless a C corporation. Service business inventory is not a material income producing factor.

Please note that there are many special rules and exceptions that apply to a business's ability to use either the cash method or accrual method of accounting. The election of which method to use is typically made with the filing of your first business income tax return. I would strongly recommend working with a tax advisor who specializes in working in your industry so that the proper and most tax effective method can be used.

Reporting Business Income and Expenses

The rules by which individuals are required to report their personal income and expenses are significantly different from the rules for business reporting. Individual taxpayers who are employees have all of their earned income reported by the employer with the issuance of a W-2 form, which is provided to both the employee and the IRS. The IRS uses this W-2 information and cross-checks it to individual taxpayers' personal income tax returns once they are filed. Individuals prepare their personal income tax returns by filing either a Form 1040 or one of the variations to this form. Individuals are required to report all of their taxable income, including W-2 earned income, on their personal income tax return.

In 2018, individuals are also allowed a standard deduction in the amount of $12,000 for single and married filing separately, $18,000 for head of household, and $24,000 for married filing jointly. The standard deduction allows taxpayers to deduct the applicable amount without listing all of their individual itemized deductions. It is an allowable personal deduction with no questions asked that will not be audited by the government. If an individual believes his or her personal itemized deductions are higher than these standard deductions, then itemizing may be beneficial. For example, if a married taxpayer has $8,000 in real estate taxes, $20,000 in home mortgage interest, and $4,000 in charitable donations, then itemized deductions would be $32,000. Since this is $8,000 higher than the $24,000 standard deduction, they would be able to deduct this additional $8,000 from their taxable income. *As of January 1, 2018, all of the miscellaneous itemized deductions subject to the 2% of AGI limitation have been eliminated.* Even if the taxpayer has $15,000 in work-related expenses, none of this would be considered tax-deductible.

Individuals that operate their own business as a sole proprietorship, partnership, limited liability company, or estate will receive a Form 1099 from the business (customer) that made payments to them. This 1099 is issued to both the business and the IRS. The IRS uses this 1099 information and cross-checks it to the business's income tax return, including Schedule C, as part of your Form 1040 for sole proprietorships and single-member LLCs, as well as Form 1065 for partnerships.

If you are set up as a C corporation, an S corporation, or an LLC or partnership that has elected to be taxed as either a C corporation or S corporation, the business (customer) is not required to provide you with a 1099 form. However, a special rule requires that fees paid to attorneys be reported on 1099s, even if they are taxed as a C corporation or an S corporation. It sounds like the government doesn't trust lawyers. Ironically, most of the politicians involved with writing the law are attorneys themselves.

You as the owner are required to report all of your business income on the appropriate business income tax return based on your entity tax status. Assuming you have a flow-through entity, all tax-deductible expenses associated with operating a business should be reported on the appropriate business income tax return, thereby reducing the actual income that is eventually reported on your personal income tax return. For example, if your business brought in $100,000 in revenues in 2018, and you had $15,000 of business expenses, you would only report and include in your personal income $85,000 ($100,000 – $15,000).

Now you as the business owner would report your net income after business expenses on your personal income tax return, as well as any other taxable income you are required to report from other sources. Using the facts from the previous example, you would be allowed a personal standard deduction in the amount of $24,000 if married filing jointly or you could itemize deductions if they are higher than the standard deduction. In this example, you would itemize, since this would result in an additional $8,000 deduction from your taxable income. As a business owner, you are also able to get the full benefit of the $15,000 in business expenses as an above-the-line deduction through your business, which reduces your adjusted gross income and taxable income. As an individual, if you had the same $15,000 in job-related expenses, you would get no benefit from this. There is a significant difference between being a W-2 employee versus being self-employed in your own business.

There are numerous other tax advantages to owning and operating your own business. We will cover many of these in the following sections. The main takeaway here is that one of the biggest advantages of owning your own business is the many tax breaks that are available to you. It is up to you to know what these tax breaks are and to take full advantage of them.

What Is the Number-One Expense in Operating a Business?

One of the most effective ways to increase your business's profits is to find ways to lower some of its most significant expenses. As you know from Chapter 2, "Understanding Taxes," your single largest personal expenditure by far is taxes. This is especially true for business owners, since you will need to deal with so many additional taxes, not to mention all of the business filing requirements. For example, if you provide a product or service that is subject to sales tax, you may be required to file monthly, quarterly, or annual sales tax reports, in addition to collecting and paying the sales tax on behalf of the state and local government. If you hire employees, you will need to withhold and pay payroll taxes on a monthly, quarterly, and annual basis. If you are set up as a corporation, you would also be required to do this, even if you are the only employee. This includes Social Security, Medicare, federal and state withholding, federal unemployment tax (FUTA), state unemployment tax (SUTA), and the list goes on and on. In essence, as a business owner, you become an agent of the government by collecting, withholding, and paying taxes over to the government on your employees' behalf. As if you were not already wearing enough hats as an entrepreneur, the government just gave you another responsibility. There are also special excise taxes and business income taxes depending on your entity choice and the state or city you are doing business in. Please refer to Appendix C, "Basic Concepts and Definitions of Various Types of Taxes" for more details. When you consider all of the taxes you are required to collect on behalf of the government as a business owner, in addition to all of the taxes you are required to pay, you can see where the most significant cash outlays of your business are going. *It is taxes, taxes, and then even more taxes!*

You should not try to tackle this subject on your own, and I would highly recommend working with a qualified certified public accounting firm that specializes in your business or profession.

Employee Versus Independent Contractor

One of the most common questions I receive from business owners is whether they can treat someone as an employee or an independent contractor. I have even had some business owners ask if they can be treated as an independent contractor through their own business. The answer to this question is *no*. By definition, you cannot be the owner of your own business and also be an independent contractor. If you are the owner of the business, you are clearly not independent of the business. The primary motivator for this question is to avoid many of the filing requirements and payroll taxes associated with employees.

In the early stages of your business, you should hire few or no employees, unless it is absolutely necessary to hire more. In fact, you should not even put yourself on the payroll until the business is generating sufficient profit. Otherwise, you will be paying unnecessary payroll taxes, and you will need to use your personal funds or additional bank loans to fund your salary and related payroll taxes. When you are in a position to hire employees, it is very important to find ways to attract the most qualified employees who possess the skills necessary to get their job done. Do not be tempted to hire employees simply because they are willing to work for the least amount of money. In life, you generally get what you pay for. You should be prepared to pay at the higher end of the pay scale for each position you are hiring to increase the chances that you are getting a quality employee. You then have to determine what benefits you will be providing. You will need to check with local state authorities to find out what, if any, benefits are required. In the early stages of your business, you may be better off hiring outside independent contractors. Even though they may be more costly per hour, you would be able to use them only as needed and would not have to provide any benefits.

A word of caution when dealing with independent contractors: Make sure that they are in fact independent contractors and not employees. There are many benefits to you as the employer and to the persons providing you the product or services to classify themselves as independent contractors. You as the employer can avoid having to pay payroll taxes and provide benefits, and the independent contractors can take a long list of business deductions that would not have been available to them if they were classified as employees. This is truer today than ever before, since unreimbursed employee business expenses are no longer deductible as a personal itemized deduction. If it was as simple as this, then there would be no employees in the world, and everyone would be an independent contractor.

The government typically looks at a list of 20 criteria to determine whether you should be treated as an independent contractor or an employee. Depending on how you answer these questions and the surrounding facts, the appropriate classification will be determined. These criteria include:

- Instructions
- Training
- Integration
- Services rendered personally

- Hiring, supervising, and paying assistants
- Continuing relationship
- Set hours of work
- Full time required
- Doing work on employer's premises
- Order or sequence set
- Oral or written reports
- Payment by hour, week, month
- Payment of business and/or traveling expenses
- Furnishing of tools and materials
- Significant investment
- Realization of profit or loss
- Working for more than one firm at a time
- Making service available to general public
- Right to discharge
- Right to terminate

You should go to your state department of labor website for more details on these criteria.

At a minimum, you, as a business owner, should not pay anyone in their personal name unless he or she is part of your payroll with the appropriate taxes withheld. If anyone wants to do business with you as an independent contractor, you should check these 20 criteria to see whether they in fact can be treated as independent contractors. The safest thing to do is to pay all individuals as employees unless they meet the majority of these criteria and have their own business entity with a separate employer identification number. The penalties and interest for not following these rules are significant and I would strongly encourage you to follow the law.

Business Tax Deduction Versus Business Tax Credit

A business tax deduction reduces the amount of income you pay taxes on; a business tax credit reduces dollar-for-dollar the amount of taxes you pay.

For example, if you have the option of taking a $5,000 business tax deduction for making your business more handicap accessible, and you are in the 24% tax bracket, you will save $1,200 ($5,000 × 24%) in taxes. Conversely, if you have the ability to take a disability access credit for $5,000, this amount is deducted, dollar-for-dollar, from your tax liability, and you would save $5,000. If given the opportunity to take advantage of a tax credit instead of a tax deduction, you should usually opt for the credit, depending on your tax bracket. With this in mind, you will always want to pay special attention to tax credits when they are discussed throughout this chapter as they relate to your business.

"Ordinary and Necessary" Test

The IRS defines a deductible business expense as follows: "To be deductible, a business expense must be both *ordinary and necessary*. An ordinary expense is one that is common and accepted in your trade or business. A necessary expense is one that is helpful and appropriate for your trade or business. An expense does not have to be indispensable to be considered necessary."

The term *ordinary and necessary* is perhaps the most subjective term used in the Internal Revenue Code. What may be considered ordinary and necessary to you in operating your business may be different from what I think is ordinary and necessary. More importantly, it may be different from what an IRS agent or ultimately a tax court judge deems ordinary and necessary, if it gets to that level.

Fortunately, most items in the Internal Revenue Code are clearly stated as being either tax-deductible or not. These deductions are very black or white. Where the gray area comes into play is for those business deductions that are more subjective and could possibly fall on either side of this scale. It is up to you as the business owner to properly document and put yourself in a position to support the tax deductibility of these expenses. By doing so, you will minimize your chances of being audited and maximize your chance of success if you are in fact audited.

The analogy I would like to draw here is that this is similar to playing a game of chess. Could you imagine playing chess against an expert when you have never played the game before? If you do not know the basics of the tax law, then what are your chances of winning against the IRS at its own game? The key here is that you must know the basic rules (tax laws), and like chess, put yourself in a proper position to take advantage of what the law allows. This is exactly what tax planning is all about: finding perfectly legal ways to avoid paying taxes. It is actually your right as a taxpayer to pay no more in taxes than the law requires. What is unfortunate here is that, in my opinion, most businesses pay significantly more in taxes than is required. In the following section, I will provide you with a list of deductible business expenses. It is up to you and your tax advisor to make sure that you take advantage of every one of them.

Deductible Business Expenses

Before purchasing any item by check, credit card, or otherwise, always ask yourself the following question first: "Is this payment somehow related to my trade or business?" If the answer is yes, and you believe it is an ordinary and necessary expense in operating your business, which facilitates your ability to provide goods or services to customers, then you should always give yourself the benefit of the doubt and pay for it through a business account. By doing so, you will be allowed to capture all possible tax-deductible business expenses. If you mistakenly pay for these items personally, you will lose out on a business tax deduction. All business expenses should be included in your business records to be provided to your business's accountant. Your accountant can then help you determine whether each item is tax-deductible or not and will assist you in preparing the necessary accounting records. We will talk more about recordkeeping for small businesses later in this chapter. Keep in mind that what might be tax-deductible in one trade or business may not be tax-deductible in another. This is another reason why it is important to work with an accountant that specializes in your particular trade or business. The following is a list of some of the most common *tax-deductible* business expenses:

- Account receivable write-offs (accrual basis only)
- Accounting fees
- Advertising
- Automobile expenses
- Bank service charges
- Cable TV
- Casualty theft and losses
- Charitable contributions
- Consulting fees
- Continuing education expenses
- Contract labor
- Credit card processing fees
- Depreciation (on fixed assets)
- Employee salary and wages
- Employer portion of Social Security, FICA, FUTA, and SUTA tax
- Equipment (under Section 179)
- Equipment rental or leases
- Fees for your trade or business

- Foreign taxes paid
- Freight and delivery charges
- Furniture (under Section 179)
- Gifts – capped at $25 per person
- Health insurance
- Home office costs
- Insurance – business liability
- Insurance – business overhead
- Insurance – business property
- Insurance – errors and omissions
- Insurance – group term life
- Insurance – malpractice
- Insurance – short-term disability
- Insurance – workers' compensation
- Interest (business debt)
- Internet and email services
- Janitorial fees
- Legal fees (with limitations)
- Magazines, newspapers, newsletters, or books
- Marketing
- Meals (50% deductible)
- Office expenses
- Office supplies
- Parking (noncommuting related)
- Payroll processing fees
- Phone – cellular and landline
- Postage
- Professional and business dues
- Public relations fees
- Relocation costs (business)
- Rent
- Retirement plan contributions
- Shipping fees
- Stationery
- Tax preparation fees
- Taxes – property (on business assets)
- Taxes – state and local
- Trade show, convention, or seminar fees
- Travel
- Uniforms
- Utilities – water, gas, electric
- Waste removal

The above list of expenses must be directly related to your trade or business and should be considered "ordinary and necessary" in order to be deductible by your business. This list of course is not all-inclusive.

Nondeductible Business Expenses

The following is a list of some of the most common *nondeductible* business expenses:

- Bribes or kickbacks
- Capital expenditures (beyond Section 179)
- Clothing that you can also use outside of the workplace
- Commute to and from work
- Country club dues
- Entertainment (as of 2018)
- Exploratory research (must be capitalized)
- Federal income tax
- Fines and penalties
- Gifts – amount over $25
- Hobby or sideline losses
- Insurance – life (except under group term)
- Insurance – long-term disability
- Interest on underpayment of taxes
- Legal fees on the purchase of property
- Lobbying expenses
- Meals (50% nondeductible)
- Medicare tax (the additional 0.9%)
- Personal expenses
- Political contributions
- Repayment of loans

This list of expenses, even if directly related to your trade or business, would be nondeductible by your business. Please understand that there are some exceptions to these items, especially with regards to C corporations and that this list is not all-inclusive.

Home Office Deduction

If you own a small business that is treated as a C corporation, S corporation, or partnership for tax purposes, you may be allowed to take a business deduction for rent paid to yourself for the business use of your home. Be sure to have a lease between yourself and your business and make these payments on a monthly basis. You can charge yourself no more than the fair market value for the rental space, and you would be required to report the rental income on Schedule E of your personal income tax return. This would give you the opportunity to deduct the appropriate percentage of your home expenses against this rental income. Therefore, your business entity would get the benefit of deducting this rent expense, and you could offset a portion of your home costs to the rental income you received personally. A word of caution here is that this may limit your ability to take the full exclusion from any gain on the sale of your primary residence (for more details, see Chapter 3 under "*Tax Alpha to the 2nd Power*[SM] Facts and Strategies"). Also, any depreciation taken on this portion of your home would have to be recaptured as ordinary income to the extent of a taxable gain upon the sale of your home.

The IRS may allow you, as a small business owner, to deduct expenses related to the business use of part of your home, but you must first meet specific requirements. Even after meeting these requirements, your deduction may be limited. If you are a sole proprietor or a single-member LLC, you would take this deduction on Schedule C (or Schedule F if your business is a farm) of your personal tax return along with IRS Form 8829. The traditional method of determining a home office deduction includes identifying all direct expenses and a portion of indirect expenses, based on a percentage of business use of your home. The relatively new simplified method allows you to deduct up to $5 per square foot on the part of your home used for business, up to a maximum deduction amount of $1,500.

To qualify to claim expenses for business use of your home, you must meet both of the following tests.

1. Your use of the business part of your home must be:
   a. Exclusive (see below for explanation)
   b. Regular
   c. For your trade or business
2. The business part of your home must be one of the following:
   a. Your principal place of business (see below for explanation)
   b. A place where you meet or deal with patients, clients, or customers in the normal course of your trade or business
   c. A separate structure (not attached to your home) you use in connection with your trade or business

To qualify under the *exclusive use test*, you must use a specific area of your home for only your trade or business. The area used for business can be a room or other separately identifiable space. The space does not need to be marked off by a permanent partition. You do not meet the requirements of the exclusive use test if you use the area in question both for business and for personal purposes.

You do *not have to meet the exclusive use test* if either of the following applies.

- You use part of your home for the storage of inventory or product samples.
- You use part of your home as a daycare facility.

Your home office will qualify as your *principal place of business* if you meet the following requirements.

- You use it exclusively and regularly for administrative or management activities of your trade or business.
- You have no other fixed location where you conduct substantial administrative or management activities of your trade or business.

Alternatively, if you use your home exclusively and regularly for your business, but your home office does not qualify as your principal place of business based on the previous rules, you can determine your principal place of business based on the following factors.

- The relative importance of the activities performed at each location.
- If the relative importance factor does not determine your principal place of business, the time spent at each location.

If, after considering your business locations, your home cannot be identified as your principal place of business, you cannot deduct home office expenses.

The majority of this information comes directly from IRS Publication 587: Business Use of Your Home. For more detailed information, you can download a PDF copy of this publication at www.irs.gov/pub/irs-pdf/p587.pdf.

We will now turn our attention to three popular business deductions available to small businesses: travel, automobile, and depreciation expenses.

Travel Expense As a Business Deduction

As the owner of a small business, you and your employees may be required to travel away from home on business as part of your work responsibilities. You can deduct ordinary and necessary business expenses you incur when you travel away from home on business. The type of expense you can deduct will of course depend on your particular facts and circumstances. Exhibit 11.1 summarizes business travel expenses you may be able to deduct. There may be other deductible business travel expenses that are not included here that may also be tax-deductible, depending on your situation.

Exhibit 11.1   Business Travel Expense Deductions

IF you have expenses for ...	THEN you can deduct the cost of ...
Transportation	Travel by airplane, train, bus, or car between your home and your business destination. If you were provided with a free ticket or you are riding free as a result of a frequent traveler or similar program, your cost is zero. If you travel by ship, there are special rules related to luxury water travel and cruise ships.
Taxi, commuter bus, and airport limousine	Fares for these and other types of transportation that take you between: • The airport or station and your hotel, and • The hotel and the work location of your customers or clients, your business meeting place, or your temporary work location.
Baggage and shipping	Sending baggage and sample or display material between your regular and temporary work locations.
Car	Operating and maintaining your car when traveling away from home on business. You can deduct actual expenses or the standard mileage rate, as well as business-related tolls and parking. If you rent a car while away from home on business, you can deduct only the business-use portion of the expenses.
Lodging and meals	Your lodging and meals if your business trip is overnight or long enough that you need to stop for sleep or rest to properly perform your duties. Meals include amounts spent for food, beverages, taxes, and related tips. There are additional rules and limitations for meals.
Cleaning	Dry cleaning and laundry.
Telephone	Business calls while on your business trip. This includes business communication by fax machine or other communication devices.
Tips	Tips you pay for any expenses in this chart.
Other	Other similar ordinary and necessary expenses related to your business travel. These expenses might include transportation to or from a business meal, public stenographer's fees, computer rental fees, and operating and maintaining a house trailer.

Source: IRS Publication 463: Travel, Entertainment, Gift, and Car Expenses

When you travel away from home on business, you are required to keep records of all the expenses you incurred. These records must include supporting documentation such as receipts, proof of payment (i.e., canceled check, credit card receipt, etc.), and an explanation as to why this was an ordinary and necessary business expense. You can also use a log, diary, notebook, your calendar, or any other written record to keep track of these expenses.

To maximize the benefit of travel expenses, you should try to combine business with pleasure. As long as the primary purpose of the trip is business, the full amount could be tax-deductible. If you spend five days on a trip and three out of the five are for business, then this may be considered the primary purpose of this trip. You must be prepared to support this position by keeping the necessary documentation, such as your agenda, which includes your scheduled meetings, and emails to and from the business associates you are meeting with.

Many small business owners have their spouses work in the business and make the mistake of not paying them a salary. You should pay your spouse a salary for actual services rendered, which will allow your spouse to join you on business trips, as long as this is part of his or her work requirement. You could then fully deduct the business travel costs associated with your spouse.

It is important to know the basics of the tax laws so that you can put yourself in a position to take full advantage of what the law allows. For example, if you are planning a trip to California for business purposes, such as to meet with one of your suppliers or a large potential customer, or simply for a business seminar or convention, you are permitted to mix business with pleasure and still get a business tax deduction.

Deducting Automobile Expenses

The cost of travel (commuting) from your home to your place of business is generally not tax-deductible. The IRS does allow some limited exceptions to this rule. If you are on a business trip and traveling away from home, you may deduct cab fares or other transportation costs to and from the airport, your home, and the hotel. Another exception to this rule is if you are using your car to transport your work tools, if the cost was incurred in addition to the ordinarily nondeductible commuting expenses. These deductions would be allowed even if you would have used the car as part of your normal nondeductible commuting costs.

If you are self-employed and are able to qualify for the home office deduction, you can then deduct all travel costs between your home office and your various job sites. For example, if you are a self-employed computer technician operating your business from your home, as soon as you leave the home and travel to your client's locations, this is now all considered business travel and not commuting. Technically, when you walk out of your bedroom and into your "den" (home office) and sit down at your desk to start your work day, your commute is over. Any travel after this will become a business tax deduction for you. This is a significant added benefit of being able to claim a home office deduction. Remember, tax planning is all about putting yourself in a position to take advantage of what the law allows.

The cost of purchasing and operating a car, truck, or van for use in your business is tax-deductible, subject to a number of restrictions. Depreciation deductions for cars, trucks, and vans may be subject to an annual limit. We will talk more about depreciation in the next section. These annual limits are reduced based on the percentage of personal use of these vehicles. You are permitted to take a percentage of the actual vehicle expenses, including depreciation, or you can take an allowance of 54.5 cents per mile (in 2018). If you use your vehicle for business, be sure to pay all costs of operating it through your business. This would include auto lease payments, gas, oil, repairs and maintenance, car washes, license plate fees, and auto insurance. Generally, if you have a relatively new vehicle, do not drive a lot of miles, or are leasing your vehicle, taking the actual expenses would be most beneficial. You should calculate this deduction under both methods and always take advantage of the one that results in the highest tax deduction to your business.

Either way, you will need to track your mileage and either use the percentage of business mileage times your auto expenses, or the allowance amount per mile times the actual number of business miles driven during the year. You are required to maintain a log or diary of your business use of your vehicle. The personal usage of this vehicle would not be tax-deductible to your business. If you operate under a corporation, you will need to report the personal use of this vehicle as wages on your year-end W-2. Thanks to technology, you can now use your smartphone to track your mileage with certain apps.

It is important to note that your business use of a vehicle is deductible against your business income and that, starting in 2018, employees are no longer allowed to claim unreimbursed vehicle expenses as personal itemized deductions. This is yet another example of how the rules for small business owners are different from those for W-2 employees.

Depreciation Deductions

Depreciation is an accounting process (also used for tax purposes) that allocates the cost of a tangible fixed asset over its useful life. A fixed asset is an item purchased for long-term use that is not easily convertible to cash. This would include items such as buildings, land, leasehold improvements, furniture, fixtures, equipment, and business vehicles. There are many special classifications, limitations, and restrictions when it comes to the appropriate depreciation method to use for tax reporting purposes. For more information, you can download a pdf copy of IRS Publication 946: How to Depreciate Property at www.irs.gov/pub/irs-pdf/p946.pdf.

The Tax Cuts and Jobs Act of 2017 removes the requirement that the original use of qualified property must commence with the taxpayer, and it now allows the additional first-year depreciation deduction for *new and used property*. A Section 179 deduction allows a business owner to immediately expense certain fixed assets, thereby avoiding the general requirement of writing off these costs over the assets useful life. Section 179 deduction has been increased to a maximum amount of $1,000,000 (with a phase-out threshold of $2,500,000), effective January 1, 2018.

The new law further allows Section 179 expensing for qualified improvement property (including leasehold improvements) made after December 31, 2017. This deduction has been expanded to include roofs; heating, ventilation, and air conditioning; fire protection and alarm systems; and security systems.

Any amount not deductible under Section 179, but still used for business, can take advantage of the bonus depreciation rules. The bonus depreciation now also applies to *new and used* vehicles, and then a six-year write-off will apply to the remaining purchase price. Bonus depreciation for property acquired after September 27, 2017, has been increased from 50% to 100% through the end of 2022, 80% in 2023, 60% in 2024, 40% in 2025, 20% in 2026, and none thereafter. I like to refer to this as depreciation on steroids. Never before has small businesses had the opportunity to write off so many fixed assets at one time.

As of 2018, accelerated depreciation expense for business vehicles (autos) has been increased to a maximum amount of $10,000 for the year they are placed in service, $16,000 for the second year,

$9,600 for the third year, and $5,760 for each year thereafter until fully depreciated. These limits will be indexed for inflation each year.

A special rule applies for sports utility vehicles (SUVs) for your business. You can take a Section 179 deduction of up to $25,000 by writing off the purchase of a new or used SUV that is utilized at least 50% of the time for business and is rated at 6,000 pounds or more when fully loaded. Check with your auto dealer for qualifying SUVs.

If you are like most business owners, you continue working at home well after your business is closed. As a result, if you must equip your home to facilitate this work with a computer, furniture, or other equipment, be sure to pay for these items through your business. These items would be fully tax-deductible, even if you do not qualify for a home office deduction.

You will be able to take a depreciation deduction if you own property used in your business or other income-producing activities, such as rental real estate. If you own the property that your business operates out of, your business may be able to pay you rent, allowing you to deduct the depreciation expense against the rental income you received. You may be able to generate a positive cash flow and actually pay no income tax on this income, after deducting this depreciation (phantom deduction) expense. Please note, a big negative here is that your cost basis in your rental property will decrease by the amount of depreciation taken each year, and you may then be required to recapture this depreciation as additional ordinary income to the extent of gain from the sale of the rental property.

When implementing these business tax strategies, you must take a multiyear approach in the planning process. You may not want to simply take the largest deduction possible in the current year to save yourself as many tax dollars as possible in the short term. You must take a long-term view and determine when the tax deduction will be most valuable to you. If this is your first or second year in business and you are reflecting a loss or simply are in a low tax bracket, this depreciation or Section 179 deduction may not be as valuable in the current year. For example, if you purchased $10,000 of equipment and took a Section 179 deduction or bonus depreciation this year when you are in the 10% tax bracket, you would save $1,000 in income tax in the current year. If you expect to be in the 37% tax bracket in one of the following years, this same $10,000 deduction could save you $3,700. So, the question is "Would you rather save $1,000 this year or $3,700 next year?" Although the general rule is to try to take every tax deduction available to you each year, you must take into consideration when the business tax deduction would be most valuable to you.

Choosing the Right Retirement Plan for Your Business

In Chapter 8, "Planning for Retirement," we covered the importance of planning and saving for your retirement as an individual. Generally, your choices are limited as an employee to what is offered through your employer, if any retirement plan is offered at all. Otherwise, you are limited to a $5,500 IRA contribution if you are under 50 years old or $6,500 if you are 50 or older (for 2018). As a business owner, you are in the driver's seat to determine the extent to which you will utilize retirement plans, since your options are significantly increased. One of the biggest benefits of being a business owner is not only the choices available to you for retirement savings, but more importantly, the amount of money you could sock away every year on a tax deferred basis.

If you refer back to Chapter 8, you will see that I provided a brief description of many of the qualified retirement plans that are offered through employers. Deciding which plan is right for you and your business is a matter of your particular facts and circumstances. These include how much your business can afford to pay based on its profitability, the age of your employees, the number of years your employees have been employed by you, your commitment to retaining your employees, your age, and your own commitment to achieving financial independence.

I am going to now take you through the natural progression of your ability to fund retirement plans for both you and your employees throughout the life of your business. If your business is not financially prepared to contribute towards funding a retirement plan for your employees and your resources are limited, then you may not want to set up a retirement plan for your business at all. It may be best to simply fund an Individual Retirement Account (IRA) personally. This will then eliminate any requirement to provide retirement plan benefits to your employees. If you are not funding a retirement plan for yourself through your business, then you are not required to fund a retirement plan for your employees.

If you decide to set up a retirement plan for the first time through your business, you can utilize the tax credit for small employer pension plan startup costs of up to $500 per year for the first three years you operate the plan, provided at least one nonowner employee earning less than $120,000 will be covered under the plan, and you have fewer than 100 employees. This is a $1,500 tax break, which is often missed by many small businesses.

All dollar amounts provided in the following retirement plan descriptions are through 2018; these amounts are usually adjusted annually for inflation.

Simplified Employee Pension (SEP)

These plans were designed to benefit owners and employees of small businesses. Like IRAs, they can provide either a lump sum payment or periodic withdrawals when you retire. They are principally funded by the employer, although some SEPs do allow employee contributions. SEPs are usually invested in the same types of accounts that hold IRAs.

If you are a small business owner and have no employees (or have employees that have been with your business for less than three years), a SEP plan may be an excellent choice, since the cost of establishing it is the same as for an IRA account. One major difference is that, with an IRA account, you are generally limited to $5,500 per year, but with a SEP you can contribute up to 25% of compensation (25% of W-2 or 20% of net self-employment earnings), to a maximum of $55,000 in 2018. This is an amazing difference between being a nonowner employee versus being a business owner. You have the opportunity to contribute 10 times more on a tax deferred basis as a business owner than you have as an individual. As I mentioned earlier in this chapter, the rules of the game are significantly better for small business owners than they are for salaried employees. The following is a summary of some of the features of SEP plans.

- Plan Setup and Operation
  - Any employer can establish this type of plan.
  - Any employee who has been employed in three of the last five years, is at least age 21, and has earned at least $600 is eligible.
  - The deadline to establish the plan is the tax-filing deadline of the employer; the plan year is typically the calendar year. (Currently, this is the ONLY form of business retirement plan that can be established after the end of the tax year to which it applies.)
  - SEP IRAs must be established for all eligible employees.
  - The participant makes his or her own investment choices.

- Annual maintenance requires no filings or required disclosures from the employer.
- Contributions
  - There are no participant pretax deferrals, except for grandfathered SARSEPs.
  - There are no participant after-tax contributions (Roth not allowed).
  - Employer contributions are discretionary.
  - Maximum contributions (employer and employee) are the lesser of 25% of compensation or $55,000 (in 2018).
  - No additional catch-up contributions are allowed for individuals age 50 or older, except for grandfathered SARSEPs.
- Distributions
  - Participant loans are not permitted.
  - Distributions can be taken at any time without restrictions, holding period, or specific qualifying event. (Taxes and penalties will apply if taken prior to age 59 1/2.)
  - Vesting is 100% immediately upon contribution to the SEP IRA account.
  - The benefit at retirement is the account balance.

If your business does not have a retirement plan, you can establish a SEP IRA up until the filing due date of your business income tax return, including extension, to still qualify for a tax-deductible contribution on your prior year's business tax return.

When you get to the point in your business that you have employees that have been with you for over three years, then continuing to maintain a SEP IRA may be cost prohibitive. If you continue with your SEP plan, you will have to contribute the same percentage to your employees from their salary. I have never met an employer willing to make a contribution of 25% on behalf of his or her employees. At this point, you will have a decision to make, since you will most likely be terminating your SEP plan. Another good option would be to set up a SIMPLE plan.

Savings Incentive Match Plans for Employees (SIMPLE)

These plans are also designed for small businesses. They can be set up either as IRAs or as 401(k)s. The employee funds them on a pretax basis, and employers are required to make matching contributions. These plans are relatively simple and inexpensive to set up, similar to a SEP plan. The major drawback is that all employees, including the business owner, will be limited to $12,500 with a $3,000 catchup if age 50 or older, in addition to a 3% match based on your salary. The following is a summary of some of the features of SIMPLE plans.

- Plan Setup and Operation
  - Any small business employer (100 or fewer employees) can establish this type of plan.
  - Any employee who has earned at least $5,000 in the prior two years and is expected to earn at least $5,000 in the current year is eligible.
  - The deadline to establish the plan is between January 1 and October 1; the plan year is always the calendar year.
  - SIMPLE investment accounts must be established for all eligible employees and/or participating employees.
  - The participant makes his or her own investment choices.
  - Annual maintenance requires a notice to eligible employees by November 1 for changes to be implemented the following year.
  - The plan is deemed to meet all nondiscrimination tests.
- Contributions
  - Participant pretax salary deferrals are limited to $12,500, with $3,000 catch-up if age 50 or older.
  - There are no participant after-tax contributions (Roth contributions not allowed).
  - Employer contributions are a dollar-for dollar match of up to 3% of compensation or 1% or 2% in no more than two of every five years; or 2% of compensation for all eligible employees on a nonmatching basis.
  - Maximum contributions are $25,000 (employer match $12,500 and employee deferral $12,500) or $31,000 including age-based catch-up age 50 and over (employer match $15,500 and employee deferral $15,500). The employer maximum is subject to a 3% employer match limit.
  - Participant loans are not permitted from SIMPLE IRAs, but may be permitted from SIMPLE 401(k) plans. SIMPLE 401(k) plans are not common.
  - Distributions can be taken at any time without restrictions, holding period, or specific qualifying event (tax and penalties will apply if taken prior to age 59½).
  - Vesting is 100% immediately upon contribution.
  - The benefit available at retirement is the account balance.

If your business has a SIMPLE plan or 401(k) plan, a tax planning strategy I recommend is to employ your spouse and increase your spouse's salary even further so that his or her tax deferral can be maximized under these plans. Please keep in mind that the salary you pay your spouse must be reasonable for actual services rendered. Although you will still have to pay the Social Security taxes on these wages, you can double the amount of tax deferral to your family.

401(k) Plan

This is a qualified plan established by employers to which eligible employees may make salary deferrals on a post-tax or pretax basis. Employers offering a 401(k) plan may make matching or nonelective (safe harbor) employer contributions to the plan on behalf of eligible employees. 401(k) plans that allow after-tax salary deferrals are known as Roth 401(k) plans. The deadline for establishing a safe harbor 401(k) plan is October 1. Traditional and Solo 401(k) plans can be established up until the end of the business year.

401(k) plans are normally provided by large corporations or small businesses that combine them with other retirement plans in order to maximize the benefit to the employee-owner. A major drawback is the high cost of establishing and the ongoing costs of maintaining these plans. I generally do not recommend switching from a SIMPLE IRA to a 401(k) plan unless the 401(k) is combined with a profit-sharing plan for larger tax-deductible contributions. In my opinion, the cost of setting up a 401(k) plan for small employers is not justified for the additional contribution that the employers can make for themselves, unless it is combined with a profit-sharing plan. The following is a summary of some of the features of 401(k) plans.

- Plan Setup and Operation
  - Any employer except government entities can establish a 401(k) plan.
  - Generally, any employee can be eligible, although you may want to apply statutory allowable exclusions (requiring age 21 and one year of service).
  - The deadline to establish the plan is the last day of the business year.
  - Participant deferrals cannot be made prior to the adoption date of the plan.

- A qualified trust must be established (can be self-trusteed).
- Generally, the participant makes his or her own investment choices.
- Annual maintenance requires Form 5500 filings, notices for safe harbor contributions, qualified default investment alternatives (QDIAs), and automatic enrollment, as applicable.
- Coverage and ACP, ADP, and top-heavy benefit nondiscrimination tests apply; if safe harbor requirements are met, the plan is deemed to satisfy the ADP and ACP tests and may qualify for top-heavy exemption.
- Contributions
  - Participant pretax salary deferrals are up to $18,500, with additional $6,000 catch-up if age 50 or older.
  - Participant after-tax salary deferrals are available as Roth contributions.
  - Employer contributions are discretionary, unless safe harbor applies.
  - Maximum contributions (employer and employee) are lesser of 100% of compensation or $55,000 ($61,000 with age-based catch-up contribution).
- Distributions
  - Participant loans are permitted.
  - Access to contributions through distributions are restricted and subject to the plan's terms.
  - Vesting is 100% immediate for the participant's own salary deferrals and any safe harbor or automatic enrollment employer matching.
  - Employer contributions may be subject to vesting schedule.
  - The benefit available at retirement is the account balance.

Profit-Sharing Plans

Profit-sharing plans are funded by the employer, who has the responsibility of determining when and how much the company will contribute to the plan. The company's contributions may depend on the company's profits and, therefore, so will the retirement benefit. When you retire, you can either receive your benefit as a lump sum or over a period of time. A profit-sharing plan can also be set up in conjunction with a 401(k) plan, which allows you to make salary deferrals from your paycheck. The following is a summary of some of the features of profit-sharing plans.

- Plan Setup and Operation
  - Any employer can establish this type of plan.
  - Generally, any employee can be eligible, although you may want to apply statutory allowable exclusions (requiring age 21 and one year of service).
  - The deadline to establish the plan is the last day of the business year.
  - A qualified trust must be established (can be self-trusteed).
  - The participant and/or plan sponsor makes investment choices.
  - Annual maintenance requires Form 5500 filings and notices for QDIAs, as applicable.
  - Coverage and benefit nondiscrimination tests apply.
- Contributions
  - Unless established in conjunction with a 401(k) feature, there are no participant pretax salary deferrals (employer contribution only).
  - Unless established in conjunction with a 401(k) feature, there are no participant after-tax salary deferrals (Roth not allowed).
  - Employer contributions are discretionary for a profit-sharing plan.
  - Maximum contributions (employer and employee) are up to $55,000 (up to 25% of compensation is deductible). Age based catch up is not available.
- Distributions
  - Participant loans are permitted.
  - Access to contributions through distributions are restricted and subject to the plan's terms.
  - Employer contributions are subject to vesting schedule.
  - The benefit available at retirement is the account balance.

If your business is not prepared to contribute a significant amount, but is still interested in getting a bigger tax deduction than would otherwise be available, you should look at a 401(k) cross-tested profit-sharing plan. This type of plan usually works well if you are over age 40 with younger employees. This will allow you to maximize tax-deductible contributions to yourself as the employer/employee, while also limiting the contribution you will be required to make for your employees. This strategy could work especially well if your spouse is also employed through your business.

Defined Benefit

With this type of plan, an employer commits to paying the employee a specific benefit for life, beginning when the employee retires. The amount of the benefit is known in advance and is usually based on factors such as the employee's age, earnings, and years of service. Defined benefit plans have benefit limits but do not have contribution limits, because they are based on a specific benefit to be paid in retirement. Today, very few private employers provide defined benefit plans, because they can be very costly. A variation to a traditional defined benefit plan is called a cash balance plan. These plans are still popular with small employers that are very profitable, have reliable and recurring income, and have an employee-owner who is interested in making large retirement plan contributions. The following is a summary of some of the features of a defined benefit plan.

- Plan Setup and Operation
  - Any employer can establish this type of plan.
  - Generally, any employee can be eligible, although you may want to apply statutory allowable exclusions (requiring age 21 and one year of service).
  - The deadline to establish the plan is the tax-filing deadline of the employer.
  - The plan year can be the calendar or fiscal year.
  - A qualified trust must be established (can be self-trusteed).
  - Only the plan sponsor makes investment decisions.
  - Annual maintenance requires Form 5500 filing and the services of a plan actuary.
  - Minimum annual contribution requirements apply.
  - Coverage and benefit nondiscrimination tests apply.
- Contributions
  - Participant pretax salary deferrals are not available (employer only).
  - Participant after-tax salary deferrals are not available (Roth not allowed).
  - Employer and employee minimum and maximum contributions are determined by an actuarial formula.
- Distributions
  - Participant loans may be permitted.
  - Access to contributions through distributions are restricted and subject to the plan's terms.

- Employer contributions are subject to vesting schedule
- The benefit available at retirement is the annuity defined by the plan's terms, which is often converted into a lump sum distribution.

Defined benefit plans can be an amazing tool for older business owners to play catch-up for lost time of not making contributions when they were younger. I have had significant success in providing clients with a combined 401(k), profit-sharing, and cash balance defined benefit plan. It is important to note that these plans are very complicated and require the involvement of plan actuaries. Having the help of a third party administrator (TPA) is essential in creating the plan designs that can meet the specific needs of the employee-owner. It is important to understand that these are not off the shelf plans and they require a high level of expertise in order to establish and continue to maintain these plans.

According to Jerrold Filipski, FSA, Vice President of TPA Solutions at Ascensus, "An older business owner with younger employees may be able to make tax-deductible retirement plan contributions substantially more than $55,000 per year by implementing a combined safe harbor 401(k) profit sharing plan with a cash balance defined benefit pension plan. For example, a 62-year-old nonprofessional may be able to contribute $55,000 to a profit-sharing plan and $270,000 to a cash-balance plan."

When it comes to planning and saving for retirement, the advantage of being self-employed is significant when compared to being a salaried employee. You are in control of your financial future because it is you, as the business owner, who will determine the type of retirement plan that will be established for your business. A business retirement plan is the single most powerful tool that the government has given you to allow you to save for retirement in pretax dollars. Depending on your personal income tax bracket, this could significantly increase your pretax return on your investments. This is because you are not only earning income on your money, but you are also earning income on the tax dollars you did not have to give to the government. This, combined with the power of compounding, will make a significant difference as to when you can achieve financial independence. As a business owner, your retirement planning strategy can exponentially be increased as a result of the significantly larger amount you will be able to contribute to your retirement plan. It is completely up to you as a small business owner to take advantage of this gift given to you by the government.

Recordkeeping

Keeping accurate records is an essential part of the success of any business. First, it is required by law that you keep accurate and complete records, so that you can properly determine your profit or loss from your business operation. These records are the foundation on which your tax returns are prepared and your tax liability to the government is determined. Furthermore, having accurate records will help you manage your business to its fullest potential. Identifying trends in revenues and costs from year to year, quarter to quarter, and month to month can help you establish goals and provide you with direction for your business. The same accounting records should be used to compare your performance to industry standards of other similar businesses. Being able to make these comparisons will help you compete more aggressively with your competitors and identify areas that may need improvement.

The key to maintaining a complete and accurate set of records starts by ensuring that you capture 100% of all of your business transactions through your business bank accounts and credit card statements. Segregating your business finances from your personal finances is critically important to ensure that you will be maintaining a complete and accurate set of records.

You should use a double-entry system, which includes both debits and credits. This balances your books and records, since all of your debits and credits must equal. Thanks to computerized small business software programs such as QuickBooks, recordkeeping has become much easier. There is a reason why 80% of small businesses use QuickBooks. If you know how to write out a check, then you should be able to work with QuickBooks in not only recording your business transactions, but also printing checks and reconciling your bank accounts.

If you are not prepared to wear this extra hat as a business owner, then you should definitely seek out help by either hiring a part-time bookkeeper or asking your accounting firm to also handle the external bookkeeping function for you. Generally, if you are prepared to write out your own checks, monitor your bills, and deal with billing and collections, then I believe the most cost-effective way to handle the rest would be to use an outside accounting firm. This is especially true since the accounting firm will most likely be responsible for preparing the business's financial statements, as well as the business's income tax returns.

Bookkeeping is only the first step to maintaining adequate records for your business. You must also be prepared to provide supporting documentation to the government in the event of an audit. Your accounting records also include your point of sale systems that tie into your cash register and inventory system. If requested by the government, you will need to provide them with receipts, sales slips, invoices, bank deposit slips, canceled checks, and any other documents to substantiate your income, deductions, and tax credits.

The key issue to remember when maintaining records to support your business *income* is that you must have the appropriate documentation to support your gross receipts. This would include such items as cash register tapes, bank deposit slips, cash receipt books, invoices, credit card charge slips, and when applicable, 1099-MISC forms issued to you by payers.

The key issue to remember when maintaining records to support your business *expenses* is that you must have a receipt that describes the product or service you purchased through your business, proof of payment (i.e., canceled check, credit card receipt, etc.), and finally, especially for those gray area deductions, an explanation as to why this was an ordinary and necessary business expense. For more details on starting a business and keeping records, you can download a copy of IRS Publication 583 at www.irs.gov/pub/irs-pdf/p583.pdf.

Financial Statements

In addition to maintaining these records for tax reporting and managing your business, you will be required to prepare business financial statements for creditors and investors. Financial statements are normally required to be prepared in accordance with generally accepted accounting principles (GAAP) in the United States. As an alternative to issuing financial statements under GAAP, statements can be provided under other comprehensive bases of accounting, including tax basis, based on the Statements on Standard for Accounting and Review Services issued by the AICPA Accounting and Review Services Committee.

When dealing with creditors or potential investors, there are four general financial statements that provide users with a financial picture of the performance, position and cash flow of a business. These financial statements are an income statement, a balance sheet, a statement of cash flow, and a statement of changes in equity.

Income Statement

An income statement gives users a picture of how a business is performing financially over a specified time period. For example, a business with a December 31 year-end would normally prepare an annual income statement that would cover the time period of January 1 through December 31 of that year. It is formatted with all income and sales items listed at the top and then subtracts out all of the categorized expenses that are associated with the business (not necessarily all tax-deductible expenses). It then would show the difference between your revenues and expenses, also known as your net income (or loss). Many creditors and investors look at an income statement as one of the most valuable financial statements in determining your ability to generate a profit.

Balance Sheet

A balance sheet shows the financial position of a company at a specific point in time (as opposed to time period). For example, a business with a December 31 year-end would normally prepare an annual balance sheet as of December 31. Unlike an income statement, a balance sheet shows certain financial data from the inception of the business up until the specified date.

A balance sheet is made up of assets (what the company owns), liabilities (debts and other obligations of the company), and equity (the difference between total assets and liabilities). This is similar to a statement of financial position that we covered in Chapter 3 regarding your own personal finances. Both assets and liabilities are laid out in order of most liquidity (for example, cash would normally be the first item listed). Another key factor of a balance sheet is that your total assets must equal your liabilities plus equity. This is where the word "balance" in *balance sheet* comes from. Many creditors and investors will also look at this very valuable financial statement, since it shows the financial position of a company. It allows the readers of your financial statements to determine your financial strength or weakness.

Statement of Cash Flow

A statement of cash flow shows all of the cash inflows and all of the cash outflows a company has over a specified time period. This shows the net effect of the changes in the business's bank balance from the beginning of the period to the end of the period. Similar to an income statement, a business with a December 31 year-end would normally prepare an annual statement of cash flow that would cover the time period of January 1 through December 31 of that year. A statement of cash flow is broken out into three categories: operating activities, investing activities, and financing activities. A potential investor or creditor would see value in this statement, because it shows how much cash a company has actually generated during the specified time period and what the actual source of this cash flow was. Creditors are most interested in the company's cash flow since their primary concern is a business's ability to repay their loan.

Statement of Changes in Equity

A statement of changes in equity shows a more detailed breakdown of the equity section of a balance sheet. However, unlike a balance sheet and similar to both an income statement and a statement of cash flow, a statement of change in equity reports all changes during the reporting period. For example, a business with a December 31 year-end would normally prepare an annual statement of changes in equity that would cover the time period of January 1 through December 31 of that year. The makeup of this statement can vary depending on the type of entity form established; however, general changes shown include change in outstanding stock (or capital), dividends issued (or distributions to shareholders/partners), and net income or loss. A potential investor or creditor would see this statement as useful in determining the financial strengths of your business.

These four statements are all interrelated. The income or loss shown on your income statement is used in the calculation on the statement of changes in equity, as well as on the balance sheet. The statement of cash flow reconciles the beginning cash balance for the reporting period with all cash-flow activity during the reporting period and then agrees this to the period-ending cash balance on the balance sheet.

Many accounting firms can be engaged to perform specific agreed-upon services in relation to your business's financial statements. These services include financial statement preparation, compilation, review, and audit engagements.

Financial Statement Preparation

Financial statement preparation is the most common of all financial statement services. Many times, when you hire a CPA firm to prepare your bookkeeping records, it will also be engaged to prepare financial statements. The main purpose of this type of engagement is for the internal business owner's use only and to assist in indicating the performance of your business and areas where you may need to improve. Some lenders may accept this level of service as sufficient documentation in obtaining a loan; however, the accounting firm gives no assurance as to whether these statements are complete and accurate, nor does it issue any formal report on these financial statements.

Compilation Engagement

A CPA firm can also be engaged to compile financial statements and issue a compilation report. A compilation engagement is very similar to a financial statement preparation engagement, but a compilation report gives more information on the relationship between the business and the CPA firm performing the work. Similar to a financial statement preparation, the accounting firm compiles the data provided and converts it into a financial statement. This type of engagement would be considered appropriate if your business was interested in obtaining some smaller financing or credit and the lender was not willing to accept basic prepared financial statements. A compilation report would also specifically state that the accounting firm did not perform an audit or a review and does not express an opinion or provide any form of assurance or conclusion on the financials.

Review Engagement

A review engagement is a more comprehensive service provided by a CPA firm. It involves the CPA firm performing analytical procedures, as well as inquiries with management and other necessary procedures, in order to obtain "limited assurance" over the accuracy of the financial statements. This is the most basic assurance service that can be provided by a CPA. In order to perform a review engagement, a CPA must be knowledgeable in both your industry and your business itself. A review would be most appropriate when a business is looking for substantial growth and is seeking larger and more complicated financing and credit from lenders.

Audit Engagement

An audit is the highest level of assurance that can be provided by a CPA firm. The main purpose of this engagement is to provide the intended users with comfort over the accuracy of these statements. A CPA obtains "reasonable assurance" over the accuracy of financial statements by obtaining comfort over the financial statement assertions. These assertions include existence and occurrence, completeness, accuracy and valuation, rights and obligations, and presentation and disclosures. Through an audit, a CPA is required to be independent of the business in which he or she is auditing. Similar to a review, the CPA is required to be knowledgeable in both the industry and the business itself, but is also required to obtain an understanding of how the business's internal controls work and assess the risk of fraud. The CPA is required to corroborate all amounts included in the financial statements and notes to the financial statements through inquiry, inspection, observation, confirmation, examination, or analytical procedures.

A CPA would issue a report on the financial statements being audited, stating an opinion on whether or not the financial statements are presented fairly in all material aspects, in accordance with the applicable financial reporting framework. This type of engagement would be most appropriate when a business is looking to obtain high levels of financing or credit or if the business owner is looking to sell the business.

Financial Management Team

Putting together and working with the right financial management team can make all of the many difficult decisions discussed throughout this chapter, as well as those that you will have to make throughout your business lifespan, much less stressful and manageable.

You would like to think that you can do all of this on your own, but the truth is that you need a team of experts to help you juggle the many responsibilities of owning a business. You need to select business advisors to help you set up your business and get you started in the right direction. They will include an accountant, attorney, banker, insurance agent, marketing firm, and others that have expertise in your line of business and industry. These experts should more than pay their fees, since they will help you avoid the many problems and pitfalls that can occur when you are going into business for the first time by yourself. For more information about selecting a trusted advisor, please refer to Appendix A, where I go into more detail about some of these financial management team advisors.

What the Tax Cuts and Jobs Act of 2017 Means for Your Small Business

On December 22, 2017, President Donald Trump signed the Tax Cuts and Jobs Act into law. It is expected that lowering taxes across the board, eliminating costly special interest tax incentives, and modernizing our international tax system so that we can compete with other countries will help create more jobs, increase pay for everyone, and make the Internal Revenue Code simpler and fairer for all Americans across the country. The following is a summary of some of the most significant changes that will affect small businesses. These changes took effect starting January 1, 2018, and have been made permanent, unlike the individual tax changes, which have a sunset provision due to expire on December 31, 2025.

The following are some highlights of the most significant changes that will affect corporations and other small business entities. For more specific details on each of these items, please refer to the following "*Tax Alpha to the 2nd Power* Facts and Strategies" section. The Tax Cuts and Jobs Act of 2017 has:

- Lowered corporate tax rates to 21% from the former 35%
- Eliminated the Alternative Minimum Tax for corporations
- Repealed the domestic production activity deduction under Section 199
- Preserved important existing business tax credits
- Allowed businesses to immediately write-off the full cost of new equipment up to $1,000,000 under Section 179 expensing
- Allowed some pass-through businesses to deduct 20% of their pass-through income
- Modernized our international tax system
- Made it easier for American businesses to bring home foreign earnings
- Discouraged American businesses from moving their headquarters, jobs, and research overseas and encouraged foreign businesses to locate within the United States

With such sweeping changes, I would highly encourage you to work with a tax professional to understand how this tax law will specifically impact your business.

TAX ALPHA TO THE 2ND POWER℠ FACTS AND STRATEGIES FOR STARTING YOUR OWN BUSINESS

Here are several tax facts and strategies that will address your wealth accumulation goals at an exponential rate, which will help put you on the path to financial independence, *point X*.

I have broken up these business *Tax Alpha to the 2nd Power* facts and strategies into **12 categories** to simplify finding the subject matter that interests you.

1. **Corporate Tax Rates**
   - **In 2018, the C corporate tax rate was changed to a flat tax of 21% on all corporate profits.** This was the most significant tax cut in corporate tax history, which dramatically simplified the corporate tax structure that existed prior. The following chart highlights these tax rate changes:

Taxable Income Range	Marginal Corporate Tax Rate (2017)	Flat Tax for 2018
$0–$50,000	15%	21%
$50,000–$75,000	25%	21%
$75,000–$100,000	34%	21%
$100,000–$335,000	39%	21%
$335,000–$10,000,000	34%	21%
$10,000,000–$15,000,000	35%	21%
$15,000,000–$18,333,333	38%	21%
$18,333,333 and above	35%	21%

2. **Business Tax Deductions**
   - Perhaps one of the biggest mistakes business owners make is paying for business expenses personally and thereby losing out on valuable tax deductions. This is why you must analyze your personal checkbook and personal credit card statements, and try to identify any expenses that were business-related and mistakenly paid for personally. You should then reimburse yourself for these expenses before the end of the year, which will allow you to take this money out of your business tax-free. This is especially important now, since unreimbursed employee business expenses are no longer deductible personally as an itemized deduction.
   - If you use your vehicle for business, be sure to pay all costs of operating it through your business. This would include auto lease payments, gas, oil,

repairs and maintenance, car washes, license plate fees, and auto insurance. You must keep a record of all business miles driven throughout the year. The personal usage of this vehicle would not be tax-deductible to your business. If you operate under a corporation, you will need to report the personal use of this vehicle as wages on your year-end W-2.

- **In 2018, the Section 199 deduction for income attributable to domestic production activities was repealed.**
- Business meals are generally only 50% deductible to your business. **This limitation has now been expanded under the new tax reform bill to include meals you provide to your employees for your convenience at or near your business premises.**
- To maximize the benefit of travel expenses, you should try to combine business with pleasure. As long as the primary purpose of the trip is business, the full amount could be tax deductible. If you spend five days on a trip and three out of the five are for business, then this may be considered the primary purpose of this trip. You must be prepared to support this position by keeping the necessary documentation, such as your agenda, which includes your scheduled meetings, and emails to and from the business associates you are meeting with.
- **As of 2018, business entertainment, as well as country club dues, are no longer tax-deductible.**
- As of 2018, net operating losses (NOL) can offset only 80% of taxable income, and **NOL carrybacks will no longer be permitted, with a few exceptions.** Existing NOL carryforwards prior to 2018 are unaffected by this change. Starting in 2018, you will no longer be required to make an election to waive carryback losses, since they will not be permitted. This change will apply on corporate, as well as individual, tax returns.
- The Tax Cuts and Jobs Act caps the deduction for business losses on individual income tax returns. **Business losses that exceed the $500,000 threshold for married filing jointly and $250,000 for all other single filers are nondeductible.** The excess loss can be carried forward to future years. This cap applies after the application of the current passive activity loss rules.
- **As of 2018, sexual harassment settlements are not tax-deductible if subject to a nondisclosure agreement.**

3. **Tax Credits**
   - The new law preserves important existing business tax credits, such as retaining the low-income housing tax credit and preserving the Research & Development Tax Credit.
   - If you make improvements to your business property, whether you own the building or you are a tenant, you may be entitled to a Disability Access Credit of up to $5,000 per year. To obtain the maximum credit,

(continued)

you must spend $10,250 or more. These improvement costs must be specifically identified to make your business more accessible to persons with disabilities. This would of course apply to some of the more obvious improvements, such as building a handicap access ramp or a new ADA-compliant bathroom. It would also apply to other less obvious improvements, such as repaving parking areas, expanding hallways, or laying new carpeting and flooring. This credit also applies to furniture and equipment purchased to provide services to the disabled.

- If you spend more than $10,250 to make your business more accessible to persons with disabilities, you should also take advantage of a Section 190 deduction. This may allow your business to immediately expense up to $15,000 of the costs that are made to remove architectural and transportation barriers for the disabled and elderly.

4. **Interest Deductions**
   - The deduction that businesses claim for interest on business debt is now limited. The net interest write-off will be capped at 30% of adjusted taxable income, with any disallowed interest carried forward to future years. Firms with $25,000,000 or less of gross receipts, real estate companies, and certain regulated public utilities will not be subject to this limitation.

5. **Health Insurance Deduction**
   - Health insurance premiums (single or family plans) that you pay for yourself through your business are 100% tax-deductible for all business owners, including sole proprietorships, partnerships, and corporations. As a sole proprietorship or partnership, you still pay Social Security and Medicare tax on the cost of this health insurance, but as a corporation (S corp or C corp), you do not. This can be a significant payroll tax savings to many small business owners.

6. **Employee Benefit Deductions**
   - **As of 2018, the tax deduction to employers for the cost of transportation-related fringe benefits, such as mass transit passes and parking, are no longer tax-deductible.** Employees are still permitted to use pretax money for parking and transit passes.
   - **Businesses that provide paid family or medical leave to workers will be entitled to a new tax credit.** Generally, it will be 12.5% of the amount of wages paid during the period of this leave. The credit is increased for employers that pay workers over 50% of their normal wages during their leave. It is important to note that many special rules and limitations may apply. This credit will apply only for 2018 and 2019, unless later extended by Congress.
   - **Under the Tax Cuts and Jobs Act, payment of cash, gift cards, and other nontangible personal property as an employee achievement award is now prohibited and, therefore, not tax-deductible to the business.**

7. **Family Tax Strategies**
   - Many small business owners have their spouses work in the business and make the mistake of not paying them a salary. You should pay your spouse at least enough to qualify for the maximum child care credit, assuming you have children age 13 or younger. Even if you do not have young children, you should still pay your spouse a salary for actual services rendered, so your spouse can join you on business trips, as long as it is part of his or her work requirement. You could then fully deduct the business travel costs associated with your spouse.
   - If your children also work in your business, be sure to include them on the payroll. You can employ children age 6 or older through your business (be sure to check your state child labor laws) in order to fund college savings, private school costs, and any other costs of raising your children on a tax-deductible basis. Since you are going to pay for these costs either way, it makes sense to pay your child for actual services rendered, which allows them to pay for that cost with the money they earned. This will also teach them the responsibility of working and the value of a dollar. **Each of your children can earn up to $12,000 federally tax-free in 2018.** If you operate as a sole proprietorship or partnership, for tax reporting purposes, any wages you pay your children also avoid Social Security and Medicare tax if they are under the age of 18. They will also be exempt from FUTA tax until age 21.
   - Your working child could fully fund the maximum annual contribution of $2,000 per year to a Coverdell Savings Account, which will shelter investment earnings for future tax-free withdrawals to cover college or private pre-K, elementary, middle school, or high school.
   - Your child could establish a Roth IRA account and contribute an amount equal to his or her earned income, up to $5,500 (for 2018). While these contributions are not deductible, the principal can be withdrawn tax-free for college, and all future earnings will be tax-free when withdrawn after age 59½. If your child does not ultimately need these funds to cover educational costs, just think of how much money will have accumulated in this account when he or she is ready for retirement in 50 or 60 years. I cannot think of a better way for your child to achieve financial independence and have the added benefit of tax-free income in retirement.
   - You should assist your children with going into business for themselves by shifting income-producing property, such as business furniture and equipment, office buildings, warehouses, or other property, into a Family Limited Partnership (FLP), Subchapter S corporation, or limited liability company (LLC). This income may be taxed at lower rates if their earned income equals more than half of their support, and they meet certain age requirements.

(continued)

8. **Business Property Strategies**
   - Under Section 280A(g) of the Internal Revenue Code, up to 14 days of rental income received by you personally can be tax-free for the rental of your personal residence or vacation home. Be sure not to rent these personal properties more than 14 days, otherwise, this special rule will not apply. To double up on this tax break, you can rent these properties to your business for legitimate business purposes such as employee training meetings, board of directors meetings, or employee retreats. *The rent paid by your business will be tax-deductible and the rental income you receive personally will be tax-free.*
   - Increase the rent you charge to your business for the use of commercial real estate property you own personally or through another business entity to the highest reasonable rate. The income from this rental property in excess of expenses (including depreciation) may not be subject to the 3.8% Medicare payroll tax if this activity is considered *nonpassive*. Normally, real estate rental is considered a passive activity, but when it is specifically related to your business in which you actively participated, then it can be viewed as nonpassive for this purpose.
9. **Depreciation Deductions**
   - **The Tax Cuts and Jobs Act of 2017 removes the requirement that the original use of qualified property must commence with the taxpayer, and it now allows the additional first-year depreciation deduction for new and used property.**
   - **The Section 179 deduction has been increased to a maximum amount of $1,000,000** (with a phase-out threshold of $2,500,000), effective January 1, 2018. **The new law further allows Section 179 expensing for qualified improvement property** (including leasehold improvements) made after December 31, 2017. This deduction has been expanded to include roofs, heating, ventilation and air conditioning, fire protection and alarm systems, and security systems.
   - You can take a Section 179 deduction of up to $25,000 by writing off the purchase of a new or used SUV that is utilized at least 50% of the time for business and is rated at 6,000 pounds or more when fully loaded. Check with your auto dealer for qualifying SUVs.
   - Any amount not deductible under Section 179 but still used for business can take advantage of the bonus depreciation rules. The bonus depreciation now applies to *new and used* vehicles, and then a six-year write-off will apply to the remaining purchase price.
   - **Bonus depreciation for new and most used property acquired after September 27, 2017, has been increased from 50% to 100%** through the end of 2022, 80% in 2023, 60% in 2024, 40% in 2025, 20% in 2026, and none thereafter.

- **As of 2018, accelerated depreciation expense for business luxury vehicles (autos) has been increased** to a maximum amount of $10,000 for the year they are placed in service, $16,000 for the second year, $9,600 for the third year, and $5,760 for each year thereafter until fully depreciated. The base amount of depreciation (before allowed bonus) has been increased and will be indexed for inflation each year after 2018. Where business use percentage is less than 50%, no additional bonus is allowed.
- If you are like most business owners, you continue working at home well after your business is closed. As a result, if you must equip your home to facilitate this work with a computer, furniture, or other equipment, be sure to pay for these items through your business. These items would be fully tax-deductible, even if you do not qualify for a home office deduction.
- You will be able to take a depreciation deduction if you own property used in your business or other income-producing activities, such as rental real estate. You may be able to generate a positive cash flow and actually pay no income tax on this income, after deducting this depreciation (phantom deduction) expense.

10. **Pension Plan Strategies**
    - If you are an older business owner with younger employees, you may be able to maximize your tax-deductible retirement plan contributions to substantially more than $55,000 per year by implementing a combined safe harbor 401(k) profit sharing plan with a cash balance defined benefit pension plan. For example, a 62-year-old nonprofessional may be able to contribute $55,000 to a profit sharing plan and $270,000 to a cash balance plan. This is a terrific way for an older business owner to make up for lost time, assuming profits allow for this level of contribution.
    - If your business is not prepared to contribute a significant amount, but is still interested in getting a bigger tax deduction than otherwise would be available, you should look at a 401(k) cross-tested profit sharing plan. This type of plan usually works well if you are over age 40 with younger employees. This will allow you to maximize tax-deductible contributions to yourself as the employer/employee, while also limiting the contribution you will be required to make for your employees. This strategy could work especially well if your spouse is also employed in your business.
    - If your business has a SIMPLE plan or 401(k) plan, you should increase your spouse's salary even further so that his or her tax deferral can be maximized under these plans. Please keep in mind that the salary you pay your spouse must be reasonable for the actual services rendered. Although you will still have to pay the Social Security taxes on these wages, you can double the amount of tax deferral to the family.

(continued)

- If your business does not have a retirement plan, set one up on or before December 31 to qualify for a business tax deduction in the current year. If you miss this deadline and your tax year has ended, you still have until the filing due date of your business income tax return to establish a SEP IRA and still qualify for a tax-deductible contribution on your prior year's income tax return. If you have employees that would qualify under this plan, it would not be advisable, since you would have to contribute up to 25% of their salary as an additional benefit.
- If this is the first time you set up a retirement plan for your business, you can utilize the tax credit for small employer pension plan startup costs of up to $500 per year for the first three years you operate the plan. This is a $1,500 tax break, which is often missed by many small businesses.

11. **Business Entity Strategies**
    - If you are a cash-basis taxpayer, delay December billing and collection activities so that you can defer income into the next year. You may want to do just the opposite with your business expenses by prepaying some of your January expenses in December to lower your profit in the current year. This strategy would defer your tax payment into the next year and is even more advantageous if you expect your income to be subject to a lower tax rate (non-C corp) in the following year.
    - **Under the new law, taxpayers with pass-through businesses, such as sole proprietorships, LLCs, partnerships, and S corporations, will be able to deduct 20% of their pass-through income.** For example, if your flow-through entity has a profit of $50,000, you will only be taxed on $40,000 (80% of the $50,000 profit) at your ordinary income tax rate. Please note that the full $50,000 will still be included in your adjusted gross income and that this tax break only affects the calculation of tax for federal tax purposes.
    - **This pass-through entity tax break does come with some strings attached to "specified service trades and businesses,"** which includes any trade or business in the field of health, law, consulting, accounting, performing arts, actuarial services, athletics, financial services, and brokerage services, and any trade or businesses where the principal asset (goodwill) of the business is the reputation or specialized skills of one or more of its employees or owners. **These flow-through entities will have this tax benefit phase out if their personal taxable income is between $157,500 and $207,500 for single filers and between $315,000 and $415,000 for married filing joint filers (in 2018).** In other words, they will get the full tax break if their personal taxable income is below this range, a partial deduction if they fall within this range, and no tax break at all if they are above this range.
    - **The tax bill excluded engineering and architectural businesses from the definition of specified service trade or business. Businesses in these fields**

may qualify for the full deduction of 20% of their pass-through income regardless of the amount of their taxable income.

- If your business is set up as a sole proprietorship, partnership, or LLC, then 100% of your profits may be subject to the 3.8% Medicare tax.

- One of the major advantages of being a Subchapter S corporation is that any profit that flows through as a distribution to shareholder (K-1) avoids the 3.8% Medicare tax on personal investment income. For those business owners earning less than the Social Security maximum, they will minimize the Social Security tax they pay (could be a 15.3% savings on this excess). By taking a lower salary, you might be able to reduce your payroll taxes significantly, since any remaining profit would not be subject to payroll taxes. Please keep in mind that you are still required to pay yourself a reasonable salary (what you would have paid an employee to perform the same services) for the work performed.

- If you operate your business through a corporate entity, you may be able to reduce any interest and penalties due on your personal income tax return for underpaying your personal taxes. You can do this by increasing your income tax withholdings on your year-end bonus, since these withholdings will be treated as if they were made equally throughout the year.

- If you are starting a business as a corporation, take advantage of Internal Revenue Code Section 1244 Stock election. Under these rules, if your business fails, you can deduct up to $50,000 of the loss against ordinary income if you file your taxes as single, and up to $100,000 if you are married and file your taxes jointly. Otherwise, the loss would be subject to the capital loss limitation rules, which state that you can take capital losses only to the extent of capital gains plus $3,000 against ordinary income in any given year; the balance of the losses can be carried to future years.

- The Tax Cuts and Jobs Act has not changed the favorable treatment to qualified small business stock (QSBS) under IRC Section 1202. The small business owner must have purchased the stock in a C corporation (not an S corporation) with assets under $50 million or less directly from the corporation. The exclusion is capped at the greater of 10 times the share basis or $10 million. Taxpayers who have held QSBS for more than five years can continue to exclude 50% of the gain upon sale if the QSBS was purchased before February 18, 2009, and 75% of the gain if the QSBS was acquired after February 17, 2009, and before September 28, 2010. The full 100% exclusion would apply to gains upon sale of QSBS purchased after September 27, 2010. Many types of businesses are excluded from the qualified category; see IRS Publication 550 to determine whether your business meets the requirements of QSBS.

(*continued*)

- The Tax Cuts and Jobs Act has not changed the favorable treatment to qualified small business stock (QSBS) under IRC Section 1045. Taxpayers who have not met the five-year holding period requirement under Section 1202, but have held the stock for more than six months, may be able to roll-over qualified small business stock gains into a new QSBS, as long as they reinvest the proceeds within 60 days.

12. **International Tax Issues**

   Since most small businesses do not have international tax consequences, I have not included this topic within this book, other than to make note of the following major changes resulting from the Tax Cuts and Jobs Act of 2017:

- **Modernizes our international tax system. The tax reform bill changes the US corporate tax system from a worldwide income tax system to a territorial income tax system after 2017.** Under a worldwide tax system, many US corporations had to pay US corporate income taxes on their profits earned abroad and were then required to pay income tax in the United States on the same income. Under the territorial income tax system, the double-taxing of most foreign profits has been substantially eliminated, after the 2017 *mandatory* taxation of foreign accumulated earnings not previously taxed since 1986. These "repatriated" earnings are subject to favorable tax rates.

- **Simplifies and encourages US businesses to bring home foreign earnings.** As a result of the worldwide tax system that previously existed, which made foreign profits subject to the 35% top corporate tax rate, there was an estimated $2.6 trillion in US corporations' foreign profits held abroad. In order to encourage US businesses to bring this money into the United States, **the new tax law sets a one-time repatriation rate of 15.5% on cash and cash equivalent foreign-held assets and 8% on illiquid assets like equipment**, which is payable over an eight-year period. This should result in not only significant amounts of assets being brought into the United States, but it will also generate tax revenues to help lower our national deficit.

- **Discourages American businesses from moving their headquarters, jobs, and research overseas and encourages foreign businesses to locate within the United States.** By lowering the corporate tax rate to 21%, the United States is now more competitive when compared to other nations, since the global corporate tax rate averages 25%. This will make US businesses more competitive, which should help keep more jobs and corporate profits in the United States. Not only will this increase the number of businesses in the United States, but it will also increase the number of people working and paying taxes.

AN ACTION PLAN FOR STARTING AND MAINTAINING YOUR OWN BUSINESS

By now, you should have a very good understanding of what is involved in starting and maintaining your own business. The challenges and risks associated with starting your own business are significant, but the rewards can clearly accelerate your journey to achieving financial independence and getting to *point X*. Here is a quick action plan to both help get your business started and keep it going:

1. **Evaluate the three pillars of establishing a successful business.** Do you possess the specialized, interpersonal, and business management skills required to succeed in business?

2. **Obtain an understanding of the risks and benefits of establishing your own business.** You will need to take the necessary steps outlined in this chapter to dramatically increase your chances of success so that you can still be in business 20 years from now.

3. **Create a business plan and put it in writing.** You must fully explain each of the seven key components included in your business plan so that someone who is not in your industry can understand it.

4. **Select the appropriate business entity form for your business.** You must understand the pros and cons of each choice and implement the one that is most suitable for you and your business.

5. **Obtain a clear understanding of the keys to reporting your business income and expenses.** One of the major advantages of owning your own business is that the rules surrounding taxation are significantly better for small business owners when compared to individuals. Be prepared to take advantage of every tax break available to you as a business owner.

6. **Educate yourself as to what is and is not tax-deductible to your business.** This includes understanding the "ordinary and necessary" test as well as how to put yourself in a position to maximize your business tax deductions.

7. **Implement the right retirement plan for you and your business.** Once you are generating sufficient profits, you will be in a position to start saving and accumulating the necessary funds towards achieving financial independence. The most tax efficient way to do so is by implementing the appropriate business retirement plan.

8. **Establish a recordkeeping and financial reporting system.** This is not only required by law, but it will also allow you to effectively manage your business by identifying strengths and weaknesses within your business and comparing your results to industry standards.

9. **Recruit a financial management team** that possesses the specialized skills necessary to assist you with juggling the many responsibilities of establishing and maintaining a successful business.

(continued)

10. **Familiarize yourself with current** *Tax Alpha to the 2nd Power* **facts and strategies.** Obtain an understanding of the basic *Tax Alpha to the 2nd Power* facts and strategies that can affect the profitability of your business. Working with a qualified tax advisor, you should be able to implement strategies that will help reduce the number-one expense in your business – taxes – thereby increasing your profitability.

12

The Time Value of Money

Compound interest is the eighth wonder of the world. He who understands it, earns it ... he who doesn't ... pays it.

—Albert Einstein,
father of modern physics

One of the most important concepts to accumulating wealth and becoming financially independent is understanding the *time value of money*. By far, the most valuable asset we have is time, but unfortunately it is usually something we take for granted and then do not fully appreciate until later in life.

The time value of money formulas are highly complex mathematical equations, beyond the scope of this book; however, I recommend you purchase a financial calculator, which can perform these calculations for you. In fact, if you are in the business world, owning a financial calculator is a necessary tool in order for you to succeed. Rather than making this a complicated chapter that sounds like calculus, I am going to give you some very simple examples and financial tables that will make this an easy concept to understand.

Before we get started, I would like to define the most basic interest formula:

$$I = P \times R \times T$$

I = Interest calculated

P = Principal

R = Annual interest rate

T = Time period covered in the interest calculation (number of months out of 12)

For example, if you have $100,000 and are earning 5% interest over one year, the components of the formula would be $P = \$100,000$, $R = 5\%$, and $T =$ one year. Therefore, $\$100,000 \times 5\% \times (12/12)$ one year = $5,000. This represents the most basic interest formula.

After one year, your principal would now be worth $105,000, which would be the original $100,000 plus $5,000 in interest.

In year two, you would have $P = \$105,000$, $R = 5\%$ and $T =$ one year. Therefore, $\$105,000 \times 5\% \times (12/12)$ one year = $5,250. As a result, in year two, your original $100,000 increased its earning power by $250 with all other factors remaining the same.

With each year that passes, the earning power increases: This is referred to as the *power of compounding.* You can truly appreciate this over time, because the outcome can be astonishing.

The Rule of 72

Before I describe how to use the financial tables provided in the following pages, I would like to explain the *Rule of 72*, which unlocks the answer to how long it will take you to double your money. Of course, the answer to this depends on your interest rate (rate of return). Simply divide the assumed rate of return into 72. For example:

- If your assumed rate of return is 10%, divide 10 into 72, which equals 7.2 years.
- If your assumed rate of return is 5%, divide 5 into 72, which equals 14.4 years.

So, for the purpose of this example, let us assume a rate of return of 10% per year and a starting point of $25,000. Based on the Rule of 72 (see Exhibit 12.1), here's how that amount will increase:

- In 7.2 years, that $25,000 will double to $50,000.
- In 14.4 years, it will double once again to $100,000.
- In 21.6 years, it will double once again to $200,000.
- In 28.8 years, it will double once again to $400,000.
- In 36 years, it will double once again to $800,000.
- In 43.2 years, it will double once again to $1.6 million.

Exhibit 12.1   Rule of 72[1]

Annual Rate of Return	Years to Increase Your Investment					
	2 times	4 times	8 times	16 times	32 times	64 times
1%	72.00	144.00	216.00	288.00	360.00	432.00
2%	36.00	72.00	108.00	144.00	180.00	216.00
3%	24.00	48.00	72.00	96.00	120.00	144.00
4%	18.00	36.00	54.00	72.00	90.00	108.00
5%	14.40	28.80	43.20	57.60	72.00	86.40
6%	12.00	24.00	36.00	48.00	60.00	72.00
7%	10.29	20.57	30.86	41.14	51.43	61.71
8%	9.00	18.00	27.00	36.00	45.00	54.00
9%	8.00	16.00	24.00	32.00	40.00	48.00
10%	**7.20**	**14.40**	**21.60**	**28.80**	**36.00**	**43.20**
11%	6.55	13.09	19.64	26.18	32.73	39.27
12%	6.00	12.00	18.00	24.00	30.00	36.00
13%	5.54	11.08	16.62	22.15	27.69	33.23
14%	5.14	10.29	15.43	20.57	25.71	30.86
15%	4.80	9.60	14.40	19.20	24.00	28.80
16%	4.50	9.00	13.50	18.00	22.50	27.00
17%	4.24	8.47	12.71	16.94	21.18	25.41
18%	4.00	8.00	12.00	16.00	20.00	24.00
19%	3.79	7.58	11.37	15.16	18.95	22.74
20%	3.60	7.20	10.80	14.40	18.00	21.60

This mathematical formula is a shortcut that approximates and simplifies the concept of the time value of money and does not represent any particular investment product. Most people are astonished when they truly understand the power of compounding and how powerful the time value of money can be.

---

[1]The rates of return shown above are purely hypothetical and do not represent the performance of any individual investment or portfolio of investments. They are for illustrative purposes only and should not be used to predict future product performance. Specific rates of return, especially for extended time periods, will vary over time. There is also a higher degree of risk associated with investments that offer the potential for higher rates of return. You should consult with your representative before making any investment decision.

In Chapter 8, "Planning for Retirement," we discussed the retirement equation to help you achieve financial independence, *point X*. Now that you have a better understanding of the time value of money, you can appreciate even more the importance of starting to save now rather than later. Achieving the highest rate of return within your risk tolerance (Chapter 9, "Managing Your Investments") is a critical component to this equation. Starting early and having a better appreciation of your most valuable asset – time – will give you a tremendous advantage in achieving your financial goals.

To do your own financial calculations to determine what it will take to achieve your own financial independence – *point X* – you need to understand how the following four financial tables work (Exhibits 12.2 – 12.5).

Future Value (FV) Factor of a Sum Certain

The Future Value (FV) factor of a sum certain will determine how large a single sum will become at the end of a specified period of time, if the amount invested earns a specified interest rate (rate of return) with compounding each period. Please refer to Exhibit 12.2, "Future Value (FV) Factors of a Sum Certain," as I take you through this example. The purpose of Exhibit 12.2 is to determine the future dollars you will have based on your *investment today* over a period of time at an assumed interest rate (rate of return).

For example, if you invested $10,000 today at 7% return per year, after 20 years, you would have $38,700. The way you would determine this is by looking at Exhibit 12.2, going down the year column to 20 years, and then going across to the 7% column per year to obtain the factor of 3.870. You then take the current single sum of $10,000 and you multiply it by the future value factor of 3.870% ($10,000 × 3.870) = $38,700.

For comparison purposes, if you take all of the same assumptions but are fortunate enough to generate a 10% return on your money, you would end up with $67,270 after the same 20-year period. If you look at Exhibit 12.2, the cross section of 20 years at 10% gives you a FV factor of 6.727%. This additional 3% return on your money over a 20-year period with compounding would result in an additional $28,570 of earnings. This example highlights the importance of trying to generate the highest possible rate of return within your risk tolerance over the long run.

Exhibit 12.2   Future Value (FV) Factors of a Sum Certain[2]

The purpose of this table is to determine the future dollars you will have based on your investment today over a period of time at an assumed interest rate (rate of return).

Insert		Your Calculation
_____ %	Step 1	Insert your expected annual return on your investment.
	Step 2	Insert the amount of years of your investment.
	Step 3	Using the table, identify the correct interest column, and insert the result for the row that has the correct number of years.
$ _____	Step 4	Insert your investment amount today.
$ _____	Step 5	Multiply the factors in steps 3 and 4. This is your future dollars.

Year	1%	2%	3%	4%	5%	6%	7%
1	1.010	1.020	1.030	1.040	1.050	1.060	1.070
2	1.020	1.040	1.061	1.082	1.103	1.124	1.145
3	1.030	1.061	1.093	1.125	1.158	1.191	1.225
4	1.041	1.082	1.126	1.170	1.216	1.262	1.311
5	1.051	1.104	1.159	1.217	1.276	1.338	1.403
6	1.062	1.126	1.194	1.265	1.340	1.419	1.501
7	1.072	1.149	1.230	1.316	1.407	1.504	1.606
8	1.083	1.172	1.267	1.369	1.477	1.594	1.718
9	1.094	1.195	1.305	1.423	1.551	1.689	1.838
10	1.105	1.219	1.344	1.480	1.629	1.791	1.967
11	1.116	1.243	1.384	1.539	1.710	1.898	2.105
12	1.127	1.268	1.426	1.601	1.796	2.012	2.252
13	1.138	1.294	1.469	1.665	1.886	2.133	2.410
14	1.149	1.319	1.513	1.732	1.980	2.261	2.579
15	1.161	1.346	1.558	1.801	2.079	2.397	2.759
16	1.173	1.373	1.605	1.873	2.183	2.540	2.952
17	1.184	1.400	1.653	1.948	2.292	2.693	3.159
18	1.196	1.428	1.702	2.026	2.407	2.854	3.380
19	1.208	1.457	1.754	2.107	2.527	3.026	3.617
20	1.220	1.486	1.806	2.191	2.653	3.207	3.870
21	1.232	1.516	1.860	2.279	2.786	3.400	4.141
22	1.245	1.546	1.916	2.370	2.925	3.604	4.430
23	1.257	1.577	1.974	2.465	3.072	3.820	4.741
24	1.270	1.608	2.033	2.563	3.225	4.049	5.072
25	1.282	1.641	2.094	2.666	3.386	4.292	5.427
26	1.295	1.673	2.157	2.772	3.556	4.549	5.807
27	1.308	1.707	2.221	2.883	3.733	4.822	6.214
28	1.321	1.741	2.288	2.999	3.920	5.112	6.649
29	1.335	1.776	2.357	3.119	4.116	5.418	7.114
30	1.348	1.811	2.427	3.243	4.322	5.743	7.612
31	1.361	1.848	2.500	3.373	4.538	6.088	8.145
32	1.375	1.885	2.575	3.508	4.765	6.453	8.715
33	1.389	1.922	2.652	3.648	5.003	6.841	9.325
34	1.403	1.961	2.732	3.794	5.253	7.251	9.978
35	1.417	2.000	2.814	3.946	5.516	7.686	10.677
36	1.431	2.040	2.898	4.104	5.792	8.147	11.424
37	1.445	2.081	2.985	4.268	6.081	8.636	12.224
38	1.460	2.122	3.075	4.439	6.385	9.154	13.079
39	1.474	2.165	3.167	4.616	6.705	9.704	13.995
40	1.489	2.208	3.262	4.801	7.040	10.286	14.974
41	1.504	2.252	3.360	4.993	7.392	10.903	16.023
42	1.519	2.297	3.461	5.193	7.762	11.557	17.144
43	1.534	2.343	3.565	5.400	8.150	12.250	18.344
44	1.549	2.390	3.671	5.617	8.557	12.985	19.628
45	1.565	2.438	3.782	5.841	8.985	13.765	21.002

(Continued)

[2]See footnote 1.

Exhibit 12.2   (*Continued*)

The purpose of this table is to determine the future dollars you will have based on your investment today over a period of time at an assumed interest rate (rate of return).

Insert		Your Calculation
_____ %	Step 1	Insert your expected annual return on your investment.
	Step 2	Insert the amount of years of your investment.
	Step 3	Using the table, identify the correct interest column, and insert the result for the row that has the correct number of years.
$ _____	Step 4	Insert your investment amount today.
$ _____	Step 5	Multiply the factors in steps 3 and 4. This is your future dollars.

Year	8%	9%	10%	12%	15%	20%	25%
1	1.080	1.090	1.100	1.120	1.150	1.200	1.250
2	1.166	1.188	1.210	1.254	1.323	1.440	1.563
3	1.260	1.295	1.331	1.405	1.521	1.728	1.953
4	1.360	1.412	1.464	1.574	1.749	2.074	2.441
5	1.469	1.539	1.611	1.762	2.011	2.488	3.052
6	1.587	1.677	1.772	1.974	2.313	2.986	3.815
7	1.714	1.828	1.949	2.211	2.660	3.583	4.768
8	1.851	1.993	2.144	2.476	3.059	4.300	5.960
9	1.999	2.172	2.358	2.773	3.518	5.160	7.451
10	2.159	2.367	2.594	3.106	4.046	6.192	9.313
11	2.332	2.580	2.853	3.479	4.652	7.430	11.642
12	2.518	2.813	3.138	3.896	5.350	8.916	14.552
13	2.720	3.066	3.452	4.363	6.153	10.699	18.190
14	2.937	3.342	3.797	4.887	7.076	12.839	22.737
15	3.172	3.642	4.177	5.474	8.137	15.407	28.422
16	3.426	3.970	4.595	6.130	9.358	18.488	35.527
17	3.700	4.328	5.054	6.866	10.761	22.186	44.409
18	3.996	4.717	5.560	7.690	12.375	26.623	55.511
19	4.316	5.142	6.116	8.613	14.232	31.948	69.389
20	4.661	5.604	6.727	9.646	16.367	38.338	86.736
21	5.034	6.109	7.400	10.804	18.822	46.005	108.420
22	5.437	6.659	8.140	12.100	21.645	55.206	135.525
23	5.871	7.258	8.954	13.552	24.891	66.247	169.407
24	6.341	7.911	9.850	15.179	28.625	79.497	211.758
25	6.848	8.623	10.835	17.000	32.919	95.396	264.698
26	7.396	9.399	11.918	19.040	37.857	114.475	330.872
27	7.988	10.245	13.110	21.325	43.535	137.371	413.590
28	8.627	11.167	14.421	23.884	50.066	164.845	516.988
29	9.317	12.172	15.863	26.750	57.575	197.814	646.235
30	10.063	13.268	17.449	29.960	66.212	237.376	807.794
31	10.868	14.462	19.194	33.555	76.144	284.852	1,009.742
32	11.737	15.763	21.114	37.582	87.565	341.822	1,262.177
33	12.676	17.182	23.225	42.092	100.700	410.186	1,577.722
34	13.690	18.728	25.548	47.143	115.805	492.224	1,972.152
35	14.785	20.414	28.102	52.800	133.176	590.668	2,465.190
36	15.968	22.251	30.913	59.136	153.152	708.802	3,081.488
37	17.246	24.254	34.004	66.232	176.125	850.562	3,851.860
38	18.625	26.437	37.404	74.180	202.543	1,020.675	4,814.825
39	20.115	28.816	41.145	83.081	232.925	1,224.810	6,018.531
40	21.725	31.409	45.259	93.051	267.864	1,469.772	7,523.164
41	23.462	34.236	49.785	104.217	308.043	1,763.726	9,403.955
42	25.339	37.318	54.764	116.723	354.250	2,116.471	11,754.944
43	27.367	40.676	60.240	130.730	407.387	2,539.765	14,693.679
44	29.556	44.337	66.264	146.418	468.495	3,047.718	18,367.099
45	31.920	48.327	72.890	163.988	538.769	3,657.262	22,958.874

Future Value (FV) of an Annuity Factor

The future value (FV) of an annuity factor will determine the future value of a stream of equal payments made at regular intervals over a specified period of time, if the amount invested earns a specified interest rate (rate of return) with compounding each period. Please refer to Exhibit 12.3, "Future Value (FV) of an Annuity Factor," as I take you through this example. The purpose of Exhibit 12.3 is to determine the future dollars you will have based on your *annual investment* over a period of time at an assumed interest rate (rate of return).

For example, if you invested $5,000 annually at 5% return per year, after 25 years, you would have $238,635. The way you would determine this is by looking at Exhibit 12.3, going down the year column to 25 years, and then going across to the 5% column per year to obtain the factor of 47.727. You then take the annual investment of $5,000 and you multiply it by the FV annuity factor of 47.727% ($5,000 × 47.727) = $238,635.

For comparison purposes, if you take all of the same assumptions but are fortunate enough to generate a 10% return on your money, you would end up with $491,735 after the same 25-year period. Look at page 2 of Exhibit 12.3; the cross section of 25 years at 10% gives you an FV annuity factor of 98.347%. This additional 5% return on your money over a 25-year period with compounding would result in an additional $253,100 of earnings. This example highlights the importance of trying to generate the highest possible rate of return within your risk tolerance over the long run.

Present Value (PV) Factor of a Sum Certain

The present value (PV) factor of a Sum Certain will determine the current value of a single sum to be paid at a specified date in the future, if the amount invested earns a specified interest rate (rate of return) with compounding each period. Please refer to Exhibit 12.4, "Present Value (PV) Factor of a Sum Certain," as I take you through this example. The purpose of this table is to determine the *present investment* needed for a future amount of dollars over a period of time at an assumed interest rate (rate of return).

Exhibit 12.3   Future Value (FV) of an Annuity Factor[3]

The purpose of this table is to determine the future dollars you will have based on your annual investment over a period of time at an assumed interest rate (rate of return).

Insert		Your Calculation
___ %	Step 1	Insert your expected annual return on your investment.
___ Years	Step 2	Insert the amount of years of your investment.
	Step 3	Using the table, identify the correct interest column, and insert the result for the row that has the correct number of years.
$ ___	Step 4	Insert your annual investment amount.
$ ___	Step 5	Multiply the factors in steps 3 and 4. This is your future dollars.

Year	1%	2%	3%	4%	5%	6%	7%
1	1.000	1.000	1.000	1.000	1.000	1.000	1.000
2	2.010	2.020	2.030	2.040	2.050	2.060	2.070
3	3.030	3.060	3.091	3.122	3.153	3.184	3.215
4	4.060	4.122	4.184	4.246	4.310	4.375	4.440
5	5.101	5.204	5.309	5.416	5.526	5.637	5.751
6	6.152	6.308	6.468	6.633	6.802	6.975	7.153
7	7.214	7.434	7.662	7.898	8.142	8.394	8.654
8	8.286	8.583	8.892	9.214	9.549	9.897	10.260
9	9.369	9.755	10.159	10.583	11.027	11.491	11.978
10	10.462	10.950	11.464	12.006	12.578	13.181	13.816
11	11.567	12.169	12.808	13.486	14.207	14.972	15.784
12	12.683	13.412	14.192	15.026	15.917	16.870	17.888
13	13.809	14.680	15.618	16.627	17.713	18.882	20.141
14	14.947	15.974	17.086	18.292	19.599	21.015	22.550
15	16.097	17.293	18.599	20.024	21.579	23.276	25.129
16	17.258	18.639	20.157	21.825	23.657	25.673	27.888
17	18.430	20.012	21.762	23.698	25.840	28.213	30.840
18	19.615	21.412	23.414	25.645	28.132	30.906	33.999
19	20.811	22.841	25.117	27.671	30.539	33.760	37.379
20	22.019	24.297	26.870	29.778	33.066	36.786	40.995
21	23.239	25.783	28.676	31.969	35.719	39.993	44.865
22	24.472	27.299	30.537	34.248	38.505	43.392	49.006
23	25.716	28.845	32.453	36.618	41.430	46.996	53.436
24	26.973	30.422	34.426	39.083	44.502	50.816	58.177
25	28.243	32.030	36.459	41.646	47.727	54.865	63.249
26	29.526	33.671	38.553	44.312	51.113	59.156	68.676
27	30.821	35.344	40.710	47.084	54.669	63.706	74.484
28	32.129	37.051	42.931	49.968	58.403	68.528	80.698
29	33.450	38.792	45.219	52.966	62.323	73.640	87.347
30	34.785	40.568	47.575	56.085	66.439	79.058	94.461
31	36.133	42.379	50.003	59.328	70.761	84.802	102.073
32	37.494	44.227	52.503	62.701	75.299	90.890	110.218
33	38.869	46.112	55.078	66.210	80.064	97.343	118.933
34	40.258	48.034	57.730	69.858	85.067	104.184	128.259
35	41.660	49.994	60.462	73.652	90.320	111.435	138.237
36	43.077	51.994	63.276	77.598	95.836	119.121	148.913
37	44.508	54.034	66.174	81.702	101.628	127.268	160.337
38	45.953	56.115	69.159	85.970	107.710	135.904	172.561
39	47.412	58.237	72.234	90.409	114.095	145.058	185.640
40	48.886	60.402	75.401	95.026	120.800	154.762	199.635
41	50.375	62.610	78.663	99.827	127.840	165.048	214.610
42	51.879	64.862	82.023	104.820	135.232	175.951	230.632
43	53.398	67.159	85.484	110.012	142.993	187.508	247.776
44	54.932	69.503	89.048	115.413	151.143	199.758	266.121
45	56.481	71.893	92.720	121.029	159.700	212.744	285.749

[3]See footnote 1.

Exhibit 12.3 (*Continued*)

The purpose of this table is to determine the future dollars you will have based on your annual investment over a period of time at an assumed interest rate (rate of return).

Insert		Your Calculation
	% Step 1	Insert your expected annual return on your investment.
	Years Step 2	Insert the amount of years of your investment.
	Step 3	Using the table, identify the correct interest column, and insert the result for the row that has the correct number of years.
$	Step 4	Insert your annual investment amount.
$	Step 5	Multiply the factors in steps 3 and 4. This is your future dollars.

Year	8%	9%	10%	12%	15%	20%	25%
1	1.000	1.000	1.000	1.000	1.000	1.000	1.000
2	2.080	2.090	2.100	2.120	2.150	2.200	2.250
3	3.246	3.278	3.310	3.374	3.473	3.640	3.813
4	4.506	4.573	4.641	4.779	4.993	5.368	5.766
5	5.867	5.985	6.105	6.353	6.742	7.442	8.207
6	7.336	7.523	7.716	8.115	8.754	9.930	11.259
7	8.923	9.200	9.487	10.089	11.067	12.916	15.073
8	10.637	11.028	11.436	12.300	13.727	16.499	19.842
9	12.488	13.021	13.579	14.776	16.786	20.799	25.802
10	14.487	15.193	15.937	17.549	20.304	25.959	33.253
11	16.645	17.560	18.531	20.655	24.349	32.150	42.566
12	18.977	20.141	21.384	24.133	29.002	39.581	54.208
13	21.495	22.953	24.523	28.029	34.352	48.497	68.760
14	24.215	26.019	27.975	32.393	40.505	59.196	86.949
15	27.152	29.361	31.772	37.280	47.580	72.035	109.687
16	30.324	33.003	35.950	42.753	55.717	87.442	138.109
17	33.750	36.974	40.545	48.884	65.075	105.931	173.636
18	37.450	41.301	45.599	55.750	75.836	128.117	218.045
19	41.446	46.018	51.159	63.440	88.212	154.740	273.556
20	45.762	51.160	57.275	72.052	102.444	186.688	342.945
21	50.423	56.765	64.002	81.699	118.810	225.026	429.681
22	55.457	62.873	71.403	92.503	137.632	271.031	538.101
23	60.893	69.532	79.543	104.603	159.276	326.237	673.626
24	66.765	76.790	88.497	118.155	184.168	392.484	843.033
25	73.106	84.701	98.347	133.334	212.793	471.981	1,054.791
26	79.954	93.324	109.182	150.334	245.712	567.377	1,319.489
27	87.351	102.723	121.100	169.374	283.569	681.853	1,650.361
28	95.339	112.968	134.210	190.699	327.104	819.223	2,063.952
29	103.966	124.135	148.631	214.583	377.170	984.068	2,580.939
30	113.283	136.308	164.494	241.333	434.745	1,181.882	3,227.174
31	123.346	149.575	181.943	271.293	500.957	1,419.258	4,034.968
32	134.214	164.037	201.138	304.848	577.100	1,704.109	5,044.710
33	145.951	179.800	222.252	342.429	664.666	2,045.931	6,306.887
34	158.627	196.982	245.477	384.521	765.365	2,456.118	7,884.609
35	172.317	215.711	271.024	431.663	881.170	2,948.341	9,856.761
36	187.102	236.125	299.127	484.463	1,014.346	3,539.009	12,321.952
37	203.070	258.376	330.039	543.599	1,167.498	4,247.811	15,403.440
38	220.316	282.630	364.043	609.831	1,343.622	5,098.373	19,255.299
39	238.941	309.066	401.448	684.010	1,546.165	6,119.048	24,070.124
40	259.057	337.882	442.593	767.091	1,779.090	7,343.858	30,088.655
41	280.781	369.292	487.852	860.142	2,046.954	8,813.629	37,611.819
42	304.244	403.528	537.637	964.359	2,354.997	10,577.355	47,015.774
43	329.583	440.846	592.401	1,081.083	2,709.246	12,693.826	58,770.718
44	356.950	481.522	652.641	1,211.813	3,116.633	15,233.592	73,464.397
45	386.506	525.859	718.905	1,358.230	3,585.128	18,281.310	91,831.496

Exhibit 12.4   Present Value (PV) Factor of a Sum Certain[4]

The purpose of this table is to determine the present investment needed for a future amount of dollars over a period of time at an assumed interest rate (rate of return).

Insert		Your Calculation
%	Step 1	Insert your expected annual return on your investment.
Years	Step 2	Insert the amount of years of your investment.
	Step 3	Using the table, identify the correct interest column, and insert the result for the row that has the correct number of years.
$	Step 4	Insert your future investment amount.
$	Step 5	Multiply the factors in steps 3 and 4. This is your present value.

Year	1%	2%	3%	4%	5%	6%	7%
1	0.99010	0.98039	0.97087	0.96154	0.95238	0.94340	0.93458
2	0.98030	0.96117	0.94260	0.92456	0.90703	0.89000	0.87344
3	0.97059	0.94232	0.91514	0.88900	0.86384	0.83962	0.81630
4	0.96098	0.92385	0.88849	0.85480	0.82270	0.79209	0.76290
5	0.95147	0.90573	0.86261	0.82193	0.78353	0.74726	0.71299
6	0.94205	0.88797	0.83748	0.79031	0.74622	0.70496	0.66634
7	0.93272	0.87056	0.81309	0.75992	0.71068	0.66506	0.62275
8	0.92348	0.85349	0.78941	0.73069	0.67684	0.62741	0.58201
9	0.91434	0.83676	0.76642	0.70259	0.64461	0.59190	0.54393
10	0.90529	0.82035	0.74409	0.67556	0.61391	0.55839	0.50835
11	0.89632	0.80426	0.72242	0.64958	0.58468	0.52679	0.47509
12	0.88745	0.78849	0.70138	0.62460	0.55684	0.49697	0.44401
13	0.87866	0.77303	0.68095	0.60057	0.53032	0.46884	0.41496
14	0.86996	0.75788	0.66112	0.57748	0.50507	0.44230	0.38782
15	0.86135	0.74301	0.64186	0.55526	0.48102	0.41727	0.36245
16	0.85282	0.72845	0.62317	0.53391	0.45811	0.39365	0.33873
17	0.84438	0.71416	0.60502	0.51337	0.43630	0.37136	0.31657
18	0.83602	0.70016	0.58739	0.49363	0.41552	0.35034	0.29586
19	0.82774	0.68643	0.57029	0.47464	0.39573	0.33051	0.27651
20	0.81954	0.67297	0.55368	0.45639	0.37689	0.31180	0.25842
21	0.81143	0.65978	0.53755	0.43883	0.35894	0.29416	0.24151
22	0.80340	0.64684	0.52189	0.42196	0.34185	0.27751	0.22571
23	0.79544	0.63416	0.50669	0.40573	0.32557	0.26180	0.21095
24	0.78757	0.62172	0.49193	0.39012	0.31007	0.24698	0.19715
25	0.77977	0.60953	0.47761	0.37512	0.29530	0.23300	0.18425
26	0.77205	0.59758	0.46369	0.36069	0.28124	0.21981	0.17220
27	0.76440	0.58586	0.45019	0.34682	0.26785	0.20737	0.16093
28	0.75684	0.57437	0.43708	0.33348	0.25509	0.19563	0.15040
29	0.74934	0.56311	0.42435	0.32065	0.24295	0.18456	0.14056
30	0.74192	0.55207	0.41199	0.30832	0.23138	0.17411	0.13137
31	0.73458	0.54125	0.39999	0.29646	0.22036	0.16425	0.12277
32	0.72730	0.53063	0.38834	0.28506	0.20987	0.15496	0.11474
33	0.72010	0.52023	0.37703	0.27409	0.19987	0.14619	0.10723
34	0.71297	0.51003	0.36604	0.26355	0.19035	0.13791	0.10022
35	0.70591	0.50003	0.35538	0.25342	0.18129	0.13011	0.09366
36	0.69892	0.49022	0.34503	0.24367	0.17266	0.12274	0.08754
37	0.69200	0.48061	0.33498	0.23430	0.16444	0.11579	0.08181
38	0.68515	0.47119	0.32523	0.22529	0.15661	0.10924	0.07646
39	0.67837	0.46195	0.31575	0.21662	0.14915	0.10306	0.07146
40	0.67165	0.45289	0.30656	0.20829	0.14205	0.09722	0.06678
41	0.66500	0.44401	0.29763	0.20028	0.13528	0.09172	0.06241
42	0.65842	0.43530	0.28896	0.19257	0.12884	0.08653	0.05833
43	0.65190	0.42677	0.28054	0.18517	0.12270	0.08163	0.05451
44	0.64545	0.41840	0.27237	0.17805	0.11686	0.07701	0.05095
45	0.63905	0.41020	0.26444	0.17120	0.11130	0.07265	0.04761

[4]See footnote 1.

Exhibit 12.4   (*Continued*)

The purpose of this table is to determine the present investment needed for a future amount of dollars over a period of time at an assumed interest rate (rate of return).

Insert		Your Calculation
	% Step 1	Insert your expected annual return on your investment.
	Years Step 2	Insert the amount of years of your investment.
	Step 3	Using the table, identify the correct interest column, and insert the result for the row that has the correct number of years.
$	Step 4	Insert your future investment amount.
$	Step 5	Multiply the factors in steps 3 and 4. This is your present value.

Year	8%	9%	10%	12%	15%	20%	25%
1	0.92593	0.91743	0.90909	0.89286	0.86957	0.83333	0.80000
2	0.85734	0.84168	0.82645	0.79719	0.75614	0.69444	0.64000
3	0.79383	0.77218	0.75131	0.71178	0.65752	0.57870	0.51200
4	0.73503	0.70843	0.68301	0.63552	0.57175	0.48225	0.40960
5	0.68058	0.64993	0.62092	0.56743	0.49718	0.40188	0.32768
6	0.63017	0.59627	0.56447	0.50663	0.43233	0.33490	0.26214
7	0.58349	0.54703	0.51316	0.45235	0.37594	0.27908	0.20972
8	0.54027	0.50187	0.46651	0.40388	0.32690	0.23257	0.16777
9	0.50025	0.46043	0.42410	0.36061	0.28426	0.19381	0.13422
10	0.46319	0.42241	0.38554	0.32197	0.24718	0.16151	0.10737
11	0.42888	0.38753	0.35049	0.28748	0.21494	0.13459	0.08590
12	0.39711	0.35553	0.31863	0.25668	0.18691	0.11216	0.06872
13	0.36770	0.32618	0.28966	0.22917	0.16253	0.09346	0.05498
14	0.34046	0.29925	0.26333	0.20462	0.14133	0.07789	0.04398
15	0.31524	0.27454	0.23939	0.18270	0.12289	0.06491	0.03518
16	0.29189	0.25187	0.21763	0.16312	0.10686	0.05409	0.02815
17	0.27027	0.23107	0.19784	0.14564	0.09293	0.04507	0.02252
18	0.25025	0.21199	0.17986	0.13004	0.08081	0.03756	0.01801
19	0.23171	0.19449	0.16351	0.11611	0.07027	0.03130	0.01441
20	0.21455	0.17843	0.14864	0.10367	0.06110	0.02608	0.01153
21	0.19866	0.16370	0.13513	0.09256	0.05313	0.02174	0.00922
22	0.18394	0.15018	0.12285	0.08264	0.04620	0.01811	0.00738
23	0.17032	0.13778	0.11168	0.07379	0.04017	0.01509	0.00590
24	0.15770	0.12640	0.10153	0.06588	0.03493	0.01258	0.00472
25	0.14602	0.11597	0.09230	0.05882	0.03038	0.01048	0.00378
26	0.13520	0.10639	0.08391	0.05252	0.02642	0.00874	0.00302
27	0.12519	0.09761	0.07628	0.04689	0.02297	0.00728	0.00242
28	0.11591	0.08955	0.06934	0.04187	0.01997	0.00607	0.00193
29	0.10733	0.08215	0.06304	0.03738	0.01737	0.00506	0.00155
30	0.09938	0.07537	0.05731	0.03338	0.01510	0.00421	0.00124
31	0.09202	0.06915	0.05210	0.02980	0.01313	0.00351	0.00099
32	0.08520	0.06344	0.04736	0.02661	0.01142	0.00293	0.00079
33	0.07889	0.05820	0.04306	0.02376	0.00993	0.00244	0.00063
34	0.07305	0.05339	0.03914	0.02121	0.00864	0.00203	0.00051
35	0.06763	0.04899	0.03558	0.01894	0.00751	0.00169	0.00041
36	0.06262	0.04494	0.03235	0.01691	0.00653	0.00141	0.00032
37	0.05799	0.04123	0.02941	0.01510	0.00568	0.00118	0.00026
38	0.05369	0.03783	0.02673	0.01348	0.00494	0.00098	0.00021
39	0.04971	0.03470	0.02430	0.01204	0.00429	0.00082	0.00017
40	0.04603	0.03184	0.02209	0.01075	0.00373	0.00068	0.00013
41	0.04262	0.02921	0.02009	0.00960	0.00325	0.00057	0.00011
42	0.03946	0.02680	0.01826	0.00857	0.00282	0.00047	0.00009
43	0.03654	0.02458	0.01660	0.00765	0.00245	0.00039	0.00007
44	0.03383	0.02255	0.01509	0.00683	0.00213	0.00033	0.00005
45	0.03133	0.02069	0.01372	0.00610	0.00186	0.00027	0.00004

For example, if you wanted $100,000 in 20 years, how much would you need to invest today at a 5% interest rate (rate of return) per year? The way you would determine this is by looking at Exhibit 12.4, going down the year column to 20 years, and then going across to the 5% column per year to obtain the factor of 0.37689. You then take the future amount of dollars needed of $100,000 and multiply it by the PV factor of 0.37689% ($100,000 × 0.37689) = $37,689. Therefore, if you would like to have $100,000 in 20 years and expect to earn a 5% return on your money, you would need to invest $37,689 today.

We can verify and cross-check this calculation by using the FV factors from Exhibit 12.2. If you now look back to Exhibit 12.2, year 20, rate of return 5%, you will come up with an FV factor of 2.653%. If you take the $37,689 and multiply this FV factor of 2.653, you come up with the same $100,000 with a small rounding difference. This not only verifies and confirms these calculations, but also proves that the PV and FV factors have an inverse relationship to one another.

It is important to note that the PV factor is used to find the PV of a future payment by discounting them at some specific rate, and this factor is always less than one, assuming positive interest rates. This is in contrast to the FV factor, which is used to find the FV of a present amount and is always greater than one.

Present Value (PV) of an Annuity Factor

The present value (PV) of an annuity factor will determine the current value of a stream of equal payments made at regular intervals over a specified period of time, if the amount invested earns a specified interest rate (rate of return) with compounding each period. Please refer to Exhibit 12.5, "Present Value (PV) on an Annuity Factor," as I take you through this example. The purpose of this table is to determine the present investment needed to have *equal future annual cash receipts* over a period of time at an assumed interest rate (rate of return).

For example, if you wanted to receive $25,000 annually for 25 years, how much would you need to invest today with a 4% interest rate (rate of return)? The way you would determine this is by looking at Exhibit 12.5, going down the year column to 25 years, and then going across to the 4% column per year to obtain the factor of 15.62208. You then take the amount you want to receive annually $25,000 and you multiply it by the PV annuity factor of 15.62208% ($25,000 × 15.62208) = $390,552. Therefore, if you would like to

Exhibit 12.5   Present Value (PV) of an Annuity Factor[5]

The purpose of this table is to determine the present investment needed to have equal future annual cash receipts over a period of time at an assumed interest rate (rate of return).

Insert		Your Calculation	
	% Step 1	Insert your expected annual return on your investment.	
	Years Step 2	Insert the amount of years of your investment.	
	Step 3	Using the table, identify the correct interest column, and insert the result for the row that has the correct number of years.	
$	Step 4	Insert your annual cash receipts you want to receive.	
$	Step 5	Multiply the factors in steps 3 and 4. You need to invest this amount.	

Year	1%	2%	3%	4%	5%	6%	7%
1	0.99010	0.98039	0.97087	0.96154	0.95238	0.94340	0.93458
2	1.97040	1.94156	1.91347	1.88609	1.85941	1.83339	1.80802
3	2.94099	2.88388	2.82861	2.77509	2.72325	2.67301	2.62432
4	3.90197	3.80773	3.71710	3.62990	3.54595	3.46511	3.38721
5	4.85343	4.71346	4.57971	4.45182	4.32948	4.21236	4.10020
6	5.79548	5.60143	5.41719	5.24214	5.07569	4.91732	4.76654
7	6.72819	6.47199	6.23028	6.00205	5.78637	5.58238	5.38929
8	7.65168	7.32548	7.01969	6.73274	6.46321	6.20979	5.97130
9	8.56602	8.16224	7.78611	7.43533	7.10782	6.80169	6.51523
10	9.47130	8.98259	8.53020	8.11090	7.72173	7.36009	7.02358
11	10.36763	9.78685	9.25262	8.76048	8.30641	7.88687	7.49867
12	11.25508	10.57534	9.95400	9.38507	8.86325	8.38384	7.94269
13	12.13374	11.34837	10.63496	9.98565	9.39357	8.85268	8.35765
14	13.00370	12.10625	11.29607	10.56312	9.89864	9.29498	8.74547
15	13.86505	12.84926	11.93794	11.11839	10.37966	9.71225	9.10791
16	14.71787	13.57771	12.56110	11.65230	10.83777	10.10590	9.44665
17	15.56225	14.29187	13.16612	12.16567	11.27407	10.47726	9.76322
18	16.39827	14.99203	13.75351	12.65930	11.68959	10.82760	10.05909
19	17.22601	15.67846	14.32380	13.13394	12.08532	11.15812	10.33560
20	18.04555	16.35143	14.87747	13.59033	12.46221	11.46992	10.59401
21	18.85698	17.01121	15.41502	14.02916	12.82115	11.76408	10.83553
22	19.66038	17.65805	15.93692	14.45112	13.16300	12.04158	11.06124
23	20.45582	18.29220	16.44361	14.85684	13.48857	12.30338	11.27219
24	21.24339	18.91393	16.93554	15.24696	13.79864	12.55036	11.46933
25	22.02316	19.52346	17.41315	15.62208	14.09394	12.78336	11.65358
26	22.79520	20.12104	17.87684	15.98277	14.37519	13.00317	11.82578
27	23.55961	20.70690	18.32703	16.32959	14.64303	13.21053	11.98671
28	24.31644	21.28127	18.76411	16.66306	14.89813	13.40616	12.13711
29	25.06579	21.84438	19.18845	16.98371	15.14107	13.59072	12.27767
30	25.80771	22.39646	19.60044	17.29203	15.37245	13.76483	12.40904
31	26.54229	22.93770	20.00043	17.58849	15.59281	13.92909	12.53181
32	27.26959	23.46833	20.38877	17.87355	15.80268	14.08404	12.64656
33	27.98969	23.98856	20.76579	18.14765	16.00255	14.23023	12.75379
34	28.70267	24.49859	21.13184	18.41120	16.19290	14.36814	12.85401
35	29.40858	24.99862	21.48722	18.66461	16.37419	14.49825	12.94767
36	30.10751	25.48884	21.83225	18.90828	16.54685	14.62099	13.03521
37	30.79951	25.96945	22.16724	19.14258	16.71129	14.73678	13.11702
38	31.48466	26.44064	22.49246	19.36786	16.86789	14.84602	13.19347
39	32.16303	26.90259	22.80822	19.58448	17.01704	14.94907	13.26493
40	32.83469	27.35548	23.11477	19.79277	17.15909	15.04630	13.33171
41	33.49969	27.79949	23.41240	19.99305	17.29437	15.13802	13.39412
42	34.15811	28.23479	23.70136	20.18563	17.42321	15.22454	13.45245
43	34.81001	28.66156	23.98190	20.37079	17.54591	15.30617	13.50696
44	35.45545	29.07996	24.25427	20.54884	17.66277	15.38318	13.55791
45	36.09451	29.49016	24.51871	20.72004	17.77407	15.45583	13.60552

(Continued)

[5]See footnote 1.

Exhibit 12.5   (*Continued*)

The purpose of this table is to determine the present investment needed to have equal future annual cash receipts over a period of time at an assumed interest rate (rate of return).

Insert		Your Calculation
%	Step 1	Insert your expected annual return on your investment.
Years	Step 2	Insert the amount of years of your investment.
	Step 3	Using the table, identify the correct interest column, and insert the result for the row that has the correct number of years.
$	Step 4	Insert your annual cash receipts you want to receive.
$	Step 5	Multiply the factors in steps 3 and 4. You need to invest this amount.

Year	8%	9%	10%	12%	15%	20%	25%
1	0.92593	0.91743	0.90909	0.89286	0.86957	0.83333	0.80000
2	1.78326	1.75911	1.73554	1.69005	1.62571	1.52778	1.44000
3	2.57710	2.53129	2.48685	2.40183	2.28323	2.10648	1.95200
4	3.31213	3.23972	3.16987	3.03735	2.85498	2.58873	2.36160
5	3.99271	3.88965	3.79079	3.60478	3.35216	2.99061	2.68928
6	4.62288	4.48592	4.35526	4.11141	3.78448	3.32551	2.95142
7	5.20637	5.03295	4.86842	4.56376	4.16042	3.60459	3.16114
8	5.74664	5.53482	5.33493	4.96764	4.48732	3.83716	3.32891
9	6.24689	5.99525	5.75902	5.32825	4.77158	4.03097	3.46313
10	6.71008	6.41766	6.14457	5.65022	5.01877	4.19247	3.57050
11	7.13896	6.80519	6.49506	5.93770	5.23371	4.32706	3.65640
12	7.53608	7.16073	6.81369	6.19437	5.42062	4.43922	3.72512
13	7.90378	7.48690	7.10336	6.42355	5.58315	4.53268	3.78010
14	8.24424	7.78615	7.36669	6.62817	5.72448	4.61057	3.82408
15	8.55948	8.06069	7.60608	6.81086	5.84737	4.67547	3.85926
16	8.85137	8.31256	7.82371	6.97399	5.95423	4.72956	3.88741
17	9.12164	8.54363	8.02155	7.11963	6.04716	4.77463	3.90993
18	9.37189	8.75563	8.20141	7.24967	6.12797	4.81219	3.92794
19	9.60360	8.95011	8.36492	7.36578	6.19823	4.84350	3.94235
20	9.81815	9.12855	8.51356	7.46944	6.25933	4.86958	3.95388
21	10.01680	9.29224	8.64869	7.56200	6.31246	4.89132	3.96311
22	10.20074	9.44243	8.77154	7.64465	6.35866	4.90943	3.97049
23	10.37106	9.58021	8.88322	7.71843	6.39884	4.92453	3.97639
24	10.52876	9.70661	8.98474	7.78432	6.43377	4.93710	3.98111
25	10.67478	9.82258	9.07704	7.84314	6.46415	4.94759	3.98489
26	10.80998	9.92897	9.16095	7.89566	6.49056	4.95632	3.98791
27	10.93516	10.02658	9.23722	7.94255	6.51353	4.96360	3.99033
28	11.05108	10.11613	9.30657	7.98442	6.53351	4.96967	3.99226
29	11.15841	10.19828	9.36961	8.02181	6.55088	4.97472	3.99381
30	11.25778	10.27365	9.42691	8.05518	6.56598	4.97894	3.99505
31	11.34980	10.34280	9.47901	8.08499	6.57911	4.98245	3.99604
32	11.43500	10.40624	9.52638	8.11159	6.59053	4.98537	3.99683
33	11.51389	10.46444	9.56943	8.13535	6.60046	4.98781	3.99746
34	11.58693	10.51784	9.60857	8.15656	6.60910	4.98984	3.99797
35	11.65457	10.56682	9.64416	8.17550	6.61661	4.99154	3.99838
36	11.71719	10.61176	9.67651	8.19241	6.62314	4.99295	3.99870
37	11.77518	10.65299	9.70592	8.20751	6.62881	4.99412	3.99896
38	11.82887	10.69082	9.73265	8.22099	6.63375	4.99510	3.99917
39	11.87858	10.72552	9.75696	8.23303	6.63805	4.99592	3.99934
40	11.92461	10.75736	9.77905	8.24378	6.64178	4.99660	3.99947
41	11.96723	10.78657	9.79914	8.25337	6.64502	4.99717	3.99957
42	12.00670	10.81337	9.81740	8.26194	6.64785	4.99764	3.99966
43	12.04324	10.83795	9.83400	8.26959	6.65030	4.99803	3.99973
44	12.07707	10.86051	9.84909	8.27642	6.65244	4.99836	3.99978
45	12.10840	10.88120	9.86281	8.28252	6.65429	4.99863	3.99983

receive $25,000 per year over the next 25 years and expect to earn a 4% return on your money, you would need to have $390,552 today.

For comparison purposes, if you take all of the same assumptions but are fortunate enough to generate a 10% return on your money, you would only need $226,926. If you look at page 2 of Exhibit 12.5, the cross section of 25 years at 10% gives you a PV annuity factor of 9.07704%. This additional 6% return on your money over a 25-year period with compounding would allow you to receive the same $25,000 annual annuity payment, with an investment of $226,926. This means you would be able to invest $163,626 ($390,552 less $226,926) less today and still manage to generate the same annual annuity payment. This example highlights the importance of trying to generate the highest possible rate of return within your risk tolerance over the long run.

Summing Up

Having a solid understanding of the tables in this chapter is essential to calculating and budgeting your way to financial independence. With the time value of money and the power of compounding, you can map out your own formula to financial success. These tables will provide you with the answers to the following essential questions:

1. How much will my current investment account be worth (see Exhibit 12.2) based on an assumed rate of return at a particular point in time (your *point X*)?
2. If I invest a fixed amount annually, how much will it be worth (see Exhibit 12.3) based on an assumed rate of return at a particular point in time (your *point X*)?
3. How much will I need to invest today (see Exhibit 12.4) based on an assumed rate of return so that I can have a certain amount of dollars at a future date (your *point X*)?
4. How much will I need to accumulate (see Exhibit 12.5) in my investment account based on an assumed rate of return so that I can receive an annual annuity payment starting at a particular point in time (*point X*) for a fixed number of years?

I recommend you reread this section until you have a full understanding of how these numbers work. Also use a number of "what-if" scenarios and test these tables to answer these questions for your particular facts and circumstances. These tables and calculations are an essential tool in Chapter 8, "Planning for Retirement," and, of course, in planning and determining your very own financial independence – *point X.*

Appendix A

Selecting a Trusted Advisor

Perhaps one of the most important decisions you will need to make in your pursuit of financial independence is the selection of a trusted advisor. This trusted advisor will be your life coach, who will be there for you during good times and bad times and whose primary goal will be to help you achieve your long-term financial objectives. This trusted advisor should be a financial planner who can analyze your financial status and assist you in setting up and implementing a financial program to achieve your ultimate goal of financial independence. Developing a close relationship is critical to your overall success, because your advisor should understand you and have a clear picture of your financial goals and dreams. This trusted advisor and his or her team must be able to provide you with comprehensive wealth management services that include financial planning, tax preparation and planning, investment advising, risk management, education planning, retirement planning, and estate planning services.

The best place to start is by asking your friends and family if they can recommend a trusted advisor with whom they have worked well. Before meeting with financial planners, you should do some research about their backgrounds, including their education and other relevant credentials. A good place to start would be visiting their websites and the licensing board website for whatever credentials they hold.

You should meet and interview a few financial planners who can meet your needs. When meeting with them, consider the following 10 questions:

1. Do you have confidence in the person who referred you to this advisor?
2. What education and credentials does this advisor hold to make him or her qualified to advise you? (Read through

the qualifications of trusted advisors listed below, and decide what is most important to you.)

3. What is the compensation model for the advice and service: fee-based, hourly, or commission? (Fee-based is a percentage of your money under management, hourly is based on time charges, and commission is transaction based.)

4. What are the financial advisor's areas of expertise, and does this line up well with your needs? (Wealth management issues go hand-in-hand with the areas of expertise.)

5. What standard of care will this advisor be held to: fiduciary or a suitability standard? (These terms are described in the next section.)

6. What is the extent of services that will be provided: is it transactional or is it truly a trusted advisor relationship? (*Transactional* means compensation is based on commissions.)

7. Is the financial decision-making customized to you, or does the advisor take a one-size-fits-all approach? One-size-fits-all is not appropriate. An 18-year-old person's goals and risk tolerance are much different from an 80-year-old retiree's.

8. Does the financial advisor provide tax advisory services such as tax planning and preparation that are integrated into your overall financial planning?

9. What is the organizational structure of the advisor's firm: will you be dealing directly with the same advisor or a junior member of the team?

10. What is the financial advisor's philosophy and approach to handling risk? Does this advisor make you comfortable?

There are more than 100 designations, or credentials, in the financial service industry, with many more being created each year. It is very important to understand the difference between these designations so that you can narrow down your search to those who are the most qualified and suitable to meet your needs. In this appendix, I provide you with a description of the designations that, in my opinion, are most respected and recognized in the financial industry. I have subdivided these into the following categories: financial planners, tax advisors, investment advisors, insurance advisors, and attorneys.

The Difference Between Suitability and Fiduciary Standards

The *suitability standard* requires a client to receive recommendations that are suitable, or appropriate, to the individual's particular circumstances. Under the suitability standard, financial professionals are not required to put the client's best interests first. Financial professionals are also not obligated to disclose conflicts of interest.

This standard is less rigorous than the *fiduciary standard*, which requires financial professionals to act in the best interests of their clients. They are required to disclose conflicts of interest. The fiduciary standard also requires that financial professionals do not maximize their own compensation ahead of their clients' best interests.

The fiduciary standard only applies to certain financial professionals and industries. There is an ongoing movement for more financial professionals to be required to be subject to this higher standard. A new Department of Labor law took effect on June 9, 2017, which increased the number of financial advisors subject to a fiduciary standard of care. Where this rule falls short is that it does not require financial advisors to provide the fiduciary level of care on all investments and advice, but, in fact, it only pertains to retirement accounts. When evaluating who you should rely on to guide you on your life journey to financial independence, selecting the proper, trusted advisor is critically important. When evaluating your choices of advisors, you should ask to what standard they are being held.

Financial Planners

The title *financial planner* frequently refers to a financial advisor who develops and implements a comprehensive wealth-management plan based on your needs analysis. This includes your long-term financial goals, together with issues pertaining to investments, estate planning, tax planning, risk management, education planning, and debt management. Many financial service providers refer to themselves as *financial planners*, but quite often, they do not consider a client's overall financial situation. A true financial planner should address all of these issues because they are interrelated, and quite often, how you deal with one will have a direct effect on the others. When choosing a financial planner, make sure you are receiving comprehensive service and not simply being sold on one particular product or service.

Certified Financial Planner™ (CFP®)

Certified Financial Planner™ (CFP®) is perhaps the most widely recognized credential in the financial planning industry. These advisors must pass a comprehensive financial planning exam and the rigorous certification requirements that are administered by the CFP board. Upon passing this painstaking two-day exam, prospective CFP® candidates must also complete at least three years of professional experience and earn a bachelor's degree in order to obtain the CFP® designation. The academic requirements for certification include courses covering insurance, estate, retirement, education, tax, and investment planning, as well as ethics and the financial planning process. CFPs must abide by a code of ethics that includes adhering to a fiduciary standard as well as complying with specific practice principles. Most Certified Financial Planners™ are also investment advisors, but not all investment advisors are Certified Financial Planners™. Financial planners may be fee-only or fee-based. For a more detailed description, visit cfp.net.

Chartered Financial Consultant® (ChFC®)

The Chartered Financial Consultant® (ChFC®) designation was originally created by the *life insurance* industry. The ChFC® designation requires the same core courses as the CFP® designation, plus two additional elective courses that tend to focus on general *financial planning* issues. There is no comprehensive board exam required for this credential. The ChFC® designations are granted by The American College. Those who earn this designation are considered knowledgeable in financial planning matters and are considered to have the ability to provide appropriate financial advice.

To be eligible for this designation, the applicant must already have a minimum of three years of relevant work experience in the financial service industry. It is also highly recommended that applicants have a degree connected to finance or business before applying, because that will make the course of study easier to master. For a more detailed description, visit theamericancollege.edu/designations-degrees/ChFC.

Tax Advisors

Tax advisors include professionals licensed or authorized by their state and/or the Internal Revenue Service, who have advanced training and are knowledgeable on the tax law. They are retained in order to legally minimize the client's tax burden and assist them in being compliant with the law.

Certified Public Accountant (CPA)

The Certified Public Accountant (CPA) designation is the oldest and most respected financial credential in the United States. This designation has long been widely recognized by the public as the definitive credential of tax expertise. CPA requirements vary by state, but generally a CPA needs 150 semester hours of undergraduate level courses that cover accounting, auditing, and business law, plus a bachelor's degree or higher in order to sit for the four-part exam. This comprehensive exam covers accounting, auditing, bookkeeping, taxes, business law, ethics, and more.

A CPA is always an accountant, but not all accountants are CPAs. CPAs handle a variety of jobs and tasks. They offer income tax preparation and advice for a range of clients including individuals, small businesses, and corporations. To maintain their license, every three years CPAs must take 120 hours of continuing education courses in order to stay abreast of changes in their profession.

Many states have a second tier of accountant qualification, usually entitled Public Accountant (PA) or Licensed Public Accountant (LPA). The majority of states have closed the designation of PA to new entrants, however, with only five states continuing to offer this designation.

Certain CPAs who are interested in specializing in financial planning can also obtain a Personal Financial Specialist (PFS) designation, which is offered by the American Institute of Certified Public Accountants (AICPA). To qualify, CPAs must be members in good standing and complete the additional educational and testing requirements. For a more detailed description, visit aicpa.org.

Enrolled Agent (EA)

EAs provide a very important service to the general public. An EA is an individual designation provided by the IRS. It is one of the few designations that signifies a concentration of proficiency in the field of taxation. Unlike CPAs, who may or may not provide tax services, all EAs specialize in taxation.

The specialized EA exam administered by the IRS is broken down into four parts of three hours each, over a two-day testing period. This exam covers personal, estate, and corporate taxes, as well as ethics and IRS regulations, but does not include accounting, auditing, bookkeeping, or business law.

EA status is awarded by the IRS to individuals who meet its requirements. Individuals who earn this designation must adhere to ethical standards and are required to complete 72 hours of continuing education credits every three years to maintain this status.

EAs are granted the same privilege as attorneys and CPAs, who have the authority to represent clients before the IRS, with a properly executed IRS Form 2848 Power of Attorney and Declaration of Representative. For a more detailed description, visit irs.gov.

Investment Advisors

An investment advisor is defined by the Investment Advisers Act of 1940 as a "person or firm that, for compensation, is engaged in the act of providing advice, making recommendations, issuing reports or furnishing analyses on securities, either directly or through publications."

In 2010, the Dodd-Frank Act amended certain provisions of the Investment Advisory Act of 1940 by delegating to the states the responsibility over certain investment advisors who have under $100 million of assets under management. This amendment to the Act increased the threshold above which all investment advisors must be registered with the Securities and Exchange Commission (SEC), from $30 million to $100 million under management. This means that state securities regulators now have the primary authority over a substantial number of investment advisors who were previously subject to primary regulation by the SEC.

Registered Investment Advisor (RIA)

Registered Investment Advisors (RIAs) are either registered with the SEC or the state securities agency in the state where they have their principal place of business. Investment advisors are prohibited from providing advice known to be deceitful or fraudulent. They are also prohibited from acting as a principal on their own accounts by buying and selling securities between themselves and their clients. Investment advisors have a fiduciary duty to their clients, which holds them to a much higher standard. This means they have a fundamental obligation to provide not only suitable investment advice, but they are always obligated to act in the client's best interests and not their own.

Most investment advisors charge either a flat fee for their services or a percentage of the assets under management. On average, fee-based advisors charge between 1% and 1.5% of the assets under management per year for providing ongoing investment advisory services, and they do not charge commissions. This typically will limit potential conflicts of interest between the investment advisors and their clients. The advisor will generally get paid more as the client's asset base grows from the advisor's recommendations, because the advisor's fees are based on assets under management. This is a significant difference when compared to transactional compensation (commissions), as is usually the case with a stockbroker.

RIAs are normally established by individuals or small investment firms that are independent of the larger financial services firms. They are also commonly known as financial advisors, asset managers, money managers, portfolio managers, investment counselors, or investment managers.

The SEC and State Security Regulators do not make any recommendation or endorsement of any investment advisor; in fact, if one is registered, it simply means that the investment advisor has fulfilled all of the necessary requirements for registration. For a more detailed description, visit sec.gov.

Chartered Financial Analyst® (CFA®)

The Chartered Financial Analyst® (CFA®) designation is considered to be one of the most elite and difficult credentials to obtain in the investment management industry, which focuses on financial analyses. The academic requirements and standards for this designation are second only to that of a CPA. This designation requires three years of coursework that covers a range of topics and disciplines, such as technical and fundamental analysis, financial accounting, and portfolio theory and analysis. Those who earn this designation frequently become portfolio managers or analysts for a variety of financial institutions. For a more detailed description, visit cfainstitute.org.

Investment Advisor Representative (IAR)

Individuals who work for investment advisory companies and whose main responsibility is to provide investment related advice are referred to as investment advisor representatives (IARs). IARs are only permitted to provide advice on topics on which they have successfully passed the appropriate examinations and are properly licensed.

An IAR is also required to be registered with the appropriate state authorities. Many IARs hold either the CFP® or ChFC® designations, to increase their credibility and financial knowledge. For a more detailed description, visit finra.org.

Stockbroker

A stockbroker is a legal term that refers to an investment professional who buys and sells securities on behalf of clients. Stockbrokers are regulated by state securities commissioners and by the SEC. They are also subject to oversight by the Financial Industry Regulatory Authority (FINRA), which is an industry self-regulatory body. Stockbrokers must recommend "suitable" investments and are required to meet the fiduciary standard only when handling retirement assets. Stockbrokers are also legally referred to as *registered representatives*. They may also call themselves *financial advisors, financial consultants,* or *investment consultants.* For a more detailed description, visit finra.org.

Insurance Advisors

Before we get into the specialized designations for insurance advisors, it is important to understand the difference between an insurance agent and an insurance broker.

Insurance Agents

Insurance agents are insurance professionals who serve as a liaison between an insurance company and the insured. Insurance agents have an administrative responsibility, which relates to the timely and accurate processing of forms, premium payments, and the related paperwork. An agent does not have a duty or responsibility to conduct a thorough examination of your finances or to make certain that you have been provided proper coverage. As the insured person, it is *your* responsibility to make sure you have purchased the necessary coverage.

Insurance agents can be captive or independent. A captive agent is an agent who works for only one company and, therefore, sells policies provided by only one insurance company. In contrast, an independent agent is one who works for many insurance providers and can provide a comparison of different insurance policies and providers.

Insurance Brokers

An insurance broker is required to have a broker's license, which normally means the broker will have additional educational qualifications and broader experience than an insurance agent. Brokers typically provide a variety of different insurance products to meet your needs. Most states require insurance brokers to have a higher duty of responsibility to their clients than an agent. Brokers have the duty to analyze your particular situation and secure the proper and adequate coverage that you may require. Typically, brokers will charge an administrative fee, or the premium payments may be higher to reflect this higher level of service.

Chartered Life Underwriter® (CLU®)

The Chartered Life Underwriter® (CLU®) designation was originally created by the life insurance industry. This is a professional designation for individuals who wish to specialize in life insurance and estate planning. Individuals must complete five core courses and three elective courses and successfully pass all eight two-hour, 100-question examinations to receive the designation. The courses required to earn this professional designation are offered through The American College. There is no comprehensive board exam required for this credential. For a more detailed description, visit theamericancollege.edu.

Chartered Property Casualty Underwriter® (CPCU®)

The Chartered Property Casualty Underwriter® (CPCU®) is respected as the premier designation in property-casualty insurance. This designation is offered by the Insurance Institute of America. This program provides a broad understanding of the property-casualty insurance industry and focuses on the legal, financial, and operational aspect of risk management and insurance. This designation requires the completion of eight courses of intensive academic study, but, as with the CLU and the ChFC, there is no comprehensive board examination required. For a more detailed description, visit cpcusociety.org.

Attorneys

To become a lawyer, you must have an undergraduate degree and then successfully complete three years of law school to earn a law degree. After law school, generally you must pass a bar examination in the state where you will be practicing law.

Tax Attorney

Tax attorneys are lawyers who have additional advanced education and training in tax law. Tax attorneys typically get involved with high-level tax matters, which may require a legal opinion or legal representation with the IRS or tax courts. Tax attorneys can negotiate settlements on your behalf and are trained to analyze complicated tax matters, allowing them to formulate a plan for resolving your problem and settling your case. Tax attorneys are most qualified to:

- Represent someone in lawsuits with the IRS.
- Represent someone in criminal IRS investigations.
- Represent someone accused of tax fraud against a taxpayer.
- Represent someone in income tax audits and appeals before the IRS.
- File estate-related tax returns and representation in estate tax audits.
- Assist with business start-ups, mergers, and acquisitions that involve complex structures.
- Handle employee payroll tax issues and disputes.
- Advise on international business transactions and related tax treaties.

Estate and Elder Law Attorneys

An attorney who specializes in estate and elder law typically has an expertise in trust, estate, and/or Medicaid planning. These attorneys will work very closely with financial planners and will draft and execute the legal documents required as part of the overall financial planning process. These attorneys are experts in drafting wills, health care proxies, power of attorneys, and trust documents. Many of these attorneys also handle transactions that involve a family business and real estate.

Some of these attorneys refer to themselves as *elder law attorneys* and will have an added level of expertise in Medicaid planning for assisted-living or nursing-home care. They can provide an asset protection plan for clients who may need long-term care. They may also represent individuals in both contested and uncontested guardianship actions.

Appendix B

101 Ways to Save $20 or More per Week

Here is a list of 101 ways you could save $20 or more. That may not sound like a lot of money to you, but watch how that $20 can grow:

- If you tuck away that extra $20 into a savings account *every week*, at the end of the year, *you will have $1,040.*
- If you are 30 years old and invest that additional $1,040 for 35 years (until you are 65) at an 8% rate of return, *you will have $179,209.*
- If you are able to save $20 or more *per day* ($7,300 per year) for 35 years at an 8% rate of return, *you will have $1,257,914.*[1]

It is pretty astonishing that as little as $20 per day has the potential of accumulating to more than $1 million over 35 years. With that said, becoming a millionaire is within almost any hard-working American's reach. All you need is the desire, willingness, discipline, and information provided throughout this book to help get you there.

Working together with your entire family, you could easily adopt several of these savings strategies, allowing you to set aside as much as $20 or more *per day*. Your family finances should be discussed and shared with your entire family so that a cooperative commitment to financial responsibility and ultimately financial independence can be achieved.

---

[1]The rates of return shown above are purely hypothetical and do not represent the performance of any individual investment or portfolio of investments. They are for illustrative purposes only and should not be used to predict future product performance. Specific rates of return, especially for extended time periods, will vary over time. There is also a higher degree of risk associated with investments that offer the potential for higher rates of return. You should consult with your representative before making any investment decision.

Go to investinganswers.com/calculators, and click on "Simple Savings Calculator: How Much Could I Save Up Over Time?" to determine just how quickly and easily you can accumulate $1 million or more based on an assumed number of years, rate of return, and dollar amount to be set aside each year. You could also use Exhibit 12.3, "Future Value (FV) of an Annuity Factor," to calculate this amount.

In Chapter 3, I showed you how to prepare your own statement of cash flow and then to analyze this statement with your family to improve and increase your discretionary cash flow. The additional cash flow provided through these cost-saving strategies should be added to your investment assets, which will lead you to financial independence. Sit down with your family and plan your goals. Save money by planning which expenses are necessary and unnecessary (needs vs. wants), and use the internet to find cheaper alternatives to the items that remain in your budget.

Regardless of your income level, you can find ways to save money by cutting costs. My parents were Italian immigrants who barely spoke English, my mother was a seamstress in a sweat shop and my father cut hair in a barber shop, and they were able to achieve financial independence within their lifetime. If they were able to reach *point X* with their limited resources, there is absolutely no excuse for you to not be able to do the same. You just have to be willing to make some adjustments to your standard of living, and I truly don't believe this will affect the quality of your life.

The following is a list of 101 basic money-saving tips that will help you find the extra money needed to start a serious savings plan. These recommendations have been listed in the same order as your statement of cash flow, shown as Exhibit 3.4 in Chapter 3.

Housing

1. Cut your cable TV costs by dropping premium TV channels or switching to basic cable. Be willing to negotiate with the cable company and even threaten to switch to a competitor service.
2. Consider dropping your TV service provider completely and joining Netflix, Hulu, Amazon Prime, and other streaming services.
3. Package your telephone bill with your cell phone, Internet, and your cable TV.

4. Buy older cell phone models and hold on to them as long as they work for you. Always buying the newest model can cost you thousands over time and is usually not necessary.

5. If you have a cell phone and rarely use your landline, consider getting rid of the landline.

6. Buy generic or store-brand products.

7. Clean your house yourself. If you must use a cleaning service, consider having them come every other week or once a month.

8. Learn to do simple home repairs yourself such as shampooing rugs, declogging a sink, and mowing your lawn. Try to avoid calling expensive plumbers, gardeners, and handymen, if possible.

9. Reduce your heat and air-conditioning costs by using a programmable thermostat to minimize your utility use.

10. Replace incandescent light bulbs with compact fluorescent bulbs (CFLs), halogen incandescent bulbs, or light-emitting diodes (LEDs). These use 25–80% less energy and last 3–25 times longer, which will save you money on the cost of light bulbs and on your electricity bill.

11. Never let the hot water run in the sink or shower unless you are actually using it, and try to cut your time in the shower by half to significantly reduce your hot water use and cost.

12. Ensure that your home – especially your attic – is sufficiently insulated. If the insulation in your attic is less than 6 inches thick, you are underinsulated. Insulation that is 12 inches thick can lower your heating and cooling costs by 25% each year.

13. Install an alarm system in your home. With monthly monitoring, you will save more on your home insurance premiums.

14. Quitting smoking can help decrease your home insurance premium. Smokers have higher premiums because of their associated risk of house fires.

15. When you leave a room in your house, turn off the light. Unplug any electronics that you rarely use.

16. Installing ceiling fans can help cut air conditioning costs.

17. Clean out the coils in your refrigerator every six months to keep it running efficiently. Having only one refrigerator in your home will cut energy costs as well.

18. You can save up to 14% or more on your energy bill by upgrading to a tankless or solar water heater.

Transportation

19. Take public transportation or join a carpool rather than driving your own vehicle to work. You can also consider carpooling with other parents or utilizing school buses for your child's school and extracurricular activities.
20. If public transportation or carpooling does not work for you, then you should consider using Uber or similar services, since this may be less expensive than taxis.
21. Find the least expensive gas stations in your neighborhood, and get into the habit of gassing up there.
22. Read your automobile owner's manual. If your car can run on regular unleaded gas, then stop paying high prices for premium gas.
23. Avoid driving over 55 miles per hour to save gas.
24. Having a good driving record can help save you money on insurance premiums. Always be alert whenever you are driving and be sure to never drink and drive.
25. You can also save money on your auto premium by qualifying for antitheft, multicar, good student, and low mileage discounts, to name a few.
26. Save money on your auto and homeowner insurance premiums by consolidating your coverages under one insurance carrier. Increase deductibles to $1,000 per auto policy and $10,000 for the homeowner policy.
27. Wash your own car. You can save anywhere from $5 to $30 on an expensive car wash, and you can usually do it just as well, if not better, on your own.
28. Buying a used car can be much less expensive than a car that is brand new.
29. If you have a car that you rarely use, consider selling it to save on insurance and maintenance costs. It may be cheaper to use Uber or similar services than to have to maintain a vehicle with all its related costs.
30. Cleaning your car's air filter when you change the oil can save you money by improving your gas mileage.
31. Ensure that you have the right amount of air pressure in your tires to improve gas mileage.

32. Join organizations such as AAA, USAA, and AARP for discounts on car repairs, auto insurance, travel, car rentals, shopping, and entertainment. These companies also offer limited free roadside assistance. Whenever getting work done on your car, booking travel or buying tickets, ask if they accept discounts for members.

Family Risk Management

33. Buy term life insurance when you are young. It is better to get as much protection as you can at a younger age when you are still healthy and the price will be locked in at a lower rate.
34. Ensure that you choose the proper length of term life insurance coverage that best suits your needs.
35. Before getting a life insurance policy, check with your employer's human resources department to find out if your company offers this coverage to employees. Companies typically get these policies at a much cheaper rate than an individual can.
36. Unfortunately, insurance companies take into account your physical health. Therefore, people who smoke, have high cholesterol levels, have high blood pressure, are overweight, and have other problems (including depression) will usually have higher insurance premiums than a person who is in good physical shape and health. Improve your health to lower your premium costs.

Food

37. Give up the $4.00 coffee you buy every morning on your way to work. Instead, pick up coffee at a less expensive coffee shop for $1.25 – or better yet, bring a thermos of coffee from home.
38. Brown-bag your lunch – and your kids' lunches, too.
39. Never throw out good food. Use leftovers for tomorrow's lunch or reheat for the next day's dinner.
40. Buy groceries and other household items in bulk from stores such as Sam's Club and Costco.
41. Most major grocery stores and drugstores offer rewards cards that make you eligible for their sales, special discounts, and rewards. Take advantage of these offers.

42. Find dual-purpose rewards cards. Many grocery stores (such as Winn-Dixie, Tom Thumb, and Stop & Shop) also give you gas discounts as well as grocery discounts.
43. Plan your weekly shopping using supermarket circulars to buy groceries that are on sale.
44. Eat at least one vegetarian meal per week. It is not only healthier, it is cheaper.
45. If you and your family eat out or order in often, commit to reducing that to a once-a-week "splurge" at a restaurant. Better yet, make that once a month!
46. When eating out with your spouse or a friend, share a meal. Portions are usually much more than you should be eating anyway so you will eat less and save money.
47. Take advantage of restaurant coupons and early bird specials.
48. Learn to cook your favorite restaurant recipes at home for a fraction of the price!
49. Make your own baby food with fresh fruits and vegetables.
50. Buy your favorite type of wine from a less expensive winery. For example, purchasing a California wine may be less expensive than a French wine, but just as tasty. Buy the cheaper brands of liquor, Scotch, gin, vodka, and so forth, especially if you use a mixer.
51. Consider cutting down your alcohol consumption altogether. This not only saves you money, but also lowers your risk of severe health issues.
52. Planning your meals can save you money and time. When grocery shopping, you will know exactly what you need to buy so there is no excess food thrown out at the end of the week.

Personal Care

53. Do not throw out torn clothing or broken items; instead, mend or repair.
54. When possible, wear clothing more than once between washes and dry cleaning. Your clothes will not only last longer, but you will cut down on cleaning costs.
55. Buy clothing that can be hand- or machine-washed to avoid dry cleaning costs.
56. Hang your clothes to dry instead of drying them in the dryer. This saves money on your utility bills as well as wear and tear on your clothing.

57. Buy clothes at discounted brand name stores, such as Marshalls, T.J. Maxx, and so forth. You can also check out resale or vintage stores.

58. Buy less clothing. Most of us already have many more outfits than we actually need. Make do with what you own, and only buy new clothes when truly necessary.

59. Try coloring your hair at home with over-the-counter hair dyes instead of professionally. If you want to have your hair colored professionally, extend the time between colorings with over-the-counter touch-ups.

60. Do your own manicures and pedicures.

61. Give up smoking, not only for health reasons but to save money on the rising price of cigarettes. Use the savings accumulation calculator to determine how much this is actually costing you over time.

62. Evaluate whether you are really getting your money's worth on gym and club memberships. If you use them rarely, you should consider canceling them.

63. Instead of paying monthly gym fees, take up walking, running, biking, or using workout videos.

64. When cleaning out your closet, sell your clothing or donate it to receive a tax deduction.

Entertainment

65. Instead of paying to see a movie in theaters, wait for them to come out on Blu-ray or streaming services.

66. Check out free events offered in your neighborhood. Many towns offer free concerts and movies in the park or at the beach during the summer.

67. Buy used books, magazines, and movies, or borrow them from your public library.

68. Support your local community theater, where you can often see high-quality shows for a fraction of what you would pay for a professional show.

Loan Payments

69. Negotiate a lower credit card interest rate. Several credit card companies will reward good credit with a lower rate.

70. If you are not paying off your credit cards each month, stop using them. Destroy them or store them in a safe place to eliminate temptation.

71. Clear your credit card debt. Even if you have a minimal 1% per month (12% per year) interest on an $8,000 balance, this will cost you more than $20 a week.

72. Do not pay unnecessary maintenance fees on your bank accounts. Switch banks or get the fees removed.

Taxes

73. Use the **Tax Alpha to the 2nd Power**^{SM} facts and strategies provided at the end of each chapter in this book to minimize your biggest expenditure, which is taxes.

Gifts and Donations

74. Do not donate money when you cannot afford it. Instead of donating money, donate your time or items that you no longer need.

75. If you want to make a big impact for your charity but don't have the means to make a large gift, see if your company will make a gift match. You can make the same impact for half the cost.

76. There is no need to buy expensive gifts for birthdays or holidays. Remember, it is not the cost of the gift that matters, it is the thoughtfulness, so save money by buying something less expensive that the receiver will still enjoy. Better yet, try thoughtful homemade gifts!

Professional Fees and Legal Obligations

77. Do not view accounting and legal fees as an expense. If your accountant or lawyer is not saving you many times the cost of their fee, then it is time to look for someone else. Make sure you are securing your professional services from a trusted advisor who can meet your professional needs (see Appendix A).

Child Care and Other Expenses

78. Save on children's toys by buying them when they are on clearance, after the holidays. Put them away to give to your child at a later date.

79. Ask family and friends for hand-me-down clothes that their children have outgrown.

Pet Care and Other Expenses

80. Shop at pet specialty stores such as Petco, which usually offer pet food, even name-brand varieties, as well as other pet supplies at much lower prices than grocery stores.

81. Cats and dogs need teeth cleanings. Instead of buying expensive pet tooth care, wash their teeth with a paste made of baking soda and water, using a soft cloth.

82. Avoid buying expensive bedding or toys for pets. Use old blankets for bedding; make play toys out of old clothes or boxes. Stuff catnip toys with bulk catnip. The animals will not know the difference.

83. Check with your local animal shelter to see if they provide annual pet vaccinations for free or for a minimal fee.

84. If you or your child is yearning for a pet, choose an animal from a shelter. It is not necessary to spend thousands on a special breed, and shelters are usually overrun with animals that need loving homes. Many shelters sponsor a Clear the Shelters Day, where pet adoptions are free.

Personal Expenses

85. Learn how to "extreme coupon." Using coupons with store sales and promotions will save you extra money. Online coupon codes are another source of savings for many people; before you make any online purchases, do a quick search to see if the retailer has any available coupons. Many websites collect a database on all the coupons available online such as RetailMeNot.com or CouponCabin.com.

86. Sign up for special online services and apps that help you find the best retail prices, such as Joinhoney.com, Shoptagr.com, and Camelcamelcamel.com.

87. Cancel your newspaper and magazine subscriptions in favor of free online articles.

88. Travel during low-demand seasons. Airfare and hotels tend to be much more expensive in the summer and around school holidays.

89. Use sites like airfarewatchdog.com to find the best times to book air travel. Flights that leave on Tuesdays, Wednesdays, or Saturdays are usually the cheapest.

90. Always compare airfare, hotel, car rental, and cruise costs through sites like Expedia® and Travelocity®. You can also get better deals when you package your travel costs through these sites.

91. Check if your company offers travel discounts. Depending on where you work, they can sometimes offer better deals on travel and activities than you would get through big name travel sites.

92. When renting a car, don't pay for rental insurance. Check with your auto insurance provider or credit card company, which probably will already cover your rental.

93. If you don't absolutely need a more expensive rental car model, reserve a cheaper model and request a free upgrade at the rental desk, if available.

94. Consider ditching the hotel and renting a vacation home or apartment through sites like Airbnb or HomeAway®. You can often get much more space and a more unique travel experience for less than you would pay at a hotel.

95. Book a rental space or hotel suite that includes a kitchen and bring your own groceries and alcohol. Since eating at restaurants for every meal can be extremely expensive, especially in tourist areas, choosing to cook throughout your vacation can save a considerable amount.

96. Join loyalty programs with hotel chains or airlines that you use frequently, or use a travel credit card. Reward points could translate to savings or even free travel down the line.

97. Consider a "staycation." Avoid the cost of travel and lodging by spending your vacation finding fun or relaxing things to do in your own area. Explore nearby parks, beaches, museums, and landmarks that you may have overlooked before.

98. If you're struggling to budget for your trip, check to see if your dream vacation is offered by Groupon and other discount travel sites. They have some amazing deals on travel packages that could potentially save you thousands on your vacation.

99. Booking a tour with a group can often be a cheaper and safer option when traveling internationally.

100. If you want full freedom when traveling abroad, consider backpacking and staying at hostels. However, be sure to always do your research and make safety a priority.

101. Know cultural differences where you're traveling. Some countries expect you to bargain for the best price. Others don't expect you to give tips for service. Not knowing these nuances could cost you more than you may realize!

Appendix C

Basic Concepts and Definitions of Various Types of Taxes

In the United States, taxes are imposed on individuals and corporations by the federal government, most state governments, and some local (or city) governments. These include income tax, property tax, sales tax, import tax, payroll tax, estate tax, gift tax, excise tax, tariffs, customs, duties, licenses, occupational taxes, and various other user fees.

Federal Income Taxes

At the federal level, the Internal Revenue Code (IRC) imposes income tax based on individuals, corporations, estates, and trusts. Income subject to tax includes almost all income from whatever source derived. With regard to income from outside the United States, US citizens and resident aliens are taxed on worldwide income, but they may be allowed a foreign tax credit if foreign taxes were paid on the same income. In addition, income earned from services performed outside the United States may be fully or partially excluded from taxable income.

The tax is based on taxable income (as defined in the IRC) multiplied by various tax rates at different levels of income, with the exception of corporations that are now taxed at a flat rate of 21%, starting January 1, 2018.

As part of President Trump's tax reform bill, the US corporate tax system is, as of 2018, substantially changed from a worldwide system to a territorial tax system. Prior to this change, many US corporations had to pay US taxes on their profits earned abroad. This new territorial system ended the effective double taxation on foreign profits accumulated but not distributed from foreign entities after 2017.

You, as an individual, are permitted to reduce your taxable income by taking a standard deduction or certain itemized deductions, such as home mortgage interest, state and local taxes, charitable contributions, and medical expenses. You can also reduce your taxes through tax credits, some of which may be refundable even if they exceed your tax liability.

In 2018, the current federal tax rates vary from 10% to 37% of taxable income.

State Income Taxes

In the United States, 43 states and many localities impose an income tax on individuals; 44 states and many localities impose a tax on the income of corporations. Tax rates vary by state and locality, and they may be fixed or graduated. State and local income taxes are imposed in addition to federal income tax and are determined under state law. Most states conform to many federal concepts and definitions, including defining income and business deductions. Some states have alternative measures of taxable income, or alternative taxes, especially for corporations.

States imposing an income tax generally tax all income of corporations organized in the state and individuals residing in the state. Taxpayers from another state are subject to tax only on income earned in the state or apportioned to the state. Businesses are subject to income tax in a state only if they have sufficient connection to the state.

Estate and Gift Taxes

Estate and gift taxes in the United States are imposed by the federal and some state governments. An *estate tax* is an excise tax levied on the right to pass on property at death. (Here, "property" does not mean real estate only; instead, it means any and all personal property, which includes real estate as well as all other assets and belongings: cars, jewelry, furniture and furnishings, investments, etc.)

The estate tax is imposed on the estate, not the beneficiary. A few states impose an *inheritance tax* on recipients of bequests. *Gift taxes* are levied on the giver (i.e., donor) of property where the property is transferred for less than it is actually worth. An additional *generation-skipping transfer (GST) tax* is imposed by the federal and some state governments on transfers to grandchildren (or their descendants).

Taxable gifts are gifts made in excess of an annual exclusion ($15,000 for gifts made in 2018) per donor per donee. The taxable amount of an estate is the gross fair market value of all rights considered property at the date of death (called the *gross estate*), plus lifetime taxable gifts, less liabilities of the descendant, costs of administration (including funeral expenses), and certain other deductions. State estate taxes are deductible, with limitations, in computing the federal taxable estate. Bequests to charities reduce the taxable estate.

Estate tax applies to all property owned in whole or in part by a citizen or resident at the time of his or her death, to the extent of the interest in the property. Generally, all types of property are subject to estate tax. Whether a descendant has sufficient interest in the property for it to be subject to gift or estate tax is determined under applicable state property laws.

Taxable values of estates and gifts are the fair market value. For some assets, such as widely traded stocks and bonds, the value may be determined by market listings. The value of other property may be determined by appraisals, which are subject to potential contest by the taxing authority. Monetary assets, such as cash, mortgages, and notes, are valued at the face amount, unless another value is clearly established. Life insurance proceeds are included in the gross estate, when owned by the descendant.

Payroll Taxes

Payroll taxes are the taxes an employer withholds and pays on behalf of its employees and are based on the wages or salary of the employee. Payroll taxes are imposed by the federal and most state governments. Revenues from these taxes are used to fund such programs as Social Security, Medicare, unemployment compensation, workers' compensation, and health care.

In the United States, payroll taxes are assessed by the federal government, all 50 states, the District of Columbia, and numerous cities. These taxes are imposed on employers and employees and on various compensation bases. They are collected and paid to the taxing jurisdiction by the employers. Most jurisdictions imposing payroll taxes require reporting quarterly and annually.

Income Tax Withholding   Federal, state, and local withholding taxes are required in those jurisdictions imposing an income tax. Employers must withhold the tax from wages paid to their employees in those jurisdictions. Computation of the amount of tax to withhold is performed by the employer, based on representations by the employee regarding his or her tax status on IRS Form W-4. Amounts of income tax withheld must be paid to the taxing jurisdiction, and they are available as refundable tax credits to employees. Income taxes withheld from payroll are not final taxes, merely estimated prepayments. Employees must still file income tax returns and self-assess tax, claiming amounts withheld as payments.

Social Security and Medicare Taxes   Federal Social Security taxes are imposed equally on employers and employees, consisting of a tax of 6.2% of wages up to an annual wage maximum ($128,400 for 2018) for Social Security, plus a tax of 1.45% of total wages for Medicare. To the extent an employee's portion of the 6.2% tax exceeds the maximum by reason of multiple employers, the employee is entitled to a refundable tax credit on filing an income tax return for the year.

Employees and the self-employed are required to pay an additional 0.9% Medicare tax on their earned wages and self-employed income in excess of limits based on their income tax return filing status ($250,000 for married filing jointly, $200,000 for single, head of household, or qualifying widow(er), or $125,000 for married filing separately). This is an additional Medicare tax that is imposed upon filing your personal income tax return above and beyond any Medicare tax already withheld throughout the year.

Unemployment Taxes   Employers are subject to unemployment taxes by the Federal and all state governments. The tax is a percentage of taxable wages with a cap, which varies by jurisdiction and by employer's industry and experience rating. Some states also impose unemployment, disability insurance, or similar taxes on employees.

Reporting and Payment   Employers must report payroll taxes to the appropriate taxing jurisdiction in the manner that each jurisdiction requires. Quarterly reporting of income tax withholding and Social Security taxes is required in most jurisdictions. Employers must also file reports of unemployment tax quarterly and annually with each applicable state, and annually at the federal level.

Each employer is required to provide each employee with an annual report on IRS Form W-2 of wages paid and federal, state, and local taxes withheld, with a copy going to the IRS and many states. These are due by January 31 following the calendar year in which wages are paid. The Form W-2 constitutes proof of payment of tax for the employee.

Severe penalties apply where federal income tax withholding and Social Security taxes are not paid to the IRS and administered properly.

Medicare Surtax on Net Investment Income

The Patient Protection and Affordable Care Act (2010) provided a new 3.8% Medicare tax surcharge on net investment income (including interest, dividends, capital gains, rental and royalty income, and passive business income). This was the first time in US history that a payroll tax was (and still is) imposed on unearned income (earnings you did not work for). This, too, is above and beyond the Medicare tax imposed on the earned income of employees and the self-employed.

This Medicare tax may be imposed on the net investment income for single and head of household taxpayers with income over $200,000, married couples and qualifying widow(er) with income over $250,000, and married filing separately with income over $125,000.

For individuals, this tax applies to the *lesser* of: (1) an individual's "net investment income" for the tax year, *or* (2) any excess of "modified adjusted gross income" (MAGI) for the tax year over the applicable threshold amount.

For example, if a single taxpayer has $180,000 of wages and also received $30,000 in net investment income, their modified adjusted gross income would be $210,000 or $10,000 above the threshold amount. The 3.8% Medicare surtax would apply to the lower of net investment income ($30,000) or the excess of modified adjusted gross income over the threshold amount ($10,000). Therefore, only the $10,000 will be subject to this 3.8% Medicare surcharge for a total of $380.

Property Taxes

Property taxes are most commonly applied to real estate and business property, including interest in land, buildings, and improvements. Ownership interests include ownership of title as well as certain other rights to property. Automobile and boat registration fees are a subset of this tax.

Property taxes are imposed on owners of property by most local governments and many special-purpose authorities. Property tax rules and rates vary widely. Taxes on property are typically imposed only at the local level, although there may be multiple local jurisdictions that tax the same property.

Property tax is based on the fair market value of the property being taxed. The amount of tax is determined annually based on the market value of each property on a particular date.

The assessment process for property taxes varies by state, and sometimes within a state. Each taxing jurisdiction determines values of property within the jurisdiction and then determines the amount of tax to assess based on the value of the property. Payment times and terms vary widely. If a property owner fails to pay the tax, the taxing jurisdiction has various remedies for collection, including seizure and sale of the property.

Sales Taxes

Sales taxes are imposed on the price at retail sale of many goods and some services by most states and some localities. Sales tax rates vary widely among jurisdictions, from 0% to more than 10%, and may vary within a jurisdiction based on the particular goods or services taxed. Most jurisdictions exempt food sold in grocery stores, prescription medications, and many agricultural supplies. Generally, cash discounts, including coupons, are not included in the price used in computing tax.

Sales tax is collected by the seller at the time of sale, or remitted as use tax by buyers of taxable items who did not pay sales tax. Sales taxes, including those imposed by local governments, are generally administered at the state level. States imposing sales tax require retail sellers to register with the state, collect tax from customers, file returns, and remit the tax to the state.

There are no federal sales taxes in the United States.

Excise Taxes

Excise taxes are imposed at the federal and state levels on the manufacture, sale, and/or consumption of a wide variety of goods, including alcohol, tobacco, tires, gasoline, diesel fuel, coal, firearms, telephone service, air transportation, unregistered bonds, and many other commodities and services. Some jurisdictions require that tax stamps be affixed to goods to demonstrate payment of the tax.

Tariffs, Customs, and Duties

The United States imposes tariffs or customs duties on the import of many types of goods from many jurisdictions. The duty is levied at the time of import and is paid by the importer of record. This tax must be paid before the goods can be legally imported. Rates of duty vary from 0% to more than 20%, based on the particular goods and country of origin. Customs duties or tariffs are imposed only by the federal government.

A wide variety of other taxes, some called *user* or *license fees,* are imposed. Failure to properly comply with customs rules can result in seizure of goods and criminal penalties against involved parties. The US Customs and Border Protection (CBP) enforces customs rules.

Licenses and Occupational Taxes

Many jurisdictions within the United States impose taxes or fees on the privilege of carrying on a particular business or maintaining a particular professional certification. Common examples include accountants, attorneys, stockbrokers, barbers, casinos, dentists, doctors, auto mechanics, and plumbers. *Licensing* or *occupational taxes* may be a fixed-dollar amount per year for the licensee, an amount based on the number of practitioners in the firm, a percentage of revenue, or any of several other bases. Persons providing professional or personal services are often subject to such fees. In addition to the tax, other requirements may be imposed for licensure.

All 50 states impose *vehicular license (license plate) fees.* Generally, the fees are based on type and size of vehicle and are imposed annually or biannually. All states and the District of Columbia also impose a fee for a driver's license, which generally must be renewed with payment of a fee every few years.

User Fees

Fees are often imposed by the federal or state governments for use of certain facilities or services. For example, fees are often imposed for use of national or state parks, use of certain highways (called *tolls* on toll roads), parking on public streets, and use of public transportation. Such fees are usually imposed at the time of use.

Administrating Taxes: Collecting and Distributing

Three different entities handle different aspects of taxes:

1. Congress, the Senate, and the President of the United States write and approve the tax laws.
2. The IRS is responsible for enforcing the laws, for collecting taxes, for processing tax returns, for issuing tax refunds, and for turning over the money collected to the US Treasury.
3. The US Treasury is responsible for paying various government expenses.

Taxes in the United States are administered by literally hundreds of tax authorities. At the federal level, there are three tax administrations:

1. The Alcohol and Tobacco Tax and Trade Bureau (TTB) administers taxes on alcohol, tobacco, and firearms. TTB is part of the US Department of Justice.
2. The Internal Revenue Service (IRS) administers all other taxes on domestic activities. The IRS is a division of the US Department of the Treasury.
3. The Customs and Border Protection (CBP) administers taxes on imports (as mentioned, as part of customs duties). The CBP belongs to the US Department of Homeland Security.

Organization of state and local tax administrations varies widely. Every state maintains a tax administration. A few states administer some local taxes in whole or in part. Most localities also maintain a tax administration or share one with neighboring localities.

Income Taxes: Concepts You Should Know

Under the US tax system, everyone is taxed, in some way or another. This includes every person, company, corporation, or nonprofit organization. (Partnerships and Subchapter S Corporations are not taxed; rather, their partners are subject to income tax at the personal level on their share of income and deductions, and they take their share of credits.)

In plain terms: *You are taxed based on your income.* Income is any money you have earned because you have worked for it or invested for it. Income includes wages, interest, dividends, profits on investments, and pension distributions; however, it does not include gifts, certain inheritances, and scholarships. People and organizations are responsible for reporting their income and calculating their tax. Some organizations are exempt from tax, but they still are legally required to file a tax return.

The amount of taxes you owe is based on your income. People who earn more income generally pay a higher tax rate than those who earn less; this means that tax rates get progressively higher the more you earn. Conversely, you can reduce your taxes by taking advantage of various tax benefits – or, to put it another way, through intelligent tax planning. It is up to you to take control of your tax situation.

The federal income tax is usually the largest tax you will have to pay every year. As mentioned, most American families pay about a third of their gross income in taxes, including federal, state, and any applicable local taxes, Social Security taxes, and Medicare tax.

President Trump signed the Tax Cuts and Jobs Act into law on December 22, 2017. It made major changes to the US tax code for both individuals and corporations. In fact, it represents the most significant tax changes in the United States in more than three decades. The majority of these tax law changes are effective January 1, 2018 (with some exceptions that are noted throughout this book). It is also important to note that most of the changes to individual taxes are temporary and set to expire after the 2025 tax year. This is referred to as a sunset provision. However, the changes that were made for corporate taxpayers are permanent. Please understand that all of these provisions can be changed in the future under a new administration.

General Payment or Withholding of Income Taxes

The US federal and state income tax systems are self-assessing systems. In other words, taxpayers must declare and pay tax, but they are not assessed by the taxing authority. Employers must withhold income tax, as well as Social Security and Medicare taxes from wages. Quarterly payments of estimated taxes are required if taxes are not paid through withholding. Married taxpayers who both work must consider if they need to raise their withholding because of the graduated tax rates. The tax withholding tables that your employer uses do not factor in the possibility that the overall family income can be in the higher tax bracket because of multiple jobs or the fact that your spouse also works.

Progressive Tax Rates

Personal income taxes are figured on a progressive rate: the larger the amount of the taxable income, the higher the rate at which it is taxed. Also, income is taxed in *brackets*. In other words, as income moves from a lower range to a higher range (or bracket), the percentage of tax goes up. The higher rate applies only to the income in that particular bracket, not the entire taxable income (see Exhibit C.1 for more detail). The tax rate for each bracket – whether it is 10%, 24%, or more – is called the *marginal tax rate*. The *total tax liability*, which is calculated by dividing the tax liability by the taxable income, is called the *average tax rate*, and is usually much less.

Filing Status

Taxes depend in part on filing status, which is based on your marital and family status as of the last day of the tax year (which is December 31). Filing status affects whether you are required to file an income tax return, the amount of your standard deduction, and your tax rate. If you have a choice (such as married, filing jointly; or married, filing separately), you should calculate your taxes both ways, and obviously choose the status that results in the lower rate.

The five filing statuses are:

1. *Single taxpayers:* Unmarried or legally separated from their spouses.
2. *Married, filing jointly:* Married couples who combine their income and allowable deductions can file one tax return.
3. *Married, filing separately:* Each spouse files his or her own return, reporting only his or her income, deductions, and so forth.
4. *Head of household:* A taxpayer who is unmarried or considered unmarried and pays more than half the cost of keeping up a home for himself or herself and a dependent child or relative.
5. *Qualifying widow or widower* with a dependent child.

Pay-As-You-Go Process

As anyone who has ever received a paycheck knows, our active wages are not the amount we actually receive; instead, our *take-home* pay is comprised of our gross wages minus our taxes. By law, you must pay your taxes throughout the year. This is called *pay-as-you-go*. For most people, this means your income taxes are taken out of your paycheck and sent directly to the federal, state, and local governments. At the end of the year, you have paid in a certain amount of money in taxes.

Self-employed persons also prepay their taxes by forwarding part of their income to the IRS, four times a year on specified dates. These are called *quarterly estimated tax payments*.

If you paid in more than you owe, the government refunds the amount in excess of what you owed. This is called a *tax refund*. If you have not paid enough to cover what you owe, then you have a balance due. You must pay this amount due by April 15 of the following year, or the government may charge you additional interest and penalties on the amount you have not paid.

Federal Withholding Tax Allowances   These taxes depend on the level of your earnings and the number of allowances you claim. (These allowances are requested on a form called a W-4, which you fill out at the behest of your employer). A taxpayer is allowed certain special allowances based on a variety of factors, such as marital status, amount of time worked during the year, large itemized deductions, and so forth.

Federal Insurance Contributions Act   All employed workers (except certain employees of the federal government) must pay taxes under the Federal Insurance Contributions Act (FICA), for old-age benefits, survivors' benefits, disability benefits, and hospital insurance benefits. This tax is commonly known as Social Security (and includes Medicare), and various percentages are allotted to both, depending on current law. The employer pays 50%, and the employee pays 50%. Self-employed people must pay the whole tax, but they can deduct 50% on their tax returns.

Other Withholding Taxes   Most states also require income taxes to be withheld, and the rates differ from state to state. Some cities and localities also impose income taxes.

Calculating Your Taxable Income and Liability

Calculating and paying income taxes is an incredibly complex process. It can be a tricky process just to define such concepts as *gross income* as well as the *true income subject to tax* (which is calculated by subtracting certain adjustments and deductions from gross income).

Beyond that, the Internal Revenue Code places all sorts of conditions and exceptions on how the idea of *income* can be defined and treated. Nevertheless, it is important that you comprehend the basic definitions of the most important terms, as well as the fundamentals of this process.

Gross Income

Gross income is all the income you receive during the year from whatever source. Personal gross income falls into three general categories:

1. *Active income:* Wages, salaries, bonuses, tips, and commissions, as well as certain business income in which you materially participate and other forms of income including pension income and alimony.
2. *Portfolio income:* Interest, dividends and profits generated from most types of investment holdings, including savings accounts, stocks, bonds, mutual funds, options, and futures.
3. *Passive income:* Income derived from real estate, limited partnerships, and other tax shelters. The deduction from income of losses derived from this type of income may have to be deferred to future tax periods.

Certain income may be *tax exempt,* including:

- Child-support payments
- Compensations from accident, health, and life insurance
- Gifts and inheritances
- Municipal bond interest
- Scholarships and fellowships
- Veteran benefits

In addition, the amount of deductions and write-offs that taxpayers can take in certain categories are subject to a number of rules, regulations, and limitations.

Capital gains is the gross income received when an individual sells an asset (such as a stock, bond, or real estate) for more than its original cost. Capital gains are taxed at different rates, depending on the holding period of the asset. Also, restrictions are imposed on the capital losses a taxpayer can take in any given year.

Adjusted Gross Income

A number of adjustments against your basic gross income are permitted, before you reach a number that represents your adjusted gross income. These elements include (with numerous limitations):

- Student loan interest
- IRA deductible contributions
- Self-employed health insurance
- Penalty on early withdrawal of savings
- Alimony paid (if divorced prior to 2019)
- Moving expenses (applies only to active duty military personnel as of 2018)
- Deductible contributions to a Health Savings Account (HSA) and Archer Medical Savings Account (MSA) that you or your spouse made

The ultimate number reached (after subtracting these adjustments from your gross income) is termed your *adjusted gross income (AGI).*

Deductions: Standard and Itemized

After you have calculated your AGI, you can consider other deductions. You can take the *standard deduction,* which is a fixed amount that depends on your filing status (for 2018 the standard deduction is: $12,000 single, $24,000 married filing jointly and surviving spouse, $12,000 married filing separately, and $18,000 head of household). *Or,* you can list *itemized deductions,* which allow taxpayers to reduce their taxable income by listing certain personal expenditures, including:

- Medical expenses (in excess of 7.5% of AGI for 2017 and 2018 and in excess of 10% beginning in 2019)
- State and local income tax or sales tax, real property taxes (capped in total at $10,000 starting 2018)
- Residential mortgage interest (can only be taken on new mortgage debt up to $750,000, down from $1,000,000 prior to 2018). Special rules apply here. Please refer to Chapter 4, "Managing Debt" for more detail.
- Charitable contributions.

These deductions are usually subject to various restrictions and limitations. Many popular personal itemized deductions have now been eliminated starting January 1, 2018, such as casualty and theft loss (except those attributable to federally declared disasters), tax preparation fees, unreimbursed employee expenses, and other miscellaneous deductions previously subject to the 2% AGI limitation.

The decision to take a standard or itemized deduction may change from year to year, depending on your needs. Starting January 1, 2018, the standard deduction has just about doubled for all filing statuses, but personal exemptions have been eliminated. Perhaps the biggest benefit to this higher standard deduction is that it dramatically simplifies the tax reporting and preparation process. Many taxpayers who have itemized their deductions in the past may no longer benefit from itemizing given the new restrictions, elimination of deductions, and the much larger standard deduction. This should also dramatically reduce the need for the IRS to conduct audits on individual taxpayers, since these items will no longer need to be questioned.

Exemptions

Exemptions allow you a deduction from your AGI based on the number of dependents an individual has. For 2017, each exemption allowed the taxpayer a $4,050 deduction. You were able to claim an exemption for yourself, your spouse, and any dependents, which can include children or other relatives earning less than a certain income. Furthermore, an exemption could have been claimed by only one taxpayer in any given tax year.

The Tax Cuts and Jobs Act of 2017 has completely eliminated personal exemptions, starting in 2018.

Calculating and Filing Your Taxes

To estimate the amount of tax you must pay, you now need to address a number of issues:

- The tax rate applicable to your personal income
- Tax credits
- Tax forms and schedules

Tax Rates

To find the amount of your taxable income, you subtract deductions (standard or itemized) from your AGI. Once you know the amount of your taxable income, you must refer to tax rate tables to find the amount of taxes you owe. Exhibit C.1 shows how you can calculate what your tax rate is at various income levels, whether you are single, married and filing jointly, married and filing separately, a head of household, or a qualifying widow or widower. The Tax Cuts and Jobs Act of 2017 has changed the tax brackets as follows: 10%, 12%, 22%, 24%, 32%, 35%, and 37%.

Alternative Minimum Tax

The Alternative Minimum Tax (AMT) was originally created to ensure that high-income taxpayers paid their fair share of taxes, regardless of how many deductions they were able to claim. Many high income earners had previously managed to pay very little tax based on the tax breaks that were available to them. Under AMT, these high income taxpayers are required to calculate their tax in two different ways. First it was calculated under the standard tax system, based on the formula we described above. This tax was then recalculated, which eliminated many of their deductions, such as state and local income tax or sales tax, real estate taxes, unreimbursed employee business expenses, and investment related expenses. This alternative minimum taxable income was then subject to tax at a lower rate. The problem that developed over the years with the AMT exemption was that it was not originally indexed for inflation every year. Over time, the AMT started to affect more and more taxpayers, including the middle class, which was never its targeted group.

Under the Tax Cuts and Jobs Act of 2017, the AMT exemption was increased to $70,300 for single or head of household, $109,400 for married filing jointly, and $54,700 for married filing separately. In essence, if your modified alternative minimum taxable income is below this amount, you will be exempt from the AMT tax. This AMT exemption will now be permanently adjusted for inflation so that middle-class taxpayers will not be affected by it going forward. Furthermore, the AMT income thresholds at which these exemption amounts begin to phase out have been dramatically increased. Starting in 2018, the new law raises the phase-out to $500,000 for individual taxpayers and $1,000,000 for married filing jointly.

Exhibit C.1   Table 1 2018 US Tax Rate Schedule for Individual: Filing Status Is Single

Example: IF you are SINGLE and your taxable income is $92,000 for 2018, your US income tax is **$16,370**

Taxable Income			The Tax Is	
$82,500			$14,090	
$9,500	Multiply by	24%	$2,280	
$92,000	Total Taxable Income		$16,370	Total Tax

2018 Schedule X: Use if your 2018 filing status is SINGLE

If Taxable Income Is						Taxable Income of the
Over	But Not Over	Then the Tax Would Be				Amount Over
$-	$9,525			10%	MULTIPLIED by	$-
$9,525	$38,700	$953	PLUS	12%	MULTIPLIED by	$9,525
$38,700	$82,500	$4,454	PLUS	22%	MULTIPLIED by	$38,700
$82,500	**$157,500**	**$14,090**	**PLUS**	**24%**	**MULTIPLIED by**	**$82,500**
$157,500	$200,000	$32,090	PLUS	32%	MULTIPLIED by	$157,500
$200,000	$500,000	$45,690	PLUS	35%	MULTIPLIED by	$200,000
$500,000	---------	$150,690	PLUS	37%	MULTIPLIED by	$500,000

Exhibit C.1   Table 2 2018 US Tax Rate Schedule for Individual: Filing Status Is Married Filing Jointly or Qualifying Widow(er)

Example: IF you are MARRIED FILING JOINTLY and your combined taxable income is $220,000 for 2018, your US income tax is **$41,379**

Taxable Income			The Tax Is	
$165,000			$28,179	
$55,000	Multiply by	24%	$13,200	
$220,000	Total Taxable Income		$41,379	Total Tax

2018 SCHEDULE Y-1: Use if your 2018 filing status is MARRIED FILING JOINTLY or QUALIFYING WIDOW(ER)

If Taxable Income Is						Taxable Income of the
Over	But Not Over	Then the Tax Would Be				Amount Over
$-	$19,050			10%	MULTIPLIED by	$-
$19,050	$77,400	$1,905	PLUS	12%	MULTIPLIED by	$19,050
$77,400	$165,000	$8,907	PLUS	22%	MULTIPLIED by	$77,400
$165,000	**$315,000**	**$28,179**	**PLUS**	**24%**	**MULTIPLIED by**	**$165,000**
$315,000	$400,000	$64,179	PLUS	32%	MULTIPLIED by	$315,000
$400,000	$600,000	$91,379	PLUS	35%	MULTIPLIED by	$400,000
$600,000	---------	$161,379	PLUS	37%	MULTIPLIED by	$600,000

Exhibit C.1   Table 3 2018 US Tax Rate Schedule for Individual: Filing Status Is Married Filing Separately

Example: IF you are MARRIED FILING SEPARATELY and your taxable income is $80,000 for 2018, your US income tax is **$13,540**

Taxable Income			The Tax Is	
$38,700			$4,454	
$41,300	Multiply by	22%	$9,086	
$80,000	Total Taxable Income		$13,540	Total Tax

2018 SCHEDULE Y-2: Use if your 2018 filing status is MARRIED FILING SEPARATELY

If Taxable Income Is		Then the Tax Would Be				Taxable Income of the Amount Over
Over	But Not Over					
$-	$9,525			10%	MULTIPLIED by	$-
$9,525	$38,700	$953	PLUS	12%	MULTIPLIED by	$9,525
$38,700	**$82,500**	**$4,454**	**PLUS**	**22%**	**MULTIPLIED by**	**$38,700**
$82,500	$157,500	$14,090	PLUS	24%	MULTIPLIED by	$82,500
$157,500	$200,000	$32,090	PLUS	32%	MULTIPLIED by	$157,500
$200,000	$300,000	$45,690	PLUS	35%	MULTIPLIED by	$200,000
$300,000	---------	$80,690	PLUS	37%	MULTIPLIED by	$300,000

Exhibit C.1   Table 4 2018 US Tax Rate Schedule for Individual: Filing Status Is Head of Household

Example: IF you are HEAD OF HOUSEHOLD and your taxable income is $60,000 for 2018, your US income tax is **$7,748**

Taxable Income			The Tax Is	
$ 51,800			$ 5,944	
$ 8,200	Multiply by	22%	$ 1,804	
$ 60,000	Total Taxable Income		$ 7,748	Total Tax

2018 SCHEDULE Z: Use if your 2018 filing status is HEAD OF HOUSEHOLD

If Taxable Income Is		Then the Tax Would Be				Taxable Income of the Amount Over
Over	But Not Over					
$-	$13,600			10%	MULTIPLIED by	$-
$13,600	$51,800	$1,360	PLUS	12%	MULTIPLIED by	$13,600
$51,800	**$82,500**	**$5,944**	**PLUS**	**22%**	**MULTIPLIED by**	**$51,800**
$82,500	$157,500	$12,698	PLUS	24%	MULTIPLIED by	$82,500
$157,500	$200,000	$30,698	PLUS	32%	MULTIPLIED by	$157,500
$200,000	$500,000	$44,298	PLUS	35%	MULTIPLIED by	$200,000
$500,000	---------	$149,298	PLUS	37%	MULTIPLIED by	$500,000

The most significant aspect to the change in the AMT tax is regarding personal itemized deductions under the standard tax system. By far, the reason that the majority of taxpayers were subject to the AMT tax in the past was because of the tax deductibility of state and local income tax, sales tax, property tax, unreimbursed work expenses and investment expenses subject to the 2% AGI limitation. Since many of these items have now been either minimized or eliminated, the vast majority of taxpayers that were subject to the AMT tax will no longer be subject to this tax going forward. *Quite frankly, this is perhaps one of the most significant changes in simplifying our existing income tax code.*

"Kiddie" Tax

Effective January 1, 2018, the "kiddie tax" has been changed to now apply ordinary and capital gains rates applicable to trusts and estates to the net unearned income of a child. Taxable income attributable to earned income is taxed according to an unmarried taxpayers' brackets and rates. The child's tax is now unaffected by the tax situation of the child's parent or the unearned income of any siblings. The kiddie tax applies to unearned income for children under the age of 18. It also applies to those who, at the end of the year, were 18 years old or full-time students age 19 to 23 and did not have earned income that was more than half of their own support.

Tax Credits

After determining taxable income and calculating tax liability (i.e., the amount you owe), you may be allowed to take certain *tax credits*. A wide variety of tax credits may reduce income tax at the federal and state levels. Some credits are available only to individuals, such as the child tax credit for each dependent child, the child care credit, and the earned income tax credit for low-income wage earners. A few credits, such as the foreign tax credit, may be available to all types of taxpayers.

Difference Between a Tax Deduction and a Tax Credit   It is important to understand the difference between a tax deduction and a tax credit. A *tax deduction* reduces the amount of income you pay taxes on; a *tax credit* reduces dollar-for-dollar the amount of taxes you pay.

For example, if you have a $1,000 tax deduction from your income, and you are in the 35% tax bracket, you will save $350

($1,000 x 35%) in taxes. Conversely, if you have a $1,000 tax credit, this amount is deducted, dollar-for-dollar, from your tax liability, and you will save $1,000. Some of these tax credits can be used only to reduce your tax liabilities. Others can be refundable after your tax liability has been reduced to zero.

Tax Forms and Schedules

The IRS requires taxpayers to file their returns using specific tax forms, usually a 1040 form or some variation. The government no longer automatically mails these tax forms to taxpayers. You should go online to www.irs.org to download the necessary forms or publications you need to prepare your tax returns. The vast majority of taxpayers use a paid preparer or an online tax program to file their tax returns.

Other Tax Considerations

As complicated as this process already is, certain other variables may need to be taken into account with regard to personal taxes.

Estimated Taxes

For most people, taxes are taken out of their paychecks by their employers. However, if you work for yourself or otherwise receive income that is not subject to withholding (investments, consulting fees, freelance jobs, etc.), you are required to pay estimated taxes to comply with the *pay-as-you-go* ruling. Estimated taxes must be paid in four installments throughout the year – on April 15, June 15, September 15, and January 15 (of the next tax year.) Failure to estimate and pay these taxes is subject to a penalty.

April 15

The tax year for personal income tax filers corresponds to the normal calendar year: January 1 through December 31. Personal taxpayers must file their returns no later than April 15 of the year immediately following the tax year. (This can be done electronically.) If you have paid taxes through the withholdings on your wages or personal estimated payments by more than your liability, you will receive a refund; if you have underpaid your tax liability, you must pay the difference.

Extensions

If needed, you can apply for a filing extension, with a due date of October 15. Nevertheless, you, the taxpayer, must estimate the taxes due and remit any estimated taxes due with the application for the extension. (In other words, a tax extension does not give a taxpayer more time to *pay* his taxes.)

Amended Returns

If you discover you have overlooked certain taxable income or potential deductions or credits, you can file an amended return up to three years from the date you filed your original return or two years from the time you paid the taxes, whichever is later.

Audited Returns

Although the chances of being audited are low, the IRS does review some returns to make sure they have been correctly calculated; this review is called an *audit*. The IRS conducts a few random checks. It also targets high-income earners. In addition, certain items can trigger an audit: a sudden increase in income, returns missing a signature, or itemized deductions that are exceedingly high or higher than previous years or the average of others in the same tax bracket.

The IRS can take three years from the date of filing to audit your return. If it does audit your taxes, the IRS will be looking to see that all income received was properly reported and that any and all deductions were legitimate. As a result, it is imperative that you keep complete and accurate records, and store them for at least three years, or to be on the safe side, for six years. I do believe that with the dramatically simplified tax filing system as a result of the Tax Cuts and Jobs Act of 2017, significantly fewer individuals will be audited going forward.

About the Author

John J. Vento[1] is the president of a New York City–based certified public accounting firm, as well as the Certified Financial Planning™ firm of Comprehensive Wealth Management Ltd. For over 30 years, his firm has worked with clients throughout the country and has focused on professional practices, high-net-worth individuals, and those committed to becoming financially independent. Mr. Vento has been a registered representative and advisor representative with HD Vest Investment Services and HD Vest Advisory Services since 2001. He has been one of their top producing advisors for over a decade.

John has been the keynote speaker at various seminars and conferences throughout the United States, which focus on tax and financial strategies that help create wealth. He frequently appears on Fox News's *Shepard Smith Reporting, the Willis Report, and the Neil Cavuto Show, NY1 News, CBSN,* and many other financial television programs. He has also published numerous articles in publications such as *Money Magazine, Reuters,* the *Wall Street Journal, Forbes, Bloomberg Businessweek,* and *MarketWatch,* to name a few. He was

---

[1]John J. Vento is an advisor with HD Vest. The views and opinions presented in this book are those of John J. Vento and not of HD Vest Financial Services® or its subsidiaries. All investment-related information in this book is for informational purposes only and does not constitute a solicitation or offer to sell securities or insurance services. The HD Vest–affiliated companies exclusively provide financial products and services, and do not provide or supervise tax or accounting services. Advisors may provide tax, accounting, or other services through their independent outside businesses, but these services are separate and apart from HD Vest. John Vento, Registered Representative, Securities offered through HD Vest Investment Services®, Member: FINRA/SIPC, Advisory Services offered through HD Vest Advisory Services, 6333 North State Highway 161, Fourth Floor, Irving, TX 75038, 972-870-6000. Investments and Insurance Products: Are not insured by the FDIC or any federal government agency Are not deposits of or guaranteed by the bank or any bank affiliate May lose value Comprehensive Wealth Management, Ltd. is not a registered broker/dealer or registered investment advisory firm.

a subject-matter expert on topics including tax saving strategies, financial planning, and various other wealth management issues.

John graduated from Pace University with a bachelor's degree in business administration in public accounting and continued on to earn an MBA in taxation from St. John's University. He is a certified public accountant (CPA) and a member of the American Institute of Certified Public Accountants and the New York State Society of Certified Public Accountants. John is also a Certified Financial Planner™ (CFP®). He holds a General Securities Representative Series 7 license, and he is an Investment Advisor Representative (IAR).

John brings with him his vast experience from working with KPMG LLP, one of the "Big Four" CPA firms, where he specialized in audits of the medical and dental profession and the financial service industry. He has been an adjunct professor at St. Francis College in Brooklyn, New York, as well as Wagner College in Staten Island, New York. John has been recognized as an advocate for promoting financial literacy and has been a lecturer throughout the New York City Public Library system.

Index